An Index to Literature in The New Yorker

Volumes XLVI-L, 1970-1975

by

Robert Owen Johnson

The Scarecrow Press, Inc.
Metuchen, N.J. 1976

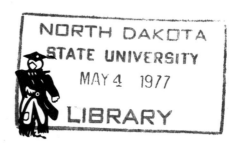

ISBN 0-8108-0905-2

LC 71-7740

Manufactured in the United States of America

to those who have helped me the most
with the preparation of this volume:
Nancy Carlson, Susan Johnson,
Suzanne Langille, Cris Busch-Lyons

CONTENTS

Introduction vii

Abbreviations ix

Part I. Original Material 1

List of Reviewers 57

Part II. Reviews of Books, Plays, Cinema and Television 57

Part III. Name Index 143

INTRODUCTION

This volume, the fourth in its series, indexes Volumes XLVI to L of The New Yorker (February 21, 1970 through February 17, 1975); like its predecessors, it is divided into three sections: Original Material, Reviews, and Author Index.

The first section, whose titles and author cross-references are numbered from 1 to 1836, lists by title every poem, short story, Profile, Reporter at Large, Letter, Onward and Upward with the Arts, Around City Hall, and similar material, as well as references to literary figures taken from Talk of the Town, Letters from Paris and London, and extended discussions in book reviews. A detailed account of the reasoning behind my decisions regarding what to include may be found in the Introduction to the second volume (1940-1955); here I should say briefly that I have not included such departments as The Art World, Musical Events, Dancing, On and Off the Avenue, The Race Track and Football. However I have included The Sporting Scene because of the extensive nature of its reportage. I have been unable to identify authorship of material appearing in Talk of the Town because The New Yorker does not wish to make this matter public.

The first section, in addition to the material listed above, includes the subject matter of all articles headed by a department title. For example, under A Reporter at Large (no. 1371), the user will find, in chronological order, the subject of each entry as printed in The New Yorker's table of contents. Under Profile (no. 1322) the user will find an alphabetical listing of persons, places and things profiled. Future separate indexes for Profiles should be unnecessary.

Section two, which lists titles of books, plays and films reviewed, is numbered from 1837 to 4578. Each reviewer's name is listed in parenthesis following the name of the author or authors, editors, translators, and adapters. I have not attempted to list writers of films.

Section three, the author index, lists all authors of original material appearing in the magazine; authors of books and plays reviewed as well as editors, translators and adapters; and authors of reviews. Thus, under George Steiner's name one will find references to articles such as "Fields of Force" which appeared in The Sporting Scene series, as well as cross-references to Mr. Steiner's discussions of such literary figures as Ford Madox Ford and Jorge Luis Borges. In addition, the user will find a reference to Mr. Steiner's book, In Bluebeard's Castle, which was reviewed anonymously, and to book reviews which Mr. Steiner wrote. Each review has the small letter "r" following the number.

During the five-year period covered by this volume, Brendan Gill and Edith Oliver wrote all the theatre reviews, and Pauline Kael and Penelope Gilliatt shared the reviewing of films, Miss Gilliatt from April through September, and Miss Kael from October through March. Because children's books received only brief discussion early each December, I have listed only the general title "Christmas Books for Children" (although the magazine used an alternate title, "Children's Books for Christmas," in 1971 and 1974).

In 1973 The New Yorker changed the date on its cover from that of Saturday to the following Monday. Thus, dates that year skip from June 23 to July 2.

I wish to express my appreciation to the Department of English at Washington State University for financial aid in getting this volume ready for publication.

Robert O. Johnson
Pullman, Washington
May 1975

ABBREVIATIONS

ACH	Around City Hall
ENC	The Enclave
OFFC	Our Far-Flung Correspondents
OLC	Our Local Correspondents
OUWA	Onward and Upward With the Arts
PR	Profile
REF	Reflections
RL	A Reporter at Large
SS	The Sporting Scene
TT	Talk of the Town

Part I

ORIGINAL MATERIAL

AWOL. RL. Daniel Lang. 48:96-133 O21'72. 1

Abraham Lincoln: lawyer, statesman, and golf nut. Prose. Thomas Meehan. 47:33-5 Ag 28'71. 2

Absolute trust. PR (Solti). Winthrop Sargeant. 50:38-62 My 27'74. 3

Academic graffiti. Verse. W. H. Auden. 47:40 My8'71. 4

An accident. Prose. Elizabeth Cullinan. 50:32-7 My27'74. 5

An accident in space. Annals of exploration. Henry S. F. Cooper, Jr. 48:48-129 N11'72; 48:75-167 N18'72. 6

Acevedo. Verse. Jorge Luis Borges. Norman Thomas di Giovanni, trans. 49:42 My 26'73. 7

Achievement. Prose. Roger Angell. 47:24-8 Ag21'71. 8

Acre. Verse. Daryl Hine. 48:42 Ap29'72. 9

Acts of witness. PR (Berrigans). Francine du Plessix Gray. 46: 44-121 Mr14'70. 10

Adam Yankev. Verse. Louis Simpson. 46:56 O24'70. 11

Address of soul to body. Verse. Robert Penn Warren. 47:46 S11'71. 12

Address to an old horse. Verse. Maxine Kumin. 49:198 N12 '73. 13

Address to the beasts. Verse. W. H. Auden. 49:44 O8'73. 14

Address to the orgiasts. Prose. Gilbert Rogin. 47:39-45 Je5 '71. 15

The admirer. Prose. Isaac Bashevis Singer. Joseph Singer, trans. 50:30-7 Ja6'75. 16

After all. Verse. William Hunt. 50:34 D30'74. 17

After all. Verse. Theodore Weiss. 49:38 S24'73. 18

After drought. Verse. Ted Walker. 47:38 Ap3'71. 19

After the creation. Verse. Paul Zweig. 49:35 Ap21'73. 20

After the flight from Rockaway. Verse. Irving Feldman. 47: 96 Mr20'71. 21

After the Japanese. Verse. Jorge Luis Borges. Norman Thomas di Giovanni, trans. 46:199 D5'70. 22

After the rain. Verse. Anthony Hecht. 48:111 S9'72. 23

Aftermath. RL. Philip Hamburger. 47:106-19 Je5'71. 24

Afternoon in Summer. Prose. Sylvia Townsend Warner. 48: 22-3 Ag26'72. 25

Afternoon of the house. Prose. Padma Perera. 50:30-6 Je 24'74. 26

An afternoon with the old man. Prose. Andre Dubus. 48:27-30 S2'72. 27

Afternoons with Hopper. OLC. James Stevenson. 47:116-28 N13'71. 28

Afterward. Verse. John Peck. 47:128 N13'71. 29

Afterward. Verse. Ted Walker. 48:140 O7'72. 30

The age of Wilmarth Lewis. OFFC. Geoffrey T. Hellman. 49:104-11 O15'73. 31

Agnes Cassilda Adams. Verse. Harold Massingham. 47:44 Mr13'71. 32

The agreement. Prose. Donald

Barthelme. 50:44-5 O14'74. 33
Ailanthus altissima. OLC. Eugene Kinkead. 46:143-55 O24 '70. 34
The air. Prose. Renata Adler. 47:46-9 D25'71; 47:74-83 F12 '72; 48:92-101 Je3'72; 48:114-22 S16'72. 35
The air. Prose. Michael J. Arlen. 50:115-18 S30'74; 50:167-73 O14'74; 50:136-47 N4'74; 50:185-94 N11'74; 50:149-55 N25'74; 50:163-70 D9'74; 50:55-9 D23'74; 50:52-6 Ja6'75; 50:73-8 Ja27'75. 36
Alaska brown bear. Verse. John Hollander. 46:42 F13'71. 37
The albatross. Prose. John Bailey. 48:28 S16'72. 38
Albee, Edward. TT. 47:33 F20 '71; 50:28-30 Je3'74. 39
Alchemist. Verse. Alan Sillitoe. 48:42 Mr11'72. 40
An alien flower. Prose. Mavis Gallant. 48:34-44 O7'72. 41
The aliens. Verse. W. H. Auden. 46:58 N21'70. 42
All dressed up and no place to go. OFFC. Whitney Balliett. 46:114-24 Ap25'70. 43
All hallows. Verse. Louise Glück. 48:44 O28'72. 44
All over (Play). TT. 47:33 F20 '71. 45
All pockets open. PR (Mekas). Calvin Tomkins. 48:31-49 Ja 6'73. 46
Allen, Woody. PR. Penelope Gilliatt. 49:39-44 F4'74. 47
Allen, Woody. TT. 48:22-3 Jy 15'72. 48
Almost (almost surely) New York, or something. Prose. Nora Ephron. 50:49 N25'74. 49
An alphabet. Verse. Al Levine. 48:33 Je10'72. 50
Altitude: 150 to 29,028. RL. Jeremy Bernstein. 46:44-81 My2'70; 46:46-94 My9'70. 51
Amazing grace, 1974. Verse. L. E. Sissman. 50:38 Je10 '74. 52
An American at the movies. Prose. H. L. Mountzoures. 49:31-4 Ja21'74. 53
The American condition. REF. Richard N. Goodwin. 49:35-60 Ja21'74; 49:36-68 Ja28'74; 49:48-91 F4'74. 54
American express. Prose. Constance Feeley. 46:50-8 N14'70. 55
American film theatre. TT. 49:31-2 O1'73. 56
The American friends service committee. RL. Gerald Jonas. 47:92-111 Mr13'71; 47:99-131 Mr20'71. 57
American women authors (collection). TT. 48:28-9 O7'72. 58
Amichai, Yehuda. Joseph Kraft. 49:70-2 Ap7'73. 59
Among schoolchildren. Verse. L. E. Sissman. 46:40 D19 '70. 60
Among the alternatives. Verse. John N. Morris. 50:75 My 27'74. 61
Amphitryon 38 (Play). S. N. Behrman. 48:41ff My20'72. 62
The analytic napkin. Prose. Marshall Brickman. 50:28-9 Ja6'75. 63
And did those feet in ancient time walk on New England's mountains green? Verse. L. E. Sissman. 47:43 F27 '71. 64
And then the whining schoolboy, with his satchel. Prose. S. J. Perelman. 50:40-3 D 9'74. 65
Anderson, Jack. TT. 47:21-3 Ja22'72. 66
Anderson, Margaret. PR. Janet Flanner. 50:44-67 Je3'74. 67
Anderson, Maxwell. S. N. Behrman. 48:54ff My27'72. 68
Anemones. Verse. Howard Moss. 50:36 Je24'74. 69
Animal. Verse. Laura Jensen. 50:127 S30'74. 70

Animal behavior. Prose. Laurie Colwin. 48:40-8 O14 '72. 71
Annals of advertising: cigarettes and television. (Also listed by title.) Prose. Thomas Whiteside. 46:42-95 D19'70. 72
Annals of diplomacy: SALT. (Also listed by title.) Prose. John Newhouse. 49:44-79 My 5'73; 49:79-117 My12'73; 49: 87-114 My19'73; 49:76-110 My 26'73; 49:68-101 Je2'73. 73
Annals of exploration: Apollo 13 accident. (Also listed by title.) Prose. Henry S. F. Cooper, Jr. 48:48-129 N11'72; 48:75-167 N18'72. 74
Annals of finance: Wall Street in the Nineteen-Sixties. (Also listed by title.) Prose. John Brooks. 49:40-67 Je23'73; 49: 35-62 Jy2'73; 49:34-63 Ag13 '73; 49:33-67 Ag20'73. 75
Annals of industry: industrial casualties. (Also listed by title.) Prose. Paul Brodeur. 49:44-106 O29'73; 49:92-142 N5'73; 49:131-77 N12'73; 49: 87-149 N19'73; 49:126-79 N26 '73. 76
Annals of justice: the Gabrielle Russier case. (Also listed by title.) Prose. Mavis Gallant. 47:47-75 Je26'71. 77
Annals of law. (Also listed by individual titles.) Prose. Richard Harris. Supreme Court decision on jury trial. 48:117-25 D16'72. Boston criminal courts. 49:45-88 Ap14'73; 49: 44-87 Ap21'73. Freedom of speech. 50:37-83 Je17'74; 50: 37-79 Je24'74. 78
Annals of law: a false arrest. (Also listed by title.) Prose. E. J. Kahn, Jr. 46:76-84 F6'71. 79
Annals of medicine. (Also listed by individual titles.) Prose. Berton Roueché. Minamata disease. 46:64-81 Ag22'70. Plague. 47:70-90 Ap10'71. Hepatitis. 47:72-86 Ag21'71. Salmonella. 47:66-81 S4'71. Electric-shock therapy. 50:84-100 S9 '74. 80
Annals of politics: Robert Moses. (Also listed by title.) Prose. Robert A. Caro. 50:32-64 Jy22'74; 50:37-65 Jy29'74; 50:40-75 Ag12'74; 50:42-77 Ag19'74. 81
Annals of politics. (Also listed by individual titles.) Prose. Richard Harris. Judge Carswell and the Senate. 46:60-161 D5'70; 46:53-131 D12'70. Senator Albert Gore. 47:34-54 Jy10'71. Campaign expenses. 47:37-64 Ag7'71. 82
Annals of politics: family assistance plan. (Also listed by title.) Prose. Daniel P. Moynihan. 48:34-57 Ja13'73; 48: 60-79 Ja20'73; 48:57-81 Ja27 '73. 83
Annals of war: Vietnam. (Also listed by title.) Prose. Frances FitzGerald. 48:36-52 Jy1'72; 48:34-54 Jy8'72; 48: 33-49 Jy15'72; 48:53-68 Jy22 '72; 48:56-69 Jy29'72. 84
Another world from mine. Prose. Padriac Colum. 46:46-9 O10 '70. 85
Anthology film archives. TT. 46:52 D5'70. 86
Anti-corporation. The marts of trade. John Brooks. 47:138-43 O9'71. 87
An antique love story. Prose. Penelope Gilliatt. 46:42-8 Ap4'70. 88
Antoon, A. J. TT. 48:18-20 S2'72. 89
Anxieties. Prose. Jorge Luis Borges. Norman Thomas di Giovanni, trans. 47:41-2 F 20'71. 90
Apartheid. Prose. Ivy Litvinov. 46:35-9 S19'70. 91
Apprehensions. Verse. Sylvia Plath. 47:37 Mr6'71. 92
Approaches. Verse. Douglas Morea. 49:54 D17'73 93

Approaching Artaud. REF. Susan Sontag. 49:39-79 My19'73. 94
Après cousin Charles. Irish sketches. John McCarten. 46: 127-9 O31'70. 95
Aptheker, Herbert. TT. 49:22-4 Jy16'73. 96
Are you enjoying this? ACH. Andy Logan. 49:127-40 Ap14'73. 97
Are you in show business? PR (Lefkowitz). William Whitworth. 47:38-44 D18'71. 98
Are you the entertainment? PR (Williamson). Kenneth Tynan. 47:35-69 Ja15'72. 99
The arena. Verse. Naomi Lazard. 50:44 Mr25'74. 100
The ariel. Prose. Ted Walker. 48:39-43 Mr25'72. 101
Aristotle contemplating the bust of Homer: after Rembrandt. Verse. J. D. O'Hara. 48:40 D9'72. 102
Arithmetic. ACH. Andy Logan. 48:102-15 O7'72. 103
Arlen, Michael. Michael J. Arlen. 46:45-79 Ap11'70; 46:41-77 Ap 18'70. 104
Around City Hall. Prose. Andy Logan. (Also listed by individual titles.) 46:101-109 F28'70; 46: 106-26 Ap18'70; 46:104-108 Je 6'70; 46:120-7 S19'70; 46:126-39 N21'70; 46:77-84 Ja16'71; 47:142-50 Mr20'71; 47:117-24 My15'71; 47:79-82 Je26'71; 47: 64-70 Ag21'71; 47:105-12 O30' 71; 47:50-6 D25'71; 47:72-8 Ja 22'72; 48:85-92 Mr11'72; 48: 111-16 Ap22'72; 48:108-20 Je 10'72; 48:38-49 Ag5'72; 48:102-15 O7'72; 48:169-82 N11'72; 48:63-70 Ja6'73; 48:68-76 F3'73; 49:76-95 Mr24'73; 49:127-40 Ap 14'73; 49:59-75 My26'73; 49: 59-66 Jy23'73; 49:50-60 S3'73; 49:120-34 O15'73; 49:209-22 N 19'73; 49:61-6 Ja14'74; 49:82-93 F11'74; 50:110-21 Mr18'74; 50:99-111 My6'74; 50:52-9 Jy 8'74; 50:66-76 Ag26'74; 50:102-11 S30'74; 50:171-81 O28'74; 50:203-13 N18'74; 50:67-73 Ja 13'75; 50:99-110 F10'75. 105
Around the bend in eighty days. Prose. S. J. Perelman. 47: 22-4 Ja1'72; 47:30-3 Ja8'72; 47:24-7 Ja15'72; 47:30-3 F5' 72; 47:32-5 F12'72; 47:36-8 F19'72. 106
Around the Horne. Prose. Garrison Keillor. 50:33-4 S30'74. 107
Arrangements. Verse. Alan Williamson. 48:36 Ja27'73. 108
Artaud, Antonin. Susan Sontag. 49:39-79 My19'73. 109
As empty as Eve. Annals of medicine. Berton Roueché. 50:84-100 S9'74. 110
As if you had never been. Verse. Richard Eberhart. 46:38 O3' 70. 111
As may be. Prose. Ted Walker. 48:40-4 Ap29'72. 112
As they were. TT. 49:36-8 O22'73. 113
As we have learnt from Freud, there are no jokes. Prose. Penelope Gilliatt. 47:36-43 O2'71. 114
The astonishment of words. OUWA. Victor Proetz. 47: 82-121 My22'71. 115
At the confluence of the Colorado and the Little Colorado. Verse. William Meredith. 48:105 Ap29'72. 116
At the dinner table. Prose. Arturo Vivante. 50:24-7 D 30'74. 117
At the masseur's. Verse. Howard Moss. 50:38-9 Ap 22' 74 118
At the opry. OUWA. Garrison Keillor. 50:46-70 My6'74. 119
At the Pines. PR (Swinburne and Watts-Dunton). Mollie Panter-Downes. 46:40-65 Ja 23'71; 46:31-43 Ja30'71; 46: 40-71 F6'71. 120
At the state mental hospital. Verse. S. J. Marks. 48:48 O14'72. 121

At the stroke of midnight. Prose. Sylvia Townsend Warner. 46: 42-62 S12'70. 122
At Vera Frost's pony farm. Verse. Peter Kane Dufault. 47: 28 Ja1'72. 123
Aubade. Verse. Seamus Heaney. 47:47 N27'71. 124
Auden, W. H. Hannah Arendt. 50:39-46 Ja20'75. 125
Auden, W. H. Mollie Panter-Downes. 50:66-8 Je10'74. 126
August. Verse. Ted Walker. 48:57 Ag26'72. 127
August: a jingle man. Verse. L. E. Sissman. 50:42 Ag12'74. 128
Augusta. SS. Herbert Warren Wind. 47:95-101 My8'71. 129
Auld lang syne. ACH. Andy Logan. 49:61-6 Ja14'74. 130
Autobiographical notes. PR (Borges). Jorge Luis Borges [and] Norman Thomas di Giovanni. 46:40-99 S19'70. 131
Autumn notes. A reporter in Washington, D. C. Elizabeth Drew. 50:42-101 Mr11'74; 50: 41-105 Mr18'74. 132
Awaiting the Copernican question. REF. Richard N. Goodwin. 50:38-49 Ja6'75. 133
Away. Verse. Mark Strand. 48: 36 Jy22'72. 134

B

The babysitters. Verse. Sylvia Plath. 47:36 Mr6'71. 135
Back home. ACH. Andy Logan. 48:111-16 Ap22'72. 136
A bad baby. Prose. Roberta Silman. 49:28-31 Jy16'73. 137
Bagnold, Enid. S. N. Behrman. 48:45ff My20'72. 138
Balcony. Prose. Henry Bromell. 50:37-9 Je10'74. 139
Ballade of sayings. Verse. W. S. Merwin. 48:46 N4'72. 140
The Baltimore Vermeers. SS. Roger Angell. 46:110-21 O31'70 141
The Baluchi Therium. Prose. John Updike. 47:39 Ag14'71. 142
The Bangor man. Prose. Garrison Keillor. 48:39 O14'72. 143
The bank drama. RL. Daniel Lang. 50:56-126 N25'74. 144
A Baptist church in Maine. Verse. David Walker. 47:34 Ag28'71. 145
Barham, Richard Harris. Edmund Wilson. 46:206-24 N21' 70. 146
Baring, Maurice. Edmund Wilson. 47:128-42 S18'71. 147
Barnes, Djuna. Janet Flanner. 48:34-6 Mr11'72. 148
The Barraclough foofarough. Verse. George Starbuck. 47:81 D18'71. 149
Bassani, Giorgio. TT. 48:33-5 Ap15'72. 150
The bats. Verse. Brendan Galvin. 50:34 Jy8'74. 151
Bay days. Verse. Howard Moss. 47:30 Ag28'71. 152
Be just and fear not. Annals of law. E. J. Kahn, Jr. 46: 76-84 F6'71. 153
Beach, Sylvia. Janet Flanner. 48:32-3 Mr11'72. 154
The beautiful lawn sprinkler. Verse. Howard Nemerov. 48:120 Je10'72. 155
Beautiful women. Verse. Marcia Nardi. 47:46 O16'71. 156
Bech swings? Prose. John Updike. 46:33-42 Mr28'70. 157
Beckett, Samuel. TT. 49:37 N 26'73. 158
Becoming you. Verse. Philip Levine. 50:117 O7'74. 159
The bed. Prose. Arturo Vivante. 46:37-9 S12'70. 160
The bedroom. Prose. Ted Walker. 50:46-8 N25'74. 161
Before fun city. Prose. Noel Perrin. 48:82-92 F26'72. 162
The beginning of grief. Prose. L. Woiwode. 46:44-7 O17'70. 163

Behind the green door (Film). Calvin Trillin. 49:74-81 F11'74. 164
Behrman, S. N. (Obituary). TT. 49:27-8 S24'73. 165
Being a lily. Prose. Sylvia Townsend Warner. 46:155-9 O10'70. 166
Beliard. Prose. Sylvia Townsend Warner. 50:32-7 Ap29'74. 167
The bell. Prose. Arturo Vivante. 48:35-9 F10'73. 168
Benediction. Verse. Donald Finkel. 50:54 N11'74. 169
Bennett, Arnold. S. N. Behrman. 48:48ff My20'72. 170
Berg Collection of English and American Literature. TT. 48: 30-1 Mr25'72; 49:45-6 D17'73. 171
Berrigan, Daniel. PR. Francine du Plessix Gray. 46:44-120 Mr14'70. 172
Berrigan, Daniel. TT. 46:20-3 Jy25'70; 49:28-30 Je23'73. 173
Berrigan, Philip. PR. Francine du Plessix Gray. 46:44-120 Mr14'70. 174
The best (Parody). Charles Mc Grath [and] Charles Menaker. 50:46 O14'74. 175
Best friend. Verse. Douglas Morea. 49:52 N5'73. 176
The best view. ENC. M. F. K. Fisher. 46:175-84 N14'70. 177
Beyle, Henri Marie. V. S. Pritchett. 50:99-102 Ja27'75. 178
A bicycle chain. Verse. John Updike. 48:48 Ap15'72. 179
Big rain. OFFC. Eugene Kinkead. 47:66-74 Jy31'71. 180
The big rock-candy mountain. Verse. L. E. Sissman. 46:28-9 Ja9'71. 181
The biggest event this year. RL. George W. S. Trow. 50:30-45 Ag26'74. 182
The biggest foundation. OLC. Edith Iglauer. 48:130-51 N4'72. 183
Billy's design. Prose. James Stevenson. 46:26-7 Ja9'71. 184
Biography (Play). S. N. Behrman. 48:68ff My20'72 185
Bioy-Casares, Adolfo. Jorge Luis Borges [and] Norman Thomas di Giovanni. 46:86-7 S19'70. 186
The birds. Verse. Nelly Sachs. Ruth Mead, trans. [and] Matthew Mead, trans. 46:48 O31'70. 187
The birds of Central Park. OLC. Eugene Kinkead. 50:78-86 Ag26'74. 188
The bird-watchers. Prose. Arturo Vivante. 50:35-7 S30'74. 189
The birth of Bangladesh. RL. Robert Shaplen. 47:40-67 F12'72; 47:89-106 F19'72. 190
The birth of love. Verse. Robert Penn Warren. 50:36 Jy22'74. 191
The bishop's robe. Prose. Isaac Bashevis Singer. Ruth Schachner Finkel, trans. 49:34-9 Je2'73. 192
The black people of Bridgehampton. PR (Bridgehampton, New York, black community). Calvin Tomkins. 49:47-101 S10'73. 193
The black plateau. Verse. W. S. Merwin. 46:39 Je6'70. 194
Blacula (Film). TT. 48:29-30 S9'72. 195
The blameless triangle. Prose. Sylvia Townsend Warner. 50: 37-45 My20'74. 196
The bloodbath. REF. William Pfaff. 48:80-9 O21'72. 197
Blue. Verse. James Schuyler. 48:32 Ag19'72. 198
Blue chip off the old block. PR (Mott). E. J. Kahn, Jr. 47: 56-87 N27'71. 199
Bluebeard (Film). TT. 48:30-1 S9'72. 200
The boat. Verse. Anne Sexton. 47:30 Ag7'71. 201
The Bobby Bison newsletter. Prose. George W. S. Trow. 50:43 Ja27'75. 202
Bobby Bison's big memory offer.

Prose. George W. S. Trow. 50:27 D30'74. 203
Bobby Shaftoe. Prose. Eli Waldron. 48:33 Jy8'72. 204
Bobst, Elmer H. TT. 49:23-4 Ja 21'74. 205
Boffos and bustos. PR (Mayer). E. J. Kahn, Jr. 50:46-66 O9' 74. 206
Bombay. Prose. R. Prawer Jhabvala. 49:38-45 O15'73. 207
Book traveller. PR (Scheer). Bruce Bliven, Jr. 49:51-113 N12'73. 208
Borges, Jorge Luis. George Steiner. 46:109-19 Je20'70. 209
The bottle. Verse. Al Levine. 48:36 My6'72. 210
Boy by a river. Verse. Ted Walker. 46:54 N14'70. 211
The boy who laughed. Prose. Ivy Litvinov. 46:43-7 O31'70. 212
Boyle, Hal (Obituary). TT. 50: 34-5 Ap15'74. 213
Brain damage. Prose. Donald Barthelme. 46:42-3 F21'70. 214
Brandt, Carl. S. N. Behrman. 48:62ff My13'72; 48:43ff My20' 72. 215
Bread. Verse. W. S. Merwin. 47:44 Ap24'71. 216
The breakfast-luncheon merger caper. Prose. Dean Vietor. 50:30-1 Jy29'74. 217
Breasts. Verse. Tess Gallagher. 49:34 Mr3'73. 218
Breath. Verse. Philip Levine. 47:40 S11'71. 219
Breath. Verse. Mark Strand. 46:41 My9'70. 220
Brief reunion. Verse. Robert Graves. 46:40 Ap11'70. 221
The briefcase. Prose. Isaac Bashevis Singer. Shulamith Charney, trans. 48:28-36 F3' 73. 222
Bright shores. Prose. Ivy Litvinov. 46:28-33 Ag1'70. 223
Bringing in the float. Verse. Louis Coxe. 49:60 N19'73. 224
The British and heroin. RL. Horace Freeland Judson. 49: 76-113 S24'73; 49:70-112 O1'73. 225
Broadway Joe. PR (Franklin). William Whitworth. 47:44-55 My22'71. 226
Browning, Robert and Elizabeth. W. H. Auden. 46:153-9 S12' 70 227
Browning Society, New York. TT. 49:36-8 My26'73. 228
The Browning-off of Pelham Manor. Prose. E. B. White. 46:49 N14'70. 229
Brownstone. Prose. Renata Adler. 48:28-34 Ja27'73. 230
Brueghel: the triumph of time. Verse. Howard Nemerov. 46:48 Ap18'70. 231
Bucolic for Sara English. Verse. Mary Haynes. 47:30 Ja15'72. 232
Bull Bailey, I love you. Prose. M. S. Tauke. 47:36-8 Je5'71. 233
Bullins, Ed. PR. Jervis Anderson. 49:40-79 Je16'73. 234
Burial. Prose. L. Woiwode. 49:50-82 N19'73. 235
Burial in Venice. OFFC. Francis Steegmuller. 47:99-103 My1'71. 236
Buried city. Verse. Howard Moss. 50:44-5 D9'74. 237
Burning the bracken. Verse. Leslie Norris. 46:180 O17'70. 238
Business hours. Verse. Keith Waldrop. 48:32 S2'72. 239
Buttercups rampant. SS. Roger Angell. 48:132-52 N11'72. 240
By candlelight. Verse. Sylvia Plath. 47:37 Mr6'71. 241
By daylight and in dream. Verse. John Hall Wheelock. 46:33 Je27'70. 242
By tens. OFFC. John Brooks. 46:182-99 N21'70. 243
By the grain elevators. Prose.

W. S. Merwin. 50:39 Ag 12'74. 244
By the Willamette. Verse. Vern Rutsala. 47:82 Ag14'71. 245
Byron exhibition (London). Mollie Panter-Downes. 50:68-72 Jy22'74. 246

C

C., again. Verse. Alan Williamson. 47:27 Ja15'72. 247
The cabalist of East Broadway. Prose. Isaac Bashevis Singer. Alma Singer, trans. [and] Herbert Lottman, trans. 47:32-4 Mr6'71. 248
Cacoyannis, Michael. TT. 48:30-2 Mr4'72. 249
A Cairo girlhood. (Also listed by title.) Prose. Suzy Eban. 50:62-73 Jy15'74. 250
California. Prose. Duncan Kennedy. 49:40-3 Mr17'73. 251
Campaign. OLC. Susan Lardner. 46:96-108 Je20'70. 252
The canal. An Ismailia childhood. Suzy Eban. 46:174-88 D5'70. 253
The cannery song. Verse. Christopher Geoffrey. 46:122 My9'70. 254
The cardplayers. Prose. Morris Lurie. 47:35-7 D18'71. 255
Carnival. Prose. Ted Walker. 46:54-9 D5'70. 256
The carol sing. Prose. John Updike. 46:36-7 D19'70. 257
The cars in Caracas. Verse. John Updike. 48:27 D30'72. 258
Castaneda, Carlos (Parody). Calvin Tomkins. 48:37-8 F3'73. 259
Castling. Prose. Renata Adler. 48:28-39 D30'72. 260
Casualties of the workplace. Annals of industry. Paul Brodeur. 49:44-106 O29'73; 49:92-142 N5'73; 49:131-77 N12'73; 49:87-149 N19'73; 49:126-79 N26'73. 261
The catechist. Prose. Donald Barthelme. 47:49-51 N13'71. 262
Catering. Prose. Penelope Gilliatt. 48:36-43 S30'72. 263
Cavalcade (Play). S. N. Behrman. 48:39ff My27'72. 264
A celebration for Autumn. Verse. Ted Walker. 46:44 S26'70. 265
Celestial events. Prose. Frank Conroy. 50:43-5 Je10'74. 266
Cemetery of childhood. Verse. Joaquim Cardozo, Elizabeth Bishop, trans. 47:52 N27'71. 267
Center. Verse. Greg Simon. 48:122 Ap22'72. 268
The center of the note. PR (Braff). Whitney Balliett. 50:41-7 Jy8'74. 269
The cerements. Verse. W. S. Merwin. 46:40 S12'70. 270
Certain hard places. Prose. Linda Arking. 50:40-76 Mr 25'74. 271
Chairman of the board. PR (Edel). Geoffrey T. Hellman. 47:43-86 Mr13'71. 272
The challenge. Prose. Jorge Luis Borges. Norman Thomas di Giovanni, trans. 46:32-3 My23'70. 273
The chance. Prose. Berry Morgan. 50:37-9 Mr4'74. 274
The chancellor. OLC. Nat Hentoff. 48:131-45 O14'72. 275
A change of hats. Verse. Theodore Weiss. 49:36 Ag20'73. 276
Chap with a good story to tell. PR (Wodehouse). Herbert Warren Wind. 47:43-101 My 15'71. 277
Chaplin, Charlie. TT. 48:36-7 Ap15'72. 278
The chart. Prose. W. S. Merwin. 49:47 O22'73. 279
Chekhov. Verse. Howard Moss. 48:36 F26'72. 280
Chekhov, Anton. W. H. Auden. 49:62-6 S3'73. 281

Children in the park. Prose. Roberta Silman. 49:43-6 O22'73. 282
Children's Theatre. TT. 47:36-8 O23'71. 283
A child's nativity. Verse. John N. Morris. 49:42 D24'73. 284
China diary. Prose. Joseph Kraft. 48:100-13 Mr11'72. 285
Chinese literature. Joseph Kraft. 48:105-108 My6'72. 286
Chomsky, Noam. OUWA. Ved Mehta. 47:44-87 My8'71. 287
Choose one from among them. Verse. Richard Shelton. 48:26 Jy29'72. 288
Choosing sides. ACH. Andy Logan. 50:102-11 S30'74. 289
Chorus of invisible things. Verse. Nelly Sachs. Ruth Mead, trans. [and] Matthew Mead, trans. 46:48 O31'70. 290
Chorus of the dead. Verse. Nelly Sachs. Ruth Mead, trans. [and] Matthew Mead, trans. 46:48 O31'70. 291
Chorus of the wanderers. Verse. Nelly Sachs. Ruth Mead, trans. [and] Matthew Mead, trans. 46:48-9 O31'70. 292
Chorus of trees. Verse. Nelly Sachs. Ruth Mead, trans. [and] Matthew Mead, trans. 46:48 O31'70. 293
Christmas Eve. Prose. Maeve Brennan. 48:27-30 D23'72. 294
Chronicle. Prose. W. S. Merwin. 49:49 D10'73. 295
Cinderella liberated. Verse. Anne Hussey. 50:77 Ag19'74. 296
The circle. Prose. Vladimir Nabokov. Dmitri Nabokov, trans. 47:32-7 Ja29'72. 297
Cité du cheval. SS. Fred Feldkamp. 46:62-83 Je6'70. 298
Citizen Kane (Film). Pauline Kael. 47:43-89 F20'71; 47:44-81 F27'71. 299
City. Verse. W. S. Merwin. 50:46 My13'74. 300
City afternoon. Verse. John Ashbery. 50:46 D2'74. 301
City in transition. PR (Louisville, Kentucky). Fred Powledge. 50:42-83 S9'74. 302
A city of churches. Prose. Donald Barthelme. 48:38-9 Ap22'72. 303
City of dreadful night. PR (Calcutta). Ved Mehta. 46:47-112 Mr21'70. 304
Civil disobedience. REF. Hannah Arendt. 46:70-105 S12'70. 305
Clamming at St. James Harbor. Verse. William Heyen. 46:34 Ag15'70. 306
Closed. RL. Richard Harris. 48:40-6 D30'72. 307
The closing circle. RL. Barry Commoner. 47:49-99 S25'71; 47:44-91 O2'71. 308
Coach. SS. Herbert Warren Wind. 50:122-50 D16'74. 309
The coat. Verse. Peter Everwine. 48:42 S23'72. 310
Coates, Robert M. (Obituary). 49:132 F24'73. 311
Cockaigne: a dream. Verse. L. E. Sissman. 49:32 Ja21'74. 312
Cocksfoot, crested dog's-tail, sweet vernal grass. Prose. Leslie Norris. 49:28-34 Jy 2'73. 313
A cold husk. Verse. Douglas Morea. 48:40 Je10'72. 314
Cold light. Our science correspondents. Eugene Kinkead. 48:92-111 S23'72. 315
Coleridge, Samuel Taylor. George Steiner. 49:77-90 Ag27'73. 316
Collage. Verse. Edwin Brock. 48:28 Jy8'72. 317
Collect calls. Prose. Renata Adler. 46:46-54 O24'70 318
The colors. Verse. William Heyen. 50:77 My6'74. 319
Come down to Queue. Prose. Peter De Vries. 50:32-3 Mr11'74. 320
Come, now! Verse. Hawley Truax. 46:30 Ag15'70. 321
Comédie française. TT. 46:31-2 Mr7'70. 322

Comfort. Verse. Richard Shelton. 48:42 Ja20'73. 323

Coming home. Verse. Tess Gallagher. 50:36 Mr25'74. 324

Commercial. Prose. John Updike. 48:30-2 Je10'72. 325

Communicating with your head. Prose. James Stevenson. 47:40-1 O16'71. 326

Compline. Verse. L. E. Sissman. 47:43 Je26'71. 327

Confabulations in Kerry. Irish sketches. John McCarten. 46:109-11 S12'70. 328

The congress. Prose. Jorge Luis Borges. Norman Thomas di Giovanni, trans. 47:50-7 N6'71. 329

Congress in crisis: the proximity bill. Prose. Garrison Keillor. 49:36-7 Ap7'73. 330

Connelly, Marc. S. N. Behrman. 48:70ff My13'72. 331

Conrad, Joseph. S. N. Behrman. 48:45-6 My13'72. 332

The consent. Verse. Howard Nemerov. 50:54 N18'74. 333

Consequences of a dime. Verse. Jonathan Aaron. 47:46 D11'71. 334

The conservative. Prose. Jose Yglesias. 47:32-9 Je12'71. 335

Constable. PR (Sawyer). John Bainbridge. 47:40-53 Ag14'71. 336

Convenient to Victoria. Verse. L. E. Sissman. 47:40 Mr20'71. 337

Conversation with a citizen. RL. Elizabeth Drew. 49:35-55 Jy 23'73. 338

Conversation with a senator. RL. Elizabeth Drew. 49:118-37 My 19'73. 339

Cooking an omelette. Verse. Jonathan Aaron. 46:40 Ap4'70. 340

Corps d'esprit. Verse. Heather McHugh. 49:40 Ja28'74. 341

Corry, John (Parody). Nora Ephron. 50:49 N25'74. 342

Cosmopolitan magazine (Parody). Lily McNeil. 49:26-7 Jy16'73. 343

A countervailing force. PR (Nader). Thomas Whiteside. 49:50-111 O8'73; 49:46-101 O15'73. 344

The counting houses. Verse. W. S. Merwin. 50:34 Ja13'75. 345

The country house. Verse. Louis Simpson. 46:42 O3'70. 346

The courage of shutting up. Verse. Sylvia Plath. 47:35-6 Mr6'71. 347

Court games. ACH. Andy Logan. 50:110-21 Mr18'74. 348

Coverup. RL. Seymour M. Hersh. 47:34-69 Ja22'72; 47:40-71 Ja29'72. 349

Coward, Noël. S. N. Behrman. 48:43ff My20'72. 350

Coward, Noël. TT. 46:30 F21'70. 351

Cowles, Gardner. TT. 46:22-3 Ja30'71. 352

Crane. Prose. Calvin Tomkins. 49:29 Ag6'73. 353

The creature. Prose. Edna O'Brien. 49:26-8 Jy30'73. 354

Cries and whispers. Prose. Ingmar Bergman. Alan Blair, trans. 48:38-74 O21'72. 355

Crimes you'll never read about. Prose. F. P. Tullius. 49:40-1 F11'74. 356

Critique de la vie quótidienne. Prose. Donald Barthelme. 47:26-9 Jy17'71. 357

The crocodile and you. Prose. Calvin Tomkins. 49:27 Ja 7'74. 358

Crosby Pond. Verse. Nina Alonso. 46:50 O24'70. 359

The crossroads. Prose. W. S. Merwin. 49:43 Mr10'73. 360

Crow and Mama. Verse. Ted Hughes. 46:30-1 Jy18'70. 361

Crow color. Verse. Ted Hughes. 46:144 N14'70. 362

Crow frowns. Verse. Ted Hughes. 46:30 Jy18'70. 363

Crow paints himself into a

Chinese mural. Verse. Ted Hughes. 46:38 Ja23'71. 364
Crow tries the media. Verse. Ted Hughes. 46:30 Jy18'70. 365
A crown of feathers. Prose. Isaac Bashevis Singer. Laurie Colwin, trans. 48:40-50 Ap 15'72. 366
Crow's fall. Verse. Ted Hughes. 46:46 D19'70. 367
Crow's undersong. Verse. Ted Hughes. 46:30 Jy18'70. 368
Crusoe in England. Verse. Elizabeth Bishop. 47:48-9 N6'71. 369
The cry. Verse. W. S. Merwin. 48:32-3 Ja13'73. 370
Crystal. Verse. James Reiss. 49:42 My12'73. 371
The cubists in Los Angeles. OUWA. Francis Steegmuller. 46:70-5 Ja23'71. 372
Cumberland station. Verse. Dave Smith. 50:42 F17'75. 373
Cupa, Davis. SS. Herbert Warren Wind. 48:159-71 N4'72. 374
The cure. Verse. Alice T. Mc Intyre. 46:38 Ag8'70. 375
Curle, Richard. S. N. Behrman. 48:45-6 My13'72. 376
Currents. Verse. Arthur Freeman. 46:32 Ag8'70. 377
A curse. Verse. W. H. Auden. 50:42 My6'74. 378
The curve of binding energy. PR (Taylor). John McPhee. 49:54-145 D3'73; 49:50-108 D10'73; 49:60-97 D17'73. 379
Custine. REF. George F. Kennan. 47:46-93 My1'71. 380
Cutting down. Annals of advertising. Thomas Whiteside. 46:42-95 D19'70. 381

D

Daddyji. PR (Mehta). Ved Mehta. 48:47-107 Ap22'72; 48:45-100 Ap29'72. 382
Daily Mirror. TT. 47:40-2 S25'71. 383
The dance of the hours. Verse. Peter Davison. 49:79 N26'73. 384
Dancing on the carpet. OLC. Whitney Balliett. 50:43-50 Ap1'74. 385
Dar. Prose. Emily Hahn. 46: 25-9 Jy18'70. 386
Dark rings. Verse. Philip Levine. 47:54 O9'71. 387
Dartmouth '70 and the war. OFFC. Noel Perrin. 46:53-8 Jy18'70. 388
Dashin' about. PR (Adams). Thomas Whiteside. 50:42-81 F25'74. 389
Daughter, last glimpses of. Prose. John Updike. 49:50-3 N5'73. 390
Daumier. Prose. Donald Barthelme. 48:31-6 Ap1'72. 391
Davenport, Tom. TT. 50:29-30 Ag5'74. 392
Dawn in Kensington Gardens. Verse. R. P. Lister. 49: 42 Mr24'73. 393
A day in Coney Island. Prose. Isaac Bashevis Singer. Laurie Colwin, trans. 47:33-7 Jy 31'71. 394
The day of the Lhasa Apso. Prose. Dan Greenburg. 47: 43-6 O23'71. 395
A day with the Duke. OLC. Whitney Balliett. 46:52-5 Je27'70. 396
Day-old baby rats. Prose. Julie Hayden. 47:28-34 Ja15'72. 397
Dayspring. Verse. Hawley Truax. 46:34 S26'70. 398
DeSica, Vittorio. Pauline Kael. 47:48-53 D18'71. 399
The deacon. Prose. John Updike. 46:38-41 F21'70. 400
Dead ringer (Radio play). TT. 49:26-7 Ja14'74. 401
Dear (name of magazine). Prose. Dan Greenburg. 47:43 Ap 24'71. 402
Death ballad. Verse. John Berryman. 46:28 Jy25'70. 403

A death in the marsh. Verse. Brendan Galvin. 50:42 Jy29'74. 404
Death of a stallion. Verse. John Peck. 48:98 Mr18'72. 405
The death of Edward Lear. Prose. Donald Barthelme. 46:21 Ja2'71. 406
The death spiral. Verse. Anne Hussey. 49:42 Mr17'73. 407
Deathwatch. Verse. Alice T. McIntyre. 46:165 N7'70. 408
Deauville. SS. Fred Feldkamp. 47:60-78 Ag14'71. 409
December river. Verse. Ted Hughes. 50:42 Je24'74. 410
December 27, 1966. Verse. L. E. Sissman. 50:42 D30'74. 411
Decision. Annals of politics. Richard Harris. 46:60-161 D 5'70; 46:53-131 D12'70. 412
The deltoid pumpkin seed. PR (Aereon). John McPhee. 48: 40-73 F10'73; 48:42-77 F17'73; 49:48-79 F24'73. 413
Department of amplification. Jeremy Bernstein. 46:93-4 Je 13'70; 47:135-6 O9'71. 414
Department of amplification. Paul Brodeur. 47:147-54 O23'71. 415
Department of amplification. Edward Jay Epstein. 47:125 My 8'71. 416
Department of amplification. Edward Kosner. 47:125 My8'71. 417
Department of amplification. Jane Kramer. 48:126-30 Ap15'72. 418
Department of amplification. Ved Mehta. 47:121-4 Mr13'71. 419
Department of amplification. Fred C. Shapiro. 49:80-3 Je9'73. 420
Department of amplification. Thomas Whiteside. 46:78-95 Je20'70; 46:64-70 Jy4'70; 47: 54-9 Ag14'71. 421
Dept. of correction and amplification. Ralph Nader. 48:48 Jy 22'72. 422
Departures. Prose. Donald Barthelme. 47:42-4 O9'71. 423
Departures. Verse. Richard Schramm. 47:88 F19'72. 424
Descent. Verse. Margaret Atwood. 46:50 Je27'70. 425
The devil's pig. Prose. W. S. Merwin. 47:33 Jy10'71. 426
The diagnostician. Prose. Arturo Vivante. 46:191-9 D5'70. 427
Dick, Philip K. TT. 50:24 F3'75. 428
Die super-schau. SS. E. J. Kahn, Jr. 48:98-108 S9'72. 429
The dilemma. Verse. Robert Graves. 48:30 Jy29'72. 430
Discobolus. Prose. Ted Walker. 48:32-7 My27'72. 431
The discovery. Prose. Donald Barthelme. 49:26-7 Ag20'73. 432
Discovery. Prose. James Stevenson. 47:30-1 Jy3'71. 433
Diversions. ACH. Andy Logan. 49:59-75 My26'73. 434
A divided party. REF. Richard N. Goodwin. 50:157-66 D2'74. 435
Division. Verse. W. S. Merwin. 47:44 Ap24'71. 436
Dr. Beeber. Prose. Isaac Bashevis Singer. Elaine Gottlieb, trans. 46:38-42 Mr7'70. 437
The doctor's doctors. Prose. H. F. Ellis. 46:114-19 S19'70. 438
Dogfish. Verse. Daniel Hoffman. 48:106 F10'73. 439
A door. Verse. W. S. Merwin. 47:44 Ap24'71. 440
The doorbell. Prose. Philip Hamburger. 48:37-8 Mr11'72. 441
Double vision. Prose. Philip Hamburger. 46:51-2 D12'70. 442
Down the [adjective deleted] road. Prose. Calvin Trillin.

50:37 My13'74. 443
Downers and séances. Prose. Renata Adler. 46:32-6 F13'71. 444
Downey, Robert. TT. 46:30-2 F28'70. 445
Dramatist. PR (Bullins) Jervis Anderson. 49:40-79 Je16'73. 446
A dream. Prose. Lily McNeil. 49:25 S3'73. 447
The dress. Verse. Mark Strand. 46:40-1 My9'70. 448
Drinking cold water. Verse. Peter Everwine. 48:42 N11'72. 449
The driver's seat. Prose. Muriel Spark. 46:38-102 My16'70. 450
The drowned children. Verse. Louise Glück. 50:58 N25'74. 451
DuBois, William Edward Burghardt. TT. 49:22-4 Jy16'73. 452
Dude (Play). TT. 48:30 S23'72. 453
The dump: a dream come true. Verse. L. E. Sissman. 47:43 F27'71. 454
Dunn, Alan (Obituary). 50:112 Je3'74. 455
Dwarf house. Prose. Ann Beattie. 50:34-8 Ja20'75. 456
Dying. Verse. Anne Hussey. 49:38 O1'73. 457
Dying away. Verse. William Meredith. 50:166 O14'74. 458

E

E. A. T. OUWA. Calvin Tompkins. 46:83-133 O3'70. 459
E. D. OFFC. Fred C. Shapiro. 46:93-105 My23'70. 460
E. P. in his silence. Verse. Barry Spacks. 46:46 N28'70. 461
The early essays. Prose. Woody Allen. 48:32-3 Ja20'73. 462
Early Sunday morning. Prose. Henry Bromell. 49:32-7 Mr3'73. 463
Early voice. PR (Randolph). Jervis Anderson. 48:60-120 D2'72; 48:48-106 D9'72; 48:40-85 D16'72. 464
The earthly paradise. Prose. Robert Hemenway. 50:40-70 O7'74. 465
East September, West October. SS. Roger Angell. 50:156-77 N11'74. 466
Ecce homo. Verse. John Berryman. 47:38 Ap10'71. 467
Echo for the promise of Georg Trakl's life. Verse. James Wright. 46:125 N21'70. 468
Edel, Leon. PR. Geoffrey T. Hellman. 47:43-86 Mr13'71. 469
Edwards, Amelia. Prose. Donald Barthelme. 48:34-5 S9'72. 470
The egotist. Prose. Isaac Bashevis Singer. Dorothea Straus, trans. 46:32-6 Ja 16'71. 471
The elder lady. Prose. Jorge Luis Borges. Norman Thomas di Giovanni, trans. 47:46-8 S25'71. 472
Elegy for Teddy Holmes, dead in a far land. Verse. Philip Levine. 50:48 Ag5'74. 473
An elegy is preparing itself. Verse. Donald Justice. 49:105 Mr3'73. 474
Eliot, T. S. George Steiner. 48:134-42 Ap22'72. 475
Eliot, T. S. John Updike. 50:137-40 Ap8'74. 476
Elisha Hospital. Prose. Mark Henry Helprin. 49:49 O8'73. 477
Elphenor and Weasel. Prose. Sylvia Townsend Warner. 50:39-45 D16'74. 478
Emblem. Verse. Richard Eberhart. 48:47 D9'72. 479
The emergency. Prose. Arturo Vivante. 48:39-40 Mr4'72. 480
An emeritus addresses the school. Verse. John Ciardi. 46:32 Je13'70. 481
Empson lieder. Verse. L. E.

Sissman. 46:42-3 O17'70. 482
The enclave. (Also listed by individual titles.) Prose. M. F. K. Fisher. 46:36-42 S5'70; 46:35-9 O3'70; 46:175-84 N14'70; 46:48-50 D12'70; 46:37-41 Ja 16'71; 47:36-42 My15'71. 483
Encounters with the archdruid. PR (Brower, Park, Fraser, Dominy). John McPhee. 47: 42-91 Mr20'71; 47:42-80 Mr 27'71; 47:41-93 Ap3'71. 484
Encyclopaedia Britannica. TT. 49:28-9 Ja28'74. 485
End of a Munich meeting. Verse. John Hollander. 47:26 Jy3'71. 486
End of May. Verse. Mona Van Duyn. 48:36 My27'72. 487
End of Summer (Play). S. N. Behrman. 48:48ff My27'72. 488
The end of the duel. Prose. Jorge Luis Borges. Norman Thomas di Giovanni, trans. 47:34-5 Mr13'71. 489
The enemy. Verse. Pablo Neruda. Ben Belitt, trans. 47:54 N20'71. 490
Engineer--private Paul Klee misplaces an aircraft between Milbertshofen and Cambrai, March 1916. Prose. Donald Barthelme. 47:33-4 Ap3'71. 491
The enigmatic enzyme. RL. Paul Brodeur. 46:42-74 Ja16'71. 492
An entirely different world. SS. Herbert Warren Wind. 48:71-83 Ap1'72. 493
Environmental impact (illusions, wonders & disappearing acts). Prose. James Stevenson. 48:51-2 N18'72. 494
Environmentalist. PR (Strong). E. J. Kahn, Jr. 48:45-75 Je 3'72. 495
Erika. Prose. Joyce Warren. 49:33-4 Ja14'74. 496
Escape from civilization. Prose. Isaac Bashevis Singer. Ruth Schachner Finkel, trans. 48: 34-6 My6'72. 497
Essential praises of silence. Verse. Barry Spacks. 50:56 O28'74. 498
Estrangement. Prose. Ted Walker. 46:30-5 Je13'70. 499
The estuary. Verse. W. S. Merwin. 50:48 D16'74. 500
The eternal present. PR (Balanchine). Bernard Taper. 49:48-90 O22'73. 501
Ethel's story. Prose. W. S. Merwin. 46:31-2 Jy25'70. 502
Ethiopia. Prose. John Updike. 49:28-32 Ja14'74. 503
The ethnic life. Verse. Daniel Halpern. 48:36 My20'72. 504
Ethnology. ACH. Andy Logan. 48:85-92 Mr11'72. 505
An E-type on the Interstate. Verse. L. E. Sissman. 46: 36 Jy25'70. 506
Evening wind. Verse. James Schuyler. 47:127 O9'71. 507
An evening with Ramón Bonavena. Prose. Jorge Luis Borges [and] Adolfo Bioy Casares. Norman Thomas di Giovanni, trans. 46:38-41 D19'70. 508
An event at Big Eddy. Verse. William Stafford. 49:28 S3'73. 509
Everding, August. TT. 47:37-9 D11'71. 510
Examining psychic phenomena. Prose. Woody Allen. 48:32-3 O7'72. 511
Excuse for an Italian sonnet. Verse. L. E. Sissman. 46: 34 Jy4'70. 512
Exiles. Prose. Michael J. Arlen. 46:45-79 Ap11'70; 46:41-77 Ap18'70. 513
Exiles. Verse. C. P. Cavafy. Edmund Keeley [and] Philip Sherrard, trans. 48:31 Je 17'72. 514
Exotica. Verse. Frederick Morgan. 49:42 F18'74. 515
Explanation. OLC. Richard N. Goodwin. 50:137-48 N25'74. 516

Explorer. PR (Ewing). William Wertenbaker. 50:54-118 N4'74; 50:52-100 N11'74; 50:60-110 N18'74. 517
Explosion. SS. Herbert Warren Wind. 48:116-34 O7'72. 518

F

F.R.A.N.K. Prose. Penelope Gilliatt. 47:34-41 My1'71. 519
A fable of the buyers. Prose. W. S. Merwin. 47:33 F5'72. 520
Fables. Prose. J. B. Handelsman. 49:40-1 S17'73. 521
Facing reality. Prose. Gilbert Rogin. 48:23-6 S2'72. 522
The fair woman. Verse. Ann Elizabeth 47:93 F27'71. 523
The falcons of Morro Rock. OFFC. Faith McNulty. 48:67-74 D23'72. 524
The fall. Prose. V. S. Pritchett. 46:34-9 Je20'70. 525
Falling. Verse. Pablo Neruda. Ben Belitt, trans. 47:54 N20'71. 526
Family walls. Prose. Maeve Brennan. 49:34-42 Mr10'73. 527
Fancy flights. Prose. Ann Beattie. 50:40-6 O21'74. 528
Farewell. Prose. J. F. Powers. 49:30-7 Ag6'73. 529
Farrell, James T. TT. 50:29-30 Mr18'74. 530
Farrell, Robert W. TT. 47:40-2 S25'71. 531
Fast food for thought. Prose. Gordon Cotler. 50:39 O7'74. 532
Fat girl. Prose. Brendan Gill. 46:32-41 S26'70. 533
Faulkner, William. TT. 46:50 N21'70. 534
The favorite. Prose. Edna O'Brien. 50:36-41 Mr11'74. 535
Fear. Verse. W. S. Merwin. 46: 35 Ag22'70. 536
Fear of death. Verse. John Ashbery. 50:50 N18'74 537
February. Verse. John Lloyd Owen. 47:87 F5'72. 538
Fellini, Federico. TT. 50:33-5 O7'74. 539
Fernández, Macedonio. Jorge Luis Borges [and] Norman Thomas di Giovanni. 46:64-8 S19'70. 540
Fiction, science. Gerald Jonas. 48:33-52 Jy29'72. 541
Fields of force. SS. George Steiner. 48:42-117 O28'72. 542
A fight between a white boy and a black boy in the dusk of a Fall afternoon in Omaha, Nebraska. Prose. Wright Morris. 46:109-11 Je6'70. 543
A film. Prose. Donald Barthelme. 46:31 S26'70. 544
Film Forum. TT. 46:51-2 D5'70. 545
"Film orgy." TT. 46:37 Mr 21'70. 546
The finder. Prose. Elizabeth Spencer. 46:30-9 Ja23'71. 547
Finding the prone landscape. Verse. Jonathan Aaron. 48: 40 O21'72. 548
A fine day for the gathering. SS. Alastair Reid. 46:60-70 Ag29'70. 549
Fire and ice. ACH. Andy Logan. 46:77-84 Ja16'71. 550
Fire in the lake. Frances FitzGerald. see Annals of war. 551
Fireside. Verse. Seamus Heaney. 49:48 My26'73. 552
Firewood. RL. John McPhee. 50:81-105 Mr25'74. 553
The first hundred years. SS. Herbert Warren Wind. 49: 114-50 O8'73. 554
The first lunar invitational. Prose. John Updike. 47:35-6 F27'71. 555
The first moon. Prose. W. S. Merwin. 47:33 Jy10'71. 556

The fish. Verse. Greg Kuzma. 47:50 D11'71. 557
The fisher cat. Verse. Richard Eberhart. 47:146 O23'71. 558
Fishing. Verse. W. S. Merwin. 50:50 Mr18'74. 559
Five. Verse. Robert Graves. 48: 42 F10'73. 560
The five black swans. Prose. Sylvia Townsend Warner. 49: 36-9 Je23'73. 561
Five flights up. Verse. Elizabeth Bishop. 50:40 F25'74. 562
Five poems. (Also listed by individual titles.) Verse. Ted Hughes. 46:30-1 Jy18'70. 563
Five poems. (Also listed by individual titles.) Verse. W. S. Merwin. 46:38-9 Je6'70; 48: 32-3 Ja13'73. 564
The Floto letters. Prose. Roger Angell. 46:34-7 F21'70. 565
Flowers. Verse. Carolyn Maisel. 48:32 Ag26'72. 566
Flying time. Verse. Alastair Reid. 47:64 Ag7'71. 566a
Flying to America. Prose. Donald Barthelme. 47:50-8 D4'71. 567
For a fatherless son. Verse. Sylvia Plath. 47:37 Mr6'71. 568
For a man who died in his sleep. Verse. David Wagoner. 47: 42 Ap3'71. 569
For Mr. Reed of Martha's Vineyard. Verse. Stephen Sandy. 46:51 Ja2'71. 570
For the record. Verse. Roy Blount, Jr. 50:42 Ap29'74. 571
Forcing the light back out. Verse. Douglas Morea. 49:38 My12'73. 572
Ford, Ford Madox. George Steiner. 47:97-102 F12'72. 573
The foregone conclusion. Prose. Sylvia Townsend Warner. 49: 45-6 N12'73. 574
Foreigners. Prose. Penelope Gilliatt. 46:36-43 Mr14'70. 575
Foreman, Richard. TT. 48:23-5 Ja27'73. 576
Foresight, nightmare, and hindsight. PR (Service). E. J. Kahn, Jr. 48:43-95 Ap8'72. 577
Foreword. Verse. W. S. Merwin. 48:32 Ja13'73. 578
Forster, E. M. George Steiner. 47:158-69 O9'71. 579
Forty flights of steps. PR (Welch, West Virginia). Berton Roueché. 49:32-44 Jy16'73. 580
Found paradise. Prose. Garrison Keillor. 47:32-3 S18'71. 581
Founding cadre. PR (Feminists). Jane Kramer. 46:52-139 N28'70. 582
The foundry. Verse. Thomas Snapp. 47:50 N13'71. 583
The fountain. Prose. W. S. Merwin. 46:28-31 Jy11'70. 584
Four figures in a room. A distant figure. Prose. Sylvia Townsend Warner. 49:46-7 F24'73. 585
Four poems. Verse. Osip Mandelstam. W. S. Merwin, trans. 49:42 Ap28'73. 586
Four songs. Verse. William Heyen. 48:26 Ag26'72. 587
The Fourth of July. Verse. Richard Wilbur. 50:28 Jy1'74. 588
Fox. Verse. Michael Dennis Browne. 50:44 Ag19'74. 589
The foxfire book (Parody). Garrison Keillor. 50:44-6 N4'74. 590
Frame, Donald M. S. N. Behrman. 48:79ff My27'72. 591
Frederic, Harold. Edmund Wilson. 46:112-34 Je6'70. 592
Freedman, Harold. S. N. Behrman. 48:62ff My13'72; 48: 51ff My27'72. 593
Fremont-Smith, Eliot. TT. 46:22 Ja30'71. 594
Fresh wind in Venice. Verse. James Wright. 50:36 Ja 6'75. 595
A friend in disguise. PR (Garlic). Berton Roueché. 50: 55-62 O28'74. 596
Friendly neighbor. Prose. Garrison Keillor. 49:23-5 D

31'73. 597
From a journal. Verse. George Amabile. 49:40 S10'73. 598
From a town trafficked by crickets. Verse. Carolyn Stoloff. 50:38 Ap1'74. 599
From Beyoglu. Verse. Richard Howard. 46:30-1 My30'70. 600
From Birnam Wood to Dunsinane. OFFC. John McPhee. 46:141-7 O10'70. 601
From the school of the renowned philosopher. Verse. C. P. Cavafy. Edmund Keeley [and] Philip Sherrard, trans. 48:31 Je17'72. 602
The fugitive. Prose. W. S. Merwin. 49:43 Mr10'73. 603
Fuller, Henry Blake. Edmund Wilson. 46:112-38 My23'70. 604
A fundamental hoax. Annals of politics. Richard Harris. 47: 37-64 Ag7'71. 605
The fury of overshoes. Verse. Anne Sexton. 48:30 Ja27'73. 606

G

Gabby. Prose. Joseph Epstein [and] Gerald Graff. 49:34-5 O1'73. 607
Game plan. Prose. Don DeLillo. 47:44-7 N27'71. 608
The gathering of the loons. Verse. David Wagoner. 47:40 My29'71. 609
The genius. Prose. Donald Barthelme. 47:38-40 F20'71. 610
Gershwin, George and Ira. S. N. Behrman. 48:64ff My27'72. 611
Getting somewhere. Verse. David Wagoner. 50:30 Jy22'74. 612
Gigolo. Verse. Sylvia Plath. 46:54 N21'70. 613
Giraffe. Verse. Stanley Plumly. 47:185 N20'71. 614
Girls' voices. Verse. Brendan Gill. 47:48 Jy17'71. 615
Glass. Verse. W. S. Merwin. 48:44 O21'72. 616
Global reach. RL. Richard Barnet [and] Ronald Müller. 50:53-128 D2'74; 50:100-59 D9'74. 617
The godfather (Film). TT. 50: 39-40 D2'74. 618
Gods must yield. Prose. Strowan Robertson. 50:34-9 Mr25'74. 619
The go-go years. Annals of finance. John Brooks. 49:40-67 Je23'73; 49:35-62 Jy2'73; 49:34-63 Ag13'73; 49:33-67 Ag20'73. 620
Gogol, Nikolai. V. S. Pritchett. 49:176-84 N5'73. 621
Going home. Verse. Philip Levine. 48:95 My20'72. 622
Gold-diggers of 1974. SS. Herbert Warren Wind. 50:118-46 O7'74. 623
Good cooking. PR (Child). Calvin Tomkins. 50:36-52 D23'74. 624
A good eye. PR (Mardersteig). Winthrop Sargeant. 46:32-47 Jy11'70. 625
Good Indians. Verse. L. E. Sissman. 47:43 F27'71. 626
The good life. Verse. Mark Strand. 46:40 My9'70. 627
The good news. PR (Hougen). Berton Roueché. 49:45-64 My12'73. 628
Good riddance. Verse. Mark Van Doren. 48:52 N18'72. 629
The gorgeous West. Prose. Sylvia Townsend Warner. 47:59-60 D4'71. 630
The gospel according to Mark. Jorge Luis Borges. Norman Thomas di Giovanni, trans. 47:40-2 O23'71. 631
Gotham Book Mart Gallery. TT. 48:30-1 D16'72. 632
Grace. Verse. Thomas Mc Namee. 48:54 D2'72. 633
Graham, Katharine. TT. 50: 32-3 S23'74. 634

The Grand Canyon. Verse. Jean Garrigue. 48:40 F17'73. 635
Grand tour de Saigon. Verse. Herbert Krohn. 46:36 Mr7'70. 636
The grandfather poem. Verse. Stephen Dobyns. 49:30 Ja14'74. 637
Grandfather, your wound. Verse. Anne Sexton. 48:40 S30'72. 638
A great flowering of free spirits. PR (Gordon). Whitney Balliett. 48:39-58 F3'73. 639
The great gulf. Verse. Richard Shelton. 48:30 Jy1'72. 640
Green: an epistle. Verse. Anthony Hecht. 47:38-9 My22'71. 641
The green torso. Prose. Sylvia Townsend Warner. 46:36-43 Ag22'70. 642
The greening of America. REF. Charles A. Reich. 46:42-111 S26'70. 643
The greening of America (Parody). E. B. White. 46:49 N14'70. 644
The greens of Ireland. SS. Herbert Warren Wind. 47:112-37 Ap3'71; 47:100-29 Ap10'71. 645
The green-sailed vessel. Verse. Robert Graves. 47:46 Mr20'71. 646
Greetings, Friends! Verse. Frank Sullivan. 46:23 D26'70; 47:31 D25'71; 48:31 D23'72; 49:37 D24'73; 50:35 D23'74. 647
Grief. Prose. Daniel Menaker. 49:34-5 Ja28'74. 648
Grief. Prose. Natacha Stewart. 47:45-9 O9'71. 649
Grifter, stay 'way from my door. Prose. S. J. Perelman. 46:40-2 O31'70. 650
Grolier Club book exhibition. TT. 49:26-7 Je9'73. 651
The grower's shadow. PR (County agents, Idaho). Berton Roueché. 49:30-45 S3'73. 652
The guard: but Ohio. Well, I guess that's one state where they elect to lock and load. RL. Renata Adler. 46:40-64 O3'70. 653
The guardian. Verse. Mark Strand. 46:40 My9'70. 654
Guardians. Verse. W. S. Merwin. 50:34 Ap29'74 655
A guide to some of the lesser ballets. Prose. Woody Allen. 48:34-5 O28'72. 656
Guilty, with an explanation. PR (Allen). Penelope Gilliatt. 49:39-44 F4'74. 657
The gun shop. Prose. John Updike. 48:42-7 N25'72. 658
The guns in the closet. Prose. Jose Yglesias. 47:50-8 N 20'71. 659

H

Hadrian's villa: water, wind & stone. Verse. George Amabile. 46:40 Mr28'70. 660
Hail, hail, the ganglia's all here. Prose. S. J. Perelman. 48:32-4 S23'72. 661
A hail of bullets. ACH. Andy Logan. 49:76-95. Mr24'73. 662
Hailing the elusory mountain lion. Prose. Edward Hoagland. 47:26-33 Ag7'71. 663
Half an hour. Verse. C. P. Cavafy. Edmund Keeley [and] Philip Sherrard, trans. 48: 31 Je17'72. 664
The hand. Verse. Howard Moss. 46:42 S5'70. 665
The handball players at Brighton Beach. Verse. Irving Feldman. 50:97 Je24'74. 666
The hands. Verse. W. S. Merwin. 46:39 Je6'70. 667
Hanging out with Blossom Dearie. PR (Dearie). Whitney Balliett. 49:46-52 My26'73. 668
Hanka. Prose. Isaac Bashevis Singer. Blanche Nevel [and] Joseph Nevel, trans. 49:32-8 F4'74. 669
A happy survival. Verse. Elizabeth Libbey. 50:34 Mr4'74. 670

Happy times. PR (Zerbe). Brendan Gill. 49:39-68 Je9'73. 671
Harper's Bazaar. TT. 48:30 D16'72. 672
Harris, Jed. S. N. Behrman. 48:42ff My13'72. 673
Harvard Crimson. TT. 48:26-7 F3'73. 674
Hassidic tales, with a guide to their interpretation by the noted scholar. Prose. Woody Allen. 46:31-2 Je20'70. 675
Having children. Verse. Douglas Morea. 50:46 S16'74. 676
The hawk and the mules. Prose. W. S. Merwin. 47:52-3 N13'71. 677
Hay fever. Verse. Leonard Nathan. 48:48 Ap22'72. 678
He knows what he's doing. Verse. Lois Moyles. 46:42 Mr21'70. 679
He who remains. Verse. Richard Shelton. 46:50 N28'70. 680
Heading for Nandi. Verse. John Updike. 50:42 D16'74. 681
The hearing. Prose. Theodore Weesner. 47:35-41 Ap10'71. 682
Hearst, William Randolph. Pauline Kael. 47:43-89 F20'71; 47:44-81 F27'71. 683
Heart of light. Prose. Henry Bromell. 49:29-34 Jy30'73. 684
Hecht, Ben. Pauline Kael. 47:46-7 F20'71. 685
Heineman collection of books and manuscripts. TT. 49:30-1 Mr 31'73. 686
Heinlein, Robert. TT. 50:17-18 Jy1'74. 687
Helburn, Theresa. S. N. Behrman. 48:72ff My13'72; 48:46ff My27'72. 688
Hemingway, Ernest. Janet Flanner. 48:32 Mr11'72. 689
Hemingway, Ernest. Peter Matthiessen. 48:68 S16'72. 690
Hemingway, Ernest. Winthrop Sargeant. 48:34-9 Jy22'72. 691
Henry W. and Albert A. Berg collection of English and American literature. TT. 49:32-3 Mr17'73. 692
Her son. Prose. Isaac Bashevis Singer. Joseph Singer, trans. 49:40-4 My12'73. 693
The Herald. TT. 47:38-40 O9'71. 694
Here is Einbaum. Prose. Wright Morris. 47:35-41 Je26'71. 695
The hermit wakes to bird sounds. Verse. Maxine Kumin. 48: 46 Ap29'72. 696
Hesse, Hermann (Parody). Roger Angell. 46:33-5 Mr 14'70. 697
The high ground, or look Ma, I'm explicating. Prose. Peter De Vries. 47:43-5 S25'71. 698
The hill. Prose. Berry Morgan. 49:38-44 Mr24'73. 699
The hill. Verse. Mark Strand. 46:40 My9'70. 700
A hill in southern England. Prose. Ted Walker. 50:32-6 Mr4'74. 701
His master's voice. Verse. John Hollander. 47:42 Ag 14'71. 702
His mother. Prose. Mavis Gallant. 49:28-33 Ag13'73. 703
Hitchcock, Alfred. Penelope Gilliatt. 47:91-3 S11'71; 50:116-19 Ap29'74. 704
Holding. Verse. Robert Grant Burns. 47:40 D18'71. 705
Holding our own. Verse. Ann Stanford. 50:36 Ag5'74. 706
Holiday. A Cairo girlhood. Suzy Eban. 50:62-73 Jy15'74. 707
Holiday Home. Prose. Ivy Litvinov. 46:42-51 N28'70. 708
The holy family. Prose. Charles Garber. 46:22-8 Ja2'71. 709
Homage to the North. Verse. Richard Eberhart. 46:54 D12'70. 710
Homage: Virgil Thomson.

Prose. Anon. 47:39 D25'71. 711
Home. Verse. Seamus Heaney. 47:48 My1'71. 712
Home. Verse. Charles Simic. 48:44 My13'72. 713
Home again. RL. Daniel Lang. 47:35-53 S4'71. 714
Home before dark. Verse. Doug Flaherty. 48:68 Ap1'72. 715
The home front. Prose. Mark Helprin. 50:27-30 F3'75. 716
Honey-moon. Prose. Katinka Loeser. 50:32-6 Jy29'74. 717
Honeymoon. Prose. Arturo Vivante. 49:43-5 N26'73. 718
Honor to the bride. RL. Jane Kramer. 46:33-49 Ag29'70; 46:43-63 S5'70; 46:112-49 S12'70. 719
Hopefuls. ACH. Andy Logan. 49:120-34 O15'73. 720
Horse sense on the gelid planet. Prose. Mark Halliday. 48:34-5 My13'72. 721
Horsepower. ACH. Andy Logan. 49:50-60 S3'73. 722
Horses. Verse. W. S. Merwin. 47:44 Ap24'71. 723
The hospital. Verse. Paul Zweig. 49:34 S3'73. 724
The house and the highway. RL. Whitney Balliett. 47:40-5. D 25'71. 725
The house growing. Verse. John Updike. 49:34 Jy23'73. 726
The house of my dreams. Prose. Edna O'Brien. 50:30-9 Ag12'74. 727
The houses of heaven. Prose. Katinka Loeser. 47:35-40 Ap 3'71. 728
How are the legs, Sam? Prose. Garrison Keillor. 46:24-5 Ja 30'71. 729
How I love you. Verse. Vladimir Nabokov. 46:44 My23'70. 730
How it might be. Verse. William Hunt. 47:48 F19'72. 731
How long. Verse. Nelly Sachs. Ruth Mead, trans. [and] Matthew Mead, trans. 46:48 O31'70. 732
How now? Prose. Calvin Tomkins. 46:28 Ja23'71. 733
How Stump stood in the water. Verse. David Wagoner. 50: 38 Ja27'75. 734
How the invalids make love. Verse. Susan Feldman. 50: 46 S2'74. 735
How the people feel. Annals of politics. Richard Harris. 47:34-54 Jy10'71. 736
How to love America and leave it at the same time. Prose. John Updike. 48:25-7 Ag19'72. 737
Howard, Sidney. S. N. Behrman. 48:48ff My27'72. 738
The human sound. PR (Short). Whitney Balliett. 46:28-35 D26'70. 739
The humanities building. Verse. Karl Shapiro. 50:40 My13'74. 740
The humblest fruit. PR (Banana). Berton Roueché. 49:43-56 O1'73. 741
A hundred thousand at a glance. Irish sketches. John McCarten. 47:131-4 My8'71. 742
Hungary. Verse. Stephen Berg. 49:52 N26'73. 743
Hunger-trace. Verse. John Peck. 47:36 Ag14'71. 744
The hunt. Prose. Cristy West. 49:35-41 S24'73. 745
Huston, John. TT. 48:19-22 Ag5'72. 746
Huxley, Aldous. George Steiner. 50:103-106 F17'75. 747
No entry 748

I

I am a cameraman. Verse. Douglas Dunn. 49:36 Je2'72. 749
I bought a little city. Prose. Donald Barthelme. 50:42-4 N11'74. 750
I thing. Prose. J. B. Handelsman. 47:72-3 Ja8'72. 751
Ibn Hakkan al-Bokhari, dead in

his labyrinth. Prose. Jorge Luis Borges. Norman Thomas di Giovanni, trans. 46:34-8 Ap25'70. 752
Ibsen, Henrik (Parody). Woody Allen. 50:44-5 O28'74. 753
Ibsen, Henrik. Brendan Gill. 48:126-9 Ap8'72. 754
The ice road. RL. Edith Iglauer. 50:28-51 D30'74. 755
Identity. Verse. Paul Petrie. 47:38 F5'72. 756
I'd know you anywhere. Prose. Charles Saxon. 50:40-2 Je10'74. 757
Idyll, with siren. Verse. Jon Swan. 46:75 F6'71. 758
If the president's half-hour press conference had been allowed to go beyond half an hour. Prose. James Stevenson. 46:35 D26'70. 759
Illich, Ivan. PR. Francine du Plessix Gray. 46:40-92 Ap25'70. 760
Immortal Gatito. Annals of justice. Mavis Gallant. 47:47-76 Je26'71. 761
In a ho-jo's by the river. Verse. L. E. Sissman. 47:43 F27'71. 762
In Baltimore--why Baltimore?--did Kahn. Verse. L. E. Sissman. 47:43 F27'71. 763
In Charlie's Bar. Verse. E. B. White. 46:36 F21'70. 764
In clover. ACH. Andy Logan. 49:209-22 N19'73. 765
In criminal court. Annals of law. Richard Harris. 49:45-88 Ap 14'73; 49:44-87 Ap21'73. 766
In Nine Sleep Valley. Verse. James Merrill. 46:34-5 Ag1'70. 767
In search of a season. SS. Roger Angell. 48:54-62 Jy1'72. 768
In snow. Verse. Lawrence Bridges. 50:36 Ja20'75. 769
In the dough. Prose. Roger Angell. 48:28-30 Je17'72. 770
In the Hamptons. Verse. John N. Morris. 48:54 Ag5'72. 771
In the hospital. Verse. Laura Jensen. 50:38 F3'75. 772
In the marriage-bed. Verse. Douglas Dunn. 49:34 Je16'73. 773
In the mental ward. Verse. Irving Feldman. 47:54 O30'71. 774
In the mountains. Prose. R. Prawer Jhabvala. 48:32-9 D16'72. 775
In the spotlight. ACH. Andy Logan. 49:82-93 F11'74. 776
In the summer house. Prose. Elizabeth Cullinan. 48:25-33 Jy 8'72. 777
In the tunnel. Prose. Mavis Gallant. 47:34-47 S18'71. 778
In the village. Verse. Andrew Oerke. 49:36 Mr31'73. 779
In the waiting room. Verse. Elizabeth Bishop. 47:34 Jy 17'71. 780
In the words of. Prose. Julie Hayden. 48:35-8 Mr25'72. 781
In thrall to fear. REF. J. William Fulbright. 47:41-62 Ja8'72. 782
Income by right. Annals of politics. Daniel P. Moynihan. 48:34-57 Ja13'73; 48:60-79 Ja20'73; 48:57-81 Ja27'73. 783
Indian journal: leaden echo, golden echo. RL. Ved Mehta. 46:94-160 Ap11'70. 784
Infinite pains. PR (Caldwell). Winthrop Sargeant. 49:43-9 D24'73. 785
Inflation meets Thoreau tactics, and is defeated. OFFC. Noel Perrin. 46:70-80 F21'70. 786
The inquiring demographer. Prose. Calvin Trillin [and] Edward Koren. 49:48-9 D17'73; 50:30-1 My27'74; 50:24-5 Ag26'74. 787
The inside-out. Prose. Sylvia Townsend Warner. 48:38-9 Ap15'72. 788

Insomnia the gem of the ocean. Verse. John Updike. 48:40 S16'72. 789
Instructions to four walls. Verse. W. S. Merwin. 48:33 Ja13'73. 790
Insufficient evidence. Annals of medicine. Berton Roueché. 46:64-81 Ag22'70. 791
The interior stadium. SS. Roger Angell. 47:92-9 F20'71. 792
Intimations of mortality. Verse. John Hall Wheelock. 50:78 Jy 22'74. 793
Into the brain. RL. Gerald Jonas. 50:52-69 Jy1'74. 794
The invention of the telephone. Verse. Peter Klappert. 47:32 Je19'71. 795
Inventory. Verse. Jacques Prévert. Natacha Stewart, trans. 50:44-5 O21'74. 796
Ionesco, Eugène. Janet Flanner. 47:117-18 Mr13'71. 797
Ip gissa gul. Prose. George Booth. 50:32-3 Ja20'75. 798
Irina. Prose. Mavis Gallant. 50:44-52 D2'74. 799
Iris. Verse. Muriel Rukeyser. 46:144 My16'70. 800
Irish sketches. (Also listed by individual titles.) Prose. John McCarten. 46:109-11 S12'70; 46:127-9 O31'70; 47:131-4 My 8'71; 47:190-9 N20'71. 801
Iron larks. Prose. Penelope Gilliatt. 48:26-30 Ja13'73. 802
The iron lung. Verse. Stanley Plumly. 50:34 Ag26'74. 803
Irvin, Rea (Obituary). 48:132 Je10'72. 804
The island. Prose. Arturo Vivante. 48:49-53 N4'72. 805
An Ismailia childhood. (Also listed by title.) Prose. Suzy Eban. 46:174-88 D5'70. 806
It is 70° in late November. Opening a window, you nearly know. Verse. Heather McHugh. 50:52 N25'74. 807
It polls for thee. Prose. Ralph Schoenstein. 48:26-7 Ja27'73. 808
It will grow on you. The marts of trade. John Brooks. 49: 106-12 Mr10'73. 809
It's detestable when you live it. PR (Charles). Whitney Balliett. 46:44-76 Mr28'70. 810

J

Jacobowsky and the colonel (Play). S. N. Behrman. 48:92ff My20'72; 48:38ff My 27'72. 811
James, Henry. Geoffrey T. Hellman. 47:43-86 Mr13'71. 812
Jesus on Honshu. Prose. John Updike. 47:29-30 D25'71. 813
Jewels and binoculars. Prose. Henry Bromell. 50:35-8 My 6'74. 814
John Chapman. Verse. Richard Wilbur. 49:32 Jy30'73. 815
John is easy to please. OUWA. Ved Mehta. 47:44-87 My8'71. 816
John 1:14. Verse. Jorge Luis Borges. Norman Thomas di Giovanni, trans. 47:38 F12'72. 817
The joke. Prose. Isaac Bashevis Singer. Dorothea Straus, trans. 46:36-44 Ap11'70. 818
Jonathan Livingston Seagull (Film). TT. 49:34-6 F24'73. 819
A journey. Prose. Edna O'Brien. 49:34-9 F11'74. 820
Journey to Eddie. Prose. Maureen Connell. 50:36-40 Mr 18'74. 821
Joyce, James. Janet Flanner. 48:33 Mr11'72. 822
Juan Muraña. Prose. Jorge Luis Borges. Norman Thomas di Giovanni, trans. 47:40-1 Mr27'71. 823
The judges. Verse. Robert Graves. 46:38 Ap25'70. 824
The judgment of Paris. Verse.

W. S. Merwin. 46:38 Je6'70. 825
The judicious observer will be disgusted. PR (Valencia). Kenneth Tynan. 46:33-53 Jy25'70. 826
July and the boat. Verse. Thomas Snapp. 46:72 Je27'70. 827
The jump. Prose. Arturo Vivante. 48:28-30 Ja6'73. 828
June bug. Verse. Anne Sexton. 49:34 Je9'73. 829
The June couple. Prose. W. S. Merwin. 46:32 Jy25'70. 830

K

Kaddish and other matters. Prose. Helen Yglesias. 50:39-45 My6'74. 831
Kafka, Franz. George Steiner. 48:75-81 Jy15'72. 832
Kalimpong Hills, West Bengal. Verse. Richard Schramm. 49:175 N5'73. 833
Kaufman, George S. Pauline Kael. 47:52-78 F20'71. 834
Keaton, Buster. Penelope Gilliatt. 46:118-23 S26'70. 835
Keep it. Verse. C. K. Williams. 47:32 Jy31'71. 836
The Kentish Sleep Journal. Prose. Marshall Brickman. 50:36-7 S16'74. 837
The key of D is daffodil yellow. PR (McPartland). Whitney Balliett. 48:43-57 Ja20'73. 838
The kind and quiet. ENC. M. F. K. Fisher. 46:36-42 S5'70. 839
A kindness. Verse. William Dickey. 50:30 S2'74. 840
King, Anthony. TT. 47:38-40 O9'71. 841
King David dances. Verse. John Berryman. 47:42 F19'72. 842
A kitchen allegory. Prose. M. F. K. Fisher. 48:37-9 Ap 1'72. 843
The kitchen, 1926-1939. Verse. John Unterecker. 48:42 Mr25'72. 844
A knack for languages. Prose. Anne Tyler. 50:32-7 Ja13'75. 845
Korty, John. TT. 46:27-8 Je 6'70. 846

L

The labors of Thor. Verse. David Wagoner. 49:46 S17'73. 847
La-dah-dah-dah-dum. Prose. Gilbert Rogin. 47:32-4 D 18'71. 848
The lady knife-thrower. Verse. Daniel Halpern. 50:28 My 27'74. 849
Lady sings the blues (Film). TT. 48:32-3 O28'72. 850
Lamentations. Prose. Hugh Nissenson. 46:32-4 S19'70. 851
Landau, Ely. TT. 49:31-2 O 1'73. 852
Landscape, with figures. SS. Roger Angell. 50:37-55 Jy 15'74. 853
Langlois, Henri. TT. 46:25 Ag8'70; 47:43-4 O30'71. 854
Langner, Lawrence. S. N. Behrman. 48:84ff My13'72; 48: 46ff My27'72. 855
The lantern. Verse. W. S. Merwin. 48:32 Ja13'73. 856
Last day there. Verse. Richard Hugo. 49:36 F18'74. 857
Last days. Prose. Arturo Vivante. 50:38-43 S16'74. 858
The last letters. Verse. Theodore Weiss. 46:38 S5'70. 859
The last of the wine. Prose. Hannah Green. 46:38-75 F28'70. 860
Last sonnet. Verse. John Hall Wheelock. 46:34 Jy11'70. 861
Late bloomers. Prose. Richard Kramer. 50:46-54 O28'74. 862
Late capital. Prose. W. S. Merwin. 50:59 N18'74. 863
Late-afternoon poem. Verse.

Sheldon Flory. 50:86 F3'75. 864
The latehomecomer. Prose. Mavis Gallant. 50:31-40 Jy8'74. 865
Later still. Verse. Philip Levine. 46:38 Je27'70. 866
Lawrence, Jim. TT. 46:33-4 Mr21'70. 867
Le poids sur le ski aval. SS. Jeremy Bernstein. 50:120-41 Ap15'74. 868
Le tourisme euphonique. Verse. Frederick Packard. 46:90 My 23'70. 869
The leap second. OFFC. E. J. Kahn, Jr. 49:50-8 Ag27'73. 870
Lear, Edward. Donald Barthelme. 46:21 Ja2'71. 871
Leaving a station--Sunday, Feb. 1, 1970. Verse. Peter Kane Dufault. 46:44 Ap18'70. 872
Leaving the church. Prose. Mark Helprin. 50:47-53 N4'74. 873
Leaving the coal cellar. Verse. John Peck. 48:32 Ag12'72. 874
Ledge Pond. Verse. Richard Sewell. 46:36 F13'71. 875
Lee, George Washington. TT. 50:23-4 S2'74 876
Les pieds noirs. PR (Martin and pieds noirs). Jane Kramer. 48:52-108 N25'72. 877
The lesson. Verse. David Wagoner. 50:44 Ap22'74. 878
Let it blow. Verse. Reed Whittemore. 49:58 N5'73. 879
Let's hear it for a beautiful guy. Prose. Bruce Jay Friedman. 50:37-9 Ap8'74. 880
Letter. Verse. W. S. Merwin. 46:40-1 S12'70. 881
Letter. Verse. Leonard Nathan. 49:94 Mr17'73. 882
The letter. Prose. Arturo Vivante. 49:26-9 S3'73. 883
Letter from an institution. Verse. Michael Ryan. 49:36 F4'74. 884
Letter from Armenia. Freeman J. Dyson. 47:126-37 N6'71. 885
Letter from Athens. Anthony Bailey. 47:130-85 N20'71. 886
Letter from Athens. Joseph Kraft. 50:82-95 F10'75. 887
Letter from Berlin. Joseph Wechsberg. 46:69-72 Je27'70; 49:86-91 Mr3'73. 888
Letter from Burma. Robert Shaplen. 49:61-70 Ag27'73. 889
Letter from Cairo. Joseph Kraft. 47:76-100 S18'71; 48:78-89 F10'73; 49:129-42 D17'73. 890
Letter from coast to coast. Verse. L. E. Sissman. 46:46 N7'70. 891
Letter from Damascus. Joseph Kraft. 50:92-106 Je17'74. 892
Letter from Dublin. Jane Kramer. 46:56-65 Jy25'70. 893
Letter from East Germany. Steven Kelman. 48:85-105 S30'72. 894
Letter from Guyana. Jane Kramer. 50:100-28 S16'74. 895
Letter from Hanoi. Joseph Kraft. 48:58-72 Ag12'72. 896
Letter from Hong Kong. Robert Shaplen. 47:58-64 Jy31'71. 897
Letter from Indo-China. Robert Shaplen. 46:130-47 My9'70; 46:125-44 My16'70; 46:57-73 Jy11'70; 46:71-82 Ag15'70; 46:116-32 D19'70; 47:78-91 Mr6'71; 47:104-29 Ap24'71; 49:40-60 Je2'73; 49:76-98 Ja28'74. 898
Letter from Indonesia. Robert Shaplen. 50:57-90 Ap1'74. 899
Letter from Ireland. Jane Kramer. 47:46-79 F19'72. 900
Letter from Israel. Joseph Kraft. 49:63-89 Ap7'73; 49:102-17 F11'74. 901
Letter from Lisbon. Jane Kramer. 50:101-32 S

23'74. 902
A letter from Little Tobago. Verse. Barbara Howes. 46:42 Mr14'70. 903
Letter from London. Mollie Panter-Downes. 46:75-8 My 30'70; 46:61-2 Jy4'70; 46:74-6 Jy25'70; 46:158-63 N14'70; 46:55-6 D26'70; 47:101-103 F27'71; 47:113-15 Ap17'71; 47:64-6 Jy3'71; 47:68-70 Ag 7'71; 47:138-42 O30'71; 47: 177-80 N13'71; 48:84-6 Mr 4'72; 48:108-11 My13'72; 48: 47-8 Jy22'72; 48:67-9 Ag26' 72; 49:131-3 Mr24'73; 49: 181-4 N12'73; 49:168-71 D 3'73; 49:45-6 D31'73; 49: 70-2 Ja28'74; 50:80-4 Mr4'74; 50:139-41 Mr18'74; 50:129-34 Ap22'74; 50:66-8 Je10'74; 50:68-72 Jy22'74; 50:182-4 O28'74; 50:142-5 D2'74; 50: 80-2 Ja27'75. 904
Letter from Long Island Sound. Morton Hunt. 47:62-74 Ag28'71. 905
Letter from Manila. Robert Shaplen. 49:97-119 Ap14'73. 906
Letter from Miami Beach. Richard H. Rovere. 48:71-7 Jy22'72; 48:56-62 S2'72. 907
Letter from Milan. William Murray. 49:76-87 Je23'73. 908
Letter from Moscow. Joseph Kraft. 47:64-76 My29'71; 48:54-60 Je 24'72; 50:68-76 Jy29'74. 909
Letter from Munich. E. J. Kahn, Jr. 48:100-107 S16'72. 910
Letter from Naples. William Murray. 50:55-65 Ag26'74. 911
Letter from New Delhi. Ved Mehta. 50:147-61 O14'74. 912
Letter from Opec. Joseph Kraft. 50:64-75 Ja20'75. 913
Letter from Oregon. E. J. Kahn, Jr. 50:88-99 F25'74. 914
Letter from Osaka. E. J. Kahn, Jr. 46:88-102 Je6'70. 915
Letter from Paris. Janet Flanner. 46:90-3 F21'70; 46:86-91 Mr 7'70; 46:141-4 Mr21'70; 46:121-7 Ap4'70; 46:128-33 Ap18'70; 46:110-17 My2'70; 46:117-21 My16'70; 46:86-9 My30'70; 46:97-102 Je13'70; 46:59-61 Je27'70; 46:50-2 Jy11'70; 46: 77-8 Jy25'70; 46:69-71 Ag 8'70; 46:85-7 Ag22'70; 46: 111-12 N21'70; 47:91-3 F 27'71; 47:116-18 Mr13'71; 47: 95-7 Mr27'71; 47:98-101 Ap 24'71; 47:130-5 My15'71; 47: 85-8 My29'71; 47:106-109 Je12'71; 47:53-6 Jy3'71; 47: 70-2 Jy10'71; 49:75-6 Ag27' 73; 50:123-4 S9'74. 916
Letter from Rome. William Murray. 48:84-95 S9'72; 50: 113-29 Ap8'74. 917
Letter from Saigon. Robert Shaplen. 47:96-118 S11'71; 50:64-75 Ja6'75. 918
Letter from Santiago. Joseph Kraft. 46:80-9 Ja30'71. 919
Letter from Scotland. Alastair Reid. 50:76-117 O7'74. 920
Letter from Selvole. William Murray. 50:178-86 N4'74. 921
Letter from Stockholm. Steven Kelman. 46:36-48 D26'70. 922
Letter from Thailand. Robert Shaplen. 49:67-83 Ja14'74. 923
Letter from the Azores. Tad Szulc. 47:54-8 Ja1'72. 924
Letter from the East. E. B. White. 47:35-7 Mr27'71; 47:27-9 Jy24'71. 925
Letter from the Middle East. Marilyn Berger. 50:140-55 N11'74. 926
Letter from the Space Center. Henry S. F. Cooper, Jr. 46:80-112 Ap4'70; 46:66-74 Ja9'71; 47:120-42 Ap17'71; 47:40-51 Jy17'71; 48:107-20 Ap8'72; 48:56-68 Ag5'72. 927
Letter from Tokyo. Joseph Kraft. 47:140-57 D11'71. 928
Letter from Tokyo. Robert

Shaplen. 50:105-23 My20'74. 929
Letter from Vienna. Joseph Wechsberg. 49:149-58 D10'73. 930
Letter from Vietnam. Robert Shaplen. 47:77-115 N13'71; 48: 114-32 My13'72; 48:70-91 Je 24'72; 48:66-84 Ja13'73; 49: 100-11 F24'73. 931
Letter from Washington. Richard H. Rovere. 46:101-109 F21'70; 46:148-55 Mr21'70; 46:138-47 Ap18'70; 46:146-51 My16'70; 46:109-16 Je13'70; 46:72-80 Jy18'70; 46:86-90 Ag15'70; 46: 130-7 S26'70; 46:131-5 O24'70; 46:187-96 N14'70; 46:137-42 D19'70; 46:85-90 Ja23'71; 47: 108-13 F20'71; 47:123-31 Mr 27'71; 47:115-17 My1'71; 47: 122-7 Je5'71; 47:70-5 Jy17'71; 47:77-81 Ag7'71; 47:116-19 S18'71; 47:155-8 O23'71; 47: 157-61 N13'71; 47:82-9 D18'71; 47:83-7 F5'72; 48:105-10 Mr 4'72; 48:84-7 Ap1'72; 48:131-4 Ap29'72; 48:115-22 My20'72; 48:83-8 Je17'72; 48:91-4 O 21'72; 48:233-7 N18'72; 48: 140-5 D16'72; 48:94-8 Ja20' 73; 48:89-92 F17'73; 49:142-4 Mr24'73; 49:124-30 Ap21'73; 49:103-109 Je9'73; 49:66-70 Jy16'73; 49:78-82 Ag13'73; 49:113-18 S10'73; 49:170-7 O15'73; 49:142-7 O22'73; 49:164-9 N5'73; 49:172-7 D 3'73; 49:54-6 D31'73; 49:97- 100 F4'74; 50:90-4 Mr4'74; 50:111-17 Ap1'74; 50:120-4 Ap29'74; 50:87-92 My27'74; 50:84-9 Je24'74; 50:80-2 Jy 22'74; 50:84-8 Ag19'74; 50: 134-5 S16'74; 50:157-63 O 7'74; 50:170-3 N4'74; 50: 187-91 N18'74; 50:87-9 Ja 20'75. 932
Letter from West Bengal. Ved Mehta. 47:166-76 D11'71. 933
Letter to Barbados. Verse. Ted Walker. 48:44 Ap15'72. 934
Letter to Zbigniew Cybulski. Verse. John Peech. 49:48 N12'73. 935
Letters to the editore. Prose. Donald Barthelme. 50:34-5 F25'74. 936
Leviathan. OLC. Whitney Balliett. 48:62-8 Je24'72. 937
Lewis, Sinclair. S. N. Behrman. 48:87ff My13'72. 938
Lewis, Wilmarth. Geoffrey T. Hellman. 49:104-11 O15'73. 939
Librairie Hachette TT. 47:35-6 O23'71. 940
The life and times of Joseph Stalin (Play). PR. Calvin Tomkins. 50:38-62 Ja13'75. 941
A life on a cloud. PR (Anderson). Janet Flanner. 50:44-67 Je3'74. 942
Life, the interesting character. Verse. Louis Simpson. 46:36 My2'70. 943
Life without mind. Verse. David Shapiro. 49:42 Mr31'73. 944
Light from Canada. Verse. James Schuyler. 47:57 Jy 31'71. 945
Lightened heart and quickened energies. ENC. M. F. K. Fisher. 46:35-9 O3'70. 946
Like a prism. Verse. Barry Spacks. 50:40 S23'74. 947
Liliom (Play). S. N. Behrman. 48:65ff My20'72. 948
The limits of duty. REF. Charles A. Reich. 47:52-9 Je19'71. 949
Link, Peter. TT. 48:35-7 N 11'72. 950
Lippmann, Walter (Obituary). TT. 50:19-20 D30'74. 951
Listening to "Pearl." Verse. Douglas Morea. 47:52 S25'71. 952
The listening woman. Prose. Sylvia Townsend Warner. 48: 34-8 My20'72. 953
Literary footnote. Prose. James Stevenson. 47:38-9 Ja29'72. 954
Literary license. Prose. John

Bailey. 48:74-8 S23'72. 955
The Little Review. Janet Flanner. 50:44-67 Je3'74. 956
The little room. PR (The Netherlands). Anthony Bailey. 46:34-57 Ag8'70; 46:32-63 Ag15'70. 957
Little tale. Verse. John Hollander. 48:89 O21'72. 958
The little wrens and robins. Prose. Benedict Kiely. 46:49-58 Ap4'70. 959
Local family keeps son happy. Prose. Garrison Keillor. 46:39 S19'70. 960
The locks that are threatened with rape. Irish sketches. John Mc Carten. 47:190-9 N20'71. 961
Loneliness. Verse. John Betjeman. 47:45 Ap17'71. 962
Long distance. Prose. Penelope Mortimer. 50:36-103 Ap15'74; 50:35-101 Ap22'74. 963
Long, Lois (Retirement). 46:138 Mr21'70. 964
Long, Lois (Obituary). 50:100 Ag12'74. 965
The long march. SS. Roger Angell. 49:183-202 N19'73. 966
Long weekend. Prose. Daniel Menaker. 50:41-3 Je3'74. 967
A look at organized crime. Prose. Woody Allen. 46:24-5 Ag15'70. 968
The look back. Verse. Arthur Gregor. 48:86 My6'72. 969
Look for the rusty lining. Prose. Ralph Schoenstein. 50:31 F3'75. 970
Look to the things around you. PR (Strand). Calvin Tomkins. 50:44-94 S16'74. 971
Looking for Itsy. Verse. Naomi Lazard. 47:42 S18'71. 972
Lord of the fish. PR (Whales). Faith McNulty. 49:38-67 Ag 6'73. 973
Lost. Prose. Isaac Bashevis Singer. Rosanna Gerber, trans. 49:31-5 Je23'73. 974
Lost in translation. Verse. James Merrill. 50:40-1 Ap8'74. 975
Lotus. Prose. Perdita Buchan. 47:36-42 Mr13'71. 976
The lotus-eater. Prose. H. L. Mountzoures. 47:36-9 F12'72. 977
Lovborg's women considered. Prose. Woody Allen. 50:44-5 O28'74. 978
Love. Prose. Sylvia Townsend Warner. 48:30-1 S16'72. 979
Love blemished but abiding. ENC. M. F. K. Fisher. 47:36-42 My15'71. 980
Love child. Prose. Edna O'Brien. 49:41-3 O29'73. 981
Love day, 1945. Verse. L. E. Sissman. 49:42-3 My5'73. 982
Love: first lessons. Prose. John Updike. 47:46-7 N6'71. 983
Love in the Hamptons. Prose. Elaine Mueller. 48:24-32 Jy29'72. 984
Love of country. RL. Daniel Lang. 49:35-48 Jy30'73. 985
A love story. Prose. Penelope Mortimer. 50:32-6 Jy15'74. 986
The lovepet. Verse. Ted Hughes. 46:24 Ja2'71. 987
The lowliest bush a purple sage would be. Prose. Garrison Keillor. 47:35 Mr6'71. 988
Lu Hsün. Joseph Kraft. 48:105-106 My6'72. 989
A lullaby. Verse. W. H. Auden. 49:32 Ag6'73. 990
Lysistrata (Play). TT. 48:30-1 S23'72. 991

M

Ma. Prose. Edna O'Brien. 48:24-6 Jy22'72. 992
Macbeth. John McPhee. 46:141-7 O10'70. 993
McCarten, John (Obituary). 50:179 O7'74. 994
Mc Govern. OLC. James Stevenson. 47:47-9 Ja1'72. 995
McGraw-Hill Company. TT. 50:

27-9 Ap29'74. 996
Mae West. Verse. Edward Field. 50:30 Jy15'74. 997
The magazine. Prose. Isaac Bashevis Singer. Laurie Colwin, trans. 47:33-7 My22'71. 998
The magic curtain. Verse. Stanley Kunitz. 46:34 F6'71. 999
Magical dangers. Verse. Ted Hughes. 46:30 Jy18'70. 1000
The magician's retreat. Verse. Marianne Moore. 46:40 F21'70. 1001
The magistrate. Prose. Alexander Frater. 48:38-44 Je3'71. 1002
Maiden's leap. Prose. Benedict Kiely. 48:26-35 Jy1'72. 1003
Mailer, Norman. TT. 47:33 O2'71. 1004
Mainly about Jones. SS. Herbert Warren Wind. 48:114-28 Ap 29'72. 1005
The makers of rain. Verse. David Wagoner. 47:40 Jy24'71. 1006
Making a noise in the world. PR (Bankhead). Brendan Gill. 48: 45-99 O7'72; 48:50-122 O14' 72. 1007
The making of the bear. Verse. Ramon Guthrie. 46:40-1 My 2'70. 1008
Malraux, André. Janet Flanner. 47:98-101 Ap24'71. 1009
A man. Prose. Donald Barthelme. 48:26-7 D30'72. 1010
Man on a hill. Prose. Ted Walker. 48:44-7 N11'72. 1011
The man on the bed. Verse. Debora Greger. 50:54 D2'74. 1012
The man on the threshold. Prose. Jorge Luis Borges. Norman Thomas di Giovanni, trans. 46:39-41 Ap4'70. 1013
Mankiewicz, Herman J. Pauline Kael. 47:46-79 F20'71; 47:44-81 F27'71. 1014
Mantras for everyone. Prose. F. P. Tullius. 50:43 D2'74. 1015
March, Saturday, 2p. m. -3p. m. Prose. James Stevenson. 46: 43 Mr28'70. 1016
Marie. Prose. L. Woiwode. 47: 32-8 D25'71. 1017
Marta and Leni. Prose. Robert Henderson. 49:26-32 Jy23'73. 1018
The marts of trade. (Also listed by individual titles.) John Brooks. The anti-corporation. 47:138-43 O9'71; Exxon. 49: 106-12 Mr10'73. 1019
Martz, Louis L. TT. 49:24-5 Ja7'74. 1020
The marvellous girl. Prose. V. S. Pritchett. 49:38-42 D24'73. 1021
Marvin Stanley Pigeon. Prose. Thomas Meehan. 48:53-4 N18'72. 1022
Mary Shellmic. Verse. Judi Croxford. 46:58 Jy18'70. 1023
The Masters--something old, something new. SS. Herbert Warren Wind. 50:102-21 My13'74. 1024
Mathematics and creativity. REF. Alfred Adler. 47:39-45 F19'72. 1025
Matins with lauds. Verse. L. E. Sissman. 47:42 Je26'71. 1026
Matthews, Brander. S. N. Behrman. 48:37ff My13'72. 1027
Matthews, Les. TT. 47:30-2 S18'71. 1028
Matura. Prose. Richard Berczeller. 48:32-8 S16'72. 1029
Maybe a quantum leap. OUWA. Calvin Tomkins. 47:42-67 F5'72. 1030
Mayer, Arthur Loeb. PR. E. J. Kahn, Jr. 50:46-66 D9'74. 1031
Mayer, Timothy. TT. 46:33 Ap11'70. 1032
Meanwhile, back at the crunch... Prose. S. J. Perelman. 48:33-5 Ap8'72. 1033
The measure of man. PR (Erikson). Robert Coles. 46:

51-131 N7'70; 46:59-138 N14'70. 1034

The meddlers. PR (Amnesty International). E. J. Kahn, Jr. 46:44-57 Ag22'70. 1035

Mediator. PR (Kheel). Fred C. Shapiro. 46:36-58 Ag1'70. 1036

The meeting. Prose. Jorge Luis Borges. Norman Thomas di Giovanni, trans. 46:30-3 Ag 8'70. 1037

The megamachine. REF. Lewis Mumford. 46:50-131 O10'70; 46:48-141 O17'70; 46:55-127 O 24'70; 46:50-98 O31'70. 1038

Mekas, Jonas. PR. Calvin Tomkins. 48:31-49 Ja6'73. 1039

Melville Society. TT. 50:29-30 Ja13'75. 1040

Memories of Lower Fifth. Verse. Howard Moss. 50:52 O14'74. 1041

The mentor. Prose. Isaac Bashevis Singer. Evelyn Torton Beck, trans. 46:40-6 Mr21'70. 1042

Mercer Arts Center. TT. 48:28-9 F26'72. 1043

Metamorphosis. Verse. Jon Swan. 46:33 Je20'70. 1044

Meteor (Play). S. N. Behrman. 48:40ff My20'72. 1045

Metropolitan comics. Prose. James Stevenson. 47:36-9 Jy 17'71. 1046

Metropolitan New York points of interest. Prose. James Stevenson. 46:38 F6'71. 1047

The Mexican peacock. Verse. Josephine Jacobsen. 48:40 Je24'72. 1048

Micheaux, Oscar. TT. 46:34-5 Ap18'70. 1049

Micronesia revisited. RL. E. J. Kahn, Jr. 47:98-115 D18'71. 1050

The milk run. Prose. Christina Stead. 48:43-7 D9'72. 1051

Milkman's boy. Prose. H. L. Mountzoures. 50:38-40 Ap29'74. 1052

Miller, Jason. TT. 48:32-3 My 20'72. 1053

The Miller's tale. SS. Herbert Warren Wind. 49:48-55 Jy9'73. 1054

Millett, Kate. Janet Malcolm. 48:128-30 Mr18'72. 1055

Mime. Prose. Henry Bromell. 49:32-5 Jy9'73. 1056

Mingus at peace. RL. Whitney Balliett. 47:42-52 My29'71. 1057

Minor heroism. Prose. Allan Gurganus. 50:49-58 N18'74. 1058

Mirror. Verse. Peter Cooley. 50:46 F25'74. 1059

Mishima, Yukio. TT. 46:39-41 D12'70. 1060

Miss Ellie's 78th Spring party. Verse. Daniel Mark Epstein. 48:44 Ap22'72. 1061

Missing masterpieces. Prose. Dean Vietor. 50:34-5 S23'74. 1062

Missing: two lollapaloozas--no reward. Prose. S. J. Perelman. 46:39-41 O17'70. 1063

Mist. Verse. W. S. Merwin. 47:44 Ap24'71. 1064

Mr. D. Verse. Ann Stanford. 49:34 Jy9'73. 1065

Mr. Parker. Prose. Laurie Colwin. 49:42-4 Ap14'73. 1066

Mrs. Blasingame Poteet. Prose. Robert D. Gorchov. 49:34-9 My12'73. 1067

Mrs. Court and Mr. Rosewall. SS. Herbert Warren Wind. 46:172-84 O10'70. 1068

Ms. magazine. TT. 50:32-3 S23'74. 1069

Mizoguchi, Kenzi. Penelope Gilliatt. 48:70-2 Jy15'72. 1070

Moment of wisdom. Prose. M. F. K. Fisher. 48:139-43 Mr18'72. 1071

Money. Prose. Arnold Sundgaard. 49:47-50 N12'73. 1072

Money music. PR (Rudman). George W. S. Trow. 48:32-49 D23'72. 1073

Monstrance. Verse. Kenneth Rosen. 50:56 N4'74. 1074
Montevideo. Verse. Jorge Luis Borges. Norman Thomas di Giovanni, trans. 48:34 Mr11'72. 1075
Moonbeam Moscowitz. PR (Syms) Whitney Balliett. 50:47-56 O21'74. 1076
The moose. Verse. Elizabeth Bishop. 48:27 Jy15'72. 1077
More ingredients. PR (Hackett). Whitney Balliett. 48:36-49 Ag 12'72. 1078
More under Saturn. Verse. William Dickey. 46:34 Ja16'71. 1079
Morgan Library. TT. 50:39-40 N4'74. 1080
Mørketiden. RL. Joseph Wechsberg. 48:103-26 Mr18'72. 1081
Morning, night, and very late. Verse. Howard Moss. 50:34 Jy29'74. 1082
The mortal milk. Prose. Sylvia Townsend Warner. 49:32-8 F18'74. 1083
The mothball fleet. Prose. Donald Barthelme. 47:34-5 S11'71. 1084
Mother Goose. Verse. Jill Hoffman. 49:35 O1'73. 1085
Mother's Day. Prose. Jessamyn West. 46:32-7 My30'70. 1086
The mountains. Verse. W. S. Merwin. 46:38 Je6'70. 1087
Mountains polecats pheasants. Verse. Leslie Norris. 47:56 D4'71. 1088
Mouth-organ tunes: the American lost and found. Verse. L. E. Sissman. 47:43 F27'71. 1089
Movies. Pauline Kael. 46:74-80 O3'70; 46:76-80 Ja23'71. 1090
Moving day. Prose. R. L. Gordon. 48:44-6 S30'72. 1091
Moving with the flow. PR (Geldzahler). Calvin Tomkins. 47:58-113 N6'71. 1092
Mū. Prose. Calvin Tomkins. 46:53 D5'70. 1093
The muse of history at Rampanalgas. Verse. Derek Walcott. 48:36-7 O28'72. 1094
Museum. Prose. Calvin Tomkins. 46:22-4 Jy18'70. 1095
The music at Long Verney. Prose. Sylvia Townsend Warner. 47:26-32 Ag28'71. 1096
Must the show go on? SS. E. J. Kahn, Jr. 48:114-23 S23'72. 1097
The mysterious case of R. Prose. Frank Conroy. 46:23-4 Ag29'70. 1098

N

Naga. Prose. R. K. Narayan. 48:24-9 Ag26'72. 1099
Nash, Ogden (Obituary). 47:92 My29'71. 1100
A nation of wheels. Prose. Donald Barthelme. 46:36-9 Je13'70. 1101
The National Star. TT. 50:30-1 F25'74. 1102
Natural history. Verse. Robert Penn Warren. 48:38 Ap1'72. 1103
Nearing the lights. Verse. Howard Moss. 48:36 O7'72. 1104
Neighbors. Prose. Isaac Bashevis Singer. Herbert R. Lottman, trans. 48:34-7 Je10'72. 1105
Networks. Verse. George Amabile. 47:97 Mr27'71. 1106
Never touch a butterfly. Prose. John Batki. 46:42-5 My9'70. 1107
The new baseball. Prose. Garrison Keillor. 47:35 My 15'71. 1108
New Books Presentation and Exhibit. TT. 49:33-5 S10'73. 1109
New chapter in Korea. RL. Robert Shaplen. 48:116-47 N25'72; 48:128-55 D2'72. 1110
New faces. ACH. Andy Logan. 50:203-13 N18'74. 1111

A new fifteenth and the old Casper. SS. Herbert Warren Wind. 46:93-101 My2'70. 1112
The new justice. REF. Richard Harris. 48:44-105 Mr25'72. 1113
The new member. Prose. Donald Barthelme. 50:28-30 Jy15'74. 1114
A new politics in Atlanta. PR (Atlanta, Georgia). Fred Powledge. 49:28-40 D31'73. 1115
The new world. Prose. W. S. Merwin. 50:35 F10'75. 1116
New year. Verse. Sheldon Flory. 46:30 Ja2'71. 1117
The new year party. Prose. Isaac Bashevis Singer. Rosanna Gerber Cohen, trans. 50:32-8 Ap1'74. 1118
New York: a Summer funeral. Verse. L. E. Sissman. 49: 26-7 Ag27'73. 1119
New York Erotic Film Festival. TT. 48:31 D16'72. 1120
The New York experience (Film). TT. 49:35-6 O8'73. 1121
New York Film Festival. TT. 46:30-1 S19'70. 1122
New York Public Library. TT. 50:46-7 N18'74 1123
New York Times (Parody). Nora Ephron. 50:49 N25'74. 1124
New York Times (Parody). Philip Hamburger. 46:51-2 D12'70. 1125
The New Yorker advisor. Prose. Roger Angell. 50:28-32 S2'74. 1126
Newsletter. Prose. Donald Barthelme. 46:23 Jy11'70. 1127
Nibbling. ACH. Andy Logan. 50:67-73 Ja13'75. 1128
Nicholson, J. Kenyon. S. N. Behrman. 48:61ff My13'72. 1129
Night city. Verse. Elizabeth Bishop. 48:122 S16'72. 1130
Night clubs. PR (Gordon and Josephson). Whitney Balliett. 47:50-92 O9'71. 1131
Night friends. Verse. S. J. Marks. 47:52 D4'71. 1132
Night out. Prose. A. Alvarez. 47:26-31. S4'71. 1133
The night out. Prose. Ted Walker. 46:26-30 Ja30'71. 1134
Night patrol. Verse. Josephine Jacobsen. 48:34 Ja6'73. 1135
Night rain on roses. Verse. Ted Walker. 47:86 Ag21'71. 1136
Night running. Verse. Thomas Snapp. 47:36 Jy31'71. 1137
Night thoughts. Prose. Gilbert Rogin. 50:33-5 S2'74. 1138
The night we rode with Sarsfield. Prose. Benedict Kiely. 49:28-32 Ag20'73. 1139
The nine. Verse. Greg Kuzma. 49:38 O29'73. 1140
Ninotchka (Film). S. N. Behrman. 48:79ff My20'72. 1141
Nixon and Lincoln. REF. Richard Harris. 50:108-14 Ap15'74. 1142
No news at all. Verse. Jack Butler. 50:42 S16'74. 1143
No, no, Nanette (Play). TT. 46:23 Ja30'71. 1144
No time for comedy (Play). S. N. Behrman. 48:59ff My27'72. 1145
Nobody's business. Prose. Penelope Gilliatt. 47:22-9 Jy3'71. 1146
Nocturne. Verse. W. H. Auden. 50:42 My6'74. 1147
Nomad. Verse. Dabney Stuart. 47:73 Ja8'72. 1148
Nones. Verse. L. E. Sissman. 47:43 Je26'71. 1149
Noon. Verse. Helen Chasin. 50:50 N4'74. 1150
Nora's friends. Prose. Elizabeth Cullinan. 46:26-32 Ag29'70. 1151
Normalcy stretching out like a clean blanket of facts. Verse. Jack Galef. 49:40 Mr10'73. 1152
North country luck. RL. Burton Bernstein. 47:100-47 N27'71. 1153

The North Sea. Verse. Howard Moss. 46:40 Mr7'70. 1154
Not dying. Verse. Mark Strand. 46:40 My9'70. 1155
Not so the chairs. Verse. Donald Finkel. 50:222 N18'74. 1156
Not you, not you. ACH. Andy Logan. 48:169-82 N11'72. 1157
Nothing: a preliminary account. Prose. Donald Barthelme. 49: 26-7 D31'73. 1158
Now it is clear. Verse. W. S. Merwin. 46:39 Je6'70. 1159
Numbers game. ACH. Andy Logan. 50:52-9 Jy8'74. 1160

O

O lasting peace. Prose. Mavis Gallant. 47:34-40 Ja8'72. 1161
Oberfest. Prose. James Stevenson. 47:43 My8'71. 1162
Objects & apparitions. Verse. Octavio Paz. Elizabeth Bishop, trans. 50:32 Je24'74. 1163
Occasional birds. Verse. P. J. Kavanagh. 47:46 Ap10'71. 1164
October ghosts. Verse. James Wright. 47:40 O2'71. 1165
Ode on insomnia. Verse. J. D. Reed. 48:49 Ag12'72. 1166
Ode to my desk. Verse. Douglas Dunn. 50:40 My20'74. 1167
O'Donoghue, Michael. TT. 46: 28-9 Je6'70. 1168
Of love and friendship. Prose. Arturo Vivante. 49:41-5 My 26'73. 1169
The oilman. Prose. Montgomery Newman. 47:120-7 S18'71. 1170
Old apple trees. Verse. W. D. Snodgrass. 47:41 My1'71. 1171
The old boat. Prose. W. S. Merwin. 49:39 F18'74. 1172
The old clothes. Verse. Brendan Galvin. 50:40 Je3'74. 1173
Old friends. Prose. Henry Bromell. 49:50-9 D17'73. 1174
The old Halvorson place. Prose. L. Woiwode. 47:35-43 My8'71. 1175
The old poet. Verse. Howard Moss. 49:50 F24'73. 1176
The old story about a path. Prose. W. S. Merwin. 46: 42-3 My2'70. 1177
Old woman. Prose. Ivy Litvinov. 49:32-6 Je16'73. 1178
Omen. Verse. Jon Swan. 48:36 S23'72. 1179
On a wagon. Prose. Isaac Bashevis Singer. Dorothea Straus, trans. 46:25-30 Jy 25'70. 1180
On actors scribbling letters very quickly in crucial scenes. Verse. Jean Garrigue. 47: 58 Ja1'72. 1181
On bail. Prose. R. Prawer Jhabvala. 49:34-44 Mr31'73. 1182
On Fourteenth Street. Verse. Douglas Morea. 47:32 Ja8'72. 1183
On going by train to White River Junction, Vt. Verse. Jean Garrigue. 47:60 N20'71. 1184
On insects. Verse. Lewis Thomas. 47:28 Jy10'71. 1185
On refusing an invitation to dine with a peer's son and some of the so-called beautiful people. Verse. Brendan Gill. 47:81 Ag28'71. 1186
On Route 202, New Hampshire. Verse. Howard Moss. 50:32 Ja6'75. 1187
On the future of movies. OUWA. Pauline Kael. 50:43-59 Ag 5'74. 1188
On the map. Prose. W. S. Merwin. 50:59 N18'74. 1189
On the mountain. Verse. W. S. Merwin. 50:39 O21'74. 1190
On the Oldpark Road, Belfast. RL. Anthony Bailey. 49:114-50 O29'73. 1191
On the road. ACH. Andy Logan. 47:72-8 Ja22'72. 1192
On the road. Verse. Pablo Neruda. Ben Belitt, trans. 47:54 N20'71. 1193
On the road, almost. Prose. Garrison Keillor. 47:45 F 19'72. 1194

On the side of the apes. RL. Emily Hahn. 47:46-97 Ap 17'71; 47:46-91 Ap24'71. 1195
On vous cherche. RL. Jeremy Bernstein. 47:118-37 O30'71. 1196
One hundred ten West Sixty-first Street. Prose. Donald Barthelme. 49:33-4 S24'73. 1197
One man's opiate. Verse. Ogden Nash. 46:56 D5'70. 1198
One of our stagecraft is missing. Prose. S. J. Perelman. 50: 32-4 D23'74. 1199
One of ours. Prose. Ted Walker. 47:36-9 O16'71. 1200
One time. Verse. W. S. Merwin. 47:44 Ap24'71. 1201
The one-legged man. Verse. Anne Sexton. 48:34 S16'72. 1202
The only bar in Dixon. Verse. Richard F. Hugo. 46:48 O10'70. 1203
The only bar in Dixon. Verse. J. D. Reed. 46:48 O10'70. 1204
The only bar in Dixon. Verse. James Welch. 46:48 O10'70. 1205
Only fitting. Verse. Jon Swan. 47:44 S25'71. 1206
Only human. Prose. Elizabeth Cullinan. 46:28-37 F6'71. 1207
Onward and upward with the arts. Prose. (Also listed by individual titles.)
Pepsi-Cola pavilion, Expo '70. Calvin Tomkins. 46:83-133 O3'70.
Cubist art exhibition in Los Angeles. Francis Steegmuller. 46:70-5 Ja23'71.
Citizen Kane. Pauline Kael. 47:43-89 F20'71; 47:44-81 F27'71.
Linguistics. Ved Mehta. 47: 44-87 My8'71.
Translation. Victor Proetz. 47:82-121 My22'71.
Earth art. Calvin Tomkins. 47:42-67 F5'72.
Science fiction. Gerald Jonas. 48:33-52 Jy29'72.
Television network news. Edward Jay Epstein. 49:41-77 Mr3'73.
Grand Ole Opry. Garrison Keillor. 50:46-70 My6'74.
Movies. Pauline Kael. 50: 43-59 Ag5'74. 1208
Opus 132. Verse. Harold Witt. 46:117 My2'70. 1209
Orchestra. PR (Cleveland Orchestra). Joseph Wechsberg. 46:38-69 My30'70. 1210
Oreads. Verse. Kathleen Raine. 48:36 D30'72. 1211
Organ transplant. Verse. J. D. Reed. 46:126 S26'70. 1212
The orphaned swimming pool. Prose. John Updike. 46:30-2 Je27'70. 1213
Orr country. SS. Herbert Warren Wind. 47:107-14 Mr27'71. 1214
The osprey suicides. Verse. Laurence Lieberman. 48:48-9 N25'72. 1215
Our far-flung correspondents. Prose. (Also listed by individual titles.)
Building a house. Noel Perrin. 46:70-80 F21'70.
Mobile jazz festival. Whitney Balliett. 46:114-24 Ap 25'70.
Environmental disruption. Fred C. Shapiro. 46:93-105 My23'70.
Dartmouth senior class. Noel Perrin. 46:53-8 Jy18'70.
Australia. Joan Colebrook. 46:70-93 S5'70.
Dunsinane. John McPhee. 46:141-7 O10'70.
British decimal currency. John Brooks. 46:182-99 N21'70.
Pigs. William Whitworth. 46: 64-9 Ja30'71.
Stravinsky. Francis Steegmuller. 47:99-103 My1'71.
Lake Baikal. Marshall I. Goldman. 47:58-66 Je19'71.
Record rainfall. Eugene Kinkead. 47:66-74 Jy31'71.

Sonic boom. William Murray. 48:85-93 S16'72.
Peregrine falcons. Faith Mc Nulty. 48:67-74 D23'72.
Leap second. E. J. Kahn, Jr. 49:50-8 Ag27'73.
Peas. Susan Sheehan. 49:103-18 S17'73.
Wilmarth S. Lewis. Geoffrey T. Hellman. 49:104-11 O 15'73. 1216
Our footloose correspondents. Prose. (Also listed by individual titles.)
General Motors stockholders' meeting. E. J. Kahn, Jr. 46:40-51 Je20'70.
Soviet cruise ship. Natacha Stewart. 50:44-99 S23'74; 50:38-93 S30'74. 1217
Our local correspondents. Prose. (Also listed by individual titles.)
New York City Assembly district campaign. Susan Lardner. 46:96-108 Je20'70.
Duke Ellington. Whitney Balliett. 46:52-5 Je27'70.
Tree champion. Eugene Kinkead. 46:143-55 O24'70.
Dennis Hopper. James Stevenson. 47:116-28 N13'71.
Senator McGovern. James Stevenson. 47:47-9 Ja 1'72.
George Wein. Whitney Balliett. 48:62-8 Je24'72.
Conversations with Red. Niccolo Tucci. 48:69-77 Ag5'72.
Harvey Scribner. Nat Hentoff. 48:131-45 O14'72
World Trade Center Foundation. Edith Iglauer. 48:130-51 N4'72.
The Eastern bluebird. Eugene Kinkead. 49:50-5 D24'73.
Jimmy Rowles. Whitney Balliett. 50:43-50 Ap1'74.
Central Park birds. Eugene Kinkead. 50:78-86 Ag26'74.
Central Park squirrels. Eugene Kinkead. 50:101-12 S9'74.
1974 election results. Richard N. Goodwin. 50:137-48 N 25'74. 1218
Our science correspondents: bioluminescence. (Also listed by title.) Prose. Eugene Kinkead. 48:92-111 S23'72. 1219
Our work and why we do it. Prose. Donald Barthelme. 49:39-41 My5'73. 1220
Out of it. RL. Daniel Lang. 46:42-68 My23'70. 1221
Out of the cocoon on the fifty-sixth floor. PR (Rockefeller). Geoffrey T. Hellman. 48:56-103 N4'72. 1222
Outgoing bag. Prose. Roger Angell. 46:32-4 O3'70 1223
The outsider. PR (Brandt). Joseph Wechsberg. 49:35-57 Ja14'74. 1224
Over. Prose. Edna O'Brien. 48:52-9 D2'73. 1225
Over by the river. Prose. William Maxwell. 50:24-44 Jy 1'74. 1226
Over the sea of hesitation. Prose. Donald Barthelme. 48:40-3 N11'72. 1227
Oxford visit. Prose. Barbara Vroom. 47:112-15 My8'71. 1228
Oya life these days. Prose. Garrison Keillor. 50:31-2 F17'75. 1229
Oz, Amos. Joseph Kraft. 49:68-70 Ap7'73. 1230
Ozu, Yasujiro. Penelope Gilliatt. 48:102-106 Ap8'72. 1231

P

Pablo. Prose. Lyll Becerra de Jenkins. 49:28-32 Ja7'74. 1232
Packard, Frederick (Obituary). 50:196 N25'74. 1233
The page-turner. Verse. David Shapiro. 48:36 D16'72. 1234
A pair. Prose. Isaac Bashevis Singer. Blanche Nevel, trans. [and] Joseph Nevel, trans. 49:48-53 D3'73. 1235
A palace incident. ENC. M. F. K.

46:37-41 Ja16'71. 1236
The Panthers and the police: a pattern of genocide? RL. Edward Jay Epstein. 46:45-77 F13'71. 1237
Parameters. Verse. Jack Butler. 50:56 O14'74. 1238
Paris Review party. TT. 49:29 Je9'73. 1239
The park. Prose. Arturo Vivante. 50:40-2 Ag5'74. 1240
Part of a season: Bay and Back Bay. SS. Roger Angell. 47:73-82 Je19'71. 1241
The party. Prose. Donald Barthelme. 48:30-1 F26'72. 1242
Passage to Ararat. Prose. Michael J. Arlen. 50:32-74 F3'75; 50:36-73 F10'75; 50:34-83 F17'75. 1243
Passell, Peter (Parody). Charles McGrath [and] Daniel Menaker. 50:46 O14'74. 1244
The passing. Prose. Berry Morgan. 47:44-6 Je26'71. 1245
Paternity. Prose. Richard Berczeller. 46:34-41 Je27'70. 1246
The path to peace. RL. Robert Shaplen. 48:184-94 N4'72. 1247
The path toward the high valley. Verse. Galway Kinnell. 47:38 Ap17'71. 1248
The patient. Prose. Barbara Lawrence. 50:162-8 N4'74. 1249
Paul, Steven. TT. 46:28-31 F13'71. 1250
The peace talks. RL. Robert Shaplen. 46:162-80 O17'70. 1251
A peaceable town. PR (Stapleton, Kansas). Berton Roueché. 46:29-40 Ja2'71. 1252
Peale, Norman Vincent. TT. 46:34-5 My9'70. 1253
Peas. OFFC. Susan Sheehan. 49:103-18 S17'73. 1254
Pebble Beach. SS. Herbert Warren Wind. 48:60-72 Jy8'72. 1255
Pelote. SS. Herbert Warren Wind. 50:85-103 Je10'74. 1256
The pen is mightier--and also pricier. Prose. S. J. Perelman. 46:21-2 D26'70. 1257
Penthouse magazine (Parody). Roger Angell. 50:28-32 S2'74. 1258
People in a diary. Prose. S. N. Behrman. 48:36-94 My13'72; 48:39-95 My20'72; 48:38-81 My27'72. 1259
The people's shopper. Prose. Garrison Keillor. 49:37-9 F24'73. 1260
Percy Colclough and the religious girls. Prose. Leslie Norris. 49:40-3 Ap28'73. 1261
The perfect crime. Prose. Elizabeth Cullinan. 49:28-45 Ag27'73. 1262
Perfection. Prose. Vladimir Nabokov. Dmitri Nabokov, trans. 49:34-8 My19'73. 1263
Peril. Verse. W. S. Merwin. 49:36 Ja7'74. 1264
Period-piece fellow. PR (Plimpton). Geoffrey T. Hellman. 47:61-126 D4'71. 1265
Peripeteia. Verse. Anthony Hecht. 49:38 F11'74. 1266
Permissiveness and rectitude. REF. Leopold Tyrmand. 46:85-96 F28'70. 1267
Perpetua. Prose. Donald Barthelme. 47:40-2 Je12'71. 1268
Person to person. Verse. William Matchett. 47:46 O 2'71. 1269
Pheasant. Verse. Sylvia Plath. 47:36 Mr6'71. 1270
Phenomena. Verse. John Updike. 49:38 F24'73. 1271
Philip and Anna. Prose. Sylvia Townsend Warner. 47:29-32 Jy31'71. 1272
The photographs. Prose. Donald Barthelme. 49:32-3 Ja28'74. 1273
Photographs. Prose. Henry Bromell. 48:36-9 Ap29'72. 1274
The pianoforte factory revisited. Prose. James

Stevenson. 46:40-1 N28'70. 1275
The pied piper. Prose. Thomas Meehan. 46:25-8 Jy4'70. 1276
The pier glass. Prose. Berry Morgan. 46:73-6 Ag29'70. 1277
Pig tale. OFFC. William Whitworth. 46:64-9 Ja30'71. 1278
Pilgrim's progress. Prose. Emily Hahn. 46:26-30 Ag15'70. 1279
Pinter, Harold (Parody). Philip Hamburger. 48:37-8 Mr11'72. 1280
Piombino's an hour from Livorno. Prose. Linda Arking. 48:30-44 Je24'72. 1281
Pipe all hands--chimeras dead ahead! Prose. S. J. Perelman. 50:35-6 My20'74. 1282
The place on the hill. RL. E. J. Kahn, Jr. 48:88-100 My27'72. 1283
Plainfolks. Prose. Garrison Keillor. 50:44-6 N4'74. 1284
A platonic relationship. Prose. Ann Beattie. 50:42-6 Ap8'74. 1285
Playboy magazine (Parody). Roger Angell. 50:28-32 S2'74. 1286
Playing. PR (Tati). Penelope Gilliatt. 48:35-49 Ja27'73. 1287
Please hang up--I'm expecting a nuisance call. Prose. Roger Angell. 47:30-1 F12'72. 1288
Plowshares, anyone? Prose. Ralph Schoenstein. 47:52-3 D11'71. 1289
Plumbing. Prose. John Updike. 47:34-7 F20'71. 1290
The plundered past. RL. Karl E. Meyer. 49:96-121 Mr24'73; 49:80-103 Mr31'73; 49:96-129 Ap7'73. 1291
Pneumonia, 1945. Prose. L. Woiwode. 46:38-44 F13'71. 1292
Poem. Verse. Elizabeth Bishop. 48:46 N11'72. 1293
The poem circling Hamtramck all night in search of you. Verse. Philip Levine. 49:142 Ap7'73. 1294
Poem of the self. Verse. Frederick Morgan. 48:75 Jy29'72. 1295
Poetic larks bid bald eagle welcome swan of Liverpool. RL. Hendrik Hertzberg. 48:138-62 D9'72. 1296
The pollution of Lake Baikal. OFFC. Marshall I. Goldman. 47:58-66 Je19'71. 1297
Pompeii revisited. Verse. Paul Roche. 47:52 O23'71. 1298
Popular Culture Association. TT. 50:29 Ja13'75. 1299
Porcupines at the university. Prose. Donald Barthelme. 46:32-3 Ap25'70. 1300
The pornography of violence. Prose. H. L. Mountzoures. 48:35-8 S23'72. 1301
Port of call. Prose. W. S. Merwin. 49:41-2 O1'73. 1302
Porter, Cole. PR. Brendan Gill. 47:48-64 S18'71. 1303
The position of the planets. Prose. Penelope Gilliatt. 47:32-8 Ag14'71. 1304
Postcard. Verse. John Fandel. 49:34 Je23'73. 1305
Postcards from the Hudson. Prose. Anthony Hiss. 47:54-65 N13'71. 1306
The potato baron and the line. Prose. Stephen Tracy. 48:32-9 F26'72. 1307
The power and the glory. PR (Sutherland). Winthrop Sargeant. 48:40-64 Ap1'72. 1308
The power broker. Annals of politics. Robert A. Caro. 50:32-64 Jy22'74; 50:37-65 Jy29'74; 50:40-75 Ag12'74; 50:42-77 Ag19'74. 1309
The prairie dog and the black footed ferret. RL. Faith McNulty. 46:40-89 Je13'70. 1310
Prayer to the good poet. Verse. James Wright. 48:42 O14'72. 1311
Preminger, Otto. TT. 46:22 Ja30'71. 1312
Presenting a watch. Verse. Richard Howard. 46:28 Ja

30'71. 1313
The presidency and the press. REF. Richard Harris. 49:122-8 O1'73. 1314
President. PR (Nyerere). William Edgett Smith. 47:42-100 O16'71; 47:47-106 O23'71; 47:53-99 O30'71. 1315
The president of the derrière-garde. PR (Wilder). Whitney Balliett. 49:36-46 Jy9'73. 1316
Primal therapy. Prose. Linda Grace Hoyer. 50:26-8 Ag26'74. 1317
Prime. Verse. L. E. Sissman. 47:42 Je26'71. 1318
The princes of exile. Verse. Richard Shelton. 49:50 O22'73. 1319
Printer. PR (Powers). Geoffrey T. Hellman. 46:43-81 Mr7'70. 1320
Priorities. ACH. Andy Logan. 48:38-49 Ag5'72. 1321
Profile. Prose. (Also listed by individual titles.)
Ted Adams. By Thomas Whiteside. 50:42-81 F25'74.
The aereon. By John McPhee. 48:40-73 F10'73; 48:42-77 F17'73; 49:48-79 F24'73.
Woody Allen. By Penelope Gilliatt. 49:39-44 F4'74.
Amnesty International. By E. J. Kahn, Jr. 46:44-57 Ag22'70.
Margaret Anderson. By Janet Flanner. 50:44-67 Je3'74.
Atlanta, Georgia. By Fred Powledge. 49:28-40 D31'73.
George Balanchine. By Bernard Taper. 49:48-90 O22'73.
The banana. By Berton Roueché. 49:43-56 O1'73.
Tallulah Bankhead. By Brendan Gill. 48:45-99 O7'72; 48:50-122 O14'72.
Tony Bennett. By Whitney Balliett. 49:33-43 Ja7'74.
Daniel Berrigan and Philip Berrigan. By Francine du Plessix Gray. 46:44-121 Mr14'70.
Bob and Ray. By Whitney Balliett. 49:42-65 S24'73.
Jorge Luis Borges. By Jorge Luis Borges and Norman Thomas di Giovanni. 46:40-99 S19'70.
Pierre Boulez. By Peter Heyworth. 49:45-71 Mr24'73; 49:45-75 Mr31'73.
Ruby Braff. By Whitney Balliett. 50:41-7 Jy8'74.
Willy Brandt. By Joseph Wechsberg. 49:35-57 Ja14'74.
Bridgehampton Black community. By Calvin Tomkins. 49:47-101 S10'73.
Ed Bullins. By Jervis Anderson. 49:40-79 Je16'73.
Sarah Caldwell. By Winthrop Sargeant. 49:43-9 D24'73.
Calcutta, India. By Ved Mehta. 46:47-112 Mr21'70.
Dick Cavett. By L. E. Sissman and Charles Saxon. 48:42-52 My6'72.
Ray Charles. By Whitney Balliett. 46:44-76 Mr28'70.
Julia Child. By Calvin Tomkins. 50:36-52 D23'74.
Robert Erskine Childers and Erskine Hamilton Childers. By Anthony Bailey. 50:44-67 Ja27'75.
Giuseppe Cipriani. By Winthrop Sargeant. 48:34-9 Jy22'72.
Cleveland Orchestra. By Joseph Wechsberg. 46:38-69 My30'70.
County agent, Idaho. By Berton Roueché. 49:30-45 S3'73.
Blossom Dearie. By Whitney Balliett. 49:46-52 My26'73.
Leon Edel. By Geoffrey T. Hellman. 47:43-86 Mr13'71.
Albert Einstein. By Jeremy Bernstein. 49:44-101 Mr10'73; 49:44-91 Mr17'73.
Erik H. Erikson. By Robert Coles. 46:51-131 N7'70; 46:59-138 N14'70.
Maurice Ewing. By William

Wertenbaker. 50:54-118 N 4'74; 50:52-100 N11'74; 50: 60-110 N18'74.
Feminists. By Jane Kramer. 46:52-139 N28'70.
Joe Franklin. By William Whitworth. 47:44-55 My22'71.
Dolores García. By Robert Coles. 49:54-86 N5'73.
Garlic. By Berton Roueché. 50:55-62 O28'74.
Henry Geldzahler. By Calvin Tomkins. 47:58-113 N6'71.
John Gordon. By Whitney Balliett. 48:39-58 F3'73.
Max Gordon and Barney Josephson. By Whitney Balliett. 47:50-92 O9'71.
Bobby Hackett. By Whitney Balliett. 48:36-49 Ag12'72.
Cyril Manton Harris. By Bruce Bliven, Jr. 48:39-67 Je17'72.
George Hartzog. By John McPhee. 47:45-89 S11'71.
Hawaii. By Francine du Plessix Gray. 48:41-79 Mr4'72; 48: 39-81 Mr11'72.
Marilyn Horne. By Winthrop Sargeant. 48:31-43 S2'72.
Edward Thomas Hougen. By Berton Roueché. 49:45-64 My12'73.
Ivan Illich. By Francine du Plessix Gray. 46:40-92 Ap25'70.
Theodore Kheel. By Fred C. Shapiro. 46:36-58 Ag1'70.
Dave Lefkowitz. By William Whitworth. 47:38-44 D 18'71.
Louisville, Kentucky. By Fred Powledge. 50:42-83 S9'74.
Marian McPartland. By Whitney Balliett. 48:43-57 Ja20'73.
Giovanni Mardersteig. By Winthrop Sargeant. 46:32-47 Jy11'70.
Arthur Loeb Mayer. By E. J. Kahn, Jr. 50:46-66 D9'74.
Amolak Ram Mehta. By Ved Mehta. 48:47-107 Ap22'72; 48:45-100 Ap29'72.
Jonas Mekas. By Calvin Tomkins. 48:31-49 Ja6'73.
Mabel Mercer. By Whitney Balliett. 48:55-64 N18'72.
Neal E. Miller. By Gerald Jonas. 48:34-57 Ag19'72; 48:30-57 Ag26'72.
Modern Jazz Quartet. By Whitney Balliett. 47:43-108 N20'71.
John Usher Monro. By E. J. Kahn, Jr. 47:43-64 Ap10'71.
Stewart Rawlings Mott. By E. J. Kahn, Jr. 47:56-87 N27'71.
Ralph Nader. By Thomas Whiteside. 49:50-111 O 8'73; 49:46-101 O15'73.
The Netherlands. By Anthony Bailey. 46:34-57 Ag8'70; 46:32-63 Ag15'70.
Julius K. Nyerere. By William Edgett Smith. 47:42-100 O16'71; 47:47-106 O23'71; 47:53-99 O30'71.
Georgia O'Keeffe. By Calvin Tomkins. 50:40-66 Mr4'74.
Charles Park, David Brower, Charles Fraser and Floyd Dominy. By John McPhee. 47:42-91 Mr20'71; 47:42-80 Mr27'71; 47:41-93 Ap 3'71.
Pieds noirs. By Jane Kramer. 48:52-108 N25'72.
Francis T. P. Plimpton. By Geoffrey T. Hellman. 47: 61-126 D4'71.
Cole Porter. By Brendan Gill. 47:48-64 S18'71.
Bertram A. Powers. By Geoffrey T. Hellman. 46: 43-81 Mr7'70.
A. Philip Randolph. By Jervis Anderson. 48:60-120 D2'72; 48:48-106 D9'72; 48:40-85 D16'72.
John D. Rockefeller, 3rd. By Geoffrey T. Hellman. 48: 56-103 N4'72.
Carol Ruckdeschel. By John McPhee. 49:44-103 Ap 28'73.
Kal Rudman. By George W.

S. Trow. 48:32-49 D23'72.
Saigon. By Robert Shaplen. 48: 51-107 Ap15'72.
Peter Roland Sawyer. By John Bainbridge. 47:40-53 Ag14'71.
George Fabian Scheer. By Bruce Bliven, Jr. 49:51-113 N12'73.
Elwood L. Schmidt. By Berton Roueché. 47:30-40 Ja1'72.
John Service. By E. J. Kahn, Jr. 48:43-95 Ap8'72.
Bobby Short. By Whitney Balliett. 46:28-35 D26'70.
Beverly Sills. By Winthrop Sargeant. 47:42-64 Mr6'71.
Georg Solti. By Winthrop Sargeant. 50:38-62 My27'74.
Stapleton, Nebraska. By Berton Roueché. 46:29-40 Ja2'71.
Stonington, Connecticut. By Anthony Bailey. 47:36-55 Jy24'71; 47:38-54 Jy31'71.
Paul Strand. By Calvin Tomkins. 50:44-94 S16'74.
Maurice Frederick Strong. By E. J. Kahn, Jr. 48:45-75 Je3'72.
Supertankers. By Noël Mostert. 50:45-100 My13'74; 50:46-99 My20'74.
Joan Sutherland. By Winthrop Sargeant. 48:40-64 Ap1'72.
Algernon Charles Swinburne and Theodore Watts-Dunton. By Mollie Panter-Downes. 46: 40-65 Ja23'71; 46:31-43 Ja 30'71; 46:40-71 F6'71.
Sylvia Syms. By Whitney Balliett. 50:47-56 O21'74.
Jacques Tati. By Penelope Gilliatt. 48:35-49 Ja27'73.
Theodore B. Taylor. By John McPhee. 49:54-145 D3'73; 49:50-108 D10'73; 49:60-97 D17'73.
Uganda Asians. By Jane Kramer. 50:47-93 Ap8'74.
Valencia, Spain. By Kenneth Tynan. 46:33-53 Jy25'70.
Welch, West Virginia. By Berton Roueché. 49:32-44 Jy16'73.
The whale. By Faith McNulty. 49:38-67 Ag6'73.
Alec Wilder. By Whitney Balliett. 49:36-46 Jy9'73.
Nicol Williamson. By Kenneth Tynan. 47:35-69 Ja15'72.
Robert Wilson. By Calvin Tomkins. 50:38-62 Ja13'75.
P. G. Wodehouse. By Herbert Warren Wind. 47:43-101 My15'71.
Jerome Zerbe. By Brendan Gill. 49:39-68 Je9'73. 1322
The prognosticators. Prose. Peter Benchley. 48:50-1 N 25'72. 1323
Promised Land Valley, June, '73. Verse. Alfred Corn. 49:54 N12'73. 1324
Promises. ACH. Andy Logan. 50:99-111 My6'74. 1325
Property. Prose. Penelope Gilliatt. 46:33-9 My2'70. 1326
Property. Prose. Isaac Bashevis Singer. Dorothea Straus, trans. 48:38-42 D9'72. 1327
Prostitutes. Prose. R. Prawer Jhabvala. 49:43-9 D10'73. 1328
Proust, Marcel. Howard Moss. 47:124-35 D18'71. 1329
Proust, Marcel (Centenary). Janet Flanner. 47:53-4 Jy 3'71. 1330
The pure suit of happiness. Verse. May Swenson. 48:38 Mr25'72. 1331
Putu. Prose. Eyre de Lanux. 48:32-8 Je17'72. 1332

Q

A quality that lets you in. PR (Bennett). Whitney Balliett. 49:33-43 Ja7'74. 1333
Quarrels. Verse. Alastair Reid. 50:42 S30'74. 1334
Queen Christina (Film). S. N. Behrman. 48:76ff My20'72. 1335
A queen remembered. Prose.

Sylvia Towsend Warner. 47:92-4 F12'72. 1336

A queenly aura. PR (Mercer). Whitney Balliett. 48:55-64 N18'72. 1337

A question answered. Prose. M. F. K. Fisher. 49:26-31 Jy9'73. 1338

Quiet. Prose. Renata Adler. 47:36-42 Ap24'71. 1339

Quiet man. PR (Harris). Bruce Bliven, Jr. 48:39-67 Je17'72. 1340

R

Rabe, David. TT. 47:48-9 N20'71. 1341

Radical departures. Verse. Howard Moss. 46:42 My16'70. 1342

Rafelson, Bob. TT. 46:41-2 O24'70. 1343

Rain. Verse. Deborah Deutschman. 48:38 My13'72. 1344

The rain guitar. Verse. James Dickey. 47:36 Ja8'72. 1345

Rainier. Verse. William Burford. 50:89 Mr4'74. 1346

The raisin. Verse. Andrew Hunt. 47:138 Ap10'71. 1347

Raising Kane. OUWA. Pauline Kael. 47:43-89 F20'71; 47:44-81 F27'71. 1348

Ranger. PR (Hartzog). John McPhee. 47:45-89 S11'71. 1349

Razzle-dazzle in the Rib Room. Prose. S. J. Perelman. 49:37-40 O29'73. 1350

Re the tower project. Prose. Garrison Keillor. 47:25 Ag 28'71. 1351

Reading late at night, thermometer falling. Verse. Robert Penn Warren. 50:34-5 Mr11'74. 1352

Reading the river. SS. John McPhee. 46:126-33 Mr21'70. 1353

Ready, aim, flee! Prose. S. J. Perelman. 49:34-6 D24'73. 1354

Real losses, imaginery gains. Prose. Wright Morris. 49:46-7 N26'73. 1355

The recipes of Chairman Mao. Prose. Marshall Brickman. 49:24-5 Ag27'73. 1356

The recovery. Verse. Mark Strand. 46:40 My9'70. 1357

Red. OLC. Niccolo Tucci. 48:69-77 Ag5'72. 1358

Red jacket's grave. Verse. James Wright. 47:40 Mr13'71. 1359

A reëxamination of the cherry tree incident. Prose. James Stevenson. 48:34-6 F17'73. 1360

Reflections. Prose. (Also listed by individual titles.)
- War and pacifism. Freeman J. Dyson. 46:44-59 F21'70.
- Permissiveness. Leopold Tyrmand. 46:85-96 F28'70.
- Civil disobedience. Hannah Arendt. 46:70-105 S12'70.
- The new generation. Charles A. Reich. 46:42-111 S 26'70.
- Science and technology. Lewis Mumford. 46:50-131 O 10'70; 46:48-141 O17'70; 46:55-127 O24'70; 46:50-98 O31'70.
- Astolphe de Custine. By George F. Kennan. 47:46-93 My1'71.
- Organization and law. Charles A. Reich. 47:52-7 Je19'71
- Vietnam. William Pfaff. 47:33-8 Jy3'71.
- U.S. foreign policy since 1945. J. William Fulbright. 47:41-62 Ja8'72.
- Mathematics. Alfred Adler. 47:39-45 F19'72.
- Anti-crime laws. Richard Harris. 48:44-105 Mr25'72.
- American Vietnam policy. William Pfaff. 48:79-80 Je3'72.
- The court-martial of Captain Ernest L. Medina. Mary McCarthy. 48:38-93 Je10'72.
- Vietnam bloodbath. William Pfaff. 48:80-9 O21'72.

Artaud. Susan Sontag. 49:39-79 My19'73.
The presidency and the press. Richard Harris. 49:122-8 O1'73.
The American social process. Richard N. Goodwin. 49:35-60 Ja21'74; 49:36-68 Ja28'74; 49:48-91 F4'74.
American presidents. Richard Harris. 50:108-14 Ap15'74.
Leningrad. George F. Kennan. 50:41-61 Ap29'74.
Watergate prosecutions. Richard Harris. 50:46-63 Je10'74.
The Democratic Party. Richard N. Goodwin. 50:157-66 D2'74.
The economy. Richard N. Goodwin. 50:38-49 Ja6'75.
W. H. Auden. By Hannah Arendt. 50:39-46 Ja20'75. 1361

The refrigerator. Verse. Howard Moss. 47:36 S18'71. 1362

The regulars. Prose. Gilbert Rogin. 46:42-5 N7'70. 1363

Reich, Charles A. (Parody). E. B. White. 46:49 N14'70. 1364

Relatives. Verse. Carl Dennis. 49:30 Jy9'73. 1365

Rembrandt's hat. Prose. Bernard Malamud. 49:34-9 Mr17'73. 1366

Remembering Wystan H. Auden, who died in the night of the twenty-eight of September, 1973. REF. Hannah Arendt. 50:39-46 Ja20'75. 1367

Remnant water. Verse. James Dickey. 49:36 Mr10'73. 1368

Renoir, Jean. Penelope Gilliatt. 50:62-7 S2'74. 1369

The rent in the screen. Verse. Howard Nemerov. 47:36 D18'71. 1370

A reporter at large. Prose. (Also listed by individual titles.)
Indian journal. Ved Mehta. 46:94-160 Ap11'70.
Nepal. Jeremy Bernstein. 46:44-81 My2'70; 46:46-94 My9'70.
Deserters in Sweden. Daniel Lang. 46:42-68 My23'70.
Prairie dogs and black footed ferrets. Faith McNulty. 46:40-89 Je13'70.
Interview with Eugene V. Rostow. William Whitworth. 46:30-56 Jy4'70.
Morocco. Jane Kramer. 46:33-49 Ag29'70; 46:43-63 S5'70; 46:112-49 S12'70.
The National Guard. Renata Adler. 46:40-64 O3'70.
Peace talks. Robert Shaplen. 46:162-80 O17'70.
Atomic bombs. Daniel Lang. 46:52-61 Ja9'71.
Enzyme detergents. Paul Brodeur. 46:42-74 Ja16'71.
Black panthers. Edward Jay Epstein. 46:45-77 F13'71.
The American Friends Service Committee. Gerald Jonas. 47:92-111 Mr13'71; 47:99-131 Mr20'71.
Primates. Emily Hahn. 47:46-97 Ap17'71; 47:46-91 Ap24'71.
Charles Mingus. Whitney Balliett. 47:42-52 My29'71.
Kent State. Philip Hamburger. 47:106-19 Je5'71.
Vietnam veteran. Daniel Lang. 47:35-53 S4'71.
Ecology. Barry Commoner. 47:49-99 S25'71; 47:44-91 O2'71.
Vietnam combat rules. Seymour M. Hersh. 47:101-19 O9'71.
International monetary fund meeting. John Brooks. 47:117-32 O23'71.
Alpine accidents and rescues. Jeremy Bernstein. 47:118-37 O30'71.
Oligocene fossils. Berton Roueché. 47:141-55 N13'71.
Essex County. Burton Bernstein. 47:100-47 N27'71.
Chimpanzees and language.

Emily Hahn. 47:54-98 D11'71.
Micronesia. E. J. Kahn, Jr. 47:98-115 D18'71.
House and highway. Whitney Balliett. 47:40-5 D25'71.
The investigations of Son My. Seymour M. Hersh. 47:34-69 Ja22'72; 47:40-71 Ja29'72.
Bangladesh. Robert Shaplen. 47:40-67 F12'72; 47:89-106 F19'72.
River life. Berton Roueché. 48:40-67 F26'72.
Mørketiden. Joseph Wechsberg. 48:103-26 Mr18'72.
Franconia College. E. J. Kahn, Jr. 48:88-100 My27'72.
The Gallup inter-tribal Indian ceremonial. Calvin Trillin and Edward Koren. 48:32-7 Ag5'72.
Atlantic City and Monopoly. John McPhee. 48:45-62 S9'72.
East Africa. Peter Matthiessen. 48:39-74 S16'72; 48:39-62 S23'72; 48:47-75 S30'72.
A Navy AWOL. Daniel Lang. 48:96-133 O21'72.
Paris peace talks. Robert Shaplen. 48:184-94 N4'72.
Korea. Robert Shaplen. 48: 116-47 N25'72; 48:128-55 D2'72.
John Lennon and Yoko Ono. Hendrik Hertzberg. 48:138-62 D9'72.
The Lobster restaurant. Richard Harris. 48:40-6 D30'72.
International art and antiquities traffic. Karl E. Meyer. 49: 96-121 Mr24'73; 49:80-103 Mr31'73; 49:96-129 Ap7'73.
Skylab. Henry S. F. Cooper, Jr. 49:110-35 My5'73.
Senator Mondale. By Elizabeth Drew. 49:118-37 My19'73.
John Gardner. By Elizabeth Drew. 49:35-55 Jy23'73.
Susan Cook Russo. By Daniel Lang. 49:35-48 Jy30'73.
Heroin in Great Britain. Horace Freeland Judson. 49:76-113 S24'73; 49:70-112 O1'73.
1970 census. E. J. Kahn, Jr. 49:137-57 O15'73; 49:105-32 O22'73.
Finiston School, Belfast. Anthony Bailey. 49:114-50 O29'73.
Oil spill. William Wertenbaker. 49:48-79 N26'73.
Cuba. Frances FitzGerald. 49:40-72 F18'74.
Firewood. John McPhee. 50:81-105 Mr25'74.
Cave art. Calvin Tomkins. 50:109-28 Ap22'74.
The human brain. Gerald Jonas. 50:52-69 Jy1'74.
Sly Stone. By George W. S. Trow. 50:30-45 Ag26'74.
The working class. Andrew Levison. 50:36-61 S2'74.
Cigarettes. Thomas Whiteside. 50:121-51 N18'74.
Swedish hostages. Daniel Lang. 50:56-126 N25'74.
Multinational corporations. Richard Barnet and Ronald Müller. 50:53-128 D2'74; 50:100-59 D9'74.
Israel. John Hersey. 50:46-82 D16'74.
Northwest Territories ice road. Edith Iglauer. 50: 28-51 D30'74. 1371

A reporter in China. (Also listed by title.) Prose. Joseph Kraft. 48:98-120 My6'72. 1372

A reporter in Washington, D. C. Prose. Elizabeth Drew. 50: 42-101 Mr11'74; 50:41-105 Mr18'74; 50:55-139 O14'74; 50:63-161 O21'74; 50:76-162 O28'74. 1373

The reprimand. RL. Seymour M. Hersh. 47:101-19 O9'71. 1374

Requiem for Sonora. Verse. Richard Shelton. 47:30 S4'71. 1375

Reruns of the mind. Prose. Arnold Sundgaard. 49:37-9 Je16'73. 1376

The rescue. Verse. Frederick Morgan. 50:137 S23'74. 1377

The rescue. Prose. V. S. Prit-

chett. 49:36-41 Ap14'73. 1378
The return. Verse. Jon Swan. 46:62 Jy4'70. 1379
Return to Merion. SS. Herbert Warren Wind. 47:56-66 Jy17'71. 1380
Reunion. Verse. Richard Shelton. 46:66 O3'70. 1381
The revolt at Brocéliande. Prose. Sylvia Townsend Warner. 49:38-42 S10'73. 1382
The rhinoceros: an appreciation. Prose. Calvin Tomkins. 47:59-61 N20'71. 1383
Rhys, Jean. Howard Moss. 50:161-6 D16'74. 1384
Ricardo Güiraldes. Verse. Jorge Luis Borges. Norman Thomas di Giovanni, trans. 49:30 Jy 2'73. 1385
Rice, Elmer. S. N. Behrman. 48:57ff My27'72. 1386
Rich people are happier than poor; healthy, happier than sick; young, happier than old. Prose. H. L. Mountzoures. 47:45-50 O30'71. 1387
Rickles, Robert N. TT. 46:33-4 My9'70. 1388
Ride. Prose. John Updike. 48:51 D2'72. 1389
Riding the elevator into the sky. Verse. Anne Sexton. 50:36 Je 3'74. 1390
The right road and the wrong road. A reporter in China. Joseph Kraft. 48:98-120 My6'72. 1391
Ripped off. Prose. Alice Adams. 47:40-3 My22'71. 1392
The rise of capitalism. Prose. Donald Barthelme. 46:45-7 D 12'70. 1393
Risk. Prose. Ruth Mackenzie. 46:56-101 N21'70. 1394
The rivals. ACH. Andy Logan. 47:79-82 Je26'71. 1395
River. Verse. Greg Kuzma. 50:44 My20'74. 1396
The river world. RL. Berton Roueché. 48:40-67 F26'72. 1397
Riverside Park. Verse. Jill Hoffman. 47:57 Jy10'71. 1398
Roberts, Bernard. TT. 48:31-2 O21'72. 1399
Romeo & Julieta. Prose. Jose Yglesias. 47:107-45 O16'71. 1400
The roofs. Prose. W. S. Merwin. 46:89-90 Ap18'70. 1401
A rookie's notebook. Prose. Gerald Graff [and] Joseph Epstein. 49:40-1 O22'73. 1402
The room. Verse. Mark Strand. 49:36 Mr17'73. 1403
A room in linden. Prose. Benedict Kiely. 48:36-44 S9'72. 1404
Room to live in. PR (Modern Jazz Quartet: Lewis, Jackson, Heath, & Kay). Whitney Balliett. 47:62-108 N20'71. 1405
Rose. Verse. Jorge Luis Borges. Norman Thomas di Giovanni, trans. 47:40 My 15'71. 1406
Rose, Carl (Obituary). 47:68 Jy3'71. 1407
The rose in the eye looked pretty fine. PR (O'Keeffe). Calvin Tomkins. 50:40-66 Mr4'74. 1408
Rose petals. Prose. R. Prawer Jhabvala. 47:24-32 Jy10'71. 1409
Roses, rhododendron. Prose. Alice Adams. 50:37-42 Ja 27'75. 1410
Ross, Harold. S. N. Behrman. 48:94 My13'72. 1411
Ross, Leonard (Parody). Charles McGrath [and] Daniel Menaker. 50:46 O14'74. 1412
Rossellini, Roberto. TT. 50:30-1 Mr4'74. 1413
Rouault. Verse. Van K. Brock. 48:38 Ja20'73. 1414
A roving commission. SS. Herbert Warren Wind. 46:154-63 D12'70. 1415
Rowse, A. L. George Steiner. 50:142-50 Mr18'74. 1416
Ruidoso. SS. John McPhee. 50:83-112 Ap29'74. 1417

The rules of the game. PR (Illich). Francine du Plessix Gray. 46:40-92 Ap25'70. 1418
A rumor in the air. OLC. Eugene Kinkead. 49:50-5 D24'73. 1419
Running. Verse. Carl Dennis. 49:44 N26'73. 1420
Running away together. Verse. Maxine Kumin. 47:38 S4'71. 1421
Running nicely. Prose. Morris Lurie. 48:38-41 My6'72. 1422
Running on the shore. Verse. May Swenson. 48:28 Ag12'72. 1423
Rural route. Verse. Charles Wright. 50:46 S9'74. 1424
Russell, Bertrand. TT. 46:29 F21'70. 1425
Ruth. Verse. Philip Levine. 48: 93 Je17'72. 1426

S

SALT. Annals of diplomacy. John Newhouse. 49:44-79 My5'73; 49:79-117 My12'73; 49:87-114 My19'73; 49:76-110 My26'73; 49:68-101 Je2'73. 1427
S. F. OUWA. Gerald Jonas. 48:33-52 Jy29'72. 1428
Sad Arthur (Go Hesse, young man). Prose. Roger Angell. 46:33-5 Mr14'70. 1429
Sam Palka and David Vishkover. Prose. Isaac Bashevis Singer. Dorothea Straus, trans. 50: 38-44 My13'74. 1430
San Juan's Day. Verse. Richard Shelton. 48:91 Je24'72. 1431
The sandpipers. Verse. David Posner. 50:40 Ap15'74. 1432
The Sans Souci launderama. Prose. Gilbert Rogin. 49:35-9 Ap28'73. 1433
The Santa Claus culture. Annals of medicine. Berton Roueché. 47:66-81 S4'71. 1434
Santa's list. Prose. William Hamilton. 50:30-1 D23'74. 1435
Saratoga. Verse. Howard Moss. 50:36 Ag19'74. 1436
Sassoon, Siegfried. S. N. Behrman. 48:38ff My13'72; 48: 45ff My20'72; 48:39ff My27'72. 1437
Saul, afterward, riding East. Verse. John Malcolm Brinnin. 46:36 F28'70. 1438
Sawdust. Verse. Howard Moss. 47:34 Jy24'71. 1439
Scenario. Prose. John Jurkowski. 47:40-5 Ap17'71. 1440
Scenes of childhood. Prose. Sylvia Townsend Warner. 49: 32-3 Je2'73. 1441
A scent of roses. Prose. Sylvia Townsend Warner. 48:44-8 N4'72. 1442
Scheer, George Fabian. Bruce Bliven, Jr. 49:51-113 N12'73. 1443
The Schemed memoirs. Prose. Woody Allen. 47:36-7 Ap17'71. 1444
The school. Prose. Donald Barthelme. 50:28 Je17'74. 1445
Science fiction. Gerald Jonas. 48:33-52 Jy29'72. 1446
A scrap of black cloth. Annals of law. Richard Harris. 50:37-83 Je17'74; 50:37-79 Je24'74. 1447
The scribe. Prose. Alexander Frater. 48:38-42 Ap8'72. 1448
The sea of lost time. Prose. Gabriel García Márquez. Gregory Rabassa, trans. 50: 32-40 Je3'74. 1449
The search. Verse. W. S. Merwin. 49:58 D17'73. 1450
The search for Joseph Tully. TT. 50:44 N25'74. 1451
The search for Marvin Gardens. RL. John McPhee. 48:45-62 S9'72. 1452
Season lightly. SS. Roger Angell. 49:50-65 Jy16'73. 1453
The second man (Play). S. N. Behrman. 48:88ff My13'72; 48:64ff My20'72. 1454
A secret gratitude. Verse. James Wright. 47:38 Mr27'71. 1455

The secrets of the old one. PR (Einstein). Jeremy Bernstein. 49:44-101 Mr10'73; 49:44-91 Mr17'73. 1456

The selection of reality. OUWA. Edward Jay Epstein. 49:41-77 Mr3'73. 1457

Selections from the Allen notebooks. Prose. Woody Allen. 49:48-9 N5'73. 1458

The sellout. REF. Freeman J. Dyson. 46:44-59 F21'70. 1459

Sembene, Ousmane. TT. 47:37-9 S25'71. 1460

Semi-private. Prose. Helen Yglesias. 47:35-41 F5'72. 1461

Sentence. Prose. Donald Barthelme. 46:34-6 Mr7'70. 1462

September, the first day of school. Verse. Howard Nemerov. 46:42 S19'70. 1463

September things. Verse. May Swenson. 48:118 S30'72. 1464

Serena Blandish (Play). S. N. Behrman. 48:58ff My20'72. 1465

Seven poems. (Also listed by individual titles.) Verse. W. S. Merwin. 47:44 Ap24'71. 1466

Seven preludes to silence. Verse. Richard Shelton. 48:36 Mr4'72. 1467

Sex tips. Prose. Garrison Keillor. 47:31 Ag14'71. 1468

Sext. Verse. L. E. Sissman. 47:42-3 Je26'71. 1469

The shades. Verse. John Hollander. 49:56 D3'73. 1470

Shades Mountain. Verse. Everette H. Maddox. 47:48 O30'71. 1471

Shades of Tlachtli. SS. Alastair Reid. 46:60-71 Jy18'70. 1472

Shadowboxing. Verse. James Tate. 46:40 F28'70. 1473

Shakespeare and Company. Janet Flanner. 48:32-3 Mr11'72. 1474

Sharon. Prose. Elizabeth Spencer. 46:36-9 My9'70. 1475

Shaw, George Bernard. W. H. Auden. 48:190-9 N25'72. 1476

She arrives at night, unexpected. Verse. William Logan. 50:38 Je17'74. 1477

Shebib, Donald. TT. 46:47-9 N21'70. 1478

The shelling machine. Verse. Louis Simpson. 49:32 Ag13'73. 1479

Sherwood, Robert E. S. N. Behrman. 48:51ff My27'72 1480

Shinoda, Masahiro. Penelope Gilliatt. 49:131-2 Ap28'73 1481

A shock. Verse. W. H. Auden. 48:40 Mr18'72. 1482

Shore. Verse. W. S. Merwin. 46:41 S12'70. 1483

A short history of the "spitball." Prose. James Stevenson. 49:36-7 S10'73. 1484

Sic transit. Prose. Daniel Menaker. 50:38-41 S9'74. 1485

Silence. Verse. Ruth Fainlight. 47:28 Je19'71. 1486

Silt shallows. Verse. Richard Schramm. 47:69 My22'71. 1487

Simon, Neil. TT. 48:30-2 F10'73. 1488

Simon, Paul. TT. 48:32-3 Ap29'72. 1489

The Simpsons and the hepatitides. Annals of medicine. Berton Roueché. 47:72-86 Ag21'71. 1490

Sir Cecil's ride. Prose. Shirley Hazzard. 50:30-6 Je17'74. 1491

Sitwell, Osbert. S. N. Behrman. 48:43ff My13'72. 1492

Six poems. (Also listed by individual titles.) Verse. Sylvia Plath. 47:36-7 Mr6'71. 1493

The size-limitation treaty. Prose. Dean Vietor. 50:36-7 S9'74. 1494

The skein. Prose. Ted Walker. 47:38-41 Mr6'71. 1495

Sketch. Prose. Robert Thompson. 46:25-7 Ag1'70. 1496

Skulls. Verse. Leslie Norris. 47:36 Ja29'72. 1497

Skylab. RL. Henry S. F. Cooper, Jr. 49:110-35 My5'73. 1498

The sleep. Verse. Mark Strand. 46:40 My9'70. 1499
Sleep tight, your honor. Prose. S. J. Perelman. 48:24-6 Ag 12'72. 1500
The sleepwalker. Verse. Greg Kuzma. 47:41 O16'71. 1501
The slightest distance. Prose. Henry Bromell. 48:25-31 Ag 5'72. 1502
Slightly exaggerated enthusiasms. RL. Frances FitzGerald. 49: 40-72 F18'74. 1503
The Slim Graves show. Prose. Garrison Keillor. 48:33-4 F 10'73. 1504
A sliver at night. Prose. Csikszentmihalyi Mihaly. 48:111-13 Ap15'72. 1505
Slow boat ride. Verse. Richard Eberhart. 50:34 Jy15'74. 1506
Slow down--dangerous footlights ahead. Prose. S. J. Perelman. 46:53-5 N21'70. 1507
A small, apprehensive child. Annals of medicine. Berton Roueché. 47:70-90 Ap10'71. 1508
A small spill. RL. William Wertenbaker. 49:48-79 N26'73. 1509
Smith, Dennis E. TT. 46:18-19 Ag29'70. 1510
Smoking still. RL. Thomas Whiteside. 50:121-51 N18'74. 1511
Snack firm maps new chip push. Prose. Garrison Keillor. 46:45 O10'70. 1512
Snake hunt. Verse. David Wagoner. 49:46 Ap14'73. 1513
Snow. Verse. Carl Dennis. 50:40 Ja13'75. 1514
Snow in southern England. Verse. Ted Walker. 46:32 Ja23'71. 1515
Snow line. Verse. Richard Schramm. 46:65 Ja9'71. 1516
Snowfall. Verse. W. S. Merwin. 46:34 Mr14'70. 1517
Sodom and Gomorrah. Prose. Richard Berczeller. 50:48-54 O14'74. 1518
The soft core. Prose. Arturo Vivante. 48:28-32 Jy15'72. 1519
Solipsism and theology. Verse. Robert Penn Warren. 47:44 Ja29'72. 1520
Solitaire. Prose. John Updike. 47:26-7 Ja22'72. 1521
Solo. PR (Schmidt). Berton Roueché. 47:30-40 Ja1'72. 1522
Solzhenitsyn, Alexander. TT. 50:27-8 Mr4'74. 1523
Solzhenitsyn, Alexander. Edmund Wilson. 47:83-7 Ag14'71. 1524
Some of us had been threatening our friend Colby. Prose. Donald Barthelme. 49:39-40 My26'73. 1525
Some Pirates and lesser men. SS. Roger Angell. 47:138-56 N6'71. 1526
Some questions about the war. RL. William Whitworth. 46: 30-56 Jy4'70. 1527
Something entirely different. Prose. Sylvia Townsend Warner. 47:28-33 Ja22'72. 1528
Son. Prose. Berry Morgan. 50:39-42 Ap1'74. 1529
Son. Prose. John Updike. 49:33-5 Ap21'73. 1530
Son and father. PR (Childers). Anthony Bailey. 50:44-67 Ja 27'75. 1531
The son from America. Prose. Isaac Bashevis Singer. Dorothea Straus, trans. 48: 37-9 F17'73. 1532
Song. Verse. Marina Tsvetayeva. Elaine Feinstein, trans. 49: 42 O15'73. 1533
Song (for lute, recorder, and deviated septum). Verse. Gerald Jonas. 46:42 Ap25'70. 1534
Song: the organic years. Verse. Marvin Bell. 47:42 Je5'71. 1535
Song with landscape and a river. Verse. Pablo Neruda. Ben Belitt, trans. 47:54 N20'71. 1536

Sonnet of intimacy. Verse. Vinícius De Moraes. Elizabeth Bishop, trans. 47:52 N27'71. 1537
Sonnet with a different letter at the end of every line. Verse. George Starbuck. 48:26 Jy22'72. 1538
Sonora for sale. Verse. Richard Shelton. 49:46 D10'73. 1539
Søren. Verse. John Peck. 48:42 My27'72. 1540
The sound of the future. OFFC. William Murray. 48:85-93 S 16'72. 1541
Soundings: Block Island. Verse. Ben Belitt. 47:29 Ag21'71. 1542
The southside. Verse. Jorge Luis Borges. Norman Thomas di Giovanni, trans. 47:40 My15'71. 1543
The Spanish house. Prose. Gilbert Rogin. 47:32-4 My15'71. 1544
Sparrow, John. TT. 48:26-8 F26'72. 1545
Speech of a guide. Prose. W. S. Merwin. 48:35 Jy1'72. 1546
Speed. Verse. May Swenson. 47: 44 O23'71. 1547
A spin around the house. Verse. Robert Pack. 50:40 S9'74. 1548
Splendid lives. Prose. Penelope Gilliatt. 50:34-9 Ag5'74. 1549
The sporting scene. Prose. (Also listed by individual titles.)
Canoeing. John McPhee. 46: 126-33 Mr21'70.
Golf. Herbert Warren Wind. 46:93-101 My2'70.
Horse racing. Fred Feldkamp. 46:62-83 Je6'70.
Soccer. Alastair Reid. 46:60-71 Jy18'70.
Golf. Herbert Warren Wind. 46:60-8 Ag1'70.
Highland Games. Alastair Reid. 46:60-70 Ag29'70.
Tennis. Herbert Warren Wind. 46:172-84 O10'70.
Baseball. Roger Angell. 46: 110-21 O31'70.
Alvin Ray Rozelle. Herbert Warren Wind. 46: 154-63 D12'70.
Baseball. Roger Angell. 47: 92-9 F20'71.
Hockey. Herbert Warren Wind. 47:107-14 Mr27'71.
Golf. Herbert Warren Wind. 47:112-37 Ap3'71; 47:100-29 Ap10'71; 47:95-101 My 8'71.
Baseball. Roger Angell. 47: 73-82 Je19'71.
Golf. Herbert Warren Wind. 47:56-66 Jy17'71.
Deauville. Fred Feldkamp. 47:60-78 Ag14'71.
Tennis. Herbert Warren Wind. 47:98-116 O2'71.
Baseball. Roger Angell. 47: 138-56 N6'71.
Golf. Herbert Warren Wind. 48:71-83 Ap1'72; 48:114-28 Ap29'72.
Baseball. Roger Angell. 48: 54-62 Jy1'72.
Golf. Herbert Warren Wind. 48:60-72 Jy8'72.
The Olympics. E. J. Kahn, Jr. 48:98-108 S9'72; 48: 114-23 S23'72.
Tennis. Herbert Warren Wind. 48:116-34 O7'72.
Chess. George Steiner. 48: 42-117 O28'72.
Tennis. Herbert Warren Wind. 48:159-71 N4'72.
Baseball. Roger Angell. 48: 132-52 N11'72.
Squash. Herbert Warren Wind. 49:92-109 Ap21'73.
Golf. Herbert Warren Wind. 49:108-25 Ap28'73; 49:48-55 Jy9'73.
Baseball. Roger Angell. 49: 50-65 Jy16'73.
Golf. Herbert Warren Wind. 49:68-76 Ag13'73.
Baseball. Roger Angell. 49: 122-50 S17'73.
Tennis. Herbert Warren Wind. 49:114-50 O8'73.

Baseball. Roger Angell. 49: 183-202 N19'73.
Football. Roger Angell. 49: 42-68 F11'74.
Skiing. Jeremy Bernstein. 50: 120-41 Ap15'74.
Quarter-horse racing. John McPhee. 50:83-112 Ap29'74.
Golf. Herbert Warren Wind. 50:102-21 My13'74.
Basque games. Herbert Warren Wind. 50:85-103 Je10'74.
Golf. Herbert Warren Wind. 50:60-70 Jy8'74.
Baseball. Roger Angell. 50: 37-55 Jy15'74.
Tennis. Herbert Warren Wind. 50:118-46 O7'74.
Baseball. Roger Angell. 50: 156-77 N11'74.
Football. Herbert Warren Wind. 50:122-50 D16'74. 1550

The sports chemist. Prose. Penelope Gilliatt. 49:41-8 O8'73. 1551

The Spring festival on the river. Verse. John Peck. 48:40 My 6'72. 1552

Spring song. Verse. L. E. Sissman. 49:40 Ap21'73. 1553

Spring trains. Verse. Alan Williamson. 50:42 Mr4'74. 1554

The springs of affection. Prose. Maeve Brennan. 48:38-83 Mr 18'72. 1555

The squirrels of Central Park. OLC. Eugene Kinkead. 50:101-12 S9'74. 1556

The stairs. Verse. Howard Moss. 47:32 Ja22'72. 1557

Star trek convention. TT. 50: 31-2 Ja27'75. 1558

Starting over. RL. John Brooks. 47:117-32 O23'71. 1559

The statesman and the conqueror. REF. William Pfaff. 48:79-80 Je3'72. 1560

Staying in bed. Prose. Penelope Gilliatt. 48:40-6 Ap22'72. 1561

Stein, Gertrude. TT. 50:27-9 Mr11'74. 1562

Stendhal. V. S. Pritchett. 50: 99-102 Ja27'75. 1563

Stephen, Steve, Stevie. Prose. Ted Walker. 47:30-5 Jy24'71. 1564

A storm in April. Verse. Richard Wilbur. 49:42 Ap7'73. 1565

A story in an almost classical mode. Prose. Harold Brodkey. 49:42-98 S17'73. 1566

The story of our lives. Verse. Mark Strand. 48:54-5 N4'72. 1567

The story of "T." Prose. F. P. Tullius. 49:26-7 Jy2'73. 1568

The story thus far: Prose. Donald Barthelme. 47:43-5 My 1'71. 1569

Strange formations. Verse. Tom McKeown. 47:156 N6'71. 1570

Strange-dreaming Charlie, cow-eyed Charlie. Prose. John Batki. 47:36-41 Mr20'71. 1571

The street. Prose. L. Woiwode. 50:89-96 Je3'74. 1572

Streets of gold forsworn. ENC. M. F. K. Fisher. 46:48-50 D12'70. 1573

Streets once really seen or seen in dreams. REF. George F. Kennan. 50:41-61 Ap29'74. 1574

Strindberg, August. Robert Coles. 49:126-32 S10'73. 1575

Study of a disaster. Prose. Max Frisch. Jessica Wolff [and] Lore Segal, trans. 48:28-33 Jy22'72. 1576

Subplot. Verse. Jack Butler. 48:40 S9'72. 1577

Subpoena. Prose. Donald Barthelme. 47:33 My29'71. 1578

Successors. RL. John Hersey. 50:46-82 D16'74. 1579

The sugar-coated fortress. PR (Hawaii). Francine du Plessix Gray. 48:41-79 Mr4'72; 48: 39-81 Mr11'72. 1580

The suicide. Verse. David Posner. 48:42 My20'72. 1581

Suicide note. Verse. Richard Eberhart. 46:36 Mr28'70. 1582

Sukhovo-Kobylin, Alexander. Edmund Wilson. 48:144-53 Mr18'72. 1583
Sundance. ACH. Andy Logan. 47:64-70 Ag21'71. 1584
Sunday lemons. Verse. Derek Walcott. 50:76 Ag26'74. 1585
Sunflowers. Verse. Charles Simic. 47:127 Je5'71. 1586
The sunshine boys (Play). TT. 48:30-2 F10'73. 1587
Super. SS. Roger Angell. 49:42-68 F11'74. 1588
Superstar. PR (Sills). Winthrop Sargeant. 47:42-64 Mr6'71. 1589
Supertankers. PR (Supertankers). Noël Mostert. 50:45-100 My13'74; 50:46-99 My20'74. 1590
The supreme option. RL. Daniel Lang. 46:52-61 Ja9'71. 1591
Survival. ACH. Andy Logan. 47:117-24 My15'71. 1592
Survivors. ACH. Andy Logan. 49:59-66 Jy23'73. 1593
The swan man. Prose. Ted Walker. 48:28-32 Ag19'72. 1594
The swastika on our door. Prose. Alice Adams. 47:36-44 S11'71. 1595
Swimming in the rock. Verse. Michael Borich. 50:28 Ag26'74. 1596
Swinburne, Algernon Charles. PR. Mollie Panter-Downes. 46:40-65 Ja23'71; 46:31-43 Ja30'71; 46:40-71 F6'71. 1597
Swindlers. Prose. Joel Gross. 49:43-6 S10'73. 1598
Szladits, Lola L. TT. 48:30-1 Mr25'72. 1599

T

Taking leave of predecessors. PR (Boulez). Peter Heyworth. 49:45-71 Mr24'73; 49:45-75 Mr31'73. 1600
The taking of Pelham one two three (Film). TT. 50:38 D2'74. 1601
Taking stock. Prose. Gilbert Rogin. 46:32-3 Ag22'70. 1602
Talking myself to sleep in the mountains. Verse. Gibbons Ruark. 50:46 S23'74. 1603
Talking to myself. Verse. W. H. Auden. 48:32 Je24'72. 1604
Talking to your veggies. Prose. F. P. Tullius. 49:26-7 Ag13'73. 1605
Tangier buzzless flies. Prose. John Hopkins. 46:40-5 O10'70. 1606
The taste. Prose. W. S. Merwin. 47:33 Jy10'71. 1607
Tati, Jacques. PR. Penelope Gilliatt. 48:35-49 Ja27'73. 1608
Tattoo. Verse. Howard Moss. 50:50 O28'74. 1609
The tattooed desert. Verse. Richard Shelton. 46:46 D12'70. 1610
The teachings of Joe Pye. Prose. Calvin Tomkins. 48:37-8 F3'73. 1611
Tempest and tempo. SS. Herbert Warren Wind. 49:68-76 Ag13'73. 1612
Temporary measures: a book of hours. Verse. L. E. Sissman. 47:42-3 Je26'71. 1613
The temptation of St. Anthony. Prose. Donald Barthelme. 48:34-6 Je3'72. 1614
Ten stories for Mr. Richard Brautigan and other stories. Prose. Garrison Keillor. 48:37 Mr18'72. 1615
Tennis troubles. SS. Herbert Warren Wind. 47:98-116 O2'71. 1616
Test: rate yourself in savoir-faire! Prose. John Bailey. 46:38-9 Ap18'70. 1617
Testimony and demeanor. Prose. John Casey. 47:24-50 Je19'71. 1618
Thank you. ACH. Andy Logan. 50:171-81 O28'74. 1619
That Cosmopolitan girl. Prose.

Lily McNeil. 49:26-7 Jy16'73. 1620
That was Paris. Prose. Janet Flanner. 48:32-6 Mr11'72. 1621
There are meadows in Lanark. Prose. Benedict Kiely. 50:26-31 Jy22'74. 1622
Their own gravity. PR (Bob and Ray). Whitney Balliett. 49:42-65 S24'73. 1623
They were expandable. Prose. Ralph Schoenstein. 50:31 Ja 13'75. 1624
Thinking in time. RL. Calvin Tomkins. 50:109-28 Ap22'74. 1625
The third one. Prose. Isaac Bashevis Singer. Laurie Colwin, trans. 47:30-5 Jy17'71. 1626
The third person. Prose. Ted Walker. 48:38-41 O28'72. 1627
Thirteen unforgettable days, twelve just as rotten nights. Prose. Gordon Cotler. 50:38-9 O21'74. 1628
This life in green. Prose. John Batki. 48:24-5 Jy15'72. 1629
This pain. Verse. John Hall Wheelock. 49:46 O22'73. 1630
Thoreau, Henry David. Noel Perrin. 46:70-80 F21'70. 1631
A thousand dragons. ACH. Andy Logan. 47:142-50 Mr20'71. 1632
A thousand words. Verse. Daryl Hine. 50:44-5 O7'74. 1633
Three encounters. Prose. Isaac Bashevis Singer. Joseph Singer, trans. 50:36-41 F 25'74. 1634
Three for the Tigers. SS. Roger Angell. 49:122-50 S17'73. 1635
Three likely lads of limbo. Prose. Eli Waldron. 46:38-9 Mr21'70. 1636
Three stories. (Also listed by individual titles.) Prose. W. S. Merwin. 46:31-2 Jy25'70; 47: 33 Jy10'71. 1637
Three Winter poems. Verse. Howard Moss. 47:46 F20'71. 1638
Through the automatic carwash. Verse. Robert Vas Dias. 46:90 Ap18'70. 1639
Thursday. Verse. Terry Stokes. 48:151 O14'72. 1640
Tide at Gloucester. Verse. Jean Garrigue. 48:24 S2'72. 1641
Tidings. Verse. Alastair Reid. 46:30 F6'71. 1642
Tierce. Verse. L. E. Sissman. 47:42 Je26'71. 1643
Till it be morrow. Prose. Richard W. O'Donnell. 46: 29 Jy4'70. 1644
Time magazine. TT. 50:40-3 O28'74. 1645
Time to think. PR (Wilson). Calvin Tomkins. 50:38-62 Ja13'75. 1646
The tin woodman and the tiger. ACH. Andy Logan. 50:66-76 Ag26'74. 1647
To have taken the trouble. Verse. C. P. Cavafy. Edmund Keeley [and] Philip Sherrard, trans. 48:31 Je 17'72 1648
To his skeleton. Verse. Richard Wilbur. 50:186 N4'74. 1649
To my god in his sickness. Verse. Philip Levine. 50: 38 F10'75. 1650
To return to the trees. Verse. Derek Walcott. 50:34 My27' 74. 1651
To Rosmarie in Bad Kissingen. Verse. Keith Waldrop. 47: 142 O30'71. 1652
To the hand. Verse. W. S. Merwin. 48:32 Ja13'73. 1653
Tom. Prose. Mary Lavin. 48: 34-42 Ja20'73. 1654
Tomorrow. Verse. Mark Strand. 46:41 My9'70. 1655
Topology. Verse. Carolyn Stoloff. 50:194 N11'74. 1656
A total disaster. Prose. F. P. Tullius. 50:29-31 Ja20'75. 1657
Totem. Verse. Richard Shelton. 47:154 O23'71. 1658
A touch of nature. Prose. Julie Hayden. 47:30-5 Ag

21'71. 1659
Tour d'argent. SS. Herbert Warren Wind. 49:108-25 Ap28'73. 1660
The trail horse. Verse. David Wagoner. 47:36 Je12'71. 1661
A transition figure. REF. Mary McCarthy. 48:38-93 Je10'72. 1662
Trastevere. Prose. Mary Lavin. 47:43-51 D11'71. 1663
Travel: a window. Verse. Howard Moss. 49:43 O29'73. 1664
Travels. ACH. Andy Logan. 48:63-70 Ja6'73. 1665
Travels in Georgia. PR (Ruckdeschel). John McPhee. 49: 44-103 Ap28'73. 1666
The tree where man was born. RL. Peter Matthiessen. 48: 39-74 S16'72; 48:39-62 S23'72; 48:47-75 S30'72. 1667
The trial. Verse. Dabney Stuart. 47:74 S18'71. 1668
Trial by jury. Annals of law. Richard Harris. 48:117-25 D16'72. 1669
Tribute. RL. Calvin Trillin. 48:32-7 Ag5'72. 1670
Triolet, Elsa. Janet Flanner. 46:50-2 Jy11'70. 1671
The trip. Prose. Berry Morgan. 49:38-40 Mr3'73. 1672
Trip South. Prose. Arturo Vivante. 47:85-8 Ja22'72. 1673
Tropical fish. Verse. Howard Moss. 49:52 D10'73. 1674
Trout. Verse. Suzanne Berger-Rioff. 48:101 Je3'72. 1675
Troy Street. Prose. Robert Hemenway. 49:30-8 Je9'73. 1676
Truffaut, François. TT. 46:35-7 O17'70; 49:34-5 O15'73. 1677
Trying to pray. Verse. David Wagoner. 47:117 S25'71. 1678
Trying to remember a town. Verse. William Stafford. 47: 116 O2'71. 1679
Turtletaub and foul distemper. Prose. Roger Angell. 46:26-9 My30'70. 1680
A tutor in the village. Prose. Isaac Bashevis Singer. Rosanna Gerber, trans. 46:33-7 Je6'70. 1681
12 o'clock news. Prose. Elizabeth Bishop. 49:37 Mr24'73. 1682
Twice-told tales. Prose. Jorge Luis Borges. Norman Thomas di Giovanni, trans. 47:25-9 Ja1'72. 1683
The two. Verse. J. F. Hendry. 49:34 Jy16'73. 1684
Two. Verse. Greg Kuzma. 50: 40 Ap1'74. 1685
Two Brazilian poems. (Also listed by individual titles.) Verse. Vinícius De Moraes [and] Joaquim Cardozo. Elizabeth Bishop, trans. 47:52 N27'71. 1686
Two dreams. Prose. Eli Waldron. 46:44-5 O24'70. 1687
Two more under the Indian sun. Prose. R. Prawer Jhabvala. 47:34-41 My29'71. 1688
Two opens to remember. SS. Herbert Warren Wind. 46: 60-8 Ag1'70. 1689
Two poems. (Also listed by individual titles.) Verse. W. H. Auden. 50:42 My6'74. 1690
Two poems. (Also listed by individual titles.) Verse. Robert Graves. 48:42 F10'73. 1691
Two stories. (Also listed by individual titles.) Prose. W. S. Merwin. 49:43 Mr10'73; 50: 59 N18'74. 1692
Tyranny. Prose. Lyll Becerra de Jenkins. 50:50-5 N25'74. 1693

U

U. S. journal. Prose. Calvin Trillin.
Albany, New York. 48:91-8 Mr18'72.
American colony, Guadalajara. 48:50-4 S2'72.
American market, London.

49:93-104 O22'73.
Arroyo Seco, New Mexico. 47:103-10 S18'71.
Atlanta. 49:101-105 Mr17'73.
Baltimore. 48:122-7 O28'72.
Biddeford, Maine. 49:160-6 D10'73.
Boston. 49:67-71 Ja21'74.
Breaux Bridge, Louisiana 48:100-106 My20'72.
Brooklyn. 48:70-6 F26'72.
Center Junction, Iowa 47:100-106 F20'71.
Cloverdale, California. 48:117-22 Ap22'72.
The coastline. 48:215-24 N18'72.
Crystal City, Texas. 47:102-107 Ap17'71.
Disney World, Fla. 47:173-80 N6'71.
Dorchester county, S. C. 47:86-92 Mr27'71.
East Hampton, L. I. 47:64-71 Ja8'72.
El Paso, Texas. 48:83-8 F17'73.
Florida. 47:104-109 My1'71.
Forest City, Iowa. 48:157-62 O14'72.
Fort Dix, New Jersey. 46:40-6 Je6'70.
Gallup, New Mexico. 47:108-14 S25'71; 49:122-32 My12'73.
Garrison, N. Y. 49:52-8 Ja7'74.
Grosvenor Square. 46:108-13 S19'70.
Houston. 46:164-71 D12'70; 50:57-60 Ja6'75.
Imperial County, California. 46:83-9 F13'71; 50:106-11 Mr11'74.
Kahoka, Missouri. 50:88-97 My6'74.
Kanawha County, West Virginia. 50:119-27 S30'74.
Kansas. 47:60-9 My22'71.
Kansas City, Missouri. 50:94-101 Ap8'74.
Lander, Wyoming. 49:114-25 N26'73.
Long Island. 46:32-40 Jy18'70.
Los Angeles. 46:92-104 Ap18'70.
The Lower East Side. 49:112-16 F24'73.
Luverne, Ala. 46:53-8 Ag29'70.
Madison, Wisconsin. 49:150-9 D3'73.
Maine. 47:70-4 F5'72.
Manhattan. 47:57-63 Jy3'71; 47:120-7 O9'71; 48:64-9 Jy15'72; 50:80-6 Je3'74; 50:76-81 F10'75.
Manhattan and Atchison, Kan. 47:90-5 Je12'71.
The Midwest. 49:84-7 Je9'73.
Missouri. 46:108-13 My16'70.
Nampa, Idaho 46:104-109 O31'70.
New Glarus, Wis. 50:48-60 Ja20'75.
New Haven. 46:170-6 N21'70.
New Orleans. 50:94-8 F17'75.
New York. 49:72-8 Ag6'73.
N. Y. / L. A. / N. Y. 46:66-77 Ap4'70.
New York, Richmond, Detroit. 48:102-107 Je3'72.
Newark. 48:62-5 D30'72.
Ohio. 48:62-7 F3'73.
Oklahoma. 49:60-6 Jy9'73.
Pasadena. 46:85-9 Ja16'71.
Pinellas County, Florida. 46:52-6 Ja2'71.
Provo, Utah. 46:120-5 Mr21'70.
Sacramento, California. 48:55-8 Ja6'73.
St. Croix, American Virgin Islands. 50:111-16 F25'74.
St. Petersburg, Florida. 48:131-8 Ap15'72.
Southern California. 49:89-96 My5'73.
Spokane, Wash. 50:60-4 Ag5'74.
Suffolk County, Long Island. 49:74-81 F11'74.
Tesuque, N. M. 47:93-7 D18'71.
Texas. 48:78-82 Je17'72.
Truth or Consequences, N. M. 50:117-24 Je10'74.
Valdez, Alaska. 50:74-8 S2'74.

Vermont. 50:128-35 N4'74.
Watts. 47:136-43 D4'71.
West Chester, Pennsylvania. 46:42-9 Je27'70.
West Forty-fourth Street. 46:148-54 O17'70.
Wheeler Lake, Alabama 50: 134-41 D2'74. 1694
U. S. still on top, says rest of world. Prose. Garrison Keillor. 47:35 O2'71. 1695
The Uganda Asians. PR (Uganda Asians). Jane Kramer. 50: 47-93 Ap8'74. 1696
Ultima thule. Prose. Vladimir Nabokov. Dmitri Nabokov, trans. 49:38-54 Ap7'73. 1697
The ultimate diary. Prose. Howard Moss. 50:33-4 F10'75. 1698
Ulysses (Novel). Janet Flanner. 48:33 Mr11'72. 1699
Una anciana. PR (García). Robert Coles. 49:54-86 N5'73. 1700
Under Libra: weights and measures. Verse. James Merrill. 48:37 Je3'72. 1701
Unpredictable but providential. Verse. W. H. Auden. 49:40 Ap14'73. 1702
Unpsychic man of the year. Prose. F. P. Tullius. 50:29 Je24'74. 1703
Unwinding the glacier. Verse. Ann Stanford. 50:44 Ap15'74. 1704
The unwritten. Verse. W. S. Merwin. 47:36 F20'71. 1705
Up and down. Verse. James Merrill. 48:36-7 Ap8'72. 1706
Up in front, please. Prose. Marshall Brickman. 49:46-7 D3'73. 1707
Upon shaving off one's beard. Verse. John Updike. 46:37 My16'70. 1708
Upstairs. ACH. Andy Logan. 47:105-12 O30'71. 1709
An upstate diary. Prose. Edmund Wilson. 47:46-99 Je5'71; 47:43-83 Je12'71. 1710
Upstate/downstate. ACH. Andy Logan. 50:99-110 F10'75. 1711
Uptown. Verse. Paul Zweig. 49:52 N19'73. 1712
Using 1957-59 as a base, try stealing home. Prose. Gordon Cotler. 46:36-7 My16'70. 1713
Ut an don an al aron. Prose. René Durel. 46:30-49 Ja9'71. 1714

V

Valediction. Verse. Richard Shelton. 46:32 Ag29'70. 1715
The valley of the Khans. SS. Herbert Warren Wind. 49: 92-109 Ap21'73. 1716
Vandergast and the girl. Verse. Louis Simpson. 46:62 D5'70. 1717
Veronese in Venice. PR (Cipriani). Winthrop Sargeant. 48:34-9 Jy22'72. 1718
Vespers. Verse. L. E. Sissman. 47:43 Je26'71. 1719
Vietnam. Annals of war. Frances FitzGerald. 48:36-52 Jy1'72; 48:34-54 Jy8'72; 48: 33-49 Jy15'72; 48:53-68 Jy22'72; 48:56-61 Jy29'72. 1720
Vietnam, Czechoslovakia, and the fitness to lead. REF. William Pfaff. 47:33-8 Jy 3'71. 1721
The view from room 9. ACH. Andy Logan. 47:50-6 D25'71. 1722
The Village. PR (Stonington, Connecticut). Anthony Bailey. 47:36-55 Jy24'71; 47:38-54 Jy31'71. 1723
The violin maker. Verse. Jack Cope. 49:36-43 Ap21'73. 1724
Vipers,. Verse. Ted Walker. 50:48 N11'74. 1725
Visceral learning. PR (Miller). Gerald Jonas. 48:34-57 Ag 19'72; 48:30-57 Ag26'72. 1726
Vision and transformation. Verse. Robert Dana. 48:62 S2'72. 1727

Visiting the oracle. Verse. Lawrence Raab. 50:28 F3'75. 1728
The visitor. Prose. W. S. Merwin. 46:31 Jy25'70. 1729
Visitors to a castle. Prose. Sylvia Townsend Warner. 49:36-40 O1'73. 1730
von Stroheim, Erich. Penelope Gilliatt. 48:81-4 Je3'72. 1731
Vonnegut, Kurt, Jr. TT. 50:29 Mr18'74. 1732
Voyage in the blue. Verse. John Ashbery. 48:60 N18'72. 1733

W

Waiting for Wingfield. Prose. James Stevenson. 46:30-5 S 5'70. 1734
Waking in the cold. Verse. Philip Schultz. 50:36 F17'75. 1735
Waking in Westchester. Verse. Sandra Hochman. 46:24 Ag29'70. 1736
Walcott, Derek. TT. 47:30-1 Je26'71. 1737
Waley, Arthur. George Steiner. 47:110-14 Je12'71. 1738
Walking in Coney Island. Verse. Irving Feldman. 50:32 Ag12'74. 1739
Walking out. Verse. Stanley Plumly. 47:34 F12'72. 1740
Walking the dog: a diatribe. Verse. Mona Van Duyn. 48:26 Ag19'72. 1741
Walking with Charlie. Prose. Julie Hayden. 46:48-50 N7'70. 1742
The walking-mort. Verse. Djuna Barnes. 47:34 My15'71. 1743
The wanderers. Prose. Robert Henderson. 47:48-55 N27'71. 1744
War. Verse. Robley Wilson, Jr. 48:44 Mr18'72. 1745
War and peace (Film). TT. 48:23-4 Ag19'72. 1746
Warming up. ACH. Andy Logan. 48:68-76 F3'73. 1747
The warrior. Verse. Douglas Morea. 49:52 D3'73. 1748
Was Blücher late at Marathon? Prose. H. F. Ellis. 47:51-2 O30'71. 1749
Washoese. RL. Emily Hahn. 47:54-98 D11'71. 1750
The waste land (Poem). George Steiner. 48:134-42 Ap22'72. 1751
The watches. Verse. Jorge Luis Borges. Norman Thomas di Giovanni, trans. 48:42 F 26'72. 1752
The Watergate elegy. Verse. Robert Dana. 49:24 D31'73. 1753
The Watergate prosecutions. REF. Richard Harris. 50:46-63 Je10'74. 1754
Watts-Dunton, Theodore. PR. Mollie Panter-Downes. 46: 40-65 Ja23'71; 46:31-43 Ja 30'71; 46:40-71 F6'71. 1755
The way ahead. Verse. W. S. Merwin. 47:44 Ap24'71. 1756
The way back. OFFC. Joan Colebrook. 46:70-93 S5'70. 1757
We have always survived. PR (Saigon). Robert Shaplen. 48: 51-107 Ap15'72. 1758
We have nothing to fear. Prose. W. S. Merwin. 46:34-6 F 28'70. 1759
We look forward to seeing you next year. Our footloose correspondents. E. J. Kahn, Jr. 46:40-51 Je20'70. 1760
The weather within. Prose. M. F. K. Fisher. 48:27-35 Ag12'72. 1761
The web. Verse. W. S. Merwin. 46:40 S12'70. 1762
Wednesday. Verse. Philip Levine. 50:112 S9'74. 1763
A week's journal. Prose. William F. Buckley, Jr. 47:36-59 Ag21'71; 47:36-57 Ag28'71. 1764
Welcome aboard the M/V Adjaria. OFC. Natacha Stewart. 50:44-94 S23'74; 50: 38-93 S30'74. 1765
Welles, Orson. Pauline Kael.

47:43-89 F20'71; 47:44-81 F27'71. 1766
We're all Democrats. ACH. Andy Logan. 48:108-20 Je10'72. 1767
Werfel, Franz. S. N. Behrman. 48:87ff My20'72. 1768
A whale of a difference. PR (Monro). E. J. Kahn, Jr. 47:43-64 Ap10'71. 1769
What, another legend? Prose. Marshall Brickman. 49:32-3 My19'73. 1770
What he must do to earn money. Verse. Sandra McPherson. 48:44 Mr4'72. 1771
What she is and isn't. Verse. Alan Campbell. 49:30 Ja21'74. 1772
What to do next. Prose. Donald Barthelme. 49:35-7 Mr24'73. 1773
When I open up down there, you'd better look out. PR (Horne). Winthrop Sargeant. 48:31-43 S2'72. 1774
Whenas in gilt my Julio goes. Prose. S. J. Perelman. 49: 28-30 Ja21'74. 1775
Where is Jenny? Prose. Mark Halliday. 50:27-9 My27'74. 1776
The whirlpool. Verse. George Amabile. 49:42 My19'73. 1777
White. Verse. Mark Strand. 48:32 F3'73. 1778
White noise. Verse. John Hollander. 47:36 My29'71. 1779
Who stole my golden undies? Prose. S. J. Perelman. 46:30-2 Je6'70. 1780
Who, what, where, how much, how many? RL. E. J. Kahn, Jr. 49:137-57 O15'73; 49:105-32 O22'73. 1781
The whore of Mensa. Prose. Woody Allen. 50:37-8 D16'74. 1782
Why haven't you written? Prose. Nadine Gordimer. 47:37-42 F27'71. 1783
Why I am an unsuccessful artist. Prose. James Stevenson. 46:47 O31'70. 1784
Wicklow. Verse. Brendan Gill. 48:35 S9'72. 1785
Wiggington, Eliot (Parody). Garrison Keillor. 50:44-6 N4'74. 1786
Wilderness child. Verse. Arthur Gregor. 47:48 O9'71. 1787
Wildfire: Berkeley, 1923. Prose. Hildegarde Flanner. 50:36-43 S23'74. 1788
Willis Avenue. Prose. Mark Helprin. 50:33 F17'75. 1789
Wilson, Edmund. V. S. Pritchett. 48:75-8 D23'72. 1790
Wilson, Edmund (Obituary). 48: 96 Je24'72. 1791
Wilson, Robert M. TT. 47:29-30 Mr27'71. 1792
Wilson, Robert M. PR. Calvin Tomkins. 50:38-62 Ja13'75. 1793
The wind-chill factor. Prose. M. F. K. Fisher. 48:24-6 Ja6'73. 1794
A window on the Oligocene. RL. Berton Roueché. 47:141-55 N13'71. 1795
Window solstice. Verse. Hawley Truax. 46:30 Jy11'70. 1796
Windy Point. Verse. Robert Grant Burns. 48:78 S23'72. 1797
Winged creatures. Prose. Sylvia Townsend Warner. 50: 32-41 Ag19'74. 1798
Winged foot: three opens. SS. Herbert Warren Wind. 50:60-70 Jy8'74. 1799
Winter. Verse. Samuel Menashe. 46:115 Mr7'70. 1800
Winter. Verse. Richard Shelton. 46:102 F13'71. 1801
The Winter and the snow. Verse. Robert Dana. 46:40 Ja16'71. 1802
Winter botany. Verse. Howard Moss. 50:46 Ja27'75. 1803
The Winter of stores. Verse. Rudy Shackelford. 50:95 F10'75. 1804
The Winter of the separation. Verse. Philip Booth. 49:42

F4'74. 1805
Winter radio. Verse. Sheldon Flory. 50:38 Mr18'74. 1806
Winter visit with an old friend. Verse. Naomi Lazard. 47:84 Ja22'72. 1807
With a gift of rings. Verse. Robert Graves. 48:42 F10'73. 1808
Wodehouse, P. G. TT. 47:40-1 O30'71. 1809
Wodehouse, P. G. PR. Herbert Warren Wind. 47:43-101 My 15'71. 1810
Wolf dreams. Prose. Ann Beattie. 50:45-51 N11'74. 1811
Wolves in the zoo. Verse. Howard Nemerov. 50:32 Je17'74. 1812
The woman on the mall. Verse. Robert Dana. 46:177 N21'70. 1813
WomenSports. TT. 50:24-5 Je24'74. 1814
Woolf, Virginia. William Maxwell. 48:88-99 F3'73. 1815
Woollcott, Alexander. S. N. Behrman. 48:77ff My13'72. 1816
Work, for the night is coming. PR (Cavett). L. E. Sissman. 48:42-52 My6'72. 1817
Working in Winter. Verse. Keith Althaus. 49:32 Ja7'74. 1818
The working-class majority. RL. Andrew Levison. 50:36-61 S2'74. 1819
The works of Li Po. Verse. Tony Towle. 48:40 O7'72. 1820
Worsening situation. Verse. John Ashbery. 50:30 Ja20'75. 1821
The worst. Prose. Charles McGrath [and] Daniel Menaker. 50:46 O14'74. 1822
Wouldn't it be fun? PR (Porter). Brendan Gill. 47:48-64 S18'71. 1823
The wound. Prose. Donald Barthelme. 49:36-7 O15'73. 1824
Wrack. Prose. Donald Barthelme. 48:36-7 O21'72. 1825

X

Xerox. Verse. Ben Belitt. 49:42 Mr3'73. 1826

Y

Yellow. Verse. Dan Gerber. 46:171 O10'70. 1827
Yellow roses. Prose. Elizabeth Cullinan. 48:34-8 Mr4'72. 1828
Yet. Verse. Harold Witt. 46:44 Ap4'70. 1829
Yevtushenko, Yevgeny. Joseph Kraft. 47:68-9 My29'71. 1830
You are as brave as Vincent Van Gogh. Prose. Donald Barthelme. 50:34 Mr18'74. 1831
You are cordially invited. Prose. Donald Barthelme. 49:33-4 Jy23'73. 1832
You steer and I'll toot. Verse. Ogden Nash. 47:92 My29'71. 1833
Your complimentary river ode. Verse. J. D. Reed. 48:28 Ag5'72. 1834
Yucca flowers. Verse. William Stafford. 48:134 My20'72. 1835

Z

Zeffirelli, Franco. TT. 48:30-2 Ap8'72. 1836

Part II

REVIEWS OF BOOKS, PLAYS, CINEMA AND TELEVISION

List of Reviewers

ANGELL, Roger
ASTRACHAN, Anthony
AUDEN, W. H.
BALLIETT, Whitney
BERNSTEIN, Jeremy
BLIVEN, Bruce, Jr.
BLIVEN, Naomi
COLES, Robert
EPSTEIN, Edward Jay
FISHER, M. F. K.
FLANNER, Janet
FRASER, Kennedy
GILL, Brendan
GILLIATT, Penelope
HARRIS, Richard
HENTOFF, Nat
HISS, Anthony
KAEL, Pauline
KRAFT, Joseph
LARDNER, Susan
MACDONALD, Dwight
MALCOLM, Janet
MAXWELL, William
MOSS, Howard
OLIVER, Edith
PANTER-DOWNES, Mollie
PERRIN, Noel
PRITCHETT, V. S.
ROSENBERG, Harold
ROVERE, Richard H.
SARGEANT, Winthrop
SISSMAN, L. E.
STAFFORD, Jean
STEINER, George
TOMKINS, Calvin
TRILLIN, Calvin
UPDIKE, John
WEST, Anthony
WHITE, Katharine S.
WILSON, Edmond

Symbols Used in Part II

B = Book Review
CC = Current Cinema
T = Theatre
TV = Television

A propos de Nice. (Gilliatt) 48:73 S23'72. CC 1837

The abbess of Crewe: a modern morality tale. by Muriel Spark. (Updike) 50:76-8 Ja 6'75. B 1838

The abdication. (Kael) 50:152-4 O7'74. CC 1839

Abelard and Heloise. by Ronald Millar. (Gill) 47:93 Mr20'71. T 1840

Abelard and Heloise. by D. W. Robertson, Jr. (Anon.) 47: 104 F12'72. B 1841

Absolutely nothing to get alarmed about. by Charles Wright. (Anon.) 49:131 Mr17'73. B 1842

Absurd person singular. by Alan Ayckbourn. (Gill) 50:

58-60 O21'74. B 1843
An accidental man. by Iris Murdoch. (Anon.) 47:102-103 F 12'72. B 1844
Acrobats. by Israel Horovitz. (Oliver) 47:82-4 F27'71. T 1845
Across from the floral park. by Kent Thompson. (Anon.) 50:63-4 D30'74. B 1846
Across the barricades. by Richard Rosenkranz. (Anon.) 47:114-15 Je12'71. B 1847
Act and the actor: making the self. by Harold Rosenberg. (Anon.) 47:140 Ap3'71. B 1848
The act of the heart. (Kael) 46: 177 D12'70. CC 1849
Act without words I. by Samuel Beckett. (Oliver) 48:123 D2'72. T 1850
Adam by Adam: the autobiography of Adam Clayton Powell, Jr. by Adam Clayton Powell, Jr. (Anon.) 47:202-203 N13'71. B 1851
Adam's rib. (Gilliatt) 48:64 S23'72. CC 1852
Addie pray. by Joe David Brown. (Anon.) 47:91 Ag21'71. B 1853
Additional dialogue: letters of Dalton Trumbo, 1942-62. by Dalton Trumbo. Helen Manfull, ed. (Anon.) 46:190-1 N28'70. B 1854
The advance man. by Jerry Bruno [and] Jeff Greenfield. (Anon.) 47:88 Jy17'71. B 1855
Advancing Paul Newman. by Eleanor Bergstein. (Anon.) 49:78-80 D24'73. B 1856
The adventurer: the fate of adventure in the western world. by Paul Zweig. (Steiner) 50:94-7 Ja20'75. B 1857
The adventurers. (Kael) 46:161-5 Mr21'70. CC 1858
The adventures of Mao on the long march. by Frederic Tuten. (Updike) 48:138-44 My13'72. B 1859
The adventures of Tom Sawyer. (Gilliatt) 49:130-4 Ap7'73. CC 1860
The adversary. (Gilliatt) 49:56-7 Jy23'73. CC 1861
The aesthetics of pornography. by Peter Michelson. (Steiner) 47:84-6 Ag28'71. B 1862
Africa counts. by Claudia Zaslavsky. (Bernstein) 50:194-9 O14'74. B 1863
Africa in prose. by O. R. Dathorne [and] Willfried Feuser, ed. (Anon.) 46:116 F28'70. B 1864
The African genius: an introduction to African social and cultural history. by Basil Davidson. (Anon.) 46:120 Je20'70. B 1865
After Claude. by Iris Owens. (Anon.) 49:76-6 Jy2'73. B 1866
After leaving Mr. Mackenzie. by Jean Rhys. (Anon.) 48: 130 Ap8'72; (Moss) 50:161-6 D16'74. B 1867
After Magritte. by Tom Stoppard. (Oliver) 48:61-2 My 6'72. T 1868
After the ball: pop music from rag to rock. by Ian Whitcomb. (Anon.) 49:124 Je2'73. B 1869
Aftermath. by Harold Owen. (Anon.) 46:99-100 Ja16'71. B 1870
Afternoon of a loser. by Tom Pace. (Anon.) 46:128 F21'70. B 1871
Against the current. by Konstantin Leontiev. George Reave, trans. (Auden) 46:133-8 Ap4'70. B 1872
Against the evidence: the Becker-Rosenthal affair. by Andy Logan. (Anon.) 46:83 Je27'70. B 1873
Agatha Moudio's son. by Francis Bebey. Joyce A. Hutchinson, trans. (Updike) 49:90-4 Ja21'74. B 1874
The age of Arthur: a history of

the British Isles from 350 to 650. by John Morris. (Anon.) 49:91-2 Ag27'73. B 1875
The age of energy: varieties of American experience, 1865-1915. by Howard Mumford Jones. (Anon.) 47:201-202 N6'71. B 1876
The age of illusion: manners and morals 1750-1848. by James Laver. (Anon.) 48:144 Ap22'72. B 1877
An age of mediocrity: memoirs and diaries, 1963-72. by C. L. Sulzberger. (Anon.) 49:199 D10'73. B 1878
The age of patronage: the arts in England 1660-1750. by Michael Foss. (Anon.) 47:116 F19'72. B 1879
The age of the Medici. (Gilliatt) 50:128-32 My13'74. CC 1880
Aguila o sol? Eagle or sun? by Octavio Paz. Eliot Weinberger, trans. (Bliven, N.) 46:91-2 Ag 15'70. B 1881
Aint supposed to die a natural death. by Melvin Van Peebles. (Gill) 47:101-102 O30'71. T 1882
The air cage. by Per Wästberg. Thomas Teal, trans. (Anon.) 48:74 Jy8'72. B 1883
Airport. (Kael) 46:165-6 Mr21'70. CC 1884
Airport 1975. (Kael) 50:71-2 O 28'74. CC 1885
Akokawe. by Afolabi Ajayi. (Oliver) 46:90 Je13'70. T 1886
The alamut ambush. by Anthony Price. (Anon.) 48:135 S23'72. B 1887
"Alas! the love of women!": Byron's letters and journals, Volume III. by George Gordon. Leslie A. Marchand, ed. (Anon.) 50:93-4 Ja13'75. B 1888
Albergo Empedocle and other writings. by E. M. Forster. George H. Thomson, ed. (Anon.) 47:136 D18'71. B 1889
Albert: a biography of the Prince Consort. by Reginald Pound. (Anon.) 50:151 Mr 18'74. B 1890
Aldous Huxley. by Sybille Bedford. (Steiner) 50:103-106 F17'75. B 1891
Alex in wonderland. (Kael) 46:62-4 Ja9'71. CC 1892
Alexander the great. by R. D. Milns. (Anon.) 46:137-8 Ap 25'70. B 1893
Alf 'n' family. (Gilliatt) 48:60-4 Ag26'72. CC 1894
Alfred Stieglitz, an American seer. by Dorothy Norman. (Malcolm) 50:223-6 N18'74. B 1895
Alfredo Alfredo. (Kael) 49:79-80 Ja21'74. CC 1896
Alice doesn't live here anymore. (Kael) 50:74-82 Ja13'75. CC 1897
Alinsky's diamond. by Tom McHale. (Sissman) 50:185 O21'74. B 1898
Alive: the story of the Andes survivors. by Piers Paul Read. (Anon.) 50:154-5 Ap 22'74. B 1899
All fires the fire. by Julio Cortázar. (Updike) 50:124-6 F25'74. B 1900
All God's dangers: the life of Nate Shaw. by Theodore Rosengarten. (Anon.) 50:234-5 N18'74. B 1901
All my friends are going to be strangers. by Larry McMurtry. (Anon.) 48:106 Ap1'72. B 1902
All my sons. by Arthur Miller. (Oliver) 50:106-107 N11'74. T 1903
All on a Summer's night. by Maurice Edelman. (Anon.) 46:154 Mr14'70. B 1904
All over. by Edward Albee. (Gill) 47:95 Ap3'71. T 1905
All over town. by Murray Schisgal. (Gill) 50:63 Ja13'75. T 1906
All said and done. by Simone

de Beauvoir. Patrick O'Brian, trans. (Anon.) 50:99 Ag12'74. B 1907
All the girls came out to play. by Richard T. Johnson [and] Daniel Hollywood [and] Jersey Meadows. (Gill) 48:103-104 Ap29'72. T 1908
All the President's men. by Carl Bernstein [and] Bob Woodward. (Rovere) 50:107-108 Je17'74. B 1909
The All-American boy. (Kael) 49: 186-7 N26'73. CC 1910
Alliance politics. by Richard E. Neustadt. (Kraft) 47:85-7 Je 19'71. B 1911
Alp murder. by Aaron Marc Stein. (Anon.) 46:120 Mr7'70. B 1912
Alpha beta. by E. A. Whitehead. (Oliver) 49:69 My12'73. T 1913
Alpha omega. by Winfield Townley Scott. Eleanor M. Scott, ed. (Anon.) 47:144 S18'71. B 1914
Alternating current. by Octavio Paz. Helen R. Lane, trans. (Anon.) 49:147-8 Ap28'73. B 1915
Amarcord. (Gilliatt) 50:95-6 S 23'74. CC 1916
Ambassador. by Don Ettlinger [and] Anna Marie Barlow [and] Don Gohman [and] Hal Hackady. (Gill) 48:123 D2'72. T 1917
America and Russia in a changing world: a half century of personal observation. by W. Averell Harriman. (Anon.) 46: 99-100 F6'71. B 1918
America, Inc. by Morton Mintz [and] Jerry S. Cohen. (Anon.) 47:76 Jy24'71. B 1919
America, my wilderness. by Frederic Prokosch. (Anon.) 48:130 Je10'72. B 1920
America the dutiful: an assessment of U.S. foreign policy since World War II. by Philip W. Quigg. (Anon.) 47:75 Jy 31'71. B 1921
The American campaigns of Rochambeau's army 1780-83. by Jean-François-Louis Clermont-Crèvecoeur [and] Jean-Baptiste-Antoine de Verger [and] Louis-Alexandre Berthier. Howard C. Rice, Jr., trans. and ed. [and] Anne S. K. Brown, trans. and ed. (Anon.) 48:177-8 D9'72. B 1922
The American corporation: its power, its money, its politics. by Richard J. Barber. (Anon.) 46:84 Je27'70. B 1923
American counterpoint: slavery and racism in the North-South dialogue. by C. Vann Woodward. (Coles) 48:143-6 Ap15'72. B 1924
An American death. by Gerold Frank. (Anon.) 48:143-4 Ap 22'72. B 1925
American graffiti. (Gilliatt) 49:66-7 Ag13'73; (Kael) 49: 154-6 O29'73. CC 1926
The American Heritage history of notable American houses. by Marshall B. Davidson. (Anon.) 47:187 N27'71. B 1927
American journey: the times of Robert Kennedy. by Jean Stein. George Plimpton, ed. (Sissman) 46:108-11 F13'71. B 1928
An American life: one man's road to Watergate. by Jeb Stuart Magruder. (Anon.) 50:104 Je24'74. B 1929
An American millionaire. by Murray Schisgal. (Gill) 50: 63 Ap29'74. T 1930
American mischief. by Alan Lelchuk. (Sissman) 49:148-50 Ap7'73. B 1931
American place names: a concise and selective dictionary for the continental United States of America. by George R. Stewart. (Anon.) 46:176 O24'70. B 1932

American popular song: The great innovators 1900-50 by Alec Wilder. (Anon.) 48: 143-4 Ap29'72. B 1933
American violence: a documentary history. Richard Hofstadter, ed. [and] Michael Wallace, ed. (Anon.) 46:96 Ja30'70. B 1934
Americans and Chinese: purpose and fulfillment in great civilizations. by Francis L. K. Hsu. (Anon.) 47:108 F27'71. B 1935
Americans and the California dream: 1850-1915. by Kevin Starr. (Coles) 49:82-7 Ag6'73. B 1936
Amigo, amigo. by Francis Clifford. (Anon.) 49:60 D31'73. B 1937
Among friends. by M. F. K. Fisher. (Anon.) 47:200 N13'71. B 1938
Amphitryon. by Peter Hacks. Ralph Manheim, trans. (Oliver) 46:92 Je13'70. T 1939
The anatomy of human destructiveness. by Erich Fromm. (Anon.) 49:103 Ja28'74. B 1940
Ancestors. by William Maxwell. (Gill) 47:88-91 Ag21'71. B 1941
The ancient historians. by Michael Grant. (Anon.) 46:64 Ja2'71. B 1942
And Miss Reardon drinks a little. by Paul Zindel. (Gill) 47:67-8 Mr6'71. T 1943
And now for something completely different. (Gilliatt) 48:60 Ag 26'72. CC 1944
And then we moved to Rossenarra. by Richard Condon. (Anon.) 49: 76 Jy2'73. B 1945
And they put handcuffs on the flowers. by Fernando Arrabal. (Oliver) 47:102-103 O30'71. T 1946
And whose little boy are you? by Rod Parker. (Oliver) 47:104-105 My15'71. T 1947
The Anderson tapes. (Kael) 47: 44 Jy3'71. CC 1948
André Kertész: sixty years of photography, 1912-72. Nicolas Ducrot, ed. (Anon.) 48:179-80 D9'72. B 1949
Andrew. by Clay Goss. (Oliver) 48:53 Jy1'72. T 1950
Andrew Carnegie. by Joseph Frazier Wall. (Anon.) 46: 210-11 N14'70. B 1951
Andromaque. by Jean Baptiste Racine. (Flanner) 46:70 Ag 8'70. T 1952
The Andromeda strain. (Kael) 47:102-103 Mr27'71. CC 1953
Aneurin Bevan: a biography, 1945-60. by Michael Foot. (Anon.) 49:120 F18'74. B 1954
The angel inside went sour. by Esther P. Rothman. (Hentoff) 47:100-101 F5'72. B 1955
Angela Davis: an autobiography. by Angela Davis. (Anon.) 50: 214 N11'74. B 1956
Angkor: an essay on art and imperialism. by Jan Myrdal [and] Gun Kessle. Paul Britten Austin, trans. (Anon.) 47:132 Mr27'71. B 1957
Angle of repose. by Wallace Stegner. (Anon.) 47:131-2 Je5'71. B 1958
The anguish of change. by Louis Harris. (Anon.) 50:123-4 Ap1'74. B 1959
Animal crackers. (Gilliatt) 50: 70-2 Jy1'74. CC 1960
Anna K. by Leo Tolstoy. Eugenie Leontovich, adapt. (Oliver) 48:96 My20'72. T 1961
Another part of the house. by Winston M. Estes. (Anon.) 46:170-1 Ap11'70. B 1962
Another self. by James Lees-Milne. (Anon.) 46:64 D26'70. B 1963
Anthony Trollope. by James Pope Hennessy. (Auden) 48: 102-104 Ap1'72. B 1964
Antigone. by Sophocles. (Gill)

47:56 My22'71. T 1965

Anti-worlds. by Andrei Voznesensky. (Kraft) 47:68 My29'71. T 1966

Antoine Bloyé. by Paul Nizan. Edmund Stevens, trans. (Anon.) 49:71 Jy30'73. B 1967

Antoine de Saint-Exupéry. by Curtis Cate. (N. Bliven) 47:133-4 Mr13'71. B 1968

Antonia: a portrait of the woman. (Gilliatt) 50:96-7 S16'74. CC 1969

Antonin Artaud: poet without words. by Naomi Greene. (Anon.) 47:144 My8'71. B 1970

Antonio das Mortes. (Gilliatt) 46:136-7 Ap18'70. CC 1971

Apostles of light. by Ellen Douglas. (Anon.) 49:113-14 Mr3'73. B 1972

Applause. by Betty Comden [and] Adolph Green [and] Charles Strouse [and] Lee Adams. (Gill) 46:81 Ap11'70. T 1973

The apprenticeship of Duddy Kravitz. (Gilliatt) 50:65-6 Jy22'74. CC 1974

Approaches to writing. by Paul Horgan. (Anon.) 49:155 S17'73. B 1975

The Arab mind. by Raphael Patai. (Anon.) 49:133-4 S10'73. B 1976

Archipenko: international visionary. Donald H. Karshan, ed. (Anon.) 46:139-40 S19'70. B 1977

Ari. by Leon Uris [and] Walt Smith. (Oliver) 46:66 Ja23'71. T 1978

Arigato. by Richard Condon. (Anon.) 48:167 O21'72. B 1979

Ark of bones. by Henry Dumas. (Anon.) 50:81-2 Ja6'75. B 1980

The armies of the streets: the New York City draft riots of 1863. by Adrian Cook. (Anon.) 50:143-4 Ap8'74. B 1981

The Arnheiter affair. by Neil Sheehan. (Anon.) 47:103-104 F12'72. B 1982

Arnold Bennett. by Margaret Drabble. (Gilliatt) 50:81-3 D23'74. B 1983

Arriving where we started. by Barbara Probst Solomon. (Anon.) 48:148 My13'72. B 1984

The art and the times of the guitar. by Frederic V. Grunfeld. (Anon.) 46:84 Jy18'70. B 1985

The Aryan myth: a history of racist and nationalist ideas in Europe. by Léon Poliakov. Edmund Howard, trans. (Anon.) 50:149-50 S16'74. B 1986

As I live and breathe: stages of an autobiography. by Malcolm Boyd. (Anon.) 46:127 F21'70. B 1987

As they were. by Tuli Kupferberg [and] Sylvia Topp. (Anon.) 49:36-8 O22'73. B 1988

As towns with fire. by Anthony C. West. (Anon.) 46:98-100 My30'70. B 1989

As we are now. by May Sarton. (Anon.) 50:141-2 Ap8'74. B 1990

As you like it. by William Shakespeare. (Oliver) 49:47 Jy9'73; (Gill) 50:86 D16'74. T 1991

Ashes of victory: World War II and its aftermath. by Quincy Howe. (Anon.) 48:133-4 S23'72. B 1992

Ashes to ashes. by Emma Lathen. (Anon.) 47:116 Je12'71. B 1993

The assassination of Henry IV. by Roland Mousnier. Joan Spencer, trans. (N. Bliven) 49:194-8 N26'73. B 1994

The assassins. by Elia Kazan. (Anon.) 48:101-102 F26'72. B 1995

Attica. (Gilliatt) 50:116-19 Ap15'74. CC 1996

Attica diary. by William R. Coons. (Anon.) 48:79-80 Ag26'72. B 1997

The au pair man. by Hugh Leonard. (Gill) 49:44 Ja7'74. T 1998

August 1914. by Alexander Solzhenitsyn. Michael Glenny, trans. (Kraft) 48:58 Je24'72; (N. Bliven) 48:178-81 O14'72. B 1999

Augustus. by John Williams. (Anon.) 48:199 N25'72. B 2000

Auprès de ma blonde. by Nicolas Freeling. (Anon.) 48:72 S2'72. B 2001

The autobiography of Miss Jane Pittman. (Kael) 49:73-5 Ja 28'74. TV 2002

The autograph hound. by John Lahr. (Anon.) 49:129-30 Mr 17'73. B 2003

An Autumn afternoon. (Gilliatt) 49:83-4 My19'73. CC 2004

Avery's mission. by J. I. M. Stewart. (Anon.) 47:130-1 O 2'71. B 2005

Awake and sing! by Clifford Odets. (Oliver) 46:52 Je6'70. T 2006

B

Baba goya. See Nourish the beast. 2007

The baby maker. (Kael). 46:137 O10'70. CC 2008

Back to the top of the world. by Hans Ruesch. (Anon.) 49:133 S10'73. B 2009

The backup men. by Ross Thomas. (Anon.) 47:184 O16'71. B 2010

Bad company. (Kael) 48:137-40 O7'72. CC 2011

Bad habits. by Terrence McNally. (Oliver) 49:74 F18'74; (Gill) 50:100 My20'74. T 2012

Bad news. by Paul Spike. (Updike) 47:131-2 S25'71. B 2013

Badge 373 (Gilliatt) 49:50-1 Jy 30'73. CC 2014

Badlands. (Kael) 50:135-8 Mr18'74. CC 2015

Ball four. by Jim Bouton. Leonard Schecter, ed. (Angell) 46:79-80 Jy25'70. B 2016

A ballet behind the bridge. by Lennox Brown. (Oliver) 48:106 Mr25'72. T 2017

Balzac. by V. S. Pritchett. (Anon.) 49:182 O29'73. B 2018

Bananas. (Gilliatt) 47:127-9 My 15'71. CC 2019

Bang the drum slowly. (Gilliatt) 49:102-104 S10'73. CC 2020

Bank shot. by Donald E. Westlake. (Anon.) 48:144 Ap29'72. B 2021

Bank shot. (Gilliatt) 50:79-80 Ag12'74. CC 2022

The bankers. by Martin Mayer. (Anon.) 50:104 Ja27'75. B 2023

Barbarians and mandarins: thirteen centuries of Western travelers in China. by Nigel Cameron. (Anon.) 46:191-2 N28'70. B 2024

Barbary shore. by Jack Gelber. (Oliver) 49:61-2 Ja21'74. T 2025

The bark tree. by Raymond Queneau. Barbara Wright, trans. (Updike) 47:134-9 S25'71. B 2026

The barn. by Eric Arthur [and] Dudley Witney. (Anon.) 48: 152 D16'72. B 2027

The barnyard epithet and other obscenities: notes on the Chicago conspiracy trial. by J. Anthony Lukas. (Anon.) 47: 124 F20'71. B 2028

The barrier and the bridge, historic Sicily. by Alfonso Lowe. (Anon.) 48:79-80 Jy 22'72. B 2029

Bartleby. (Kael) 48:91-2 Mr 4'72. CC 2030

The basic training of Pavlo Hummel. by David Rabe. (Oliver) 47:55 My29'71. T 2031

The battle of Algiers. (Kael) 49:236-44 N19'73. CC 2032

The battle Stalin lost: memories of Yugoslavia, 1948-53. by

Vladimir Dedijer. (Anon.) 47:155-6 Ap10'71. B 2033
The bay of noon. by Shirley Hazzard. (Sissman) 46:117 Je 13'70. B 2034
The beauty part. by S. J. Perelman. (Oliver) 50:105-106 N11'74. T 2035
Beaverbrook. by A. J. P. Taylor. (Anon.) 48:168 O21'72. B 2036
Because it is absurd. by Pierre Boulle. Elisabeth Abbott, trans. (Anon.) 47:135 D18'71. B 2037
Bed and board. (Kael) 46:89 F6'71. CC 2038
Bednobs and broomsticks. (Kael) 47:138-9 D11'71. CC 2039
The bee sting. by George Beare. (Anon.) 48:184 O14'72. B 2040
Before civilization: the radiocarbon revolution and pre-historic Europe. by Colin Renfrew. (Anon.) 49:72-4 Ja7'74. B 2041
Before my time. by Maureen Howard. (Anon.) 50:93 F3'75 B 2042
Before the deluge: a portrait of Berlin in the 1920s. by Otto Friedrich. (Anon.) 48:80 Ag 12'72. B 2043
Beg. (Kraft) 47:67 My29'71. CC 2044
A beggar in Jerusalem. by Elie Wiesel. Lily Edelman, trans. (Anon.) 46:134 Je6'70. B 2045
Beggar on horseback. by George S. Kaufman [and] Marc Connelly [and] Stanley Silverman [and] John Lahr. (Gill) 46:73-4 My 23'70. T 2046
The beggar's opera. by John Gay. (Oliver) 48:97 Ap8'72. T 2047
Beginning to end. by Samuel Beckett. Jack MacGowran, ed. (Flanner) 46:120-1 My16'70. T 2048
Behind the door. by Giorgio Bassani. William Weaver, trans. (Anon.) 48:157-9 O7'72. B 2049
Behind the green door. (Trillin) 49:74-81 F11'74. CC 2050
Behold! Cometh the Vanderkellans. by William Wellington Mackey. (Oliver) 47:67-8 Ap10'71. T 2051
Being there. by Jerzy Kosinski. (Updike) 47:132-4 S25'71. B 2052
Bell: Alexander Graham Bell and the conquest of solitude. by Robert V. Bruce. (Anon.) 49:91-2 Je23'73. B 2053
The bell jar. by Sylvia Plath. (Moss) 47:73-5 Jy10'71. B 2054
Belloc: a biographical anthology. by Hilaire Belloc. Herbert van Thal, ed. (Anon.) 46:192 O17'70. B 2055
Below stairs. by Margaret Powell. (Anon.) 46:138 Ap 25'70. B 2056
Beneath the planet of the apes. (Gilliatt) 46:55-6 Je20'70. CC 2057
Benedict Arnold: the dark eagle. by Brian Richard Boylan. (Anon.) 49:71-2 Jy30'73. B 2058
Benjamin Franklin: a biography in his own words. by Benjamin Franklin. Thomas Fleming, ed. (Anon.) 48:200 N25'72. B 2059
Bérénice. by Jean Racine. (Flanner) 46:98-102 Je13'70. T 2060
The Beria papers. by Alan Williams. (Anon.) 49:75 Ja7'74. B 2061
Berlin to Broadway with Kurt Weill. by Kurt Weill. (Oliver) 48:125 O14'72. T 2062
Bernard Shaw: collected letters 1898-1910. by George Bernard Shaw. Dan H. Laurence, ed. (Auden) 48: 190-9 N25'72. B 2063
Bertram Cope's year. by Henry

Blake Fuller. (Wilson) 46: 131-4 My23'70. B 2064
Bessie. by Chris Albertson. (Balliett) 49:128-9 F24'73. B 2065
The best in "The World." John K. Hutchens, ed. [and] George Oppenheimer, ed. (Anon.) 49: 104 Ja28'74. B 2066
Betty. by Georges Simenon. (Anon.) 50:94 F3'75. B 2067
Between enemies: a compassionate dialogue between an Israeli and an Arab. by Amos Elón [and] Sana Hassan. (Anon.) 50:94 Ja13'75. B 2068
Beyond a reasonable doubt. by Sandor Frankel. (Anon.) 48: 126 Mr11'72. B 2069
Beyond freedom and dignity. by B. F. Skinner. (Anon.) 47:170-1 O9'71. B 2070
Beyond reductionism. Arthur Koestler, ed. [and] J. R. Smythies, ed. (Steiner) 47: 104-10 Mr6'71. B 2071
Beyond the tumult. by Barry Winchester. (Anon.) 48:140 My 20'72. B 2072
Bijou. by David Madden. (Anon.) 50:105 My27'74. B 2073
Billion dollar baby. by Bob Greene. (Anon.) 50:194-6 D9'74. B 2074
Billy Jack. (Kael) 47:148-52 N 27'71. CC 2075
Billy Noname. by William Wellington Mackey [and] Johnny Brandon. (Oliver) 46:122 Mr 14'70. T 2076
The bind. by Stanley Ellin. (Anon.) 46:192 O17'70. B 2077
A Bintel brief: Sixty years of letters from the lower east side to the Jewish Daily Forward. Isaac Metzker, ed. Diana Shalet Levy, trans. (Anon.) 47:75 Jy31'71. B 2078
Biology and the future of man. Philip Handler, ed. (Bernstein) 47:124-6 My22'71. B 2079
A bird in the hand. by Donald Wetzel. (Anon.) 48:93 Ja 27'73. B 2080
The bird of night. by Susan Hill. (Anon.) 48:110 F17'73. B 2081
The bird of paradise. by Lily Powell. (Anon.) 47:135 Ap 24'71. B 2082
The bird with the crystal plumage. (Gilliatt) 46:70 Ag1'70. CC 2083
The birds on the trees. by Nina Bawden. (Anon.) 47:87-8 Je 19'71. B 2084
The birthday party. by Harold Pinter. (Oliver) 46:78 F 13'71. T 2085
Black as he's painted. by Ngaio Marsh. (Anon.) 50:88 Ag5'74. B 2086
Black conceit. by John Leonard. (Anon.) 49:196-8 D10'73. B 2087
Black freedom: the nonviolent abolitionists from 1830 through the civil war. by Carlton Mabee. (Anon.) 46:127-8 My2'70. B 2088
Black girl. by J. E. Franklin. (Oliver) 47:76 Je26'71. T 2089
Black girl. (Kael) 48:159-60 D 2'72. CC 2090
Black Odyssey: the case of the slave ship Amistad. by Mary Cable. (Anon.) 47:76 Jy24'71. B 2091
Black picture show. by Bill Gunn. (Gill) 50:61 Ja20'75. T 2092
The black press. Martin E. Dann, ed. (Anon.) 47:92 Ag 21'71. B 2093
The black prince. by Iris Murdoch. (Fraser) 49:69-71 Jy 30'73. B 2094
Black sun. by Edward Abbey. (Anon.) 47:87-8 Jy17'71. B 2095
Black sunlight. by Al Davis. (Oliver) 50:52 Ap1'74. T 2096

The black terror. by Richard Wesley. (Oliver) 47:119-20 N20'71. T 2097

The black vanguard: origins of the Negro social revolution, 1900-60. by Robert H. Brisbane. (Anon.) 46:226 N21'70. B 2098

Black visions. by Sonia Sanchez [and] Neil Harris [and] Richard Wesley. (Oliver) 48:97-9 Ap 8'72. T 2099

The black windmill. (Gilliatt) 50:97-9 Je3'74. CC 2100

Blackberry Winter: my earlier years. by Margaret Mead. (Anon.) 48:200 N25'72. B 2101

Blaming the victim. by William Ryan. (Anon.) 46:100 F6'71. B 2102

Blasts and bravos: an evening with H. L. Mencken. by Paul Shyre. (Gill) 50:69-70 Ja27'75. T 2103

Blazing saddles. (Kael) 49:100-103 F18'74. CC 2104

The blind horn's hate. by Richard Hough. (Anon.) 47:92 Ja15'72. B 2105

Blind husbands. (Gilliatt) 48:81-4 Je3'72. CC 2106

The blind junkie. Everyman Company. (Oliver) 47:54 S4'71. T 2107

Blood. Blood Company. (Oliver) 47:96 Mr20'71. T 2108

Blood red roses. by John Lewin. (Gill) 46:82-3 Mr28'70. T 2109

Blood red, sister rose. by Thomas Keneally. (Anon.) 50:115 F 10'75. B 2110

The blossoming world. by H. E. Bates. (Anon.) 47:86-7 Ja8'72. B 2111

Blue dreams. by William Hanely. (Steiner) 47:86-8 Ag28'71. B 2112

The blue knight. by Joseph Wambaugh. (Anon.) 48:105 Ap1'72. B 2113

Bluebeard. (Gilliatt) 48:67-8 S9'72. CC 2114

The bluest eye. by Toni Morrison. (Sissman) 46:93-4 Ja 23'71. B 2115

Blume in love. (Gilliatt) 49:69-71 Je23'73. CC 2116

Bob and Ray--the two and only. by Bob Elliott [and] Ray Goulding. (Gill) 46:66 O3'70. T 2117

Bodies in motion. by Zane Kotker. (Anon.) 48:74 Jy1'72. B 2118

The body of a girl. by Michael Gilbert. (Anon.) 48:108 Ap 1'72. B 2119

Boesman and Lena. by Athol Fugard. (Oliver) 46:57 Jy4'70. T 2120

Bolingbroke and Harley. by Sheila Biddle. (Anon.) 50: 94-5 Ja13'75. B 2121

Bombay talkie. (Kael) 46:172-5 N28'70. CC 2122

Bomber. by Len Deighton. (Anon.) 46:189-90 N28'70. B 2123

Bone. (Kael) 49:83 Ja21'74. CC 2124

Bonecrack. by Dick Francis. (Anon.) 48:80 Jy22'72. B 2125

The book of imaginary beings. by Jorge Luis Borges. Norman Thomas di Giovanni, trans. (Steiner) 46:116-19 Je20'70. B 2126

The book of Sansevero. by Andrea Giovene. Marguerite Waldman, trans. (Anon.) 46:190 O10'70. B 2127

Books do furnish a room. by Anthony Powell. (N. Bliven) 47:150-4 O30'71. B 2128

Boom boom room. <u>See</u> In the boom boom room. T 2129

The Borgias. by Clemente Fusero. Peter Green, trans. (Anon.) 49:148 Ap28'73. B 2130

The born exile: George Gissing. by Gillian Tindall. (Anon.) 50:83-4 S2'74. B 2131

Born to rebel: an autobiography. by Benjamin E. Mays. (Anon.) 47:138 Ap3'71. B 2132
Born to win. (Kael) 47:170-2 D4'71. CC 2133
Born yesterday. (Gilliatt) 46:54-5 Jy25'70. CC 2134
Borstal boy. by Frank McMahon. (Gill) 46:81-2 Ap11'70. T 2135
Boss. by Mike Royko. (Harris) 47:137-42 My8'71. B 2136
Boswell in extremes: 1776-78. by James Boswell. Charles McC. Weis, ed. [and] Frederick A. Pottle, ed. (Anon.) 46:100 Ja 16'71. B 2137
Boulanger. by James Harding. (Anon.) 47:141 S25'71. B 2138
Bound to violence. by Yambo Ouologuem. Ralph Manheim, trans. (Updike) 47:187-90 N 13'71. B 2139
Boundaries. by Robert Jay Lifton. (Coles) 47:193-7 N6'71. B 2140
The boy friend. by Sandy Wilson. (Gill) 46:95 Ap25'70. T 2141
The boy friend. (Kael) 47:74-7 Ja 8'72. CC 2142
The boys in the band. (Kael) 46: 166-7 Mr21'70. CC 2143
The boys on the bus. by Timothy Crouse. (Anon.) 49:153-4 D 17'73. B 2144
Brahmin in revolt: a biography of Herbert C. Pell. by Leonard Baker. (Anon.) 48:115-16 Mr 4'72. B 2145
Brand X (Gilliatt) 46:115-16 My 16'70. CC 2146
Bread. by David Scott Milton. (Oliver) 49:74 F18'74. T 2147
Breakfast of champions. by Kurt Vonnegut, Jr. (Anon.) 49: 146 My12'73. B 2148
The breast. by Philip Roth. (Anon.) 48:199-200 N25'72. B 2149
A breeze from the Gulf. by Mart Crowley. (Oliver) 49:110 O29'73. T 2150
Brewster McCloud. (Kael) 46: 64-5 Ja9'71. CC 2151
The bride wore the traditional gold. by Talbot Spivak. (Anon.) 48:138-9 My20'72. B 2152
Brides of price. by Dan Davin. (Anon.) 48:99-100 F3'73. B 2153
The bridge. by H. L. Mountzoures. (Anon.) 48:102-103 Je17'72. B 2154
The bridge of beyond. by Simone Schwarz-Bart. Barbara Bray, trans. (Updike) 50:96-8 Ag 12'74. B 2155
A bridge too far. by Cornelius Ryan. (Anon.) 50:131-2 S 30'74. B 2156
Brief lives. by Patrick Garland. (Gill) 50:65-6 O28'74. T 2157
Bright particular star: the life and times of Charlotte Cushman. by Joseph Leach. (Anon.) 46:181-2 N7'70. B 2158
Bring me a unicorn: diaries and letters of Anne Morrow Lindbergh, 1922-28. by Anne Morrow Lindbergh. (Anon.) 48:108 Ap1'72. B 2159
Bring us together. by Leone Panetta [and] Peter Gall. (Anon.) 47:91-2 My29'71. B 2160
Bronco Bullfrog. (Panter-Downes) 46:161-2 N14'70; (Gilliatt) 48:96-8 Je10'72. CC 2161
Brotherhood. by Douglas Turner Ward. (Oliver) 46:84 Mr28'70. T 2162
Buchanan dying: a play. by John Updike. (Anon.) 50:80 Jy8'74. B 2163
Bucky: a guided tour of Buckminster Fuller. by Hugh Kenner. (Anon.) 49:130-1 F24'73. B 2164
Bukharin and the Bolshevik revolution: a political biography, 1888-1938. by Stephen F. Cohen. (Anon.) 49:128 F11'74.

B 2165
Bunraku. by Chikamatsu. (Gill) 49:91 Ap14'73. T 2166
A burial in Portugal. by Noah Webster. (Anon.) 50:151 S16'74. B 2167
Burn! (Kael) 46:159-62 N7'70. CC 2168
The burnt orange heresy. by Charles Willeford. (Anon.) 47: 199-200 N6'71. B 2169
Burr. by Gore Vidal. (Anon.) 49:198-9 N26'73. B 2170
Bury my heart at Wounded Knee. by Dee Brown. (Anon.) 46:111-12 F13'71. B 2171
The bushwhacked piano. by Thomas McGuane. (Sissman) 47:124-6 S11'71. B 2172
Butley. by Simon Gray. (Gill) 48: 130 N11'72. T 2173
Byron's letters and journals, volumes I and II. by George Gordon. Leslie A. Marchand, ed. (Anon.) 50:123 Ap1'74. B 2174

C

C. C. and company. (Kael) 46:132-5 O31'70. CC 2175
C. S. Lewis: a biography. by Roger Lancelyn Green [and] Walter Hooper. (Anon.) 50: 210-11 N4'74. B 2176
Cabaret. (Kael) 47:84-8 F19'72. CC 2177
The cage. by Rick Cluchey. (Oliver) 46:50 Je27'70. T 2178
Cages. by Paul Covert. (Anon.) 47:64 Ja1'72. B 2179
California split. (Gilliatt) 50:78-80 Ag19'74. CC 2180
The call girls. by Arthur Koestler. (Anon.) 49:134 Ap21'73. B 2181
The Camerons. by Robert Crichton. (Anon.) 48:189-90 N11'72. B 2182
Camus and Sartre: crisis and commitment. by Germaine Brée. (Anon.) 48:127 S30'72. B 2183
The cancer ward. by Alexander Solzhenitsyn. (Wilson) 47:83-4 Ag14'71. B 2184
Candida. by George Bernard Shaw. (Gill) 46:79 Ap18'70. T 2185
The candidate. (Gilliatt) 48:64-5 Jy1'72. CC 2186
Candide. by Voltaire. (Oliver) 47:94-5 Ap24'71. T 2187
Candide. by Hugh Wheeler [and] Leonard Bernstein [and] Richard Wilbur. (Oliver) 49: 42-4 D31'73; (Gill) 50:108 Mr18'74. T 2188
The candyapple. by John Grissmer. (Oliver) 46:162 D5'70. T 2189
The cannibal isle. by William Stevens. (Anon.) 46:88 Ag 22'70. B 2190
Capital punishment: the inevitability of caprice and mistake. by Charles L. Black, Jr. (Anon.) 50:64 D30'74. B 2191
Caprifoil. by William P. McGivern. (Anon.) 48:182-4 O14'72. B 2192
Captain Bligh & Mr. Christian: the men and the mutiny. by Richard Hough. (Anon.) 48: 115-16 F10'73. B 2193
Captain Brassbound's conversion. by George Bernard Shaw. (Gill) 48:103 Ap29'72. T 2194
Captain Cook. by Alistair Maclean. (Anon.) 48:182 O14'72. B 2195
The captive dreamer. by Christian de La Mazière. Francis Stuart, trans. (Anon.) 50:90-1 Ag19'74. B 2196
Car. by Harry Crews. (Anon.) 48:104-105 Ap1'72. B 2197
The car thief. by Theodore Weesher. (Anon.) 48:81 Jy 15'72. B 2198
Caravan to Vaccares. by Alistair Maclean. (Anon.) 46:64 Ja

2'71. B 2199
The Carey treatment. (Gilliatt) 48:122-3 Ap15'72. CC 2200
Carnal knowledge. (Kael) 47:43-4 Jy3'71. CC 2201
Carnival. by Arthur H. Lewis. (Anon.) 46:156 My16'70. B 2202
Caro: the fatal passion; the life of Lady Caroline Lamb. by Henry Blyth. (Anon.) 49:131 F24'73. B 2203
The carpenters. by Steven Tesich. (Oliver) 46:75-6 Ja16'71. T 2204
Carry it on. (Gilliatt) 46:66 S5'70. CC 2205
Carrying the fire: an astronaut's journeys. by Michael Collins. (Anon.) 50:84 S2'74. B 2206
Casanova in London. by Peter Quennell. (Anon.) 47:116 Je 12'71. B 2207
The case for black reparations. by Boris I. Bittker. (Anon.) 49:135-6 Mr10'73. B 2208
The case of Robert Quarry. by Andrew Garve. (Anon.) 48:148 My13'72. B 2209
The case of Sukhovo-Kobylin. by Viktor Grossman. (Wilson) 48:146-9 Mr18'72. B 2210
The case of the midwife toad. by Arthur Koestler. (Anon.) 48:131-2 Ap8'72. B 2211
The case worker. by George Konrád. Paul Aston, trans. (Anon.) 50:134 Mr11'74. B 2212
The Castro complex. by Mel Arrighi. (Oliver) 46:142-3 N28'70. T 2213
Cat on a hot tin roof. by Tennessee Williams. (Gill) 50:73-4 O7'74. T 2214
Catch-22. (Lardner) 46:62-3 Je 27'70. CC 2215
Catholics. by Brian Moore. (Anon.) 49:149 My5'73. B 2216
Celebration of awareness. by Ivan D. Illich. (Coles) 47:191-3 N 6'71. B 2217
The Cerberus murders. by Rodney Quest. (Anon.) 47:132 My 1'71. B 2218
A ceremony for our times. by Aeschylus. John Lewin, trans. and adapt. (Oliver) 46:96-7 Ap25'70. T 2219
A certain world: a commonplace book. by W. H. Auden. (Anon.) 46:76 Ag1'70. B 2220
Cervantes. by Richard L. Predmore. (Anon.) 49:188 O15'73. B 2221
César and Rosalie. (Kael) 48:85 Ja13'73. CC 2222
The chairs. by Eugène Ionesco. (Gill) 46:105 My16'70. T 2223
The challenge of world poverty: a world anti-poverty program in outline. by Gunnar Myrdal. (Anon.) 46:79 Ag29'70. B 2224
Chance and necessity: an essay on the natural philosophy of modern biology. by Jacques Monod. Austryn Wainhouse, trans. (N. Bliven) 48:75-7 Ag12'72. B 2225
Change at Shebika. by Jean Duvignaud. Frances Frenaye, trans. (Anon.) 46:168 Ap18'70. B 2226
The changing room. by David Storey. (Gill) 49:92 Mr17'73. T 2227
Changing sources of power: American politics in the 1970's. by Frederick G. Dutton. (Anon.) 47:82 Ag7'71. B 2228
Charles dead or alive. (Gilliatt) 48:46-9 S2'72. CC 2229
Charles of Orleans: prince and poet. by Enid McLeod. (Anon.) 46:83-4 Je27'70. B 2230
Charley Varrick. (Kael) 49:188-95 N12'73. CC 2231
Charley's aunt. by Brandon Thomas. (Oliver) 46:48 Jy 11'70. T 2232
Charlie was here ... and now

he's gone. by Dennis Turner. (Oliver) 47:51 Je19'71. T 2233

Charmed circle: Gertrude Stein & company. by James R. Mellow. (Anon.) 50:127-8 F25'74. B 2234

Charulata. (Gilliatt) 50:48-50 Jy8'74. CC 2235

Chemin de fer. by Georges Feydeau. Suzanne Grossmann, adapt. [and] Paxton Whitehead, adapt. (Gill) 49:111 D10'73. T 2236

The cherry orchard. by Anton Chekhov. (Oliver) 48:59 Ja 20'73. T 2237

Chicago 70. Toronto Workshop Company. (Oliver) 46:51-2 Je 6'70. T 2238

The chicken coop Chinaman. by Frank Chin. (Oliver) 48:46 Je24'72. T 2239

Chien blanc. by Romain Gary. (Flanner) 46:116-17 My2'70. B 2240

Child of God. by Cormac McCarthy. (Coles) 50:87-90 Ag26'74. B 2241

Children are civilians too. by Heinrich Böll. Leila Vennewitz, trans. (Anon.) 46:114-16 F28'70. B 2242

The children of Frankenstein: a primer on modern technology and human values. by Herbert J. Muller. (Anon.) 46:163 My9'70. B 2243

Children of the wind. by Jerry Devine. (Gill) 49:89 N5'73. T 2244

Children's games in street and playground. by Iona Opie [and] Peter Opie. (Steiner) 46:146-53 Mr14'70. B 2245

The children's mass. by Frederick Combs. (Oliver) 49:54-6 My26'73. T 2246

The child's conception of time. by Jean Piaget. (Anon.) 46:128 My2'70. B 2247

Child's play. by Robert Marasco. (Gill) 46:77 F28'70. T 2248

Child's play. (Kael) 48:131-2 D16'72. CC 2249

Chimera. by John Barth. (Anon.) 48:125 S30'72. B 2250

A China passage. by John Kenneth Galbraith. (Anon.) 49:151 My5'73. B 2251

China perceived: images and policies in Chinese-American relations. by John K. Fairbank. (Anon.) 50:178 O7'74. B 2252

Chinatown. (Gilliatt) 50:70 Jy 1'74. CC 2253

The Chinese. by Murray Schisgal. (Gill) 46:115 Mr 21'70. T 2254

The chip-chip gatherers. by Shiva Naipaul. (Anon.) 49: 87 Ag6'73. B 2255

Chloe in the afternoon. (Kael) 48:135-7 O7'72. CC 2256

A choice of masks. by Oscar Pinkus. (Anon.) 46:171 Ap 11'70. B 2257

Christmas books for children. (Stafford) 46:200-20 D5'70; 47:177-214 D4'71; 48:190-212 D2'72; 49:194-220 D3'73; 50: 170-204 D2'74. B 2258

Cinderella liberty. (Kael) 49:80 Ja21'74. CC 2259

The circle. by W. Somerset Maugham. (Oliver) 50:64 Ap 29'74. T 2260

Cities in the sand. by Aubrey Menen. (Anon.) 49:187-8 O 15'73. B 2261

Cities of light and sons of the morning: a cultural psychology for an age of revolution. by Martin Green. (N. Bliven) 48:89-90 Ja13'73. B 2262

The city. by John V. Lindsay. (Anon.) 46:163-4 My9'70. B 2263

City lights. (Gilliatt) 48:123-4 Ap15'72. CC 2264

The city of Dickens. by Alexander Welsh. (Anon.) 47:202 N6'71. B 2265

The Civil War: a narrative; Red River to Appomattox. by

Shelby Foote. (Anon.) 50:82 Ja6'75. B 2266
Civilisation. by Kenneth Clark. (Anon.) 46:134-5 Je6'70. B 2267
Civilized man's eight deadly sins. by Konrad Lorenz. (Anon.) 50:144 Ap8'74. B 2268
Claire's knee. (Kael) 47:137-8 Mr20'71. CC 2269
Clarence Darrow. by David W. Rintels. (Gill) 50:103 Ap8'74. T 2270
Claudine. (Gilliatt) 50:115-16 Ap29'74. CC 2271
Clausewitz. by Roger Parkinson. (Anon.) 47:83-4 Ag7'71. B 2272
Cleopatra Jones. (Kael) 49:73 Ja28'74. CC 2273
The clock winder. by Anne Tyler. (Anon.) 48:140 Ap29'72. B 2274
A clockwork orange. (Kael) 47:50-3 Ja1'72. CC 2275
Close up. by Len Deighton. (Anon.) 48:94 Je24'72. B 2276
The clowns. (Flanner) 47:96-7 Mr27'71; (Gilliatt) 47:96-100 Je12'71. CC 2277
Cobra. by Severo Sarduy. Suzanne Jill Levine, trans. (Anon.) 50:102-103 Ja27'75. B 2278
Cockfighter. by Charles Willeford. (Anon.) 48:81-2 Jy15'72. B 2279
Cocteau. by Francis Steegmuller. (N. Bliven) 47:130-2 Mr13'71. B 2280
Cocteau's world: an anthology of writings by Jean Cocteau. by Jean Cocteau. Margaret Crosland, ed. (Anon.) 49:152 My 5'73. B 2281
Cogan's trade. by George V. Higgins. (Anon.) 50:103-104 Je24'74. B 2282
Cold feet. by Marvin Pletzke. (Oliver) 48:62 My6'72. T 2283
Cold war and counterrevolution: the foreign policy of John F. Kennedy. by Richard J. Walton. (Anon.) 48:103 F26'72. B 2284
Cole. Robert Kimball, ed. (Anon.) 47:104 F12'72. B 2285
Coleridge, the damaged archangel. by Norman Fruman. (Steiner) 49:77-90 Ag27'73. B 2286
Colette. by Harvey Schmidt [and] Tom Jones. Elinor Jones, adapt. (Oliver) 46:105-106 My16'70. T 2287
Colette: the difficulty of loving. by Margaret Crosland. (Anon.) 49:59 D31'73. B 2288
Colette: the thousand and one mornings. by Sidonie Gabrielle Colette. Margaret Crosland, trans. [and] David Le Vay, trans. (Anon.) 49:99 Ja14'74. B 2289
The colony. by John Bowers. (Anon.) 47:155-6 O30'71. B 2290
The color dictionary of flowers and plants, for home and garden. by Roy Hay [and] Patrick M. Synge. (White) 46:120-1 Mr28'70. B 2291
The Columbus tree. by Peter Feibleman. (Anon.) 49:130 F24'73. B 2292
Come into the garden Maud. by Nöel Coward. (Gill) 50: 102 Mr11'74. T 2293
The coming of age. by Simone de Beauvoir. Patrick O'Brian, trans. (Flanner) 46:87-90 Mr7'70; (Coles) 48:68-79 Ag19'72. B 2294
The coming of post-industrial society: a venture in social forecasting. by Daniel Bell. (N. Bliven) 49:151-4 S17'73. B 2295
The coming of the golden age. by Gunther S. Stent. (Anon.) 46:168 Ap18'70. B 2296
The common insects of North America. by Lester A. Swan [and] Charles S. Papp. (Anon.)

48:179 D9'72 B 2297
Common or garden. by Tyler Whittle. (White) 46:126-7 Mr 28'70. B 2298
Company. by George Furth. (Gill) 46:83 My2'70. T 2299
The company and the union. by William Serrin. (N. Bliven) 49:69-70. Jy9'73. B 2300
The complete "Greed." Herman G. Weinberg, ed. (Anon.) 49: 152 Ap7'73. B 2301
The complete stories. by Franz Kafka. Nahum Glatzer, ed. (Steiner) 48:75-81 Jy15'72. B 2302
The complete works of Kate Chopin. by Kate Chopin. Per Seyersted, ed. (Anon.) 46:155 Mr14'70. B 2303
A concise history of Germany. by Constantine FitzGibbon. (Anon.) 49:79-80 Jy16'73. B 2304
A concise history of Scotland. by Fitzroy Maclean. (Anon.) 46: 100 My30'70. B 2305
Condemned to freedom. by William Pfaff. (Anon.) 47:88 Ag28'71. B 2306
Conduct unbecoming. by Barry England. (Gill) 46:129 O24'70. T 2307
The confession. (Flanner) 46: 119-20 My16'70; (Kael) 46: 172-7 D12'70. CC 2308
Confession from the Malaga madhouse: a Christmas diary. by Charlotte Painter. (Anon.) 47: 199 N13'71. B 2309
Confessions of a white racist. by Larry L. King. (Anon.) 47:92 Je26'71. B 2310
Confessions of cherubino. by Bertha Harris. (Anon.) 48:130-1 Ap8'72. B 2311
The confessions of Edward Dahlberg. by Edward Dahlberg. (Anon.) 47:124 F20'71. B 2312
The confessions of Lady Nijō. by Lady Nijō. Karen Brazell, trans. (Anon.) 49:60 D31'73. B 2313
The conformist. (Flanner) 47: 118 Mr13'71; (Kael) 47:99-102 Mr27'71. CC 2314
Confrontations with myself: an epilogue. by Helene Deutsch. (Anon.) 49:76 Jy2'73. B 2315
The connoisseur by Evan S. Connell, Jr. (Anon.) 50:199-200 O14'74. B 2316
The conquest of the Incas. by John Hemming. (Anon.) 46: 207-208 N14'70. B 2317
Conrack. (Kael) 50:119-22 Mr 11'74. CC 2318
Conrad's romanticism. by David Thorburn. (Anon.) 50:201-202 O14'74. B 2319
The consent of the governed. by Arthur Krock. (Anon.) 47:76 Jy10'71. B 2320
Constantine the great. by John Holland Smith. (Anon.) 47: 91-2 Ag21'71. B 2321
The continuing battle: memoirs of a European 1936-66. by Paul-Henri Spaak. Henry Fox, trans. (Anon.) 47:116 F19'72. B 2322
The contractor. by David Storey. (Oliver) 49:107-109 O29'73. T 2323
The contrast. by Royall Tyler. Anthony Stimac, adapt. (Oliver) 48:110 D9'72. T 2324
Contribution. by Ted Shine. (Oliver) 46:118 Mr21'70. T 2325
Conventional wisdom. by John Bart Gerald. (Anon.) 48:110 Je3'72. B 2326
The conversation. (Gilliatt) 50: 116 Ap15'74. CC 2327
Cop and blow. by Neil Harris. (Oliver) 48:98-9 Ap8'72. T 2328
Coping: essays on the practice of government. by Daniel P. Moynihan. (N. Bliven) 50:151-3 Ap22'74. B 2329
Cops and robbers. (Gilliatt)

49:46-7 Ag27'73. CC 2330
The corner. by Ed Bullins. (Oliver) 48:53 Jy1'72. T 2331
The cornucopia, being a kitchen entertainment and cookbook. by Judith Herman [and] Marguerite Shalett Herman. (Fisher) 50:95-7 My27'74. B 2332
The corrupt kingdom: the rise and fall of the United Mine Workers. by Joseph E. Finley. (Anon.) 49:151 Ap7'73. B 2333
Corsica: portrait of a granite island. by Dorothy Carrington. (Anon.) 50:90 Ag19'74. B 2334
The cotillion, or one good bull is half the herd. by John Oliver Killens. (Anon.) 47:90-1 My29'71. B 2335
Cotton comes to Harlem. (Lardner). 46:64 Je27'70. CC 2336
Counselor Ayres' memorial. by Joachim Maria Machado de Assis. (West) 49:117-18 Mr 31'73. B 2337
Count Julian. by Juan Goytisolo. Helen R. Lane, trans. (Pritchett) 50:173-5 O7'74. B 2338
The country and the city. by Raymond Williams. (N. Bliven) 49:83-6 Ag13'73. B 2339
The country girl. by Clifford Odets. (Gill) 48:106 Mr25'72. T 2340
A country journal. by Michael Harwood [and] Mary Durant. (Anon.) 50:135 S9'74. B 2341
Couplings and groupings. by Megan Terry. (Anon.) 48:116 F10'73. B 2342
The courageous and the proud. by Samuel Vance. (Anon.) 46:140 My23'70. B 2343
The court-martial of Lt. Calley. by Richard Hammer. (Anon.) 47:88 Ag28'71. B 2344
The cousinhood. by Chaim Bermant. (Anon.) 48:94 Je 24'72. B 2345
The cowboys. (Kael) 47:83-4 Ja 22'72. CC 2346
The creation of the world and other business. by Arthur Miller. (Gill) 48:109 D9'72. T 2347
Creeps. by David E. Freeman. (Oliver) 49:99-100 D17'73. T 2348
Creezy. by Félicien Marceau. J. A. Underwood, trans. (N. Bliven) 46:74-6 Ag1'70. B 2349
Cries and whispers. (Kael) 48:50-4 Ja6'73. CC 2350
Crime and compromise: Janos Kadar and the politics of Hungary since revolution. by William Shawcross. (Anon.) 50:149 S16'74. B 2351
The crime of Sukhovo-Kobylin. by Leonid Grossman. (Wilson) 48:145-6 Mr18'72. B 2352
The criminals. by José Triana. Adrian Mitchell, trans. (Oliver) 46:83-4 Mr7'70. T 2353
Crises of the republic. by Hannah Arendt. (Anon.) 48:132 Je10'72. B 2354
Crisis in the classroom: the remaking of American education. by Charles E. Silberman. (Anon.) 46:208-209 N14'70. B 2355
Crisis 1918. by Joseph Gies. (Anon.) 50:110-11 Je3'74. B 2356
Croesus and the witch. by Vinnette Carroll [and] Micki Grant. (Oliver) 47:54 S4'71. T 2357
Cromwell. (Kael) 46:163-4 N7'70. CC 2358
Cromwell: the lord protector. by Antonia Fraser. (N. Bliven) 49:95-7 Ja14'74. B 2359
The crook. (Gilliatt) 47:85-6 Je26'71. CC 2360
The crouching future: international politics and U.S. foreign policy. by Roger Hilsman. (Anon.) 50:95

F3'75. B 2361
Crown matrimonial. by Royce Ryton. (Gill) 49:102 O15'73. T 2362
The crown of Mexico: Maximillian and his empress Carlota. by Joan Haslip. (Anon.) 48:146-7 My13'72. B 2363
The crucible. by Arthur Miller. (Gill) 48:54-6 My6'72. T 2364
Cry for us all. by William Alfred [and] Albert Marre [and] Mitch Leigh [and] Phyllis Robinson. (Gill) 46:79-80 Ap18'70. T 2365
A cry of angels. by Jeff Fields. (Anon.) 50:130 S30'74. B 2366
A cry of crickets. by Brian Glanville. (Anon.) 46:166 Ap18'70. B 2367
Crystal and fox. by Brian Friel. (Oliver) 49:82 My5'73. T 2368
The crystal garden. by Elaine Feinstein. (Anon.) 50:109-10 Je3'74. B 2369
Cuba: the pursuit of freedom. by Hugh Thomas. (N. Bliven) 48:68-71 S2'72. B 2370
Cults of unreason. by Christopher Evans. (Anon.) 50:112 Je3'74. B 2371
Culture and society in Italy 1290-1420. by John Larner. (Anon.) 47:183-4 O16'71. B 2372
Cyrano. by Edmond Rostand. Anthony Burgess, adapt. [and] Michael J. Lewis, adapt. (Gill) 49:54 My26'73. T 2373

D

D. H. Lawrence: novelist, poet, prophet. Stephen Spender, ed. (Anon.) 49:80 D24'73. B 2374
Daddy was a number runner. by Louise Meriwether. (Sissman) 46:77 Jy11'70. B 2375
Daisy Bates. by Elizabeth Salter. (Anon.) 48:104 Je17'72. B 2376
Daisy Miller. (Gilliatt) 50:69-75 My27'74. CC 2377
The damnation of Theron Ware. by Harold Frederic. (Wilson) 46:123-6 Je6'70. B 2378
Dance hall of the dead. by Tony Hillerman. (Anon.) 49:60 D31'73. B 2379
Dance of death. by August Strindberg. (Gill) 47:89-90 My8'71; 50:104 Ap15'74. T 2380
The dance of legislation. by Eric Redman. (Anon.) 49:170 O8'73. B 2381
Dance of the happy shades. by Alice Munro. (Anon.) 49:186 N5'73. B 2382
Dance the eagle to sleep. by Marge Piercy. (Updike) 47:143-53 Ap10'71. B 2383
Dance wi' me; or, the fatal twitch. by Greg Antonacci. (Oliver) 47:51 Je19'71; (Gill) 50:77 F3'75 T 2384
Dancing lady. (Gilliatt) 47:93-4 S11'71. CC 2385
The Danziger transcript. by Carl Fick. (Anon.) 47:64 Ja1'72. B 2386
Dark and bloody ground: a guerrilla diary of the Spanish Civil War. by Francisco Pérez López. Joseph D. Harris, trans. Victor Guerrier, ed. (Anon.) 48:110-11 Je3'72. B 2387
A dark corner. by Celia Dale. (Anon.) 48:131 Mr25'72. B 2388
The dark night of resistance. by Daniel Berrigan. (Anon.) 47:88 Jy17'71. B 2389
A darkening green: notes from the silent generation. by Peter S. Prescott. (Anon.) 50:143-4 My6'74. B 2390
Darkness in Summer. by Takeshi Kaiko. Cecilia Segawa Seigle, trans. (Anon.) 49:109-10 F 4'74. B 2391
Darling Lili. (Gilliatt) 46:70 Ag1'70. CC 2392
Darwin on Man: a psychological study of scientific creativity.

by Howard E. Gruber. (Anon.) 50:158-9 My13'74. B 2393
Daughter buffalo. by Janet Frame. (Anon.) 48:125 S30'72. B 2394
Daughters of darkness. (Gilliatt) 47:69 Je19'71. CC 2395
The dawn's early light. by Walter Lord. (Anon.) 48:82-3 Jy15'72. B 2396
Day for night. (Kael) 49:160-5 O15'73. CC 2397
A day in the death of Joe Egg. (Gilliatt) 48:95-6 Je10'72. CC 2398
A day in the life of just about everyone. by Earl Wilson, Jr. (Oliver) 47:96 Mr20'71. T 2399
A day no pigs would die. by Robert Newton Peck. (Anon.) 48:100 F3'73. B 2400
Day of absence. by Douglas Turner Ward. (Oliver) 46:84 Mr28'70. T 2401
The day of the dolphin. (Kael) 49:50 D31'73. CC 2402
The day of the Jackal. by Frederick Forsyth. (Anon.) 47:88 Ag28'71. B 2403
The day of the Jackal. (Gilliatt) 49:66-7 Je2'73. CC 2404
Days and nights in the forest. (Kael) 49:121-6 Mr17'73. CC 2405
A day's march nearer home. by Roger Parkinson. (Anon.) 50:99-100 Ag12'74. B 2406
DeGaulle. by Brian Crozier. (Anon.) 49:72 Ja7'74. B 2407
De Kooning. by Harold Rosenberg. (Anon.) 50:168 D16'74. B 2408
Deadly night shade. by James Fraser. (Anon.) 46:192 O17'70. B 2409
Deafman glance. by Robert M. Wilson. (Oliver) 47:95-6 Mr 20'71. T 2410
Dear Janet Rosenberg, dear Mr. Kooning. by Stanley Eveling. (Oliver) 46:87-8 Ap18'70. T 2411
Dear Miss Weaver: Harriet Shaw Weaver, 1876-1961. by Jane Lidderdale [and] Mary Nicholson. (Anon.) 47:151 Mr20'71. B 2412
Dear nobody. by Fanny Burney. Jane Marla Robbins, adapt. (Oliver) 50:69-70 Mr4'74. T 2413
Dear Oscar. by Caryl Gabrielle Young [and] Addy O. Fieger. (Gill) 48:123 D2'72. T 2414
The death and life of Malcolm X. by Peter Goldman. (Anon.) 48:92 Ja13'73. B 2415
The death and rebirth of the Seneca. by Anthony F. Wallace. (Anon.) 46:126-7 F 21'70. B 2416
Death claims. by Joseph Hansen. (Anon.) 49:132 Mr17'73. B 2417
Death cracks a bottle. by Kenneth Giles. (Anon.) 46:128 F21'70. B 2418
Death in Venice. (Panter-Downes) 47:114-15 Ap17'71; (Gilliatt) 47:85 Je26'71. CC 2419
Death in Willow Pattern. by W. J. Burley. (Anon.) 46:164 My9'70. B 2420
Death of a schoolboy. by Hans Koning. (Anon.) 50:142 My 6'74. B 2421
The death of me yet. by Whit Masterson. (Anon.) 46:143-4 S26'70. B 2422
The death of the detective. by Mark Smith. (Anon.) 50:147 S16'74. B 2423
The death of the imperial dream: the British Commonwealth and Empire 1775-1969. by Edward Grierson. (Anon.) 48:72 S2'72. B 2424
The death of the past. by J. H. Plumb. (Anon.) 46:127 F 21'70. B 2425
A death out of season. by Emanuel Litvinoff. (Anon.) 50:89 Ag19'74. B 2426
Death wish. (Gilliatt) 50:48-50 Ag26'74. CC 2427

Death's bright dart. by V. C. Clinton-Baddeley. (Anon.) 46:139-40 Ap25'70. B 2428

The début. (Kael) 47:143-4 O23'71. CC 2429

Decent and indecent. by Benjamin Spock. (Anon.) 46:156 Mr14'70. B 2430

The decline of the wasp. by Peter Schrag. (Anon.) 48:116 Mr4'72. B 2431

Deep end. (Gilliatt) 47:56-7 S4'71. CC 2432

Defeated: inside America's military machine. by Stuart H. Loory. (Anon.) 49:74-5 Ja7'74. B 2433

The defector. by Charles Collingwood. (Anon.) 46:120 Mr7'70. B 2434

Deliverance. by James Dickey. (Sissman) 46:123-6 My2'70. B 2435

Deliverance. (Gilliatt) 48:52-3 Ag5'72. CC 2436

Demon. by Wilford Leach [and] John Braswell. (Oliver) 47:70 Ja22'72. T 2437

Derby. (Gilliatt) 47:129 My15'71. CC 2438

The descent of woman. by Elaine Morgan. (Anon.) 48:139-40 My20'72. B 2439

The desert world. by David F. Costello. (Anon.) 48:126-7 S9'72. B 2440

The deserters and the nomads. (Gilliatt) 50:129-30 My20'74. CC 2441

Desperate characters. (Gilliatt) 47:101-104 S25'71. CC 2442

Desperate games. by Pierre Boulle. Patricia Wolf, trans. (Anon.) 49:72 Ja7'74. B 2443

The destiny waltz. by Gerda Charles. (Anon.) 48:125-6 S16'72. B 2444

Destroy, she said. (Gilliatt) 46:135-6 Ap18'70. CC 2445

A detective's story. by George Hatherill. (Anon.) 49:151-2 Ap7'73. B 2446

The devil and John Foster Dulles. by Townsend Hoopes. (Anon.) 49:246 N19'73. B 2447

The devil catchers. by Anon. (Oliver) 46:132 D12'70. T 2448

The devils. (Gilliatt) 47:58-61 Jy24'71. CC 2449

The devil's decade. by Claud Cockburn. (Anon.) 50:151-2 My20'74. B 2450

The diamond of Jannina: Ali Pasha 1741-1822. by William Plomer. (Anon.) 46:139 S 19'70. B 2451

Diamond studs: the life of Jesse James. by Jim Wann [and] Bland Simpson. (Gill) 50:70 Ja27'75. T 2452

Diamonds are forever. (Kael) 47:81-2 Ja15'72. CC 2453

Diane Arbus. by Diane Arbus. (Anon.) 48:80 D23'72. B 2454

Diaries of Sir Alexander Cadogan. by Alexander Cadogan. David Dilks, ed. (Panter-Downes) 48:148-58 O28'72. B 2455

Diary of a mad housewife. (Gilliatt) 46:68-9 Ag15'70. CC 2456

Diary of a man in despair. by Friedrich Percyval Reck-Malleczewen. Paul Rubens, trans. (Coles) 46:92-5 Ja 30'71. B 2457

The diary of Anaïs Nin: Volume V, 1947-55. by Anaïs Nin. Gunther Stuhlmann, ed. (Anon.) 50:159 My13'74. B 2458

The dice of war. by Andrea Giovene. Bernard Wall, trans. (N. Bliven) 50:187-9 D9'74. B 2459

Dickie's list. by Ann Birstein. (Anon.) 49:174-5 O22'73. B 2460

A dictionary of slang and unconventional English. by Eric Partridge. (Anon.) 46:112 F 13'71. B 2461

Diderot. by Arthur M. Wilson. (Anon.) 48:80 Jy29'72. B 2462

Different times. by Michael Brown. (Gill) 48:99 My13'72. T 2463
A different woman. by Jane Howard. (Anon.) 49:198-9 D 10'73. B 2464
The digger's game. by George V. Higgins. (Anon.) 49:150 Ap7'73. B 2465
Dillinger. (Gilliatt) 49:64-6 Ag 13'73. CC 2466
Dingdong. by Arthur Maling. (Anon.) 50:108 My27'74. B 2467
The dirtiest show in town. by Tom Eyen. (Oliver) 46:57 Jy4'70. T 2468
Dirty Harry. (Kael). 47:78-81 Ja 15'72; 49:87-9 Ja14'74. CC 2469
The disciple and his devil. by Valerie Pascal. (Anon.) 46:104 S5'70. B 2470
The discovery of the asylum: social order and disorder in the new republic. by David J. Rothman. (Anon.) 47:67 Jy3'71. B 2471
The discreet charm of the bourgeoisie. (Kael). 48:153 N11'72. CC 2472
Discretions. by Mary de Rachewiltz. (Anon.) 47:202 N13'71. B 2473
Discriminations: essays & afterthoughts, 1938-74. by Dwight Macdonald. (Anon.) 50:168 D16'74. B 2474
The divided self. by R. D. Laing. (Anon.) 46:155-6 Mr14'70. B 2475
Divided soul: the life of Gogol. by Henri Troyat. Nancy Amphoux, trans. (Pritchett) 49:176-84 N5'73. B 2476
The divine mistress. by Samuel Edwards. (Anon.) 46:136 Je 6'70. B 2477
Divine Right's trip. by Gurney Norman. (Updike) 48:115-21 S9'72. B 2478
The diviners. by Margaret Laurence. (Anon.) 50:79 Jy8'74. B 2479
The divorce of Judy and Jane. by Arthur Whitney. (Oliver) 48:62 My6'72. T 2480
Do with me what you will. by Joyce Carol Oates. (Anon.) 49:185-6 O15'73. B 2481
Do you hear them? by Nathalie Sarraute. Maria Jolas, trans. (N. Bliven) 49:128 Mr17'73. B 2482
Do you remember England? Derek Marlowe. (Anon.) 48:81 Jy15'72. B 2483
Do you sincerely want to be rich? The full story of Bernard Cornfeld and I. O. S. by Charles Raw [and] Bruce Page [and] Godfrey Hodgson. (Anon.) 47:183 O16'71; (Epstein) 47:90-9 Ja22'72. B 2484
Doc (Gilliatt) 47:60-2 Ag21'71. CC 2485
Doctor Cobb's game. by R. V. Cassill. (Anon.) 46:98-9 F 6'71. B 2486
Dr. Fish. by Murray Schisgal. (Gill) 46:115 Mr21'70. T 2487
Doctor Frigo. by Eric Ambler. (Anon.) 50:177-8 O7'74. B 2488
The doctor in spite of himself. by Jean Baptiste Pouquelin Molière. (Oliver) 49:105 Ap 28'73. T 2489
Doctor Selavy's magic theatre. by Richard Foreman [and] Stanley Silverman [and] Tom Hendry. (Oliver) 48:109-10 D9'72. T 2490
Doctors' wives. (Kael) 47:89 Mr13'71. CC 2491
Dog soldiers. by Robert Stone. (Anon.) 50:166-7 O16'74. B 2492
A dog's ransom. by Patricia Highsmith. (Anon.) 48:128 S16'72. B 2493
A doll's house. by Henrik Ibsen. (Oliver) 46:66-7 Ja 23'71. T 2494

A doll's house. (Gilliatt) 49: 65-6 Je2'73. CC 2495
Don Juan. by Jean Baptiste Pouquelin Molière. (Gill) 48: 86 D16'72. T 2496
Don Juan in hell. by George Bernard Shaw. (Gill) 48:50 Ja 27'73. T 2497
Don't bother me, I can't cope. by Vinnette Carroll. (Oliver) 46:144-5 O17'70; 48:104-105 Ap29'72. T 2498
Don't drop dead tomorrow. by Hugh Pentecost. (Anon.) 47:87 Ja8'72. B 2499
Don't let it go to your head. by J. E. Gaines. (Oliver) 47:72-4 Ja29'72. T 2500
Don't look now. (Kael) 49:68-72 D24'73. CC 2501
Don't play us cheap. by Melvin Van Peebles. (Gill) 48:82 My 27'72. T 2502
Doom's caravan. by Geoffrey Household. (Sissman) 47:125-8 My1'71. B 2503
Dorothy Richardson: a critical biography. by John Rosenberg. (Anon.) 49:98 Ja14'74. B 2504
Dostoevsky: works and days. by Avrahm Yarmolinsky. (Anon.) 47:92 Ja15'72. B 2505
The double-cross system in the war of 1939 to 1945. by J. C. Masterman. (Anon.) 48:155-6 Mr18'72. B 2506
Down there. by Jose Yglesias. (Anon.) 46:190 O17'70. B 2507
Dragon by the tail: American, British, and Russian encounters with China and one another. by John Paton Davies, Jr. (Anon.) 48:131-2 S23'72. B 2508
The dragon wakes: China and the West, 1793-1911. by Christopher Hibbert. (Anon.) 46:95-6 Ja 30'71. B 2509
Drat! by Fred Bluth [and] Steven Metcalf. (Oliver) 47:104 O30'71. T 2510
The dream and the deal. by Jerre Mangione. (Rosenberg) 48:99-102 Ja20'73. B 2511
The dream on Monkey Mountain. by Derek Walcott. (Oliver) 47:83-5 Mr27'71. T 2512
Dress and society, 1560-1970. by Geoffrey Squire. (Anon.) 50:131 S30'74. B 2513
Drew Pearson diaries, 1949-59 by Drew Pearson. Tyler Abell, ed. (Anon.) 50:127 F25'74. B 2514
Dreyfus in rehearsal. by Jean-Claude Grumberg. Garson Kanin, adapt. (Gill) 50:65 O28'74. T 2515
Drive, he said. (Gilliatt) 47:55-6 Jy10'71. CC 2516
The drunkard. by W. H. S. Smith [and] Bro Herrod [and] Barry Manilow. (Oliver) 46: 97 Ap25'70. T 2517
The drunks. by Donald Newlove. (Anon.) 50:193-4 D9'74. B 2518
Dubcek. by William Shawcross. (Anon.) 47:132 Je5'71. B 2519
Ducca and the Milan murders. by Giorgio Scerbanenco. Eileen Ellenbogen, trans. (Anon.) 46:64 Ja2'71. B 2520
Duce! a biography of Benito Mussolini. by Richard Collier. (Anon.) 47:68 D25'71. B 2521
Dudder love. by Walter Jones. (Oliver) 48:121 O28'72. T 2522
Dude. by Gerome Ragni [and] Galt MacDermot. (Gill) 48: 76 O21'72. T 2523
The duel: De Gaulle and Pompidou. by Philippe Alexandre. Elaine P. Halperin, trans. (Anon.) 48:79 Jy22'72. B 2524
Duel of eagles. by Peter Townsend. (Anon.) 47:124 F20'71. B 2525

Duet. by Nathan Teitel. (Oliver) 50:60 O21'74. T 2526
Dummy. by Ernest Tidyman. (Anon.) 50:136 Mr11'74. B 2527
Dunelawn. by Terrence McNally. (Oliver) 49:74 F18'74. T 2528
The duplex. by Ed Bullins. (Oliver) 48:85 Mr18'72. T 2529
Duty, honor, empire: the life and times of Colonel Richard Meinertzhagen. by John Lord. (Anon.) 46:137-8 S19'70. B 2530
Dylan. by Sidney Michaels. (Oliver) 47:80-2 F19'72. T 2531

E

Eagle eye. by Hortense Calisher. (Anon.) 49:217 N12'73. B 2532
The earl of Ruston. by C. C. Courtney [and] Ragan Courtney [and] Peter Link. (Gill) 47:102-103 My15'71. T 2533
Early American gardens, "For meate or medicine." by Ann Leighton. (White) 46:127-8 Mr28'70. B 2534
Earthkeeping: the war with nature and a proposal for peace. by Gordon Harrison. (Anon.) 47:127 S11'71. B 2535
Earthquake. (Kael) 50:152-4 D2'74. CC 2536
Easter Island: island of enigmas. by John Dos Passos. (Anon.) 47:131 My1'71. B 2537
Easy living. (Gilliatt) 48:51-2 Jy22'72. CC 2538
Eat of me, I am the Savior. by Arnold Kemp. (Anon.) 48:78 Jy22'72. B 2539
The ebony tower. by John Fowles. (Anon.) 50:83-4 D23'74. B 2540
The echoing green: memories of Victorian youth. by Gillian Avery. (Anon.) 50:178-9 O7'74. B 2541
Economics and the public purpose. by John Kenneth Galbraith. (N. Bliven) 49:57-9 D31'73. B 2542
Economics, peace, and laughter. by John Kenneth Galbraith. (Anon.) 47:92 My29'71. B 2543
Eden End. by J. B. Priestley. (Panter-Downes) 50:133-4 Ap22'74. T 2544
Edith Sitwell: selected letters, 1919-64. by Edith Sitwell. John Lehmann, ed. [and] Derek Parker, ed. (Anon.) 47:156 Ap10'71. B 2545
Edward Hopper. by Lloyd Goodrich. (Anon.) 48:126-7 Mr11'72. B 2546
Edward II. by Harold H. Hutchison. (Anon.) 48:141-2 Ap29'72. B 2547
Edward II. by Christopher Marlowe. (Oliver) 50:141-2 O14'74. T 2548
Edward Weston: fifty years. by Ben Maddow. (Malcolm) 50:226-33 N18'74. B 2549
Edwardian life and leisure. by Ronald Pearsall. (Anon.) 50:133-4 S9'74. B 2550
Edwardian occasions. by Samuel Hynes. (Anon.) 48:104 Ja20'73. B 2551
The Edwardians. by J. B. Priestley. (Anon.) 46:225-6 N21'70. B 2552
The effect of gamma rays on man-in-the-moon marigolds. by Paul Zindel. (Oliver) 46:82-7 Ap18'70. T 2553
The effect of gamma rays on man-in-the-moon marigolds. (Kael) 48:52-3 D23'72. CC 2554
The ego and the mechanisms of defense. by Anna Freud. (Coles) 48:125-6 S23'72. B 2555
18/44. by Etienne Leroux. Cassandra Perrey, trans. (Anon.) 48:78 Jy22'72. B 2556
Einstein: the life and times.

by Ronald W. Clark. (Anon.) 47:92 Ag21'71. B 2557
El grande de Coca-Cola. by Ron House [and] Diz White. (Oliver) 49:81-2 F24'73. T 2558
El hajj malik. by N. R. Davidson, Jr. (Oliver) 47:102 D11'71. T 2559
El topo. (Kael) 47:212-20 N20'71. CC 2560
Eleanor and Franklin. by Joseph P. Lash. (Gill) 47:177-81 O 16'71. B 2561
Eleanor: the years alone. by Joseph P. Lash. (Anon.) 48:80 Ag19'72. B 2562
The electric waxer. (Gilliatt) 50: 112 My6'74. CC 2563
The elements of style. by William Strunk, Jr. [and] E. B. White. (Anon.) 48:95 Je24'72. B 2564
Elephant bangs train. by William Kotzwinkle. (Sissman) 47:90 My29'71. B 2565
11 Harrowhouse. (Kael) 50:170-3 O21'74. CC 2566
Elizabeth I. by Paul Foster. (Gill) 48:108 Ap15'72. T 2567
The Elizabethan renaissance: the cultural achievement. by A. L. Rowse. (Anon.) 48:78-80 D 23'72. B 2568
The Elizabethan renaissance: the life of the society. by A. L. Rowse. (Anon.) 48:115-16 My 27'72. B 2569
The embassy madonna. by Lydia Kirk. (Anon.) 47:180 O23'71. B 2570
The emerging Japanese superstate: challenge and response. by Herman Kahn. (Anon.) 46:95-6 Ja23'71. B 2571
The emigrants. (Kael) 48:115-18 S30'72. CC 2572
Emlyn: an early autobiography, 1927-35. by Emlyn Williams. (Anon.) 50:104 Je24'74. B 2573
Emperor Henry IV. by Luigi Pirandello. (Gill) 49:57 Ap 7'73. T 2574
Emperor of China: self-portrait of K'ang-hsi. by K'ang-hsi. Jonathan D. Spence, ed. (Pritchett) 50:201-208 N4'74. B 2575
Emperor of the North Pole. (Gilliatt) 49:71-2 Je9'73. CC 2576
The enclave. by Arthur Laurents. (Oliver) 49:147 D3'73. T 2577
Encounters with Stravinsky. by Paul Horgan. (Anon.) 48:82 Jy15'72. B 2578
End of a priest. (Gilliatt) 46: 111-13 Ap25'70. CC 2579
End zone. by Don DeLillo. (Anon.) 48:145-6 My6'72. B 2580
Endgame. by Samuel Beckett. (Oliver) 46:90 Je13'70; 48: 80 F17'73. T 2581
Ending up. by Kingsley Amis. (Sissman) 50:185 O21'74. B 2582
Enemies. by Maxim Gorky. Jeremy Brooks, adapt. [and] Kitty Hunter-Blair, adapt. (Gill) 48:69 N18'72. T 2583
Enemies, a love story. by Isaac Bashevis Singer. (Sissman) 48:70-1 D30'72. B 2584
An enemy of the people. by Henrik Ibsen. Arthur Miller, adapt. (Gill) 47:93-4 Mr20'71. T 2585
The enemy: what every American should know about imperialism. by Felix Greene. (Anon.) 47:128 My22'71. B 2586
The engagement baby. by Stanley Shapiro. (Gill) 46:70 My30'70. T 2587
England. by Angus Wilson [and] Edwin Smith [and] Olive Cook. (Anon.) 47:148 My15'71. B 2588
England in the age of Hogarth. by Derek Jarrett. (Anon.) 50:94-5 F3'75. B 2589

England made me. (Kael) 49:187-8 N12'73. CC 2590
The English country house. by Olive Cook. (Anon.) 50:196 D 9'74. B 2591
Enid Starkie. by Joanna Richardson. (Anon.) 50:142 Ap8'74. B 2592
Enquiry. by Dick Francis. (Anon.) 46:156 O31'70. B 2593
Enter a free man. by Tom Stoppard. (Gill) 50:50 Ja6'75. T 2594
Entertaining Mr. Sloane. (Gilliatt) 46:69-70 Ag1'70. CC 2595
Eothen. by A. W. Kinglake. (Anon.) 46:88 Ja9'71. B 2596
Ephemeral folk figures. by Avon Neal [and] Ann Parker. (Anon.) 46:168 Mr21'70. B 2597
Equus. by Peter Shaffer. (Panter-Downes) 49:184 N12'73; (Gill) 50: 123-4 N4'74. T 2598
Erasmus. by George Faludy. (Anon.) 47:130 My1'71. B 2599
Escape from the planet of the apes. (Gilliatt) 47:102-104 Je 5'71. CC 2600
Escape to nowhere. (Gilliatt) 50: 78-9 Ag12'74. CC 2601
The Etruscans. by Werner Keller. Alexander Henderson, trans. [and] Elizabeth Henderson, trans. (Anon.) 50:146 S23'74. B 2602
The European discovery of America: the northern voyages. by Samuel Eliot Morison. (Anon.) 47:143-4 My8'71. B 2603
The European discovery of America: the southern voyages, 1492-1616. by Samuel Eliot Morison. (Anon.) 50:200-201 O14'74. B 2604
Eva Peron. Grotowski Troupe. (Flanner) 46:124 Ap4'70. T 2605
The eve of Saint Venus. by Anthony Burgess. (Anon.) 47: 135 Mr13'71. B 2606
Evelyn Waugh and his world. David Pryce-Jones, ed. (Sissman) 49:107-109 F4'74. B 2607
The evening colonnade. by Cyril Connolly. (Anon.) 50:103-104 Ja27'75. B 2608
Evening in Byzantium. by Irwin Shaw. (Anon.) 49:90 Je23'73. B 2609
The evening star. by Sidonie Gabrielle Colette. David LeVay, trans. (Anon.) 50: 213 N11'74. B 2610
An evening with Richard Nixon and ... by Gore Vidal. (Gill) 48:54 My6'72. T 2611
An evening with the poet-senator. by Leslie Weiner. (Oliver) 49:77 Mr31'73. T 2612
Event 1000. by David Lavallee. (Anon.) 47:68 D25'71. B 2613
Events. (Gilliatt) 46:71-2 Jy4'70. CC 2614
Evergreen. (Gilliatt) 49:137-9 My5'73. CC 2615
Evers. by Charles Evers. Grace Halsell, ed. (Anon.) 47:132 Je5'71. B 2616
Everybody knows and nobody cares. by Mason Smith. (Anon.) 47:87 Je19'71. B 2617
Everyman and roach. by Geraldine Fitzgerald [and] Jonathan Brother. (Oliver) 47:101 O16'71. T 2618
Everything you always wanted to know about sex but were afraid to ask. (Gilliatt) 48: 58-61 Ag19'72. CC 2619
The evolution of man and society. by C. D. Darlington. (Steiner). 47:110-15 Mr6'71. B 2620
Executive privilege: a constitutional myth. by Raoul Berger. (Anon.) 50:111-12 Je3'74. B 2621
Exiles from paradise: Zelda and Scott Fitzgerald. by Sara Mayfield. (Anon.) 47:88 Ag 14'71. B 2622
Existential errands. by Norman

Mailer. (Anon.) 48:103-104 Je17'72. B 2623

The exorcist. (Kael) 49:59-62 Ja7'74. CC 2624

An experience of India. by R. Prawer Jhabvala. (Anon.) 48: 110 Je3'72. B 2625

The exterminating angel. (Kael) 48:153-5 N11'72. CC 2626

Exterminator! by William S. Burroughs. (Anon.) 49:246 N19'73. B 2627

An eye for the dragon: Southeast Asia observed: 1954-70. by Dennis Bloodworth. (Anon.) 46:143 S26'70. B 2628

The eye of the storm. by Patrick White. (Steiner) 50:109-13 Mr 4'74. B 2629

F

F. Jasmine Addams. by Carson McCullers [and] G. Wood [and] Theodore Mann. (Oliver) 47:115-116 N6'71. T 2630

Fabre, poet of science. by G. V. Legros. Bernard Miall, trans. (Moss) 48:109-14 My27'72. B 2631

Fabrications. by Michael Ayrton. (Updike) 49:147-9 My5'73. B 2632

The fabulous ego: absolute power in history. Milton Klonsky, ed. (Anon.) 50:82 Ja6'75. B 2633

The fabulous Miss Marie. by Ed Bullins. (Oliver) 47:94-5 Mr 20'71. T 2634

The face of defeat: Palestinian refugees and guerrillas. by David Pryce-Jones. (Anon.) 49:146-7 My12'73. B 2635

Faces from the past. by Richard M. Ketchum. (Anon.) 46:160 S12'70. B 2636

Facets of comedy. by Walter Sorell. (Anon.) 48:126-7 S16'72. B 2637

Facing the lions. by Tom Wicker. (Anon.) 49:76 Jy2'73. B 2638

Fadeout. by Joseph Hansen. (Anon.) 46:192 O17'70. B 2639

The faggot. by Al Carmines. (Oliver) 49:82 My5'73. T 2640

A fairly good time. by Mavis Gallant. (Gill) 46:132-3 S 19'70. B 2641

Fairy tale. by Erich Segal. (Anon.) 49:151 Ap7'73. B 2642

A fairy tale of New York. by J. P. Donleavy. (Sissman) 49:168-9 O8'73. B 2643

The fall of New York. by Miles Donis. (Anon.) 47:153 Ap 10'71. B 2644

Falling bodies. by Sue Kaufman. (Anon.) 49:126-7 F11'74. B 2645

Fame. by Anthony J. Ingrassia. (Gill) 50:132 D2'74. T 2646

Families and survivors. by Alice Adams. (Anon.) 50: 115 F10'75. B 2647

The family Guareschi: chronicles of the past and present. by Giovanni Guareschi. L. K. Conrad, trans. (Anon.) 46: 88 Ja9'71. B 2648

Family letters of Robert and Elinor Frost. by Robert Frost [and] Elinor Frost. Arnold Grade, ed. (Anon.) 48:95 Ja27'73. B 2649

Family portrait. by Catherine Drinker Bowen. (Anon.) 46: 76 Jy4'70. B 2650

The fan man. by William Kotzwinkle. (Anon.) 50:142 Mr 25'74. B 2651

Fanny Kemble and the lovely land. by Constance Wright. (Anon.) 48:72 D30'72. B 2652

Farewell to Manzanar. by Jeanne Wakatsuki Houston [and] James D. Houston. (Anon.) 49:186-7 N5'73. B 2653

Farewell to the South. by Robert Coles. (Anon.) 48:71-2 S2'72. B 2654

Farewell Uncle Tom. (Kael) 48: 163-4 D2'72. CC 2655
Farragan's retreat. by Tom McHale. (Sissman) 47:145 Ap 17'71. B 2656
Fashion. by Don Pippin [and] Steve Brown [and] Anthony Stimac. (Oliver) 50:68-9 Mr 4'74. T 2657
Fat city. (Gilliatt) 48:53 Jy29'72. CC 2658
The fatal friendship. by Stanley Loomis. (Anon.) 48:147-8 My6'72. B 2659
The fate of Sukhovo-Kobylin. by Isador Kleiner. (Wilson) 48: 149 Mr18'72. B 2660
The father. by August Strindberg. (Oliver) 49:109-10 O29'73. T 2661
Fathering. by Nicholas Delbanco. (Anon.) 49:196 D10'73. B 2662
Father's day. by Oliver Hailey. (Gill) 47:83 Mr27'71. T 2663
Faulkner: a biography. by Joseph Blotner. (Anon.) 50:132-3 S9'74. B 2664
Fear and loathing: on the campaign trail '72. by Hunter S. Thompson. (Anon.) 49:88 Ag13'73. B 2665
The fear of conspiracy: images of un-American subversion from the revolution to the present. David Brion Davis, ed. (Anon.) 47:131 My1'71. B 2666
Fear of flying. by Erica Jong. (Updike) 49:149-53 D17'73. B 2667
Fedayeen. by Zeev Schiff [and] Raphael Rothstein. (Anon.) 48:72 S2'72. B 2668
Felix. by Claude McNeal. (Oliver) 49:69 Ja28'74. T 2669
Felled oaks: conversation with de Gaulle. by André Malraux. Irene Clephane, trans. [and] Linda Asher, trans. (Anon.) 48:115 My27'72. B 2670
Fellini satyricon. (Kael) 46:134-40 Mr14'70. CC 2671
Fellini's Roma. (Kael). 48:137-40 O21'72. CC 2672
Fellow passenger. by Geoffrey Household. (Sissman) 47:127 My1'71. B 2673
Feral. by Berton Roueché. (Anon.) 50:215 N11'74. B 2674
A few virtuous men. by Ben Morreale. (Anon.) 49:59 D 31'73. B 2675
Fiddler on the roof. (Kael) 47:133-9 N13'71. CC 2676
Fifth business. by Robertson Davies. (Anon.) 46:63 D26'70. B 2677
The fifth world of Forster Bennett: portrait of a Navaho. by Vincent Crapanzano. (Anon.) 48:131-2 Je10'72. B 2678
Figure 8. by Mark Dintenfass. (Anon.) 50:210 N4'74. B 2679
Figures in a landscape. (Gilliatt) 47:56-7 Jy31'71. CC 2680
Figures in the sand. by Nathan Teitel. (Oliver) 50:60 O21'74. T 2681
Final analysis. by Lois Gould. (Anon.) 50:154 Ap22'74. B 2682
Find your way home. by John Hopkins. (Gill) 49:58 Ja14'74. T 2683
The finger. by Aaron Marc Stein. (Anon.) 49:136 Mr 10'73. B 2684
Finishing touches. by Jean Kerr. (Gill) 48:79 F17'73. T 2685
Fire sermon. by Wright Morris. (Anon.) 47:142 S18'71. B 2686
The first Bourbon: Henri IV, king of France and Navarre. by Desmond Seward. (Anon.) 47:186-7 N27'71. B 2687
The first circle. by Alexander Solzhenitsyn. (Wilson) 47:85 Ag14'71. B 2688
The first circle. (Kael) 48:80-6 Ja20'73. CC 2689
The first deadly sin. by Law-

rence Sanders. (Anon.) 49:174 O22'73. B 2690

The first decade: a report on independent black Africa. by E. J. Kahn, Jr. (Anon.) 48:146 My6'72. B 2691

The first four Georges. by J. H. Plumb. (Anon.) 50:108 F17'75. B 2692

First love. (Kael) 46:157-8 O17'70. CC 2693

The first trial of Mary, Queen of Scots. by Gordon Donaldson. (Anon.) 46:138-9 Ap4'70. B 2694

Five easy pieces. (Gilliatt) 46: 101-103 S19'70. CC 2695

Five million words later. by Bruce Bliven, Jr. (Anon.) 46:96 Ja23'71. B 2696

Five patients. by Michael Crichton. (Anon.) 46:83-4 Jy18'70. B 2697

Flags in the dust. by William Faulkner. (Anon.) 49:66-7 S 3'73. B 2698

Flaubert in Egypt: a sensibility on tour. by Gustave Flaubert [and] Maxime du Camp. Francis Steegmuller, trans & ed. (Auden) 49:72-5 Jy2'73. B 2699

Flaubert: the master. by Enid Starkie. (Anon.) 47:64 Ja1'72. B 2700

A flawed escape. by Boris Kidel. (Anon.) 50:106-107 F17'75. B 2701

Flight. (Kraft) 47:67 My29'71. CC 2702

Flight into Egypt. by Philippe Jullian. John Haylock, trans. (Anon.) 46:76 Ag8'70. B 2703

The flight of Icarus. by Raymond Queneau. Barbara Wright, trans. (Updike) 50:122-4 F25'74. B 2704

Flower decoration in European homes. by Laurence Buffet-Challié. (White) 46:122 Mr 28'70. B 2705

Flowers. by Jean Genet. Lindsay Kemp, adapt. (Gill) 50:58 O21'74. T 2706

Flowers in the garden. by Dorothy Jacob. (White) 46: 122-5 Mr28'70. B 2707

The fly on the wall. by Tony Hillerman. (Anon.) 47:142-3 S25'71. B 2708

Flying. by Kate Millett. (Anon.) 50:92 Ag26'74. B 2709

Follies. by George Furth [and] Stephen Sondheim. (Gill) 47: 67 Ap10'71. T 2710

Follow the drum. by James Leasor. (N. Bliven) 49:128-9 Mr17'73. B 2711

Food in history. by Reay Tannahill. (Fisher) 49:213-17 N 12'73. B 2712

Foolish wives. (Gilliatt) 48:81-4 Je3'72. CC 2713

The fools in town are on our side. by Ross Thomas. (Anon.) 47:108 F27'71. B 2714

For Pete's sake. (Gilliatt) 50: 50-1 Jy8'74. CC 2715

For reasons of state. by Noam Chomsky. (Anon.) 49:72 Jy 30'73. B 2716

For the good of the cause. by Alexander Solzhenitsyn. Max Hayward, trans. [and] David Floyd, trans. (Anon.) 47: 147 Ap17'71. B 2717

For the President, personal and secret: correspondence between Franklin D. Roosevelt and William C. Bullitt. by Franklin D. Roosevelt [and] William C. Bullitt. Orville H. Bullitt, ed. (Anon.) 48:75-6 Ja6'73. B 2718

For those I loved. by Martin Gray [and] Max Gallo. Anthony White, trans. (Anon.) 48:72 D30'72. B 2719

The Forbin Project. (Gilliatt) 46:114-15 My16'70. CC 2720

Forensic and the navigators. by Sam Shepard. (Oliver) 46:83-4 Ap11'70. T 2721

Foreplay. by Robert M. Lane.

(Oliver) 46:96 D19'70. T 2722
The forests and wetlands of New York City. by Elizabeth Barlow. (Anon.) 47:187 N27'71. B 2723
Forever flowering. by Vasily Grossman. Thomas P. Whitney, trans. (Anon.) 48:144-5 My 13'72. B 2724
Forever panting. by Peter De Vries. (Gilliatt) 49:76-8 Jy 16'73. B 2725
The forgotten soldier. by Guy Sajer. Lily Emmet, trans. (Anon.) 46:100 F6'71. B 2726
Fortune made his sword. by Martha Rofheart. (Anon.) 48: 105-106 Ap1'72. B 2727
Four against the Bank of England. by Ann Huxley. (Anon.) 47:92 My29'71. B 2728
Four frightened people. (Gilliatt) 48:50-1 Jy22'72. CC 2729
Four on a garden. by Abe Burrows. (Gill) 46:72 F6'71. T 2730
Four reforms: a guide for the Seventies. by William F. Buckley, Jr. (Anon.) 49:119-20 F18'74. B 2731
The four suns: recollections and reflections of an ethnologist in Mexico. by Jacques Soustelle. E. Ross, trans. (Anon.) 47: 75-6 Jy24'71. B 2732
The foursome. by E. A. Whitehead. Anon., adapt. (Oliver) 49:80-2 N26'73. T 2733
Foxfire 2. Eliot Wigginton, ed. (Anon.) 49:87-8 Ag13'73. B 2734
Fragments. by Euripides [and] Sophocles. Andrei Serban, adapt. [and] Elizabeth Swados, adapt. (Oliver) 50:56 Jy15'74. T 2735
Fragments from my diary. by Maxim Gorky. Moura Budberg, trans. (Anon.) 48:196 N4'72. B 2736
Frank Lloyd Wright. by Robert C. Twombly. (Anon.) 49:124 Je2'73. B 2737
Frank Merriwell. by Skip Redwine [and] Larry Frank [and] Heywood Gould. (Gill) 47:94 My 1'71. T 2738
Franklin D. Roosevelt: launching the New Deal. by Frank Freidel. (Anon.) 49:186-7 O15'73. B 2739
The Fred Astaire and Ginger Rogers book. by Arlene Croce. (Kael) 48:183-7 N 25'72. B 2740
Frederick Douglass ... through his own words. by Frederick Douglass. (Oliver) 48:96 My 20'72. T 2741
Fredi & Shirl & the kids: the autobiography in fables of Richard M. Elman, a novel. by Richard M. Elman. (Anon.) 48:82 Ag5'72. B 2742
Free schools. by Jonathan Kozol. (Anon.) 48:148 Ap 15'72. B 2743
A free woman. (Gilliatt) 50:72 Jy1'74. CC 2744
The freedom of the city. by Brian Friel. (Gill) 50:68 Mr4'74. T 2745
Freeman. by Phillip Hayes Dean. (Oliver) 48:75 F10'73. T 2746
The freeways. by Viña Delmar. (Anon.) 47:126-7 S11'71. B 2747
The French connection. (Kael) 47:113-16 O30'71. CC 2748
The French conspiracy. (Kael) 49:236 N19'73. CC 2749
French without tears. by Terence Rattigan. (Oliver) 50:52 Ap1'74. T 2750
Frenzy. (Gilliatt) 48:51-2 Je24'72. CC 2751
The Freud-Jung letters: the correspondence between Sigmund Freud and C. G. Jung. by Sigmund Freud and C. G. Jung. Ralph Manheim, trans. [and] R. F. C.

Hull, trans. William McGuire, ed. (Anon.) 50:151-2 Ap15'74. B 2752
Friends. (Gilliatt) 47:109 Ap3'71. CC 2753
The friends of Eddie Coyle. by George V. Higgins. (Anon.) 48:113-14 Mr4'72. B 2754
Fritz the cat. (Gilliatt) 48:88-94 My6'72. CC 2755
From Caesar to the Mafia. by Luigi Barzini. (Anon.) 47:148 My15'71. B 2756
From colony to country: the revolution in American thought, 1750-1820. by Ralph Ketcham. (Anon.) 50:132 S30'74. B 2757
From Columbus to Castro: the history of the Caribbean, 1492-1969. by Eric Williams. (Anon.) 47:68 Jy3'71. B 2758
From honey to ashes. by Claude Lévi-Strauss. (Anon.) 49:92 Je23'73. B 2759
From Palo Alto to Brooklyn. by Gerald Hiken [and] Paul Richards. (Oliver) 49:77-8 Mr31'73. T 2760
From the diary of a snail. by Günter Grass. Ralph Manheim, trans. (Updike) 49:182-5 O15'73. B 2761
The front page. (Kael) 50:94-8 Ja27'75. CC 2762
The fruit of paradise. (Gilliatt) 50:130-1 My20'74. CC 2763
The frying-pan: a prison and its prisoners. by Tony Parker. (Anon.) 46:63 Ja2'71. B 2764
Full circle. by Erich Maria Remarque. Peter Stone, adapt. (Gill) 49:84 N19'73. T 2765
Fun city. by Joan Rivers [and] Lester Colodny [and] Edgar Rosenberg. (Gill) 47:63 Ja8'72. T 2766
A funny thing happened on the way to the Forum. by Burt Shevelove [and] Larry Gelbart [and] Stephen Sondheim. (Gill) 48:108-109 Ap15'72. T 2767
The future. by Al Carmines. (Oliver) 50:106 Ap15'74. T 2768

G

G. by John Berger (Steiner) 48:90-3 Ja27'73. B 2769
G. K. Chesterton. by Dudley Barker. (Anon.) 49:170 O 8'73. B 2770
The gambler. by Fydor Dostoevski. Edward Wasiolek, ed. Victor Terras, trans. (Updike) 49:145-54 Ap14'73. B 2771
The gambler. (Kael) 50:174-5 O14'74. CC 2772
The game of the foxes. by Ladislas Farago. (Anon.) 47:94-5 Ja29'72. B 2773
Gandhi. by Gurney Campbell. (Oliver) 46:101 O31'70. T 2774
The gang and the establishment. by Richard W. Poston. (Anon.) 47:82-3 Ag7'71. B 2775
Gantry. by Peter Bellwood [and] Stanley Lebowsky [and] Fred Tobias. (Gill) 46:62-7 F21'70. T 2776
Garbage: the history and future of garbage in America. by Katie Kelly. (Anon.) 49:91-2 Ag20'73. B 2777
The garden of delights. (Kael) 47:90-1 Mr13'71. CC 2778
The garden of the Finzi-Continis. (Kael) 47:48-53 D18'71. CC 2779
The gasp. by Romain Gary. (Anon.) 49:118 Mr31'73. B 2780
Gather together in my name. by Maya Angelou. (Anon.) 50:87-8 Jy15'74. B 2781
The general was a spy. by Heinz Höhne [and] Hermann Zolling. (Anon.) 48:147-8 My13'72. B 2782
George C. Marshall: organizer of victory, 1943-45. by Forrest C. Pogue. (Anon.) 48:110-11 F17'73. B 2783
George IV: Prince of Wales, 1762-1811. by Christopher Hibbert. (Anon.) 50:126-7 F25'74. B 2784

George Grosz, by Hans Hess. (Anon.) 50:104 Ja27'75. B 2785

George M. Cohan. by John Mc Cabe. (Anon.) 49:119 Mr31'73. B 2786

George Meredith and English comedy. by V. S. Pritchett. (Maxwell) 46:77-8 Ag29'70. B 2787

George S. Kaufman. by Howard Teichmann. (Anon.) 48:79 Jy22'72. B 2788

George III and the mad business. by Richard Hunter [and] Ida Macalpine. (Coles) 47:89-92 Je 26'71. B 2789

George Washington and the new nation. by James Thomas Flexner. (Anon.) 46:189-90 O17'70. B 2790

George Washington: anguish and farewell (1793-1799). by James Thomas Flexner. (B. Bliven) 49:131-4 Mr10'73. B 2791

Georgy. by Tom Mankiewicz [and] George Fischoff [and] Carol Bayer. (Gill) 46:83 Mr7'70. T 2792

The Germans. by Erich Kahler. Robert Kimber, ed. [and] Rita Kimber, ed. (Anon.) 50: 145-6 S23'74. B 2793

Geronimo rex. by Barry Hannah. (Updike) 48:121-4 S9'72. B 2794

Gertrude. by Wilford Leach [and] John Braswell. (Oliver) 47:70 Ja22'72. T 2795

Gertrude Stein in pieces. by Richard Bridgman. (Anon.) 47:88 Je19'71. B 2796

The getaway. (Kael) 48:55 D23' 72. CC 2797

Gettin' it together. by Richard Wesley. (Oliver) 48:99 Ap8'72. T 2798

Getting married. by August Strindberg. Mary Sandbach, trans. (Coles) 49:126-32 S 10'73. B 2799

Getting straight. (Gilliatt) 46:108-10 My23'70. CC 2800

Gettysburg: the final fury. by Bruce Catton. (Anon.) 50:143 Mr25'74. B 2801

Giambattista Vico, an international symposium. Giorgio Tagliacozzo, ed. (Steiner) 46:154-62 My9'70. B 2802

Gideon's fog. by J. J. Marric. (Anon.) 50:83 Ja6'75. B 2803

Gideon's sport. by J. J. Marric. (Anon.) 47:132 My1'71. B 2804

The gift horse: report on a life. by Hildegard Knef. David Cameron Palastanga, trans. (Anon.) 47:76 Jy10'71. B 2805

Gigi. by Alan Jay Lerner [and] Frederick Loewe. (Gill) 49: 80 N26'73. T 2806

Gimme shelter. (Kael) 46:112-15 D19'70. CC 2807

The gingerbread lady. by Neil Simon. (Gill) 46:96 D19'70. T 2808

The girl from Petrovka. by George Feifer. (Sissman) 48:78-82 Ag5'72. B 2809

Girl, 20. by Kingsley Amis. (Anon.) 47:102-103 F5'72. B 2810

Girls at war and other stories. by Chinua Achebe. (Anon.) 49:155 Ap14'73. B 2811

Give me combat: the memoirs of Julio Alvarez del Vayo. by Julio Alvarez del Vayo. Donald D. Walsh, trans. (Anon.) 49:67-8 S3'73. B 2812

The glass cage. by Georges Simenon. Antonia White, trans. (Anon.) 49:88 Ag13'73. B 2813

The glass menagerie. (Kael) 49:50-1 D31'73. CC 2814

Glass people. by Gail Godwin. (Anon.) 48:159 O7'72. B 2815

Gloria mundi. by Harold Frederic. (Wilson) 46:131-2 Je 6'70. B 2816

Glory. by Vladimir Nabokov. Dmitri Nabokov, trans. (Updike) 48:96-101 F26'72. B 2817

The glory of the hummingbird. by Peter DeVries. (Anon.) 50:194 D9'74. B 2818

The glory of the violin. by Joseph Wechsberg. (Anon.) 50:152 Ap 15'74. B 2819

Go East, young man. by William O. Douglas. (N. Bliven) 50: 74-9 Jy8'74. B 2820

The goalie's anxiety at the penalty kick. by Peter Handke. Michael Roloff, trans. (Anon.) 48:93-4 Je24'72. B 2821

The go-between. (Gilliatt) 47:55-6 Jy31'71. CC 2822

'God save this honourable court!' by Louis M. Kohlmeier. (Anon.) 48:100 F3'73. B 2823

God says there is no Peter Ott. by Bill Hare. (Oliver) 48:105 Ap29'72. T 2824

God stand up for bastards. by David Leitch. (Anon.) 49:134-5 Ap21'73. B 2825

A god within. by René Dubos. (Anon.) 48:132 S23'72. B 2826

The godfather. (Kael) 48:133-8 Mr18'72. CC 2827

The godfather, part II. (Kael) 50: 63-6 D23'74. CC 2828

God's favorite. by Neil Simon. (Gill) 50:53-4 D23'74. T 2829

The godson. (Gilliatt) 48:71-2 Jy 15'72. CC 2830

Godspell. by Stephen Schwartz [and] John-Michael Tebelak. (Oliver) 47:56 My29'71. T 2831

Godspell. (Gilliatt) 49:134-5 Ap 7'73. CC 2832

Goin' a buffalo. by Ed Bullins. (Oliver) 48:83 Mr4'72. T 2833

Goin' down the road. (Kael) 46:130-1 O31'70. CC 2834

Going home. (Kael) 47:173 D4'71. CC 2835

Going places. (Gilliatt) 50:124-6 My20'74. CC 2836

Going thru changes. by Richard Wesley. (Oliver) 49:69 Ja 28'74. T 2837

Gold. (Kael) 50:168-70 O21'74. CC 2838

The gold in the glass. by Virginia Chaquet. (Anon.) 46:103 S5'70. B 2839

The golden age; a climate for greatness: Virginia, 1732-75 by Clifford Dowdey. (Anon.) 46:62-3 Ja2'71. B 2840

Golden bat. by Tokyo Kid Brothers. (Oliver) 46:59 Ag 1'70. T 2841

The golden road to Samarkand. by Wilfrid Blunt. (Anon.) 49:79 Jy23'73. B 2842

Golf in the kingdom. by Michael Murphy. (Updike) 48:76-8 Jy 29'72. B 2843

A good day to die. by Jim Harrison. (Anon.) 49:185-6 N 5'73. B 2844

The good doctor. by Neil Simon. (Gill) 49:111-12 D10'73. T 2845

Good evening. by Peter Cook [and] Dudley Moore. (Gill) 49:80 N26'73. T 2846

The good life ... or what's left of it. by Phyllis Feldkamp [and] Fred Feldkamp. (Anon.) 48:134 S23'72. B 2847

Good morning, midnight. by Jean Rhys. (Moss) 50:161-6 D16'74. B 2848

Good news. by Laurence Schwab [and] B. G. De Sylva [and] Frank Mandel [and] Lew Brown [and] Ray Henderson [and] Garry Marshall, adapt. (Gill) 50:50 Ja6'75. T 2849

Good night, Jupiter. by Raymond Kennedy. (Anon.) 46:87 Ja 9'71. B 2850

Good old Modern: an intimate portrait of the Museum of Modern Art. by Russell Lynes. (Anon.) 49:72 Jy30'73. B 2851

The good woman of Setzuan. by Bertolt Brecht. (Gill) 46:141

N14'70. T 2852
Goodbye, Bobby Thomson! Goodbye, John Wayne! by Alan S. Foster. (Anon.) 49:134 Mr10'73. B 2853
Goodbye, Mr. Christian: a personal account of McGovern's rise and fall. by Richard Dougherty. (Anon.) 49:182-3 O29'73. B 2854
Goodbye to an old friend. by Brian Freemantle. (Anon.) 49:136 Ap21'73. B 2855
Good-bye, Union Square. by Albert Halper. (Anon.) 46:225 N21'70. B 2856
The goon show scripts. by Spike Milligan. (Sissman) 49:77-8 D24'73. B 2857
Gordon's war. (Kael) 49:73 Ja 28'74. CC 2858
Goshawk squadron. by Derek Robinson. (Anon.) 47:102 F 12'72. B 2859
The governor. by Edward R. F. Sheehan. (Anon.) 47:123-4 F 20'71. B 2860
Graffiti: two thousand years of wall writing. by Robert Reisner. (Anon.) 47:76 Jy31'71. B 2861
Grand opera: the story of the world's leading opera houses and personalities. by Anthony Gishford. (Anon.) 49:135-6 Ap21'73. B 2862
The grand original: portraits of Randolph Churchill by his friends. Kay Halle, ed. (Anon.) 47:231 N20'71. B 2863
The grand tradition: seventy years of singing on record. by J. B. Steane. (Anon.) 50:146-7 S 23'74. B 2864
The grande bouffe. (Gilliatt) 49:73-5 S24'73. CC 2865
Grant as military commander. by James Marshall-Cornwall. (Anon.) 46:104 S5'70. B 2866
The grass harp. by Kenward Elmslie [and] Claibe Richardson. (Gill) 47:66 N13'71. T 2867
The grass of oblivion. by Valentin Katayev. Robert Daglish, trans. (Anon.) 46:154-5 My16'70. B 2868
A grave affair. by Shelley Smith. (Anon.) 49:72 Jy9'73. B 2869
Gravity's rainbow. by Thomas Pynchon. (Sissman) 49:138-40 My19'73. B 2870
Grease. by Jim Jacobs [and] Warren Casey. (Oliver) 48: 68 F26'72. T 2871
Greaser's palace. (Gilliatt) 48: 53-4 Ag5'72. CC 2872
The great American motion sickness: or why you can't get there from here. by John Burby. (Anon.) 47:172 O9'71. B 2873
The great American shooting prints. Robert Elman, ed. (Anon.) 48:180 D9'72. B 2874
The great bridge. by David McCullough. (N. Bliven) 48:187-9 N11'72. B 2875
The great coalfield war. by George S. McGovern [and] Leonard F. Guttridge. (Anon.) 48:111 Je3'72. B 2876
The great dictator. (Gilliatt) 48:68-9 Je17'72. CC 2877
The great fear of 1789. by Georges Lefebvre. Joan White, trans. (Anon.) 49: 155 S17'73. B 2878
The great Gatsby. (Gilliatt) 50:93-8 Ap1'74. CC 2879
The great god Brown. by Eugene O'Neill. (Gill) 48:86 D16'72. T 2880
The great MacDaddy. by Paul Carter Harrison [and] Coleridge-Taylor Perkinson. (Oliver) 50:84-5 F25'74. T 2881
The great Northfield Minnesota raid. (Gilliatt) 48:52-3 Je 24'72. CC 2882
The great ponds. by Elechi Amadi. (Updike) 49:84-9 Ja 21'74. B 2883
The great school wars: New

York City, 1805-1973. by Diane Ravitch. (Anon.) 50:151 Ap15'74. B 2884
Great Tom: notes toward the definition of T. S. Eliot. by T. S. Matthews. (Updike) 50: 137-40 Ap8'74. B 2885
The great transfer. by V. S. Yanovsky. (Anon.) 49:103 Ja 28'74. B 2886
The great white hope. (Kael) 46: 155-7 O17'70. CC 2887
The greatest men's party on earth: inside the Bohemian Grove. by John van der Zee. (Anon.) 50: 83 Jy22'74. B 2888
The greatest thing that almost happened. by Don Robertson. (Anon.) 47:151 Mr20'71. B 2889
Greed. (Gilliatt) 48:81-4 Je3'72. CC 2890
Green Julia. by Paul Ableman. (Oliver) 48:110 D9'72. T 2891
The green man. by Kingsley Amis. (Sissman) 46:205-206 N14'70. B 2892
Grendel. by John Gardner. (Anon.) 47:142-3 S18'71. B 2893
The Grimké sisters from South Carolina. by Gerda Lerner. (Anon.) 48:132 Mr25'72. B 2894
Grin and bare it! by Tom Cushing. Ken McGuire, adapt. (Gill) 46:81 Mr28'70. T 2895
The groove tube. (Kael) 50:184 N25'74. CC 2896
Groupies. (Kael) 46:167-8 D5'70. CC 2897
The guiltless: a novel in eleven stories. by Hermann Broch. Ralph Manheim, trans. (Anon.) 50:150-1 Ap15'74. B 2898
The Gulag archipelago. by Alexander Solzhenitsyn. (Steiner) 50:78-87 Ag5'74. B 2899
Gumshoe. (Gilliatt) 48:93-6 Ap 1'72. CC 2900
A gun play. by Yale M. Udoff. (Oliver) 47:116 N6'71. T 2901
Gypsy. by Jule Styne [and] Stephen Sondheim [and] Arthur Laurents. (Gill) 50: 74 O7'74. T 2902
The gypsy's curse. by Harry Crews. (Anon.) 50:86-7 Jy 15'74. B 2903

H

Hadley: the first Mrs. Hemingway. by Alice Hunt Sokoloff. (Anon.) 49:111 Je16'73. B 2904
Hail to the chief. (Gilliatt) 49: 49-50 Jy30'73. CC 2905
Half of Spain died: a reappraisal of the Spanish Civil War. by Herbert L. Matthews. (Anon.) 49:118-19 Mr31'73. B 2906
Hallelujah, I'm a bum. (Gilliatt) 49:71-2 Je23'73. CC 2907
Hamlet. by William Shakespeare. (Flanner) 47:91 F27'71; (Oliver) 48:50 Jy15'72. T 2908
Hammarskjöld. by Brian Urquhart. (Auden) 49:130-5 My26'73. B 2909
Hannibal. by Gavin De Beer. (Anon.) 46:126 F21'70. B 2910
The happiness cage. by Dennis J. Reardon. (Oliver) 46:143 O17'70. T 2911
Happy birthday, Wanda June. by Kurt Vonnegut, Jr. (Oliver) 46:143-4 O17'70. T 2912
Happy days. by Samuel Beckett. (Oliver) 48:123 D2'72. T 2913
A happy death. by Albert Camus. Richard Howard, trans. (Updike) 48:157-167 O21'72. B 2914
Hard job being God. by Tom Martel. (Gill) 48:82 My27'72. T 2915
Hard scrabble: observations on a patch of land. by John Graves. (Anon.) 50:91 Ag 19'74. B 2916
Hard times: an oral history of

the great depression. by Studs Terkel. (Sissman) 46:152-4 My 16'70. B 2917
The harder they come. (Kael) 49:120-2 F24'73. CC 2918
Hark! by Dan Goggin [and] Marvin Solley [and] Robert Lorick. (Oliver) 48:77 Je3'72. T 2919
Harlequin. by Morris West. (Anon.) 50:167 O16'74. B 2920
Harriet said. by Beryl Bainbridge. (Anon.) 49:180-2 O29'73. B 2921
Harry & Tonto. (Gilliatt) 50:46-8 Ag26'74. CC 2922
Harry S. Truman. by Margaret Truman. (Anon.) 48:71 D30'72. B 2923
Harvest home. by Thomas Tryon. (Anon.) 49:77-8 Jy23'73. B 2924
Harvey. by Mary Chase. (Gill) 46:83 Mr7'70. T 2925
The hashish club. by Lance Larsen. (Gill) 50:63 Ja13'75. T 2926
Hawks & harriers. by Page Stegner. (Anon.) 48:114-15 Mr4'72. B 2927
Hay fever. by Noël Coward. (Gill) 46:103 N21'70. T 2928
The heart of the battle: for a new social contract. by Edgar Faure. Gill Manning, trans. (Anon.) 49:131-2 F24'73. B 2929
A heartbeat away: the investigation and resignation of Vice-President Spiro T. Agnew. by Richard M. Cohen and Jules Witcover. (Anon.) 50:110 Je3'74. B 2930
The heartbreak kid. (Kael) 48:126-8 D16'72. CC 2931
Heartland. by Saul Maloff. (Anon.) 49:185 N5'73. B 2932
Heathen! by Robert Helpmann [and] Eaton Magoon, Jr. (Gill) 48:82-4 My27'72. T 2933
Heaven and hell's agreement. by J. E. Gaines. (Oliver) 50:103 Ap22'74. T 2934
Heavy traffic. (Gilliatt) 49:68-9 Ag20'73. CC 2935
Heck. by Morris Renek. (Anon.) 47:198 N13'71. B 2936
Hedda Gabler. by Henrik Ibsen. (Oliver) 47:84-5 F27'71. T 2937
Hello-goodbye. (Gilliatt) 46:46-7 Jy18'70. CC 2938
The Hellstrom chronicle. (Gilliatt) 47:54 Jy17'71. CC 2939
Henry in a silver frame. by James Eastwood. (Anon.) 48:71 S2'72. B 2940
The Henry Miller odyssey. (Gilliatt) 50:97-8 S16'74. CC 2941
Here are ladies. by Siobhan McKenna [and] Sean Kenny. (Oliver) 47:68 Mr6'71; (Gill) 49:57-8 Ap7'73. T 2942
The hermit. by Eugène Ionesco. Richard Seaver, trans. (N. Bliven) 50:187 D9'74. B 2943
The hero and the blues. by Albert Murray. (Anon.) 49:88 Ag6'73. B 2944
Hi, Mom! (Gilliatt) 46:118-20 My9'70. CC 2945
The hidden crisis in American politics. by Samuel Lubell. (Anon.) 46:76 Ag1'70. B 2946
The hidden injuries of class. by Richard Sennett [and] Jonathan Cobb. (Anon.) 48:80 D23'72. B 2947
The Hindenburg. by Michael M. Mooney. (Anon.) 48:148 Ap15'72. B 2948
The hired hand. (Gilliatt) 47:62-3 Ag21'71. CC 2949
The hireling. (Gilliatt) 49:83-5 Je16'73. CC 2950
His first step (part I). by Oyamo. (Oliver) 48:53 Jy 1'72. T 2951
Historians' fallacies: toward a logic of historical thought. by David Hackett Fischer. (Anon.) 46:172 Ap11'70. B 2952

Historical memoirs: 1691-1723. by Louis De Rouvroy Saint-Simon. Lucy Norton, trans. (N. Bliven) 48:122-5 S30'72. B 2953
A history of gardens and gardening. by Edward Hyams. (Anon.) 47:203-204 N13'71. B 2954
History of the Second World War. by B. H. Liddell Hart. (Anon.) 47:144 My8'71. B 2955
A history of the umbrella. by T. S. Crawford. (Anon.) 46:140 S19'70. B 2956
Hitler: the last ten days. (Gilliatt) 49:123-4 My26'73. CC 2957
Hoa-Binh. (Flanner) 46:132-3 Ap18'70; (Gilliatt) 47:69-70 S18'71. CC 2958
Hogan's goat. by William Alfred. (Oliver) 47:102 O16'71. T 2959
Hogarth on high life: the "marriage à la mode" series. by Georg Christoph Lichtenberg. Arthur S. Wensinger, trans. and ed. [and] W. B. Coley, trans. and ed. (Anon.) 46:196 D12'70. B 2960
Holiday. by Philip Barry. (Gill) 49:44-6 Ja7'74. T 2961
The holiday friend. by Pamela Hansford Johnson. (Anon.) 49:145 Ap28'73. B 2962
The hollow crown. by John Barton. (Oliver) 50:64-6 Ap29'74. T 2963
Hollywood: stars and starlets. by Garson Kanin. (Anon.) 50:236 N18'74. B 2964
Homage to Daniel Shays: collected essays 1952-72. by Gore Vidal. (Anon.) 48:72 D30'72. B 2965
Homage to Theodore Dreiser. by Robert Penn Warren. (Anon.) 47:131-2 O2'71. B 2966
The home. by Penelope Mortimer. (Anon.) 48:153-4 Mr18'72. B 2967
Home. by David Storey. (Gill) 46:141-2 N28'70. T 2968
Home comfort: stories and scenes of life on Total Loss Farm. by Total Loss Farm. (Anon.) 49:134-5 Mr10'73. B 2969
A home for the heart. by Bruno Bettelheim. (Anon.) 50:155-6 Ap22'74. B 2970
Home from the war; Vietnam veterans: neither victims nor executioners. by Robert Jay Lifton. (Anon.) 49:90 Ag20'73. B 2971
The homecoming. by Harold Pinter. (Oliver) 47:55-6 My29'71. T 2972
The homecoming. (Kael) 49:185-6 N26'73. CC 2973
Hope abandoned. by Nadezhda Mandelstam. Max Hayward, trans. (Steiner) 49:113-18 F18'74. B 2974
Hope against hope. by Nadezhda Mandelstam. Max Hayward, trans. (Steiner) 46:59-63 D26'70. B 2975
Horatia Nelson. by Winifred Gérin. (Anon.) 46:142-3 S26'70. B 2976
Hosanna. by Michel Tremblay. John Van Burek, trans. [and] Bill Glassco, trans. (Gill) 50:65 O28'74. T 2977
The hospital. (Kael) 47:74 Ja8'72. CC 2978
The hostage. by Brendan Behan. (Oliver) 48:76-7 O21'72. T 2979
The Hot L Baltimore. by Lanford Wilson. (Oliver) 49:77 Mr31'73. T 2980
The hot rock. (Kael) 47:76-9 F5'72. CC 2981
Hot to trot. by John Lahr. (Anon.) 50:93-4 F3'75. B 2982
Hotel for criminals. by Richard Foreman [and] Stanley Silverman. (Gill) 50:65 Ja13'75. T 2983
Hour of gold, hour of lead: diaries and letters, 1929-32. by Anne Morrow Lindbergh. (Anon.) 49:156 Ap14'73. B 2984
The hour of the furnaces.

(Kael) 47:95-7 Mr6'71. CC 2985
House of blue leaves. by John Guare. (Oliver) 47:90 F20'71. T 2986
The house of leather. by Frederick Gaines. (Oliver) 46:86-8 Mr 28'70. T 2987
The house of Northcliffe: a biography of an empire. by Paul Ferris. (Anon.) 48:142-3 Ap 29'72. B 2988
House party. by Ed Bullins. (Oliver) 49:89-91 N5'73. T 2989
How she died. by Helen Yglesias. (Anon.) 48:101 F26'72. B 2990
How the other half loves. by Alan Ayckbourn. (Gill) 47:95 Ap3'71. T 2991
How to survive in your native land. by James Herndon. (Hentoff) 47:99-100 F5'72. B 2992
How to talk back to your television set. by Nicholas Johnson. (Anon.) 46:138 Ap25'70. B 2993
How 2 gerbils 20 goldfish 200 games 2,000 books and I taught them how to read. by Steven Daniels. (Hentoff) 47: 101-102 F5'72. B 2994
The hunter. by Murray Mednick. (Oliver) 48:77 Je3'72. T 2995
Hurricane! by Joe McCarthy. (Anon.) 46:140 My23'70. B 2996
Hurry, Harry. by Jeremiah Morris [and] Lee Kalcheim [and] Susan Perkis. (Gill) 48:76 O 21'72. T 2997
Husbands. (Kael) 46:48-51 Ja2'71. CC 2998

I

I. F. Stone's Weekly. (Gilliatt) 50:135-6 Ap22'74. CC 2999
I am a cat. by Sōseki Natsume. Aiko Itō, trans. [and] Graeme Wilson, trans. (Anon.) 48:80 Ag19'72. B 3000
I am Elijah Thrush. by James Purdy. (Anon.) 48:114-15 My27'72. B 3001
I chose prison. by James V. Bennett. (Anon.) 46:168 Mr 21'70. B 3002
I come as a thief. by Louis Auchincloss. (Anon.) 48:78-9 Ag26'72. B 3003
I could never have sex with any man who has so little regard for my husband. (Gilliatt) 49:49 Jy30'73. CC 3004
I dreamt I dwelt in Bloomingdale's. by Ernest McCarty [and] Jack Ramer. (Oliver) 46:67 F21'70. T 3005
I give you my word. by Françoise Giroud. Richard Seaver, trans. (Anon.) 50:211 N4'74. B 3006
I love you, I kill you. (Gilliatt) 48:106 My27'72. CC 3007
I never sang for my father. (Kael) 46:130 O31'70. CC 3008
I walk the line. (Kael) 46:168-9 D5'70. CC 3009
Ibsen. by Michael Meyer. (Gill) 48:129-30 Ap8'72. B 3010
Ice. (Kael) 46:136-9 O24'70. CC 3011
The iceman cometh. (Kael) 49: 149-157 N5'73. CC 3012
The iceman cometh. by Eugene O'Neill. (Gill) 49:56-8 D 24'73. T 3013
Idle passion: chess and the dance of death. by Alexander Cockburn. (Anon.) 50:107-108 F17'75. B 3014
If Beale Street could talk. by James Baldwin. (Anon.) 50: 79-80 Jy8'74. B 3015
If I die in a combat zone, box me up and ship me home. by Tim O'Brien. (Anon.) 49:80 Jy16'73. B 3016
If I had a gun. (Kael) 48:98-9

F17'73. CC 3017

Images. (Kael) 48:55-6 D23'72. CC 3018

Images and shadows: part of a life. by Iris Origo. (Anon.) 47:126-7 My22'71. B 3019

The imperial presidency. by Arthur Schlesinger, Jr. (Rovere) 49:190-6 D10'73. B 3020

Imperial sunset. Volume one: Britain's liberal empire, 1897-1921. by Max Beloff. (Anon.) 46:154-5 Mr14'70. B 3021

The impossible friendship: Boswell and Mrs. Thrale. by Mary Hyde. (Anon.) 49:150-1 My5'73. B 3022

Impressionism. by Editors of Réalités. (Anon.) 49:220 N 12'73. B 3023

In Bluebeard's castle: some notes toward the redefinition of culture. by George Steiner. (Anon.) 47:156 O30'71. B 3024

In case of accident. by Peter Simon. (Oliver) 48:99-100 Ap 8'72. T 3025

In hiding: the life of Manuel Cortes. by Ronald Fraser. (Anon.) 48:79-80 Jy29'72. B 3026

In New England Winter. by Ed Bullins. (Oliver) 46:72 F6'71. T 3027

In praise of love. by Terence Rattigan. (Gill) 50:53 D23'74. T 3028

In pursuit of relevance. by Herbert J. Muller. (Anon.) 47:64 Ja1'72. B 3029

In red and black: Marxian explorations in Southern and Afro-American history. by Eugene D. Genovese. (Anon.) 47:75-6 Jy 31'71. B 3030

In search of the red ape. by John MacKinnon. (Anon.) 50:145 S23'74. B 3031

In spite of myself: a personal memoir. by Winthrop Sargeant. (Anon.) 46:104 S5'70. B 3032

In the boom boom room. by David Rabe. (Gill) 49:84 N19'73; 50:69 D9'74. T 3033

In the bunker. by Constantine FitzGibbon. (Anon.) 49:87 Ag6'73. B 3034

In the days of Simon Stern. by Arthur A. Cohen. (Anon.) 49:79 Jy16'73. B 3035

In the deepest part of sleep. by Charles Fuller. (Oliver) 50:84 Je17'74. T 3036

In the fog of the season's end. by Alex LaGuma. (Updike) 49:89-90 Ja21'74. B 3037

In the name of profit: profiles in corporate irresponsibility. David Obst, ed. (N. Bliven) 48:73-4 Jy8'72. B 3038

In the name of the father. (Gilliatt) 50:109-11 Ap8'74. CC 3039

In the service of their country: war resisters in prison. by Willard Gaylin. (Coles) 46: 98-103 S5'70. B 3040

In the springtime of the year. by Susan Hill. (Anon.) 50: 147-8 S16'74. B 3041

In the Twenties. by Harry Kessler. Charles Kessler, trans. (N. Bliven) 47:87-91 Ja15'72. B 3042

In their wisdom. by C. P. Snow. (Anon.) 50:90 Ja13'75. B 3043

In transit. by Brigid Brophy. (Anon.) 46:153-4 Mr14'70. B 3044

The incomparable Max. by Jerome Lawrence [and] Robert E. Lee. (Gill) 47: 101 O30'71. T 3045

The Indian sign. by John Gunther. (Anon.) 46:79-80 Jy11'70. B 3046

Infinite riches: the adventures of a rare book dealer. by David Magee. (Anon.) 49: 112 Je16'73. B 3047

The Ingoldsby legends. by Richard Harris Barham. (Wilson) 46:206-24 N21'70. B 3048

The inheritor. (Kael) 49:157-8 N5'73. CC 3049
Inner city. by Helen Miller [and] Eve Merriam. (Gill) 47:42 Ja1'72. T 3050
The innocent bystanders. by James Munro. (Anon.) 46:140 Ap25'70. B 3051
The innocents. by Margery Sharp. (Anon.) 48:74 Jy1'72. B 3052
Innocents at home: America in the 1970's. by Tad Szulc. (Anon.) 50:130-1 S30'74. B 3053
Inquest. by Donald Freed. (Gill) 46:83-5 My2'70. T 3054
An inquiry into the human prospect. by Robert L. Heilbroner. (Anon.) 50:155 Ap22'74. B 3055
Inside, looking out: a personal memoir. by Harding Lemay. (Anon.) 47:115-16 Je12'71. B 3056
Inside the Third Reich. by Albert Speer. Clara Winston, trans. [and] Richard Winston, trans. (Steiner) 47:70-5 Jy24'71. B 3057
Inspector Ghote trusts the heart. by H. R. F. Keating. (Anon.) 49:92 Ag20'73. B 3058
Inspector's holiday. by Richard Lockridge. (Anon.) 47:132 My 1'71. B 3059
Instant lives. by Howard Moss. (Anon.) 50:112 Je3'74. B 3060
Interrogating the oracle. by William S. Peterson. (Anon.) 46:80 Ag29'70. B 3061
Intervention and negotiation: the United States and the Dominican revolution. by Jerome Slater. (Anon.) 47:151-2 Mr20'71. B 3062
Investigation of a citizen above suspicion. (Kael) 46:48 Ja2'71. CC 3063
The investigation of Ralph Nader: General Motors vs. one determined man. by Thomas Whiteside. (Anon.) 48:74-5 Jy1'72. B 3064
The invisible pyramid. by Loren Eiseley. (Coles) 47:194-9 N6'71. B 3065
Inward hunger: the education of a prime minister. by Eric Williams. (Anon.) 48:116 Mr 4'72. B 3066
The inward turn of narrative. by Erich Kahler. Richard Winston, trans. [and] Clara Winston, trans. (Updike) 50:133-40 Mr25'74. B 3067
Ionescopade. by Eugène Ionesco [and] Mildred Kayden [and] Robert Allan Ackerman. (Oliver) 50:76-7 My6'74. T 3068
Irascible genius: the life of Charles Babbage. by Maboth Moseley. (Anon.) 46:138-9 Ap25'70. B 3069
Ireland's civil war. by Calton Younger. (Anon.) 46:116 F 28'70. B 3070
Irene. by Hugh Wheeler [and] Joseph Stein [and] Charles Gaynor [and] Otis Clements. (Gill) 49:74 Mr24'73. T 3071
Irish houses and castles. by Desmond Guinness [and] William Ryan. (Anon.) 48:103-104 F26'72. B 3072
The Irish: portrait of a people. by Richard O'Connor. (Anon.) 47:155 O30'71. B 3073
Is there sex after death? (Kael) 47:188-90 N6'71. CC 3074
The island. by Athol Fugard [and] John Kani [and] Winston Ntshona. (Gill) 50:69 D9'74. T 3075
Islands in the stream. by Ernest Hemingway. (Wilson) 46:59-62 Ja2'71. B 3076
The Israelis: founders and sons. by Amos Elon. (Anon.) 47:132 Je5'71. B 3077
Italia, Italia: modern Italy and the contemporary Italians. by Peter Nichols. (Anon.) 50:159-60 My13'74. B 3078

J

J. M. Barrie: the man behind the image. by Janet Dunbar. (Anon.) 46:79-80 Ag29'70. B 3079
J. W. Coop. (Gilliatt) 48:106-107 My13'72. CC 3080
Jack MacGowran in the works of Samuel Beckett. by Samuel Beckett. (Oliver) 46:142 N28'70. T 3081
Jack the bear. by Dan McCall. (Anon.) 50:134-5 Ap29'74. B 3082
Jakey fat boy. by Stanley Eveling. (Oliver) 46:88 Ap18'70. T 3083
The James Joyce memorial liquid theatre. by Stephen Kent [and] Jack Rowe [and] Robert Walker [and] Lance Larsen. (Oliver) 47:101-102 O16'71. T 3084
Jamimma. by Martie Evans-Charles. (Oliver) 48:106-108 Mr25'72. T 3085
Japan: the story of a nation. by Edwin O. Reischauer. (Anon.) 46:80 Ag29'70. B 3086
Japan's imperial conspiracy. by David Bergamini. (N. Bliven) 48:128-31 Mr25'72. B 3087
Jarano. by Ramón Beteta. John Upton, trans. (Anon.) 46:137 S19'70. B 3088
Jaws. by Peter Benchley. (Anon.) 49:118 F18'74. B 3089
Jazznite. by Walter Jones. (Oliver) 47:96 My1'71. T 3090
Je t'aime, je t'aime. (Gilliatt) 46:103-104 S19'70. CC 3091
Jefferson the President: first term, 1801-05. by Dumas Malone. (Anon.) 46:126 F21'70. B 3092
Jeremiah Johnson. (Kael) 48:51 D30'72. CC 3093
Jeremy. (Gilliatt) 49:47-8 Ag27'73. CC 3094
Jesus Christ superstar. by Tom Rice [and] Andrew Lloyd Webber. (Gill) 47:109 O23'71. T 3095
Jesus Christ superstar. (Gilliatt) 49:71 Ag20'73. CC 3096
Joan. by Al Carmines. (Oliver) 47:101-102 D11'71; 48:46 Je24'72. T 3097
Joan, maid of Orléans. by Henri Guillemin [and] Harold J. Salemson. (Anon.) 49:147 My12'73. B 3098
The job. by Daniel Odier [and] William S. Burroughs. (Anon.) 46:84 Jy18'70. B 3099
The Jockey Club stakes. by William Douglas Home. (Gill) 48:59 F3'73. T 3100
Joe. (Gilliatt) 46:65-6 Ag15'70. CC 3101
John Adams: a biography in his own words. by John Adams. James Bishop Peabody, ed. (Anon.) 49:89-90 Ag20'73. B 3102
John Donne: a life. by R. C. Bald. (Anon.) 46:139 My23'70. B 3103
John Frum he come. by Edward Rice. (Anon.) 50:159 My13'74. B 3104
John Strachey. by Hugh Thomas. (Anon.) 49:175-6 O22'73. B 3105
John Thomas and Lady Jane. by D. H. Lawrence. (Sissman) 48:73-5 Ja6'73. B 3106
Johnny got his gun. (Gilliatt) 47:65-6 Ag7'71. CC 3107
Johnny Johnson. by Paul Green [and] Kurt Weill. (Gill) 47:94 Ap24'71. T 3108
Joiner. by James Whitehead. (Anon.) 47:198-9 N13'71. B 3109
The joke. (Gilliatt) 46:110-11 Ap25'70. CC 3110
The Jones men. by Vern E. Smith. (Anon.) 50:177 O7'74. B 3111
A journal of the plague years. by Stefan Kanfer. (Anon.) 49:135-6 My26'73. B 3112
Journey between two Chinas. by

Seymour Topping. (Anon.) 48:181-2 O14'72. B 3113

Journey for myself. by Sidonie Gabrielle Colette. David Le Vay, trans. (Anon.) 48:160 O28'72. B 3114

Journey from the North: autobiography of Storm Jameson. by Storm Jameson. (Anon.) 47:201-202 N13'71. B 3115

The journey not the arrival matters: an autobiography of years 1939 to 1969. by Leonard Woolf. (Anon.) 46:127 My2'70. B 3116

The journey of Snow White. by Al Carmines. (Oliver) 47:96 Mr20'71. T 3117

Journey to heartbreak: the crucible years of Bernard Shaw, 1914-18. by Stanley Weintraub. (Anon.) 47:82 Ag7'71. B 3118

Juggernaut. (Kael) 50:154-6 O 7'74. CC 3119

Julia in Ireland. by Ann Bridge. (Anon.) 49:133 S10'73. B 3120

Jumpers. by Tom Stoppard. (Gill) 50:75 My6'74. T 3121

Junior Bonner. (Gilliatt) 48:53-4 Ag12'72. CC 3122

Juror number four: the trial of thirteen Black Panthers as seen from the jury box. by Edwin Kennebeck. (Anon.) 49: 130-1 Mr17'73. B 3123

The justice box. by Michael Robert David [and] Basheer Quasar (Oliver) 47:84 Je12'71. T 3124

Justices and Presidents: a political history of appointments to the Supreme Court. by Henry J. Abraham. (Anon.) 50:106 My 27'74. B 3125

K

Kaddish. by Allen Ginsberg. (Oliver) 47:82 F19'72. T 3126

Kafka's other trial: the letters to Felice. by Elias Canetti. Christopher Middleton, trans. (Anon.) 50:83 Ja6'75. B 3127

The Kaisers. by Theo Aronson. (Anon.) 47:156 O30'71. B 3128

The Karl Marx play. by Rochelle Owens [and] Galt MacDermot. (Oliver) 49:58-60 Ap7'73. T 3129

Kaspar. by Peter Handke. (Oliver) 49:83 F24'73. T 3130

Kate Chopin: a critical biography. by Per Seyersted. (Anon.) 46:155 Mr14'70. B 3131

Katherine Mansfield: the memories of LM. by LM (Anon.) 48:127-8 S9'72. B 3132

Kathleen and Frank: the autobiography of a family. by Christopher Isherwood. (Anon.) 47:100 Ja22'72. B 3133

The Kennedy promise: the politics of expectation. by Henry Fairlie. (Anon.) 48: 93-4 Ja27'73. B 3134

Kentucky ham. by William Burroughs, Jr. (Anon.) 49: 91 Ag20'73. B 3135

Kenyatta. by Jeremy Murray-Brown. (Anon.) 49:90-1 Ag 20'73. B 3136

Kerouac. by Ann Charters. (Anon.) 49:147-8 My12'73. B 3137

Kes. (Gilliatt) 46:124-6 S26'70. CC 3138

A key to Laurels. by March Cost. (Anon.) 49:129-30 F 24'73. B 3139

Khrushchev remembers: the last testament. by Nikita Khrushchev. Strobe Talbott, trans. and ed. (Anon.) 50: 83-4 Jy22'74. B 3140

The kid. by John Seelye. (Anon.) 47:115-16 F19'72. B 3141

The killdeer. by Jay Broad. (Oliver) 50:104-105 Ap8'74.

T 3142
The killing zone. by William Crawford Woods. (Sissman) 46:92-3 Ja23'71. B 3143
Kinds of love. by May Sarton. (Anon.) 46:143 D19'70. B 3144
King Henry VIII's Mary Rose. by Alexander McKee. (Anon.) 50:134-5 S9'74. B 3145
King Lear. (Kael) 47:135-6 D 11'71. CC 3146
King Lear. by William Shakespeare. (Oliver) 49:74 F18'74. T 3147
King of the hill. by A. E. Hotchner. (Anon.) 48:124-5 S9'72. B 3148
The king of Yvetot. (Gilliatt) 50:114-15 My6'74. CC 3149
Kissinger. by Marvin Kalb [and] Bernard Kalb. (Anon.) 50:91-2 Ag26'74. B 3150
Kissinger: the uses of power. by David Landau. (Anon.) 48:167-8 O21'72. B 3151
Klute. (Kael) 47:42-3 Jy3'71. CC 3152
The knight and chivalry. by Richard W. Barber. (Anon.) 46:64 D26'70. B 3153
Knots. by R. D. Laing. Edward Petherbridge, adapt. (Oliver) 49:71-2 F11'74. T 3154
Krapp's last tape. by Samuel Beckett. (Oliver) 48:123-4 D 2'72. T 3155
Krazy kat. by George Herriman. Woody Gelman, ed. [and] Joseph Greene, ed. [and] Rex Chessman, ed. (Anon.) 46:156 Mr 14'70. B 3156

L

La collectionneuse. (Gilliatt) 47:119-21 My8'71. CC 3157
La jeune fille à marier. by Eugène Ionesco. (Gill) 46:105 My16'70. T 3158
La lacune. by Eugène Ionesco. (Gill) 46:105 My16'70. T 3159
La religieuse. (Gilliatt) 47:54-5 Jy17'71. CC 3160
La salamandre. (Gilliatt) 48:50-3 Ag12'72. CC 3161
La vieillesse. See The coming of age. B 3161a
Lacombe, Lucien. (Kael) 50:94-100 S30'74. CC 3162
Ladies in waiting. by Peter DeAnda. (Oliver) 49:110 O 29'73. T 3163
Lady Audley's secret. by George Goehring [and] John B. Kuntz. Douglas Seale, adapt. (Oliver) 48:126 O14'72. T 3164
Lady Caroline Lamb. (Kael) 48:90-2 F10'73. CC 3165
Lady day: a musical tragedy. by Aishah Rahman [and] Archie Shepp. (Oliver) 48:105-108 N4'72. T 3166
The lady from the sea. by Henrik Ibsen. (Oliver) 49:112 O 8'73. T 3167
Lady sings the blues. (Kael) 48:152-8 N4'72. CC 3168
The lady: studies of certain significant phases of her history. by Emily James Putnam. (Anon.) 46:212 N14'70. B 3169
L'amante anglaise. by Marguerite Duras. (Flanner) 47:91-2 F 27'71; (Gill) 47:93 Ap24'71. T 3170
The landlocked man. by Alfred Coppel. (Anon.) 48:159 O 7'72. B 3171
The landlord. (Gilliatt) 46:110-11 My23'70. CC 3172
Landscape. by Harold Pinter. (Oliver) 46:84 Ap11'70. T 3173
Langdon, Harry. (Gilliatt) 47:130-4 Ap24'71. CC 3174
The language of cities: a glossary of terms. by Charles Abrams [and] Robert Kolodny. (MacDonald) 48:130-45 My 6'72. B 3175
Lassiter's folly. by Nathaniel Benchley. (Anon.) 47:153 Ap10'71. B 3176
The last American hero. (Kael)

49:114-18 O1'73. CC 3177
The last Christmas Eve. (Gilliatt) 50:112 My6'74. CC 3178
The last days of Louisiana Red. by Ishmael Reed. (Anon.) 50: 208-10 N4'74. B 3179
The last detail. (Kael) 49:95-6 F11'74. CC 3180
The last, long journey. by Ernie Maher. (Anon.) 46:125-6 F 21'70. B 3181
The last movie. (Kael) 47:152-4 O9'71. CC 3182
The last of Mrs. Lincoln. by James Prideaux. (Gill) 48:50 D23'72. T 3183
The last of Shelia. (Gilliatt) 49: 68-9 Je23'73. CC 3184
The last of the giants. by C. L. Sulzberger. (Anon.) 46:143 D 19'70. B 3185
The last of the southern girls. by Willie Morris. (Anon.) 49:123 Je2'73. B 3186
The last picture show. (Kael) 47:145-52 O9'71. CC 3187
Last respects. by Jerome Weidman. (Anon.) 47:116 F 19'72. B 3188
The last secret: the delivery to Stalin of over two million Russians by Britain and the United States. by Nicholas Bethel. (Anon.) 50:115-16 F10'75. B 3189
The last Stuart: the life and times of Bonnie Prince Charlie. by David Daiches. (Anon.) 49:111-12 Je16'73. B 3190
The last supper. by Chaim Bermant. (Anon.) 49:118-19 F18'74. B 3191
Last tango in Paris. (Kael) 48: 130-8 O28'72. CC 3192
The last valley. (Kael) 46:90 F13'71. CC 3193
The last year of Leo Tolstoy. by Valentin Bulgakov. Ann Dunnigan, trans. (Anon.) 47: 135-6 Ap24'71. B 3194
A late education: episodes in a life. by Alan Moorehead. (Anon.) 47:135 Ap24'71. B 3195
The late great creature. by Brock Brower. (Anon.) 48: 106 Ap1'72. B 3196
The late Harvey Grosbeck. by Gilbert Millstein. (Sissman) 50:130-2 S9'74. B 3197
Laughing all the way. by Barbara Howar. (Anon.) 49:80 Jy16'73. B 3198
The laughing policeman. (Kael) 49:80-3 Ja21'74. CC 3199
Law and disorder. (Kael) 50: 164-8 O21'74. CC 3200
Law and order. by Dorothy Uhnak. (Anon.) 49:145-6 Ap 28'73. B 3201
Lawyer's lawyer: the life of John W. Davis. by William H. Harbaugh. (Anon.) 49:80 D24'73. B 3202
Le boucher. (Kael) 47:79-80 F5'72. CC 3203
Le Caporal Epinglé. (Gilliatt) 50:62-7 S2'74. CC 3204
Le chagrin et la pitié. (Flanner) 47:134-5 My15'71. CC 3205
Le conformiste. See The conformist. CC 3206
Le fantôe de la liberté. (Kael) 50:71 O28'74. CC 3207
Le médecin malgré lui. See The doctor in spite of himself. T 3208
Le portrait d'un C.R.S. (Flanner) 46:97-8 Je13'70. TV 3209
Le retour d'Afrique. (Gilliatt) 49:101-102 S17'73. CC 3210
Le roi des aulnes. See The ogre. B 3211
Le samouraï. See The godson. CC 3212
Le sex shop. (Gilliatt) 49:68-70 Ag6'73. CC 3213
Le souffleau coeur. (Flanner) 47:130-4 My15'71. CC 3214
Le tréteau de Paris. (Gill) 46:81-2 Ap18'70. T 3215
[No entry] 3216
Leaf storm and other stories. by Gabriel García Márquez.

Gregory Rabassa, trans. (Anon.) 48:125-6 Mr11'72. B 3217
Leaving home. by Arthur Cavanaugh. (Anon.) 46:111 F13'71. B 3218
L'école des femmes. See The school for wives. T 3219
L'effort. by Charles de Gaulle. (Flanner) 47:98-101 Ap24'71. B 3220
Legacy of glory. by Michael Glover. (Anon.) 47:92 Ja15'72. B 3221
The legend of John Brown: a biography and a history. by Richard O. Boyer. (Anon.) 48:115 F10'73. B 3222
Legends of the South Seas. by Antony Alpers. (Anon.) 46:156 My16'70. B 3223
Lemmings. by Sean Kelly [and] Tony Hendra [and] Christopher Guest [and] Paul Jacobs. (Oliver) 48:59 F3'73. T 3224
The lemon. by Mohammed Mrabet. Paul Bowles, trans. and ed. (Anon.) 48:78 D23'72. B 3225
Lemon sky. by Lanford Wilson. (Oliver) 46:72 My30'70. T 3226
L'enfant sauvage. (Flanner) 46: 144 Mr21'70; (Gilliatt) 46:67-9 S12'70. CC 3227
Leningrad. by Wright Miller. (Anon.) 46:80 Ag29'70. B 3228
Lenin's childhood. by Isaac Deutscher. (Anon.) 47:108 F27'71. B 3229
Lenny. by Julian Barry. (Gill) 47:100 Je5'71. T 3230
Lenny. (Kael) 50:194-202 N18'74. CC 3231
Leo & Theodore. by Donald Newlove. (Anon.) 48:93 Ja 27'73. B 3232
Leo the last. (Gilliatt) 46:111 My 23'70. CC 3233
Les blancs. by Lorraine Hansberry. Robert Nemiroff, adapt. (Gill) 46:104 N21'70. T 3234
Les femmes noires. by Edgar White. (Oliver) 50:52 Ap1'74. T 3235
Les femmes savantes. by Jean Baptiste Poquelin Molière. (Gill) 46:60-2 F21'70. T 3236
Les fourberies de Scapin. See Scapino and Tricks. T 3237
Les violons du bal. (Kael) 50: 78-80 Ja20'75. CC 3238
Lesclarcissement de la langue Francoyse. by John Palsgrave. (Perrin) 48:82-92 F26'72. B 3239
Lesser lives. by Diane Johnson. (Anon.) 48:150-2 D16'72. B 3240
The Lester affair. by Andrew Garve. (Anon.) 50:144 My 6'74. B 3241
Let it be. (Gilliatt) 46:86-7 Je6'70. CC 3242
Let me hear you smile. by Leonora Thuna [and] Harry Cauley. (Gill) 48:50 Ja27'73. T 3243
Let's fall in love. by Carol Hill. (Anon.) 50:157-8 My13'74. B 3244
Letter and image. by Massin. Caroline Hillier, trans. [and] Vivienne Menkes, trans. (Anon.) 46:191-2 O17'70. B 3245
Letter of intent. by Ursula Curtiss. (Anon.) 47:76 Jy 24'71. B 3246
Letters from England. by José Eça de Queiroz. Ann Stevens, trans. (Anon.) 46:175-6 O 24'70. B 3247
Letters from Liselotte: Elizabeth Charlotte, Princess Palatine and Duchess of Orléans. by Elizabeth Charlotte, Princess Palatine. Maria Kroll, trans. and ed. (Anon.) 47:139-40 Ap3'71. B 3248
The letters of A. E. Housman. by A. E. Housman. Henry Maas, ed. (Auden) 47:111-

14 F19'72. B 3249
Letters of Aldous Huxley. by Aldous Huxley. Grover Smith, ed. (N. Bliven) 46:81-3 Jy 18'70. B 3250
Letters of Anton Chekhov. by Anton Chekhov. Michael Henry Heim, trans. Simon Karlinsky, ed. (Anon.) 49:78-9 Jy23'73. B 3251
The letters of Anton Chekhov. by Anton Chekhov. Avrahm Yarmolinsky, trans. and ed. (Auden) 49:62-6 S3'73. B 3252
Letters of Hart Crane and his family. by Hart Crane. Thomas S. W. Lewis, ed. (Anon.) 50: 190-1 O21'74. B 3253
The letters of Robert Browning and Elizabeth Barrett, 1845-1846. by Robert Browning [and] Elizabeth Barrett Browning. Elvan Kintner, ed. (Auden) 46: 153-9 S12'70. B 3254
Letters of Roger Fry. by Roger Fry. Denys Sutton, ed. (Anon.) 49:130 Mr17'73. B 3255
The letters of Sigmund Freud and Arnold Zweig. by Sigmund Freud [and] Arnold Zweig. Ernst L. Freud, ed. Elaine Robson-Scott, trans. [and] William Robson-Scott, trans. (Anon.) 46:76 Ag8'70. B 3256
Letters of Thomas Mann: 1889-1955. by Thomas Mann. Clara Winston, trans. [and] Richard Winston, trans. (Anon.) 47: 129-30 My1'71. B 3257
Letters to Felice. by Franz Kafka. James Stern, trans. [and] Elisabeth Duckworth, trans. (Anon.) 49:187 N5'73. B 3258
The levanter. by Eric Ambler. (Anon.) 48:84 Jy15'72. B 3259
Lewis Namier. by Julia Namier. (Steiner) 47:61-3 Ja1'72. B 3260
L'Idiot de la famille. by Jean-Paul Sartre. (Flanner) 47:106-109 Je12'71. B 3261
The life and destiny of Isak Dinesen. by Clara Svendsen. Frans Lasson, ed. (Anon.) 46:88 Ja9'71. B 3262
The life and times of J. Walter Smintheus. by Edgar White. (Oliver) 47:96 My1'71. T 3263
The life and times of Joseph Stalin. by Robert Wilson. (Oliver) 49:44 D31'73; (Tomkins) 50:38-62 Ja13'75. T 3264
The life and times of Judge Roy Bean. (Kael) 48:86-8 Ja13'73. CC 3265
Life in Mexico: the letters of Fanny Calderón de la Barca. by Fanny Calderón de la Barca. Howard T. Fisher, ed. [and] Marion Hall Fisher, ed. (Anon.) 46:191 O17'70. B 3266
The life of a man. by Al Carmines. (Oliver) 48:125-6 O14'72. T 3267
The life of Captain James Cook. by J. C. Beaglehole. (Anon.) 50:142-3 My6'74. B 3268
The life of Emily Dickinson. by Richard B. Sewall (Anon.) 50:98-9 Ja20'75. B 3269
The life of Ivy Compton-Burnett. by Elizabeth Sprigge. (Updike) 49:119-22 Je2'73. B 3270
The life of Mayakovsky. by Wiktor Woroszylski. Boleslaw Taborski, trans. (Anon.) 47: 132 Mr27'71. B 3271
The life of the spider. by Jean Henri Fabre. Alexander Teixeira de Mattos, trans. (Moss) 48:109-14 My27'72. B 3272
Life signs. by Johanna Davis. (Anon.) 49:70-1 Jy9'73. B 3273
Lifelines. by James Mossman. (Anon.) 47:127 S11'71. B 3274
The light garden of the angel king. by Peter Levi. (Anon.) 48:111 F17'73. B 3275

Like to the lark: the early years of Shakespeare. by Frederick J. Pohl. (Anon.) 48:104 Ja 20'73. B 3276
Limbo. (Kael) 48:77-80 F3'73. CC 3277
Limehouse nights. by Thomas Burke. (Anon.) 50:150 My20'74. B 3278
The Lincoln mask. by V. J. Longhi. (Gill) 48:130 N11'72. T 3279
Lincoln Steffens. by Justin Kaplan. (Anon.) 50:150-1 My 20'74. B 3280
Line. by Israel Horovitz. (Oliver) 47:82-4 F27'71. T 3281
The lion in the lei shop. by Kay Starbird. (Anon.) 46:224-5 N21'70. B 3282
Listen to me. by Gertrude Stein [and] Al Carmines. (Oliver) 50:126 N4'74. T 3283
Listening to America. by Bill Moyers. (Anon.) 47:135 Ap 24'71. B 3284
Little big man. (Kael) 46:50-2 D26'70. CC 3285
The little black book. by Jean-Claude Carrière. Jerome Kilty, adapt. (Gill) 48:56 My 6'72. T 3286
Little Fauss and Big Halsy. (Kael) 46:132 O31'70. CC 3287
A little girl under a mosquito net. by Monique Lange. Patsy Southgate, trans. (Anon.) 49: 59 D31'73. B 3288
The little girl who lives down the lane. by Laird Koenig. (Anon.) 50:152 Mr18'74. B 3289
Little murders. (Kael) 47:92-5 Mr 6'71. CC 3290
A little night music. by Stephen Sondheim [and] Hugh Wheeler. (Gill) 49:78-80 Mr3'73. T 3291
Little prayers & finite experience. by Paul Goodman. (Anon.) 48: 246 N18'72. B 3292
The little prince. (Kael) 50:154-6 D2'74. CC 3293
The little theatre of Jean Renoir. (Gilliatt) 46:58-60 Ag8'70; 50:112-15 My6'74. CC 3294
Live and let die. (Gilliatt) 49: 56-7 Jy9'73. CC 3295
The lives of a cell: notes of a biology watcher. by Lewis Thomas. (Updike) 50:83-6 Jy15'74. B 3296
The lives of children. by George Dennison. (Hentoff) 46:116-20 Mr7'70. B 3297
Lives of girls and women. by Alice Munro. (Anon.) 48:75 Ja6'73. B 3298
Living together. by Alan Ayckbourn. (Panter-Downes) 50: 142-4 D2'74. T 3299
Livingstone: and his African journeys. by Elspeth Huxley. (Anon.) 50:235-6 N18'74. B 3300
Lloyd George: a diary by Frances Stevenson. by Frances Stevenson. (Anon.) 47:85-6 Ja8'72. B 3301
Local anaesthetic. by Günter Grass. Ralph Manheim, trans. (Updike) 46:133-6 Ap25'70. B 3302
Locked rooms and open doors. by Anne Morrow Lindbergh. (Anon.) 50:143-4 Mr25'74. B 3303
The logic of life: a history of heredity. by François Jacob. (Bernstein) 50:88-90 Ja13'75. B 3304
Lola Montez. by Amanda Darling. (Anon.) 48:78-80 Ag12'72. B 3305
London assurance. by Dion Boucicault. (Gill) 50:86 D 16'74. T 3306
London: the biography of a city. by Christopher Hibbert. (Anon.) 46:160 S12'70. B 3307
Long ago, tomorrow. (Kael) 47:183-8 N6'71. CC 3308
Long day's journey into night. by Eugene O'Neill. (Oliver) 47:94-6 My1'71. T 3309

Long division. by Anne Roiphe. (Anon.) 48:195 N4'72. B 3310
The long fuse. by Alan White. (Anon.) 50:200 O14'74. B 3311
The long goodbye. (Kael) 49:133-9 O22'73. CC 3312
The long march, 1935: the epic of Chinese Communism's survival. by Dick Wilson. (Anon.) 48:154-5 Mr18'72. B 3313
Long pants. (Gilliatt) 47:133-4 Ap24'71. CC 3314
The long revolution. by Edgar Snow. (Anon.) 48:159 O28'72. B 3315
The long shot: George McGovern runs for President. by Gordon L. Weil. (Anon.) 49:182-3 O 29'73. B 3316
The long watch. by Alan White. (Anon.) 47:88 Je19'71. B 3317
The longer the thread. by Emma Lathen. (Anon.) 48:144 Ap29'72. B 3318
The longest yard. (Kael) 50:175-81 O14'74. CC 3319
Longtime Californ': a documentary study of an American Chinatown. by Victor G. Nee [and] Brett de Bary Nee. (Anon.) 49:134-5 S10'73. B 3320
A look at the Fifties. by Al Carmines. (Oliver) 48:105 Ap29'72. T 3321
Look at the harlequins! by Vladimir Nabokov. (Updike) 50:209-12 N11'74. B 3322
Look away. by Jerome Kilty. (Gill) 48:59 Ja20'73. T 3323
Look for me in the whirlwind: the collective biography of the New York 21. by New York 21. (Anon.) 47:128 S11'71. B 3324
Look to the lilies. by Leonard Spigelgass [and] Jule Styne [and] Sammy Cahn. (Gill) 46:61-2 Ap4'70. T 3325
Look what they done to my song. by John McCluskey. (Anon.) 50:194 N25'74. B 3326
Looking at photographs. by John Szarkowski. (Anon.) 49:187-8 N5'73. B 3327
The looking glass war. (Kael) 46:99-100 F21'70. CC 3328
Loophole. by Arthur Maling. (Anon.) 47:184 O16'71. B 3329
Loot. (Gilliatt) 48:110-13 Ap 29'72. CC 3330
Lord Hervey: eighteenth-century courtier. by Robert Halsband. (Anon.) 50:134-5 Mr11'74. B 3331
Lord Palmerston. by Jasper Ridley. (Anon.) 47:68 Jy3'71. B 3332
Lord Rochester's monkey. by Graham Greene. (Steiner) 50:185-8 O28'74. B 3333
The lord's woods: the passing of an American woodland. by Robert Arbib. (Anon.) 47:88 S4'71. B 3334
Lorelei. by Anita Loos [and] Joseph Fields [and] Kenny Solms [and] Gail Parent. (Gill) 49:46 F4'74. T 3335
Losing battles. by Eudora Welty. (Moss) 46:73-5 Jy 4'70. B 3336
The loss of El Dorado. by V. S. Naipaul. (Updike) 46:72-6 Ag 8'70. B 3337
Lost horizon. (Kael) 49:119-21 Mr17'73. CC 3338
Lost in the stars. by Kurt Weill [and] Maxwell Anderson (Gill) 48:103 Ap29'72. T 3339
Lost names. by Richard E. Kim. (Anon.) 46:159-60 S 12'70. B 3340
Lotta; or, the best thing evolution's ever come up with. by Robert Montgomery. (Oliver) 49:147 D3'73. T 3341
Louis XI. by Paul Murray Kendall. (Anon.) 46:96 Ja

23'71. B 3342
Louis XIV. by Philippe Erlanger. Stephen Cox. trans. (Anon.) 46:156 O 31'70. B 3343
Louise Nevelson. by Arnold B. Glimcher. (Anon.) 48: 80 D23'72. B 3344
Love. (Gilliatt) 49:89-90 Ap 21'73. CC 3345
Love affair--a Venetian journal. by Wright Morris. (Anon.) 48:191 N11'72. B 3346
Love and pain. (Gilliatt) 49: 136-7 My5'73. CC 3347
Love feast. by Frederick Buechner. (Anon.) 50:189 O21'74. B 3348
Love for love. by William Congreve. (Gill) 50:113 N18'74. T 3349
Love in the afternoon. by Ed Zimmermann. (Anon.) 47:88 S4'71. B 3350
Love in the ruins. by Walker Percy. (Sissman) 47:121-4 S11'71. B 3351
Love is a funny thing. (Gilliatt) 46:116-18 Ap4'70. CC 3352
The love life of a Cheltenham lady. by Dinah Brooke. (Anon.) 47:100 Ja22'72. B 3353
The love machine. (Gilliatt) 47:69 S18'71. CC 3354
Love me, love my children. by Robert Swerdlow. (Oliver) 47:66-8 N13'71. T 3355
Love story. by Erich Segal. (Anon.) 46:116 F28'70. B 3356
Love story. (Kael) 46:52-4 D26'70. CC 3357
The love suicide at Schofield Barracks. by Romulus Linney. (Gill) 47:80 F19'72. T 3358
Lovely ladies, kind gentlemen. by John Patrick [and] Stan Freeman [and] Franklin Underwood. (Gill) 46:51 Ja 9'71. T 3359
Lovers and other strangers. (Gilliatt) 46:67-8 Ag15'70. CC 3360
Lovin' Molly. (Gilliatt) 50: 136-40 Ap22'74. CC 3361
Loving. (Kael) 46:92-4 Mr7'70. CC 3362
Lucia. (Gilliatt) 50:108-109 Ap 8'74. CC 3363
Ludwig. (Kael) 49:122-7 Mr24' 73. CC 3364
Luis Agassiz Fuentes & the singular beauty of birds. by George Marcham, ed. (Anon.) 47:204 N13'71. B 3365
Lumumba: the last 50 days. by G. Heinz [and] H. Donnay. Jane Clark Seitz, trans. (Anon.) 46:135-6 Je6'70. B 3366
Luther: his life and times. by Richard Friedenthal. John Nowell, trans. (Anon.) 46:87-8 Ja9'71. B 3367
Lying woman. by Jean Giraudoux. Richard Howard, trans. (Anon.) 47: 103 F12'72. B 3368
The lynching of Orin Newfield. by Gerald Jay Goldberg. (Anon.) 47:138 Ap3'71. B 3369
Lyndon. by Richard Harwood [and] Haynes Johnson. (Anon.) 49:183-4 O29'73. B 3370
Lysistrata. by Aristophanes. (Gill) 48:112 N25'72. T 3371

M

Macaulay: the shaping of the historians. by John Clive. (Anon.) 49:155-6 Ap14'73. B 3372
Macbeth. by William Shakespeare. (Oliver) 46:75 Ja 16'71. T 3373
Macbeth. (Kael) 47:76 F5'72. CC 3374
McCabe and Mrs. Miller. (Kael) 47:40-2 Jy3'71. CC 3375

Mack and Mabel. by Michael Stewart [and] Jerry Herman. (Gill) 50:141 O14'74. T 3376

The mackintosh man. (Gilliatt) 49:70-1 Ag6'73. CC 3377

The McMasters. (Gilliatt) 46: 61-2 Ag22'70. CC 3378

McQ. (Kael) 49:96 F11'74. CC 3379

The mad adventures of "Rabbi" Jacob. (Gilliatt) 50:66-7 Jy 22'74. CC 3380

Mad dogs & Englishmen. (Gilliatt) 47:98 Ap17'71. CC 3381

Mad ducks and bears. by George Plimpton. (Anon.) 49:154-6 D17'73. B 3382

Mad in pursuit. by Violette Leduc. Derek Coltman, trans. (N. Bliven) 48:111-13 Mr4'72. B 3383

Made for each other. (Kael) 47: 59-62 D25'71. CC 3384

Mademoiselle Chanel. by Pierre Galante. Eileen Geist, trans. [and] Jessie Wood, trans. (Anon.) 49:134 S10'73. B 3385

The madhouse company of London. by The madhouse company of London. (Gill) 50:70 D9'74. T 3386

Madly singing in the mountains. Ivan Morris, ed. (Steiner) 47:110-14 Je12'71. B 3387

The madwoman of Chaillot. by Jean Giraudoux. (Oliver) 46:64 Ap4'70. T 3388

The magic Christian. (Kael) 46: 95 Mr7'70. CC 3389

The magic garden of Stanley Sweetheart. (Lardner) 46:64 Je27'70. CC 3390

The magic show. by Bob Randall [and] Stephen Schwartz. (Gill) 50:64 Je10'74. T 3391

Magnum force. (Kael) 49:84-9 Ja14'74. CC 3392

The mahabharata. J. A. B. van Buitenen, trans. (Sargeant) 50:131-4 Mr11'74. B 3393

Mahagonny. by Kurt Weill [and] Bertolt Brecht. (Oliver) 46: 97 My9'70. T 3394

Mahler: Volume I. by Henri-Louis de la Grange. (Anon.) 49:248 N19'73. B 3395

Maigret and the bum. by Georges Simenon. Jean Stewart, trans. (Anon.) 49:184 O29'73. B 3396

Maigret and the madwoman. by Georges Simenon. Eileen Ellenbogen, trans. (Anon.) 48:135 S23'72. B 3397

Maigret hesitates. by Georges Simenon. Lyn Moir, trans. (Anon.) 46:139 Ap25'70. B 3398

Maigret loses his temper. by Georges Simenon. Robert Eglesfield, trans. (Anon.) 50:114 Mr4'74. B 3399

The making of a surgeon. by William A. Nolen. (Anon.) 46:94-5 Ja23'71. B 3400

The making of Americans. by Al Carmines. (Oliver) 48: 126 D2'72. T 3401

The making of an ex-astronaut. by Brian O'Leary. (Anon.) 46:100 My30'70. B 3402

The making of the president: 1972. by Theodore H. White. (Anon.) 49:171 O8'73. B 3403

Malcolm Lowry. by Douglas Day. (Anon.) 49:217-18 N 12'73. B 3404

The malcontents. by C. P. Snow. (Anon.) 48:145-6 My 13'72. B 3405

Malizia. (Gilliatt) 50:90-1 Je 17'74. CC 3406

Maltaverne. by François Mauriac. Jean Stewart, trans. (N. Bliven) 46:141-2 S26'70. B 3407

Mame. (Kael) 50:122-4 Mr11'74. CC 3408

The man. (Gilliatt) 48:54 Jy 29'72. CC 3409

Man about Paris: the confessions of Arsène Houssaye. by Arsène Houssaye. Henry

Knepler, trans. & ed. (Anon.) 46:143-4 D19'70. B 3410
Man and superman. by George Bernard Shaw. (Gill) 48:50 Ja27'73. T 3411
A man called horse. (Gilliatt) 46:118 My9'70. CC 3412
Man in the wilderness. (Kael) 47:136-8 D11'71. CC 3413
Man of LaMancha. (Kael) 48:54-5 D23'72. CC 3414
Man on the moon. by John Phillips. (Gill) 50:74 F10'74. T 3415
The man who liked women. by Marc Brandel. (Anon.) 48:190 N11'72. B 3416
The man who loved zoos. by Malcolm Bosse. (Anon.) 50:136 S9'74. B 3417
The man with the tiny head. by Ivor Drummond. (Anon.) 46:139-40 Ap4'70. B 3418
The manipulated man. by Esther Vilar. (Anon.) 48:103-104 Ja 20'73. B 3419
The manticore. by Robertson Davies. (Anon.) 48:176-7 D 9'72. B 3420
The manuscripts of Pauline Archange. by Marie-Claire Blais. Derek Coltman, trans. (N. Bliven) 46:138-41 S 26'70. B 3421
Many deadly returns. by Patricia Moyes. (Anon.) 46:136 Je6'70. B 3422
Mao's great revolution. by Robert Elegant. (Anon.) 47:127-8 My 22'71. B 3423
Marceau, Marcel. (Gill) 46:80-1 Ap18'70. T 3424
Marcel Proust. by Roger Shattuck. (Anon.) 50:95 F3'75. B 3425
Marcel Proust 1871-1922: a centennial volume. Peter Quennell, ed. (Moss) 47:127-35 D18'71. B 3426
Marilyn. by Norman Mailer. (Anon.) 49:87-8 Ag6'73. B 3427
Marinetti: selected writings. R. W. Flint, ed. (Anon.) 49:116 Mr3'73. B 3428
Marjoe. (Gilliatt) 48:50-2 Ag 5'72. CC 3429
Mark Twain and his world. by Justin Kaplan. 50:84 D23'74. B 3430
The market-place. by Harold Frederic. (Wilson) 46:132-3 Je6'70. B 3431
The marriage of a young stockbroker. by Charles Webb. (Anon.) 46:88 Ag22'70. B 3432
The married lovers. by Julius Horwitz. (Anon.) 49:90-1 Ag 27'73. B 3433
Martin Buber: an intimate portrait. by Aubrey Hodes. (Anon.) 47:88 Ag28'71. B 3434
Mary. by Vladimir Nabokov. Michael Glenny, trans. (Anon.) 46:181 N7'70. B 3435
Mary Stuart. by Johann Christoph Schiller. Stephen Spender, trans. (Gill) 47:111-12 N 20'71. T 3436
Masks in brown. by Al Fann Theatrical Ensemble. (Oliver) 46:42-3 Ja2'71. T 3437
The master builder. by Henrik Ibsen. (Oliver) 47:103-104 O30'71. T 3438
The master: 1901-1916. by Leon Edel. (N. Bliven) 48:137-40 Ap29'72. B 3439
The master of go. by Yasunari Kawabata. (Steiner) 48:89-90 Ja27'73. B 3440
Maurice. by E. M. Forster. (Steiner) 47:158-69 O9'71. B 3441
Maurice Baring restored. by Paul Horgan. (Wilson) 47:128-42 S18'71. B 3442
Max Jamison. by Wilfrid Sheed. (Gill) 46:133-7 S19'70. B 3443
Mayakovsky: a poet in the revolution. by Edward J. Brown. (Anon.) 49:103 Ja28'74. B 3444
The me nobody knows. Gary

William Friedman, adapt. (Oliver) 46:70-2 My30'70. T 3445
Mean streets. (Kael) 49:157-62 O8'73. CC 3446
Meany: the unchallenged strong man of American labor. by Joseph C. Goulden. (Anon.) 49:115-16 Mr3'73. B 3447
The measures taken. by Bertolt Brecht. (Oliver) 50:66-8 O 28'74. T 3448
The mechanisms of perception. by Jean Piaget. (Anon.) 46: 128 My2'70. B 3449
Medea. (Flanner) 46:90-2 F21'70. CC 3450
Medea. by Euripides; Seneca. Andrei Serban, adapt. (Oliver) 47:69 F12'72. T 3451
Medea. by Euripides. Minos Volanakis, adapt. (Gill) 48:50 Ja27'73. T 3452
The medieval castle: life in a fortress in peace and war. by Philip Warner. (Anon.) 48:108 Ap1'72. B 3453
Meditations on hunting. by José Ortega y Gasset. Howard B. Wescott, trans. (Anon.) 48:79 Jy22'72. B 3454
The Mediterranean and the Mediterranean World in the age of Philip II. by Fernand Braudel. Siân Reynolds, trans. (N. Bliven) 50:118-22 Ap1'74. B 3455
The Medvedev papers. by Zhores A. Medvedev. (Anon.) 47:135-6 D18'71. B 3456
The meeting point. by Austin Clarke. (Anon.) 48:142 Ap22'72. B 3457
Melody. (Gilliatt) 47:98 Ap17'71. CC 3458
The member of the wedding. by Carson McCullers. (Gill) 50: 63-4 Ja13'75. T 3459
Memo from David O. Selznick. by David O. Selznick. Rudy Behlmer, ed. (Anon.) 48:246 N18'72. B 3460
Memoirs: 1885-1967. by André Maurois. Denver Lindley, trans. (Anon.) 46:78-9 Ag 29'70. B 3461
Memoirs: 1950-1963. by George F. Kennan. (Anon.) 48:125-6 S30'72. B 3462
Memoirs of a captivity among the Indians of North America. by John Dunn Hunter. Richard Drinnon, ed. (Anon.) 50:113 Mr4'74. B 3463
Memoirs of an aesthete 1936-1969. by Harold Acton. (Steiner) 47:63-4 Ja1'72. B 3464
Memoirs of an ex-prom queen. by Alix Kates Shulman. (Anon.) 48:130 Je10'72. B 3465
Memoirs of hope: renewal and endeavor. by Charles de Gaulle. Terence Kilmartin, trans. (Anon.) 48:126 Mr 11'72. B 3466
The memoirs of Lord Gladwyn. by Hubert Miles Gladwyn Jebb Gladwyn. (Anon.) 48: 190 N11'72. B 3467
The memoirs of Marshal Zhukov. by Georgii K. Zhukov. Novosti Press Agency, trans. (Anon.) 47:76 Jy24'71. B 3468
Memoirs of Waldo Frank. by Waldo Frank. Alan Trachtenberg, ed. (Anon.) 49:170-1 O8'73. B 3469
Memories of underdevelopment. (Gilliatt) 49:122-3 My26'73. CC 3470
Men and the Matterhorn. by Gaston Rébuffat. Eleanor Brockett, trans. (Anon.) 49:110-11 F4'74. B 3471
Men, ideas and politics. by Peter F. Drucker. (Anon.) 47:88 S4'71. B 3472
The merchant of Venice. by William Shakespeare. (Gill) 49:102-104 Mr10'73. T 3473
Merchants and masterpieces: the story of the Metropolitan Museum of Art. by Calvin

Tomkins. (Anon.) 46:168 Ap18'70. B 3474
Mert & Phil. by Anne Burr. (Gill) 50:105 N11'74. T 3475
Metamorphoses. by Ovid. Arnold Weinstein, adapt. & trans. (Gill) 47:89 My8'71. T 3476
Midnight oil. by V. S. Pritchett. (Maxwell) 48:94-102 Je17'72. B 3477
The midnight Raymond Chandler. by Raymond Chandler. (Sissman) 48:124-5 Mr11'72. B 3478
A midsummer night's dream. by William Shakespeare. (Gill) 46:54 Ja30'71; 50:70-1 Ja27'75. T 3479
The Miernik dossier. by Charles McCarry. (Anon.) 49:88 Ag 13'73. B 3480
Milton's Paradise Lost: screenplay for cinema of the mind. by John Collier. (Updike) 49:84-9 Ag20'73. B 3481
The mind of Chesterton. by Christopher Hollis. (Anon.) 46:100 F6'71. B 3482
Minnie's boys. by Arthur Marx [and] Robert Fisher. (Gill) 46:61 Ap4'70. T 3483
The mirror of souls and other essays. by Félix Martí-Ibáñez. (Anon.) 48:72 D30'72. B 3484
The Mississippi Chinese. by James W. Loewen. (Coles) 48:135-8 My20'72. B 3485
Mississippi mermaid. (Gilliatt) 46:134 Ap18'70. CC 3486
Mr. Bone's retreat. by Margaret Forster. (Anon.) 47:142-3 My 8'71. B 3487
Mr. Crook lifts the mask. by Anthony Gilbert. (Anon.) 46:192 O17'70. B 3488
Mister Doctor Blo. by John Tyne. (Sissman) 49:147-8 Ap 7'73. B 3489
Mr. Esteban. by Anon. (Oliver) 47:54 S4'71. T 3490
Mr. Sermon. by R. F. Delderfield. (Anon.) 46:168 Mr21'70. B 3491
Mrs. Starr lives alone. by Jon Godden. (Anon.) 48:79-80 Ag 19'72. B 3492
Mrs. Wallop. by Peter DeVries. (Gilliatt) 46:95-8 Ja16'71. B 3493
Mod Donna. by Myrna Lamb. (Oliver) 46:107 My16'70. T 3494
Mohammed. by Maxime Rodinson. Anne Carter, trans. (Anon.) 48:139 My20'72. B 3495
Molly. by Jerry Livingston [and] Leonard Adelson [and] Mack David. (Gill) 49:114 N12'73. T 3496
Money in politics. by Herbert E. Alexander. (Anon.) 48:147-8 Ap15'72. B 3497
Money, money, money. (Gilliatt) 49:90 Ap21'73. CC 3498
Money talks. (Gilliatt) 48:69-70 S9'72. CC 3499
Monte Walsh. (Kael) 46:157 O 17'70. CC 3500
A moon for the misbegotten. by Eugene O'Neill. (Gill) 49:58 Ja14'74. T 3501
Moon mysteries: three visionary plays by W. B. Yeats. by W. B. Yeats. Jean Erdman, adapt. (Oliver) 48:50 D23'72. T 3502
Moonchildren. by Michael Weller. (Gill) 48:81-2 Mr4'72. T 3503
Mooncranker's gift. by Barry Unsworth. (Anon.) 50:157 My13'74. B 3504
More classic trains. by Arthur D. Dubin. (Anon.) 50:196 D9'74. B 3505
More than you deserve. by Jim Steinman [and] Michael Weller. (Oliver) 49:58-60 Ja14'74. T 3506
The morning deluge: Mao Tse-Tung and the Chinese revolution, volume I, 1893-1954. by Han Suyin. (Anon.) 48:195-6 N4'72. B 3507
Morning without noon. by

Salvador de Madariaga. (Anon.) 50:106-107 My27'74. B 3508
Mortal consequences. by Julian Symons. (Anon.) 48:107-108 Ap1'72. B 3509
Moscow Central Puppet Theatre. (Kraft) 47:66-7 My29'71. T 3510
The most dangerous man in America: scenes from the life of Benjamin Franklin. by Catherine Drinker Bowen. (Anon.) 50:213-14 N11'74. B 3511
Most deadly hate. by Harry Carmichael. (Anon.) 50:108 My 27'74. B 3512
The mother and the whore. (Kael) 50:85-9 Mr4'74. CC 3513
Mother earth. by Ron Thronson [and] Toni Shearer. (Gill) 48: 119 O28'72. T 3514
The mound builders. by Lanford Wilson. (Oliver) 50:84-5 F 17'75. T 3515
The mountain people. by Colin M. Turnbull. (Anon.) 48:246-7 N18'72. B 3516
Mourning becomes Electra. by Eugene O'Neill. (Gill) 48:111 N25'72. T 3517
Mourning pictures. by Honor Moore. (Gill) 50:113 N18'74. T 3518
Move. (Gilliatt) 46:60-1 Ag8'70. CC 3519
Much ado about nothing. by William Shakespeare. (Oliver) 48: 58 Ag26'72; (Gill) 48:69-70 N 18'72. T 3520
Much entertainment, a visual and culinary record of Johnson and Boswell's tour of Scotland in 1773. by Virginia Maclean. (Fisher) 50:97-105 My27'74. B 3521
Mudie's circulating library and the Victorian novel. by Guinevere L. Griest. (Anon.) 46:211-12 N14'70. B 3522
The mugging. by Morton Hunt. (Anon.) 48:83-4 Jy15'72. B 3523
Mumbo jumbo. by Ishmael Reed. (Anon.) 48:125 S16'72. B 3524
Mundome. by A. G. Mojtabai. (Anon.) 50:108-109 Je3'74. B 3525
Murder on the Orient Express. (Kael) 50:171-2 D9'74. CC 3526
Murder to go. by Emma Lathen. (Anon.) 46:128 F21'70. B 3527
Murderous angels. by Conor Cruise O'Brien. (Gill) 47: 41-2 Ja1'72. T 3528
Murder's a waiting game. by Anthony Gilbert. (Anon.) 48: 84 Jy15'72. B 3529
Murmur of the heart. (Kael) 47:139-43 O23'71. CC 3530
Music and musical life in Soviet Russia 1917-70. by Boris Schwarz. (Anon.) 48:148 My 6'72. B 3531
The music lovers. (Kael) 46: 76-9 Ja30'71. CC 3532
Music! music! by Alan Jay Lerner. (Gill) 50:103 Ap22'74. T 3533
Mussolini and facism: the view from America. by John P. Diggins. (Anon.) 48:106-107 Ap1'72. B 3534
My days. by R. K. Narayan. (Updike) 50:80-2 S2'74. B 3535
My fat friend. by Charles Laurence. (Gill) 50:103 Ap 8'74. T 3536
My father: Joseph Conrad. by Borys Conrad. (Anon.) 46: 62 Ja2'71. B 3537
My galleries and painters. by Daniel-Henry Kahnweiler [and] Francis Crémieux. Helen Weaver, trans. (Anon.) 47:202-203 N6'71. B 3538
My grandfather, his wives and loves. by Diana Holman-Hunt. (Anon.) 46:191-2 O10'70. B 3539
My land is dying. by Harry M. Caudill. (Tomkins) 48:125-30 Je10'72. B 3540

My last two thousand years. by Herbert Gold. (Anon.) 48:182 O14'72. B 3541
My life. by Oswald Mosley. (Anon.) 47:103-104 F5'72. B 3542
My life and "The Times." by Turner Catledge. (Anon.) 46:112 F13'71. B 3543
My life as a man. by Philip Roth. (Anon.) 50:102-103 Je24'74. B 3544
My life on the Mississippi; or, why I am not Mark Twain. by Richard Bissell. (Anon.) 49:80 D24'73. B 3545
My name is Asher Lev. by Chaim Potok. (Anon.) 48:114 My27'72. B 3546
My name is Nobody. (Gilliatt) 50:66 Jy29'74. CC 3547
My night at Maud's. (Gilliatt) 46:115-16 Ap4'70. CC 3548
My past and thoughts: the memoirs of Alexander Herzen. by Alexander Herzen. Constance Garnett, trans. Dwight Macdonald, ed. (Anon.) 49:246 N19'73. B 3549
My sister, my sister. by Ray Aranha. (Oliver) 50:104 Mr 11'74. T 3550
My travel diary: 1936. by Paul Tillich. Jerald C. Brauer, ed. Maria Pelikan, trans. (Anon.) 46:80 Jy11'70. B 3551
My uncle. (Gilliatt) 47:58-61 Ag 28'71. CC 3552
My Uncle Antoine. (Gilliatt) 48:125-7 Ap22'72. CC 3553
My young years. by Arthur Rubinstein. (Anon.) 49:115 Je9'73. B 3554
Myselves when young. by Frank Budgen. (Anon.) 46:155-6 My 16'70. B 3555
Mysteries. by Knut Hamsun. Gerry Bothmer, trans. 47:169-70 O9'71. B 3556
Mystery play. by Jean-Claude van Itallie. (Oliver) 48:59-60 Ja13'73. T 3557
The myth of France. by Raymond Rudorff. (Anon.) 46:120 Je20'70. B 3558
The myth of the guerrilla. by J. Bowyer Bell. (Anon.) 47:86 Ja8'72. B 3559
Mythologies. by Roland Barthes. Annette Lavers, trans. (Anon.) 48:128 S9'72. B 3560
Myths to live by. by Joseph Campbell. (Anon.) 48:111-12 Je3'72. B 3561

N

Naked is the best disguise: the death and resurrection of Sherlock Holmes. by Samuel Rosenberg. (Anon.) 50:104 Je24'74. B 3562
Napoleon. by André Castelot. Guy Daniels, trans. (Anon.) 47:136 D18'71. B 3563
Napoleon is dead in Russia. by Guido Artom. Muriel Grindrod, trans. (Anon.) 46:139-40 My 23'70. B 3564
Napoleon symphony: a novel in four movements. by Anthony Burgess. (Anon.) 50:80 Jy 8'74. B 3565
The Napoleonists: a study in political disaffection, 1760-1960. by E. Tangye Lean. (Anon.) 47:153-5 Ap10'71. B 3566
Narrow road to the deep North. by Edward Bond. (Gill) 47:70-2 Ja15'72. T 3567
Nash at nine. by Ogden Nash. Martin Charnin, adapt. (Gill) 49:54 My26'73. T 3568
Nasser. by Anthony Nutting. (Anon.) 48:126 S9'72. B 3569
Nasser: a biography. by Jean Lacouture. Daniel Hofstadter, trans. (Anon.) 49:68 S3'73. B 3570
Natalie Natalia. by Nicholas Mosley. (Anon.) 47:91 Ja 15'72. B 3571

Nathanael West: the art of his life. by Jay Martin. (Sissman) 46:185-90 O10'70. B 3572
The national health. by Peter Nichols. (Gill) 50:60 O21'74. B 3573
Natives of my person. by George Lamming. (Anon.) 48:140-1 Ap29'72. B 3574
Nature of the crime. by Larry Cohen. (Oliver) 46:62-4 Ap 4'70. T 3575
Navigating the rapids, 1918-71. by Adolf A. Berle. Beatrice Bishop Berle, ed [and] Travis Beal Jacobs, ed. (Anon.) 49:115-16 Je9'73. B 3576
Nayak the hero. (Gilliatt) 50:66-7 Jy29'74. CC 3577
The needle's eye. by Margaret Drabble. (Fraser) 48:146-9 D16'72. B 3578
Nellie Toole & Co. by Peter Keveson. (Oliver) 49:112 O 8'73. T 3579
The Nelson affair. (Gilliatt) 49:90-1 Ap21'73. CC 3580
The neophiliacs. by Christopher Booker. (Anon.) 46:88 Ag22'70. B 3581
Nethergate. by Norah Lofts. (Anon.) 49:110 Je16'73. B 3582
The new centurions. (Gilliatt) 48:54-5 Ag12'72. CC 3583
The new chastity and other arguments against women's liberation. by Midge Decter. (Anon.) 48:159-60 O7'72. B 3584
The new land. (Kael) 49:165-9 O15'73. CC 3585
A new leaf. (Kael) 47:140 Mr20'71. CC 3586
The new populism. by Fred R. Harris. (Anon.) 49:87 Ag13'73. B 3587
New reformation: notes of a neolithic conservative. by Paul Goodman. (Anon.) 46:138-9 S19'70. B 3588
The new woman: feminism in Greenwich village, 1910-20. by June Sochen. (Anon.) 48:159-60 O28'72. B 3589
The New York school: a cultural reckoning. by Dore Ashton. (Anon.) 49:71-2 Jy9'73. B 3590
Ni Marx ni Jésus. See Without Marx or Jesus. B 3591
Nicholas and Alexandra. (Kael) 47:58-9 D25'71. CC 3592
Nickel mountain. by John Gardner. (Anon.) 49:94 Ja 21'74. B 3593
Nicol Williamson's late show. by Nicol Williamson. (Oliver) 49:47 Jy9'73. T 3594
The nigger factory. by Gil Scott-Heron. (Anon.) 48:139 My20'72. B 3595
Night. by Edna O'Brien. (Anon.) 48:114-15 F10'73. B 3596
The night of the assassins. See The criminals. T 3597
The night porter. (Kael) 50:151-2 O7'74. CC 3598
Night watch. by Lucille Fletcher. (Gill) 48:82-3 Mr11'72. T 3599
Nightmares and human conflict. by John E. Mack. (Coles) 48:70-4 Jy1'72. B 3600
1919: red mirage. by David Mitchell. (Anon.) 46:63-4 Ja2'71. B 3601
Ninety-two in the shade. by Thomas McGuane. (Sissman) 49:88-9 Je23'73. B 3602
Niño: child of the Mexican revolution. by Andrés Iduarte. James F. Shearer, trans. (N. Bliven) 47:85-7 Jy17'71. B 3603
Nixon in the White House: the frustration of power. by Roland Evans, Jr. [and] Robert D. Novak. (Anon.) 47:201 N6'71. B 3604
No cause for indictment: an autopsy of Newark. by Ron Porambo. (Anon.) 47:68 D 25'71. B 3605
No final victories. by Lawrence F. O'Brien. (Anon.) 50:189-

90 O21'74. B 3606
No hail, no farewell. by Louis Heren. (Anon.) 46:192 O10'70. B 3607
No hard feelings. by Sam Bobrick [and] Ron Clark. (Gill) 49:91 Ap14'73. T 3608
No known survivors. by David Levine. (Anon.) 46:96 Ja30'71. B 3609
No loaves, no parables: liberal politics and the American language. by Clifford Adelman. (Anon.) 50:116 F10'75. B 3610
No more reunions. by John Bowers. (Anon.) 49:150-1 Ap7'73. B 3611
No neutral ground. by Joel Carlson. (Anon.) 49:151-2 My5'73. B 3612
No, no, Nanette. by Otto Harbach [and] Frank Mandel [and] Vincent Youmans [and] Irving Caesar. Burt Shevelove, adapt. (Gill) 46:54 Ja30'71. T 3613
No peace, no place: excavations along the generational fault. by Jeff Greenfield. (Anon.) 49:116 Je9'73. B 3614
No way. by Natalia Ginzburg. (Sissman) 50:185-8 O21'74. B 3615
Nobody ever died of old age. by Sharon R. Curtin. (Anon.) 48:103 Ja20'73. B 3616
Nobody hears a broken drum. by Jason Miller. (Oliver) 46:84-6 Mr28'70. T 3617
Noël Coward in two keys. by Noël Coward. (Gill) 50:102 Mr 11'74. T 3618
Normality and pathology in childhood. by Anna Freud. (Coles) 48:126-9 S23'72. B 3619
The Norman achievement. by David C. Douglas. (Anon.) 46:127-8 F21'70. B 3620
The Norman conquests. by Alan Ayckbourn. (Panter-Downes) 50:142-4 D2'74. T 3621
Norman, is that you? by Ron Clark [and] Sam Bobrick. (Gill) 46:77-8 F28'70. T 3622
North. by Louis-Ferdinand Céline. Ralph Manheim, trans. (Anon.) 48:114 Mr 4'72. B 3623
Not I. by Samuel Beckett. (Oliver) 48:124-6 D2'72. T 3624
Not now, darling. by Ray Cooney [and] John Chapman. (Gill) 46:133 N7'70. T 3625
Not on the screen. by Henry Blake Fuller. (Wilson) 46: 134-7 My23'70. B 3626
The nothing kid. by Julie Bovasso. (Gill) 50:65-6 Ja 13'75. T 3627
Nourish the beast. by Steve Tesich. (Oliver) 49:88-9 Je9'73; 49:102 O15'73. T 3628
The novel as faith: the gospel according to James, Hardy, Conrad, Joyce, Lawrence, and Virginia Woolf. by John Paterson. (Anon.) 49:95 Ja 21'74. B 3629
Novella. by Johann Wolfgang von Goethe. Elizabeth Mayer, trans. [and] Louise Bogan, trans. (Anon.) 47:106-108 F27'71. B 3630
Nowhere to run, nowhere to hide. by Herman Johnson. (Oliver) 50:103 Ap22'74. T 3631

O

O Congress. by Donald Riegle [and] Trevor Armbrister. (Anon.) 48:78-9 Jy22'72. B 3632
O Jerusalem! by Larry Collins [and] Dominique Lapierre. (Anon.) 48:94-5 Je24'72. B 3633
O lucky man! (Gilliatt) 49:80-3 Je16'73. CC 3634
The obscene bird of night. by José Donoso. (Anon.) 49:

78-9 Jy16'73. B 3635
Odd girl out. by Elizabeth Jane Howard. (Anon.) 48:102 F26'72. B 3636
The odd woman. by Gail Godwin. (Anon.) 50:234 N18'74. B 3637
Ododo. by Joseph A. Walker [and] Dorothy A. Dinroe. (Oliver) 46:162 D5'70. T 3638
Of a fire on the moon. by Norman Mailer. (Anon.) 47:136 Mr13'71. B 3639
Of light and sounding brass. by V. S. Yanovsky. Isabella Levitin, trans. (Anon.) 48:102-103 Ja20'73. B 3640
Of mice and men. by John Steinbeck. George S. Kaufman, adapt. (Gill) 50:52 D30'74. T 3641
Off the middle way: report from a Swedish village. by Sture Källberg. Angela Gibbs, trans. (Anon.) 48:127 S9'72. B 3642
Off-Broadway: the prophetic theatre. by Stuart W. Little. (Anon.) 48:142 Ap29'72. B 3643
The ogre. by Michel Tournier. Barbara Bray, trans. (Flanner) 47:116-17 Mr13'71; (Sissman) 48:68-70 D30'72. B 3644
Oh Coward! by Noël Coward. (Oliver) 48:125 O14'72. T 3645
Oh, lady! lady! by P. G. Wodehouse [and] Guy Bolton [and] Jerome Kern. (Oliver) 50:108 Mr25'74. T 3646
Oh, what a blow that phantom gave me! by Edmund Carpenter. (Anon.) 49:92 Ag27'73. B 3647
The old ones of New Mexico. by Robert Coles. (Anon.) 49:98-9 Ja14'74. B 3648
Old times. by Harold Pinter. (Panter-Downes) 47:64-5 Jy 3'71; (Gill) 47:89 N27'71. T 3649
Older people. by John Ford Noonan. (Oliver) 48:84-5 My 27'72. T 3650
The Omni-Americans. by Albert Murray. (Coles) 46:185-9 O 17'70. B 3651
On a clear day you can see forever. (Lardner) 46:64 Je 27'70. CC 3652
On culture and communication. by Richard Hoggart. (N. Bliven) 49:143-5 Ap28'73. B 3653
On directing. by Harold Clurman. (Anon.) 48:94-5 Ja 27'73. B 3654
On instructions of my government. by Pierre Salinger. (Anon.) 47:67 Jy3'71. B 3655
On the shady side. by Frank Swinnerton. (Anon.) 47:146 My15'71. B 3656
On the town. by Adolph Green [and] Betty Comden. (Gill) 47:115 N6'71. T 3657
On violence. by Hannah Arendt. (Anon.) 46:168 Ap18'70. B 3658
On wings of song: a biography of Felix Mendelssohn. by Wilfrid Blunt. (Anon.) 50:89-90 Ag19'74. B 3659
Once upon a pedestal. by Emily Hahn. (Anon.) 50:89 Ag19'74. B 3660
One across, two down. by Ruth Rendell. (Anon.) 47:193 S 25'71. B 3661
One day in the life of Ivan Denisovich. (Gilliatt) 47:71-2 My22'71. CC 3662
One for the money. by Nancy Hamilton [and] Morgan Lewis. (Oliver) 47:74 Ja29'72; 48:77-8 Je3'72. T 3663
One hand clapping. by Anthony Burgess. (Anon.) 48:154 Mr 18'72. B 3664
One hundred years of solitude. by Gabriel García Márquez. (Updike) 47:93-4 Ja29'72. B 3665
One million. by Hendrik Hertzberg. (Anon.) 46:191 O10'70.

B 3666
One of our own. (Kraft) 47:67-8 My29'71. CC 3667
One woman's Arctic. by Sheila Burnford. (Coles) 50:138-44 S23'74. B 3668
One time, one place. by Eudora Welty. (Gill) 47:66-8 D25'71. B 3669
One-night stands of a noisy passenger. by Shelley Winters. (Oliver) 46:76 Ja16'71. T 3670
One's own island. (Kraft) 47:67 My29'71. T 3671
Only a novel: the double life of Jane Austen. by Jane Aiken Hodge. (Anon.) 48:84 Ag5'72. B 3672
The only way to cross. by John Maxtone-Graham. (Anon.) 48:76 Ja6'73. B 3673
Open heart. by Frederick Buechner. (Anon.) 48:78 Jy 22'72. B 3674
Operation overflight: the U-2 spy pilot tells his story for the first time. by Francis Gary Powers [and] Curt Gentry. (Anon.) 46:83 Jy18'70. B 3675
Operation rhino. by John Gordon Davis. (Anon.) 49:147 Ap28'73. B 3676
Operation sidewinder. by Sam Shepard. (Gill) 46:115-16 Mr 21'70. T 3677
Ophélia. (Gilliatt) 50:76-8 Ag12'74. CC 3678
Opium and the romantic imagination. by Alethea Hayter. (Anon.) 46:99 Ja16'71. B 3679
Optimism one: the emerging radicalism. by F. M. Esfandiary. (Anon.) 46:228 N21'70. B 3680
Ordeal of ambition: Jefferson, Hamilton, Burr. by Jonathan Daniels. (Anon.) 46:176 O 24'70. B 3681
Orlando furioso. by Lodovico Ariosto. (Flanner) 46:88 My 30'70; (Gill) 46:141-2 N14'70. T 3682
The orphan. by David Rabe. (Oliver) 49:105 Ap28'73. T 3683
Orphans and other children. by Charles Webb. (Anon.) 50:82-3 S2'74. B 3684
Orpheus in the New World: the symphony orchestra as an American cultural institution. by Philip Hart. (Anon.) 49: 218-19 N12'73. B 3685
Othello. by William Shakespeare. (Gill) 46:112 S26'70. T 3686
The other de Gaulle: diaries 1944-54. by Claude Mauriac. Moura Budberg, trans. [and] Gordon Latta, trans. (Anon.) 49:94-5 Ja21'74. B 3687
The other Germans: report from an East German town. by Hans Axel Holm. Thomas Teal, trans. (Anon.) 46:98-9 Ja16'71. B 3688
Other men's daughters. by Richard Stern. (Anon.) 49: 246 N19'73. B 3689
The other one. by Julian Green. Bernard Wall, trans. (Anon.) 49:122-3 Je2'73. B 3690
The other South: Southern dissenters in the Nineteenth Century. by Carl N. Degler. (Anon.) 50:150-1 Mr18'74. B 3691
Our Kate. by Catherine Cookson. (Anon.) 47:232 N20'71. B 3692
Our late night. by Wallace Shawn. (Gill) 50:62-3 Ja20'75. T 3693
Ourselves. by Jonathan Strong. (Anon.) 47:200 N6'71. B 3694
Out cry. by Tennessee Williams. (Gill) 49:104 Mr10'73. T 3695
Out of my time. by Marya Mannes. (Anon.) 47:136 D 18'71. B 3696
Out of this world. by Cole Porter [and] George Oppenheimer. (Oliver) 49:94 Mr

17'73. T 3697
Out back. (Kael) 48:89-91 Mr4'72. CC 3698
The out-of-towners. (Lardner) 46: 64 Je27'70. CC 3699
Over here! by Will Holt [and] Richard M. Sherman [and] Robert B. Sherman. (Gill) 50:107-108 Mr18'74. T 3700
The owl and the pussycat. (Kael) 46:165-6 N14'70. CC 3701
Owners. by Caryl Churchill. (Oliver) 49:56 My26'73. T 3702
The Oxford book of twentieth-century English verse. Philip Larkin, ed. (Sissman) 49:110-13 Je9'73. B 3703

P

Paine. by David Freeman Hawke. (Anon.) 50:152 My20'74. B 3704
Painter's progress. by Maurice Grosser. (Flanner) 48:92-3 Je24'72. B 3705
The pajama game. by Richard Bissell [and] George Abbott [and] Richard Adler [and] Jerry Ross. (Gill) 49:56 D24'73. T 3706
The Pallisers. by Anthony Trollope. Simon Raven, adapt. (Panter-Downes) 50:84 Mr4'74. TV 3707
The paper chase. (Kael) 49:153-4 O29'73. CC 3708
The paper house. by Françoise Mallet-Joris. Derek Coltman, trans. (Anon.) 47:76 Jy31'71. B 3709
Paper moon. (Gilliatt) 49:124-5 My26'73. CC 3710
The paperhanger. by Suzanne Prou. Adrienne Foulke, trans. (Anon.) 50:208 N4'74. B 3711
The papers and the papers. by Sanford J. Ungar. (Harris) 48:73-8 Ag26'72. B 3712
Papers on the war. by Daniel Ellsberg. (Anon.) 48:83 Ag 5'72. B 3713
Papillon. (Kael) 49:72-3 D24'73. CC 3714
Parades. (Gilliatt) 48:53-4 Jy 29'72. CC 3715
Paradise lost: the decline of the auto-industrial age. by Emma Rothschild. (Anon.) 49:200 N26'73. B 3716
The parallax view. (Gilliatt) 50:82-3 Je24'74. CC 3717
Parentheses. by Jay Neugeboren. (Anon.) 46:80 Jy11'70. B 3718
Park. by Paul Cherry [and] Lance Mulcahy. (Gill) 46: 85 My2'70. T 3719
A part of myself: portrait of an epoch. by Carl Zuckmayer. Richard Winston, trans. [and] Clara Winston, trans. (Anon.) 46:62 Ja2'71. B 3720
Parthian words. by Storm Jameson. (Anon.) 47:142 S 25'71. B 3721
The partners. by Louis Auchincloss. (Anon.) 50:126 F25'74. B 3722
Pascal. (Gilliatt) 50:132-5 My 13'74. CC 3723
The passenger. (Gilliatt) 46:85-6 Je6'70. CC 3724
The passion of Anna. (Gilliatt) 46:103-108 Je13'70. CC 3725
Passmore. by David Storey. (Anon.) 50:141-2 Mr25'74. B 3726
The past is the past. by Richard Wesley. (Oliver) 49:69 Ja 28'74. T 3727
Pat and Mike. (Gilliatt) 48:66-71 S23'72. CC 3728
Patriotism, Inc., and other tales. by Paul van Ostaijen. E. M. Beekman, trans. (Updike) 48:135-8 My13'72. B 3729
Paul Ehrenfest: the making of a theoretical physicist. by Martin Klein. (Bernstein) 46:95-8 F6'71. B 3730

Pavilions of the heart: the four walls of love. by Leslie Blanch. (Anon.) 50:104 Je 24'74. B 3731
Pawns: the plight of the citizen-soldier. by Peter Barnes. (Anon.) 47:95 Ja29'72. B 3732
Payday. (Kael) 49:119-20 F24'73. CC 3733
Peace and counterpeace: from Wilson to Hitler. by Hamilton Fish Armstrong. (Anon.) 47:75-6 Jy10'71. B 3734
Peary at the North Pole: fact or fiction? by Dennis Rawlins. (Anon.) 49:72 Jy30'73. B 3735
A peck of salt. by John T. Hough. (Anon.) 46:143 D19'70. B 3736
A peep into the past: and other prose pieces. by Max Beerbohm. (Anon.) 48:196 N4'72. B 3737
People are living there. by Athol Fugard. (Oliver) 47:131 D4'71. T 3738
The people in Glass House. by June Drummond. (Anon.) 46:144 S26'70. B 3739
People who pull you down. by Thomas Baird. (Anon.) 46:126-7 My2'70. B 3740
People will always be kind. by Wilfrid Sheed. (Anon.) 49:133-4 Ap21'73. B 3741
A percentage of the take. by Walter Goodman. (Anon.) 47:135-6 Mr13'71. B 3742
Perfect Friday. (Kael) 46:125 N21'70. CC 3743
Perfectly clear: Nixon from Whittier to Watergate. by Frank Mankiewicz. (Anon.) 49:80 D24'73. B 3744
Performance. (Gilliatt) 46:61 Ag 8'70. CC 3745
Pericles. by William Shakespeare. (Oliver) 50:56 Jy15'74. T 3746
Perry's mission. by Clarence Young, III (Oliver) 46:54-6 Ja 30'71. T 3747
The Persians. by Aeschylus. See A ceremony for our time. T 3748
A personal country. by A. C. Greene. (Anon.) 46:156 Mr 14'70. B 3749
Pete 'n' Tillie. (Kael) 48:49-50 D30'72. CC 3750
A phantasmagoria historia of D. Johann Fausten Magister. by Anon. (Oliver) 49:82 My 5'73. T 3751
Phantom India. (Gilliatt) 48:55-7 Jy8'72. CC 3752
Phantom of the Paradise. (Kael) 50:178-82 N11'74. CC 3753
The philanthropist. by Christopher Hampton. (Panter-Downes) 47:103 F27'71; (Gill) 47:83 Mr 27'71. T 3754
Philemon. by Tom Jones [and] Harvey Schmidt. (Gill) 50:63 Ja20'75. T 3755
Philosophers of the earth: conversations with ecologists. by Anne Chisholm. (Anon.) 49:136 My26'73. B 3756
Physics and beyond: encounters and conversations. by Werner Heisenberg. Arnold J. Pomerans, trans. (Bernstein) 47:128-31 Je5'71. B 3757
The physiology of taste: or meditations on transcendental gastronomy. by Jean Anthelme Brillat-Savarin. M. F. K. Fisher, trans. (Anon.) 47:100 Ja22'72. B 3758
Piaf. by Simone Berteaut. (Anon.) 48:76 Jy8'72. B 3759
Picasso says... by Hélène Parmelin. Christine Trollope, trans. (Anon.) 46:120 Mr7'70. B 3760
Pick up sticks. by Emma Lathen. (Anon.) 46:64 Ja2'71. B 3761
A pictorial history of English architecture. by John Betjeman. (Anon.) 48:178-9 D 9'72. B 3762

Pictures and conversations. by Elizabeth Bowen. (Anon.) 50: 99 Ja20'75. B 3763
Pictures in the hallway. by Paul Shyre. (Oliver) 47:90 My8'71. T 3764
Pictures of the past. by Alexander Sukhovo-Kobylin. (Wilson) 48: 149-53 Mr18'72. B 3765
A piece of truth. by Amalia Fleming. (Anon.) 49:135 Ap 21'73. B 3766
The pig pen. by Ed Bullins. (Oliver) 46:72-3 My30'70. T 3767
Pink Floyd. (Gilliatt) 50:117 S9'74. CC 3768
Pippin. by Roger O. Hirson [and] Stephen Schwartz. (Gill) 48:105 N4'72. T 3769
The pizza triangle. (Kael) 46:170-2 N28'70. CC 3770
A place for Polly. by Lonnie Coleman. (Gill) 46:95-6 Ap 25'70. T 3771
A place in England. by Melvyn Bragg. (Anon.) 47:87-8 Ag14'71. B 3772
A place without doors. by Marguerite Duras. (Oliver) 46:42 Ja2'71. T 3773
Places. by Sidonie Gabrielle Colette. David LeVay, trans. (Anon.) 47:68 D25'71. B 3774
Places where I've done time. by William Saroyan. (Anon.) 48:142 Ap29'72. B 3775
Plain speaking: an oral biography of Harry S. Truman. by Harry S. Truman [and] Merle Miller. (Anon.) 49:127 F11'74. B 3776
Plantation. by Ted Shine. (Oliver) 46:116-18 Mr21'70. T 3777
Play it again, Sam. (Gilliatt) 48: 104-106 My13'72. CC 3778
Play it as it lays. (Kael) 48:155-8 N11'72. CC 3779
Play Strindberg. by Friedrich Dürrenmatt. James Kirkup, trans. (Oliver) 47:84 Je12'71. T 3780
The playboy of the western world. by John Millington Synge. (Gill) 46:75 Ja16'71. T 3781
Players inn. by Neil Harris. (Oliver) 48:98 Ap8'72. T 3782
The play's the thing. by Ferenc Molnár. P. G. Wodehouse, adapt. (Oliver) 48:75 F10'73. T 3783
Playtime. (Gilliatt) 49:63-6 Jy 2'73. CC 3784
Plaza suite. (Gilliatt) 47:129 My15'71. CC 3785
Please don't cry and say no. by Townsend Brewster. (Oliver) 48:88 D16'72. T 3786
Pleasure and repentance. by Terry Hands. (Oliver) 50: 75-6 My6'74. T 3787
The plot against Roger Rider. by Julian Symons. (Anon.) 49:200 D10'73. B 3788
The plot that thickened. by P. G. Wodehouse. (Anon.) 49:86-7 Ag13'73. B 3789
The plough and the stars. by Sean O'Casey. (Gill) 48:59 Ja13'73. T 3790
Pocahontas and her world. by Philip L. Barbour. (Anon.) 46:119 Je13'70. B 3791
Poetic justice. by Amanda Cross. (Anon.) 47:152 Mr20'71. B 3792
A poet's journal: days of 1945-1951. by George Seferis. Athan Anagnostopoulos, trans. (Anon.) 50:87-8 Ag5'74. B 3793
A political education. by Harry McPherson. (Anon.) 48:75-6 Jy8'72. B 3794
The politics of heroin in Southeast Asia. by Alfred W. McCoy [and] Cathleen B. Read [and] Leonard P. Adams, II. (Anon.) 48:126-7 S30'72. B 3795
The polygamist. by Ndabaningi Sithole. (Anon.) 48:82-3 Ag 5'72. B 3796

Popular prints of the Americas. by A. Hyatt Mayor. (Anon.) 50:136 Mr11'74. B 3797
A populist manifesto: the making of a new majority. by Jack Newfield [and] Jeff Greenfield. (Anon.) 48:79 Jy22'72. B 3798
The porkchoppers. by Ross Thomas. (Anon.) 48:94 Je 24'72. B 3799
Portnoy's complaint. (Gilliatt) 48:63 Jy1'72. CC 3800
The portrait game. Marion Mainwaring, ed. and trans. (Anon.) 49:96 Ja21'74. B 3801
Portrait of a marriage. by Nigel Nicolson. (Gill) 49:173-9 O 29'73. B 3802
The Portuguese seaborne empire: 1415-1825. by Charles R. Boxer. (Anon.) 46:171-2 Ap 11'70. B 3803
The Poseidon adventure. (Kael) 48:128-31 D16'72. CC 3804
Postcards. by James Prideaux. (Gill) 46:81 Mr28'70. T 3805
Pound. (Gilliatt) 46:50-1 Ag29'70. CC 3806
The Pound era. by Hugh Kenner. (N. Bliven) 48:90-2 Ja13'73. B 3807
Power and innocence: a search for the sources of violence. by Rollo May. (Anon.) 48:149-50 D16'72. B 3808
Practice to deceive. by Elizabeth Linington. (Anon.) 46:96 Ja30'71. B 3809
Prague: the mystical city. by Joseph Wechsberg. (Anon.) 47:67-8 Jy3'71. B 3810
Pravda. (Gilliatt) 46:81-4 My 30'70. CC 3811
The preachers. by James Morris. (Anon.) 49:67 S3'73. B 3812
The President's war: the story of the Tonkin Gulf Resolution and how the nation was trapped in Vietnam. by Anthony Austin. (Anon.) 47:131 O2'71. B 3813
Pretzels. by John Forster, et al. (Gill) 50:53 D30'74. T 3814
A pride of lions: the Astor orphans. by Lately Thomas. (Anon.) 47:200-201 N13'71. B 3815
The princess bride. by William Goldman. (Anon.) 49:217 N 12'73. B 3816
Princess Yang Kwei Fei. (Gilliatt) 48:70-1 Jy15'72. CC 3817
Principles of American nuclear chemistry. by Thomas Mc Mahon. (Steiner) 46:175-81 N7'70. B 3818
The prisoner of Second Avenue. by Neil Simon. (Gill) 47:111 N20'71. T 3819
Private faces/public places. by Abigail McCarthy. (Anon.) 48:84 Ag5'72. B 3820
The private life of Sherlock Holmes. (Kael) 46:168 N14'70. CC 3821
Private lives. by Noël Coward. (Gill) 50:84 F17'75. T 3822
Private worlds. by Sarah Gainham. (Anon.) 47:75 Jy31'71. B 3823
A problem in angels. by Leonard Holton. (Anon.) 46:140 Ap25'70. B 3824
The prodigal sister. by J. E. Franklin [and] Micki Grant. (Gill) 50:69-70 D9'74. T 3825
The professor's daughter. by Piers Paul Read. (Anon.) 47:199 N6'71. B 3826
Promenade, all! by David V. Robison. (Gill) 48:108 Ap 22'72. T 3827
Promise at dawn. (Kael) 46: 89-92 F6'71. CC 3828
Promised lands. (Gilliatt) 50: 58 Jy15'74. CC 3829
Promises to keep: my years in public life, 1941-69. by Chester Bowles. (Anon.) 47: 148 Ap17'71. B 3830
Prophets with honor: great dissents and great dissenters in the Supreme Court. by Alan Barth. (Anon.) 50:92 Ag26'74.

B 3831
The proposition. by Allan Albert. (Oliver) 47:97 Ap3'71. T 3832
The proselytizer. by D. Keith Mano. (Anon.) 48:130 Ap8'72. B 3833
Proust and his world. by William Sansom. (Anon.) 50:91 Ag19'74. B 3834
The psychology of consciousness. by Robert E. Ornstein. (Hiss) 49:65-72 Ja7'74. B 3835
The public eye. (Gilliatt) 48:54 Jy29'72. CC 3836
Purlie. by Ossie Davis [and] Gary Geld [and] Peter Udell. (Gill) 46:81-2 Mr28'70. T 3837
Puzzle of a downfall child. (Kael) 46:90-5 F13'71. CC 3838

Q

Quackser Fortune has a cousin in the Bronx. (Gilliatt) 46:55 Jy25'70. CC 3839
The quality of hurt. by Chester Himes. (Anon.) 48:155 Mr 18'72. B 3840
Quartet. by Jean Rhys. (Moss) 50:161-6 D16'74. B 3841
Queen Anne. by David Green. (Anon.) 47:148 Ap17'71. B 3842
The queen of a distant country. by John Braine. (Anon.) 49:149-50 My5'73. B 3843
Queen of the head hunters. by Sylvia Brooke. (Sissman) 48:108-10 Je3'72. B 3844
Queen Victoria and the Bonapartes. by Theo Aronson. (Anon.) 48:95 Je24'72. B 3845
Queen Victoria: from her birth to the death of the prince consort. by Cecil Woodham-Smith. (N. Bliven) 48:173-6 D9'72. B 3846
Querelle. by Jean Genet. Anselm Hollo, trans. (Anon.) 50:188-9 O21'74. B 3847
The quest for mind: Piaget, Lévi-Strauss, and the structuralist movement. by Howard Gardner. (Anon.) 48:100 F 3'73. B 3848
A question of judgment: the Fortas case and the struggle for the Supreme Court. by Robert Shogan. (Anon.) 48:104 Je17'72. B 3849
The quiet end of evening. by Honor Tracy. (Anon.) 48:74-5 Jy8'72. B 3850
A quiet voyage home. by Richard Jessup. (Anon.) 46:80 Jy 25'70. B 3851

R

Rabbit redux. by John Updike. (Gill) 47:83-4 Ja8'72. B 3852
Rabelais. Jean-Louis Barrault, adapt. (Gill) 46:70 My30'70. T 3853
The Rachel papers. by Martin Amis. (Sissman) 50:102 Je 24'74. B 3854
Rafferty and the Gold Dust Twins. (Kael) 50:82-3 F3'75. CC 3855
The raft of the Medusa. by Vercors. Audrey C. Foote, trans. (Anon.) 47:88 S4'71. B 3856
Rail facts and feats. by John Marshall. (Anon.) 50:95 Ja 13'75. B 3857
Rain. by W. Somerset Maugham. John Colton, adapt. (Oliver) 48:67 Ap1'72. T 3858
Rainbow. by James Rado [and] Ted Rado. (Oliver) 48:47 D30'72. T 3859
Rainbow Jones. by Jill Williams. (Gill) 50:83 F25'74. T 3860
Raisin. by Robert Nemiroff [and] Charlotte Zaltzberg [and] Judd Woldin [and] Robert Brittan. (Gill) 49:107 O29'73. T 3861
A rap on race. by Margaret

Mead [and] James Baldwin. (Anon.) 47:116 Je12'71. B 3862

Rat race. by Dick Francis. (Anon.) 47:132 My1'71. B 3863

Raven's End. (Gilliatt) 46:80-1 My30'70. CC 3864

Ravenswood. by Terrence Mc Nally. (Oliver) 49:74 F18'74. T 3865

Raw material. by Alan Sillitoe. (Anon.) 49:59-60 D31'73. B 3866

The real inspector hound. by Tom Stoppard. (Oliver) 48:61-2 My6'72. T 3867

The real Isadora. by Victor Seroff. (Anon.) 47:127-8 S11'71. B 3868

The real majority: an extraordinary examination of the American electorate. by Richard M. Scammon [and] Ben J. Wattenberg. (Anon.) 46:139-40 O3'70. B 3869

The real world of the public schools. by Harry S. Broudy. (Anon.) 48:160 O7'72. B 3870

Reason awake. by René Dubos. (Anon.) 46:118-19 Je13'70. B 3871

A recent killing. by Le Roi Jones. (Oliver) 48:75 F10'73. T 3872

Recollections. by Alexis de Tocqueville. George Lawrence, trans. J. P. Mayer, ed. [and] A. P. Kerr, ed. (Anon.) 46:76 Jy4'70. B 3873

Recollections of Virginia Woolf by her contemporaries. Joan Russell Noble, ed. (Maxwell) 48:96-9 F3'73. B 3874

Recovery. by John Berryman. (Anon.) 49:114 Je9'73. B 3875

The red and the white: report from a French village. by Edgar Morin. A. M. Sheridan-Smith, trans. (Anon.) 47:138 Ap3'71. B 3876

The red house. by Derek Lambert. (Anon.) 48:110 Je3'72. B 3877

The red tent. (Gilliatt) 47:57 S4'71. CC 3878

The rediscovery of black nationalism. by Theodore Draper. (Anon.) 46:76 Ag 8'70. B 3879

Reed: insurgent Mexico. (Gilliatt) 50:95-6 S16'74. CC 3880

Reflections on the causes of human misery and upon certain proposals to eliminate them. by Barrington Moore. (Coles) 49:106-13 Mr3'73. B 3881

Regiment of women. by Thomas Berger. (Anon.) 49:109-10 Je16'73. B 3882

Reinhold Niebuhr: prophet to politicians. by Ronald Stone. (Coles) 48:153-7 O7'72. B 3883

The reluctant rapist. by Ed Bullins. (Anon.) 49:186 O 15'73. B 3884

Remembering the answers: essays on the American student revolt. by Nathan Glazer. (Anon.) 46:191 N28'70. B 3885

Renaissance exploration. by J. R. Hale. (Anon.) 48:83 Jy15'72. B 3886

René Leys. by Victor Segalen. J. A. Underwood, trans. (N. Bliven) 50:189-93 D9'74. B 3887

Report from Engine Co. 82. by Dennis Smith. (Anon.) 47:116 F19'72. B 3888

Report to the commissioner. (Kael) 50:96-8 F10'75. CC 3889

The republic. by Aristophanes. Ed Wode, adapt. (Oliver) 46:97 My9'70. T 3890

Requiem for a Spanish village. by Barbara Norman. (Anon.) 48:71-2 D30'72. B 3891

The resurrection of Richard Nixon. by Jules Witcover. (Anon.) 46:103-104 S5'70. B 3892

Retreat from love. by Sidonie

Gabrielle Colette. Margaret Crosland, trans. (Anon.) 50: 90-1 Ag26'74. B 3893

Return to black America. by William Gardner Smith. (Anon.) 46:137 Ap25'70. B 3894

The revenge of heaven: journal of a young Chinese. by Ken Ling. Miriam London, ed. and trans. [and] Ta-ling Lee, ed. and trans. (Anon.) 48:102-103 F26'72. B 3895

The revolutionary. (Gilliatt) 46: 45-6 Jy18'70; 46:60-1 Ag22'70. CC 3896

The Rhinemann exchange. by Robert Ludlum. (Anon.) 50: 202-203 O14'74. B 3897

Rich man, poor man. by Irwin Shaw. (Anon.) 47:134-5 Mr 13'71. B 3898

Richard Lion Heart. by James A. Brundage. (Anon.) 50:100 Ag12'74. B 3899

Richard II. by William Shakespeare. (Oliver) 49:61 Ja21'74. T 3900

Richard III. by William Shakespeare. (Oliver) 50:124 N4'74. T 3901

Richelieu and his age, Vol. I. by Carl J. Burckhardt. Edwin Muir, trans. [and] Willa Muir, trans. (Anon.) 48:125-6 S9'72. B 3902

Richelieu and his age, Vols. II and III. by Carl J. Burckhardt. Bernard Hoy, trans. (Anon.) 48:125-6 S9'72. B 3903

The riddle of the pyramids. by Kurt Mendelssohn. (Anon.) 50:104 Je24'74. B 3904

Ride a black horse. by John Scott. (Oliver) 47:100 Je5'71. T 3905

The ride across Lake Constance. by Peter Handke. (Oliver) 47: 70 Ja22'72. T 3906

Rider on the rain. (Gilliatt) 46:56 Je20'70. CC 3907

Riding the rails. by Michael Mathers. (Anon.) 49:60 D31'73. B 3908

Riding the storm, 1956-1959. by Harold Macmillan. (Anon.) 47:229-30 N20'71. B 3909

Rigadoon. by Louis-Ferdinand Céline. (N. Bliven) 50:129-32 Je10'74. B 3910

Right on! (Gilliatt) 47:135-6 Ap10'71. CC 3911

Ring round the bathtub. by Jane Trahey. (Gill) 48:56-61 My 6'72. T 3912

Ringolevio: a life played for keeps. by Emmett Grogan. (Anon.) 48:130-1 Je10'72. B 3913

Ripley's game. by Patricia Highsmith. (Anon.) 50:107-108 My27'74. B 3914

The rise of Louis XIV. (Gilliatt) 46:58-60 Ag22'70. CC 3915

The rise of New York port, 1815-60. by Robert Greenhalgh. (Anon.) 46:192 O10'70. B 3916

Rites of passage. by Joanne Greenberg. (Anon.) 48:147 Ap15'72. B 3917

The Ritz. by Terrence McNally. (Gill) 50:76-7 F3'75. T 3918

Rivals. (Gilliatt) 48:68-9 S9'72. CC 3919

The rivals. by Richard Brinsley Sheridan. (Gill) 50:69 Ja27'75. T 3920

The river gets wider. by R. L. Gordon. (Anon.) 50:123 Ap 1'74. B 3921

The River Niger. by Joseph A. Walker. (Oliver) 48:86-8 D16'72; (Gill) 49:57 Ap7'73. T 3922

Riverrun. (Gilliatt) 46:120-2 My9'70. CC 3923

The Riverside Villas murder. by Kingsley Amis. (Anon.) 49:169-70 O8'73. B 3924

Robert Browning: a portrait. by Betty Miller. (Anon.) 49: 148 My12'73. B 3925

Robert Burns and his world. by David Daiches. (Anon.) 47:100 Ja22'72. B 3926

Robert, Earl of Essex. by Robert Lacey. (Anon.) 47:92 Je26'71. B 3927
Rogue male. by Geoffrey Household. (Sissman) 47:125-7 My 1'71. B 3928
Roll, Jordan, roll: the world the slaves made. by Eugene D. Genovese. (Anon.) 50:167-8 D16'74. B 3929
The romantic rebellion: romantic versus classic art. by Kenneth Clark. (Anon.) 50:160 My13'74. B 3930
Room service. by John Murray [and] Allen Boretz. (Gill) 46: 73 My23'70. T 3931
Roosevelt: the soldier of freedom, 1940-1945. by James MacGregor Burns. (N. Bliven) 46:81-7 Ja 9'71. B 3932
The Roosevelts of Hyde Park: an untold story. by Elliott Roosevelt [and] James Brough. (Anon.) 49:123-4 Je2'73. B 3933
The roots of civilization. by Alexander Marshack. (Anon.) 48:74 Jy1'72. B 3934
The roots of coincidence. by Arthur Koestler. (N. Bliven) 48:75-7 Ag12'72. B 3935
Roots of involvement: the U.S. in Asia, 1784-1971. by Marvin Kalb [and] Elie Abel. (Anon.) 47:76 Jy10'71. B 3936
Rosalee Pritchett. by Carlton Molette [and] Barbara Molette. (Oliver) 46:56-7 Ja30'71. T 3937
Rosalind passes. by Frank Swinnerton. (Anon.) 50:153-4 Ap 22'74. B 3938
Rose, where did you get that red? by Kenneth Koch. (Anon.) 49:246-8 N19'73. B 3939
Rosebloom. by Harvey Perr. (Oliver) 47:72-3 Ja15'72. T 3940
Rosencrantz and Guildenstern are dead. by Tom Stoppard. (Oliver) 50:70 Mr4'74. T 3941
Ross and Tom: two American tragedies. by John Leggett. (Anon.) 50:148 S16'74. B 3942
The Rothschilds. by Jerry Bock [and] Sheldon Harnick [and] Sherman Yellen. (Gill) 46: 101 O31'70. T 3943
The Rothschilds: family of fortune. by Virginia Cowles. (Anon.) 49:103-104 Ja28'74. B 3944
Round and round the garden. by Alan Ayckbourn. (Panter-Downes) 50:142-4 D2'74. T 3945
The royal house. by Eric Linklater. (Anon.) 46:119-20 Je13'70. B 3946
Rule Britannia. by Daphne du Maurier. (Anon.) 48:110 F 17'73. B 3947
Rules for radicals. by Saul D. Alinsky. (Anon.) 47:92 Ag21'71. B 3948
The rules of the game. by Luigi Pirandello. (Gill) 50:54 D 23'74. T 3949
The ruling class. (Gilliatt) 48: 79-82 S16'72. CC 3950
Rumour in Orléans. by Edgar Morin. Peter Green, trans. (Anon.) 47:200-201 N6'71. B 3951
Runaway horses. by Yukio Mishima. Michael Gallagher, trans. (Anon.) 49:89-90 Je 23'73. B 3952
Running out. by Christopher Brookhouse. (Fraser) 46:170-5 O24'70. B 3953
Russian prospect. by Erik de Mauny. (Anon.) 46:116 F 28'70. B 3954
Russian writers: notes and essays. by Helen Muchnic. (Anon.) 47:130-1 My1'71. B 3955
Ruth Benedict. by Margaret Mead. (Bernstein) 50:92-3 F3'75. B 3956
Ryan's daughter. (Kael) 46:116-25 N21'70. CC 3957

S

Sabbatai Sevi: the mystical messiah. by Gershom Scholem. (Steiner) 49:152-74 O22'73. B 3958
The sacred and profane love machine. by Iris Murdoch. (Updike) 50:78-81 Ja6'75. B 3959
The sacred mushroom and the cross. by John M. Allegro. (Anon.) 46:209-10 N14'70. B 3960
The saddest story: a biography of Ford Madox Ford. by Arthur Mizener. (Anon.) 47:143 My8'71. B 3961
St. George and the godfather. by Norman Mailer. (Anon.) 48: 158-9 O28'72. B 3962
Saint Jack. by Paul Theroux. (Anon.) 49:132-3 S10'73. B 3963
The salamander. by Morris West. (Anon.) 49:184-5 N5'73. B 3964
The Salisbury manuscript. by William M. Green. (Anon.) 50:115 Mr4'74. B 3965
Sammy. by Sammy Davis, Jr. (Gill) 50:75 My6'74. T 3966
Samuel de Champlain: father of New France. by Samuel Eliot Morison. (Anon.) 48:94 Je 24'72. B 3967
Samuel Johnson and the life of writing. by Paul Fussell. (Anon.) 47:155 Ap10'71. B 3968
Samuel Johnson: his friends and enemies. by Peter Quennell. (Anon.) 49:147 Ap28'73. B 3969
The San Francisco earthquake. by Gordon Thomas [and] Max Morgan Witts. (Anon.) 47:180 O23'71. B 3970
The Santa Claus bank robbery. by A. C. Greene. (Anon.) 48:127-8 S16'72. B 3971
The saphead. (Gilliatt) 50:115-17 S9'74. CC 3972
Sarah Siddons: portrait of an actress. by Roger Manvell. (Anon.) 47:128 My22'71. B 3973
Saturday morning. (Gilliatt) 47: 121-2 My8'71. CC 3974
Saturday Sunday Monday. by Eduardo de Filippo. (Gill) 50:132 D2'74. T 3975
The savage is loose. (Kael) 50:183-4 N25'74. CC 3976
Savage messiah. (Kael) 48:225-32 N18'72. CC 3977
Savages. (Gilliatt) 48:63-4 Jy 1'72. CC 3978
Save the tiger. (Kael) 48:95-6 F17'73. CC 3979
Saved. by Edward Bond. (Oliver) 46:133-5 N7'70. T 3980
Scapegoats. by George Mandel. (Anon.) 46:190 O10'70. B 3981
Scapino. by Jean Baptiste Poquelin Molière. Jim Dale, adapt. (Oliver) 50:107-108 Mr25'74; (Gill) 50:64 My 27'74. T 3982
Scars on the soul. by François Sagan. Joanna Kilmartin, trans. (Updike) 50:95-6 Ag 12'74. B 3983
Scenes from a marriage. (Gilliatt) 50:96-8 S23'74. CC 3984
Scenes from American life. by A. R. Gurney, Jr. (Oliver) 47:95-7 Ap3'71. T 3985
A scent of lilies. by Claire Gallois. Elizabeth Walter, trans. (Anon.) 47:91 Ag21'71. B 3986
The school for scandal. by Richard Brinsley Sheridan. (Oliver) 48:100 O7'72. T 3987
The school for wives. by Jean Baptiste Poquelin Molière. Richard Wilbur, trans. (Gill) 47:82 F27'71. T 3988
The schoolgirl murder case. by Colin Wilson. (Anon.) 50:150-1 S16'74. B 3989

Science and philosophy in the Soviet Union. by Loren R. Graham. (Astrachan) 49:117-40 S24'73. B 3990
Scorpion. by Christopher Hill. (Anon.) 50:147 S23'74. B 3991
The scorpion god. by William Golding. (Anon.) 47:94 Ja29'72. B 3992
The scoundrel. (Gilliatt) 48:51 Jy22'72. CC 3993
Scramble for Africa: the great trek to the Boer War. by Anthony Nutting. (Anon.) 47:88 Jy17'71. B 3994
Scratch. by Archibald MacLeish. (Gill) 47:102 My15'71. T 3995
Scrooge. (Kael) 46:175-6 N28'70. CC 3996
Scuffler. by Harvey Orkin. (Anon.) 50:194 N25'74. B 3997
The sea horse. by James Irwin. (Oliver) 50:63-4 Ap29'74. T 3998
The seagull. by Anton Chekhov. Andre Gregory, adapt. (Gill) 50:62 Ja20'75. T 3999
Seascape. by Edward Albee. (Gill) 50:75-6 F3'75. T 4000
The season of the witch. by James Leo Herlihy. (Sissman) 47:89-90 My29'71. B 4001
The second death of Ramón Mercader. by Jorge Semprun. Len Ortzen, trans. (Anon.) 49:75 Ja7'74. B 4002
A second flowering: works and days of the lost generation. by Malcolm Cowley. (Anon.) 49:90-1 Je23'73. B 4003
The secret affairs of Mildred Wild. by Paul Zindel. (Gill) 48:111-12 N25'72. T 4004
The secret conferences of Dr. Goebbels: the Nazi propaganda war, 1939-43. Willi Boelcke, ed. Edward Osers, trans. (Anon.) 46:112 F13'71. B 4005
The seduction of Mimi. (Gilliatt) 50:80-2 Je24'74. CC 4006
See no evil. (Gilliatt) 47:69 S18'71. CC 4007
See you at Mao. (Gilliatt) 46:84-5 My30'70. CC 4008
Seesaw. by Michael Bennett [and] Cy Coleman [and] Dorothy Fields. (Gill) 49:74 Mr 24'73. T 4009
The selected letters of Lady Mary Wortley Montagu. by Mary Wortley Montagu. Robert Halsband, ed. (Anon.) 47:146-7 My15'71. B 4010
Selected prose, 1909-65. by Ezra Pound. William Cookson, ed. (Anon.) 49:91 Ag27'73. B 4011
The self-inflicted wound. by Fred P. Graham. (Anon.) 46:63-4 D26'70. B 4012
Selma, 1965. by Charles E. Fager. (Anon.) 50:134 S9'74. B 4013
The seminarian. by Michel del Castillo. George Robinson, trans. (Anon.) 46:138 Ap4'70. B 4014
Sensations. by Wally Harper [and] Paul Zakrzewski. (Oliver) 46:135 N7'70. T 4015
A sense of loss. (Kael) 48:135-7 O21'72. CC 4016
A sense of place: the artist and the American land. by Alan Gussow. (Sissman) 48:123-5 S16'72. B 4017
A sense of the Senate. by Seymour K. Freidin. (Anon.) 48:78 Ag12'72. B 4018
The serpent. by Jean-Claude van Itallie. (Oliver) 46:90 Je13'70. T 4019
Serpico. by Peter Maas. (Anon.) 49:76 Jy2'73. B 4020
Serpico. (Kael) 49:107-10 D17'73. CC 4021
Seven houses: a memoir of time and places. by Josephine W. Johnson. (Anon.) 49:150 My 5'73. B 4022
Seven voices: seven Latin American writers talk to Rita

Guibert. by Rita Guibert. Frances Partridge, trans. (Anon.) 48:92 Ja13'73. B 4023
1776. (Kael) 48:180-3 N25'72. CC 4024
70, girls, 70. by Fred Ebb [and] Norman L. Martin [and] John Kander. Joseph Masteroff, adapt. (Gill) 47:93-4 Ap24'71. T 4025
Sextet. by Harvey Perr [and] Lee Goldsmith [and] Lawrence Hurwit. (Oliver) 50:109 Mr 18'74. T 4026
Sexual politics. by Kate Millett. (Anon.) 46:137 S19'70. B 4027
Sexual suicide. by George F. Gilder. (Anon.) 49:154 D17'73. B 4028
The shadow of a gunman. by Sean O'Casey. (Oliver) 48:83-4 Mr 11'72. T 4029
The shadow war: European resistance 1939-45. by Henri Michel. Richard Barry, trans. (Anon.) 48:116 F10'73. B 4030
Shaft. (Gilliatt) 47:67 Ag7'71. CC 4031
Shakespeare the man. by A. L. Rowse. (Steiner) 50:142-50 Mr18'74. B 4032
Shakespeare's flowers. by Jessica Kerr. (White) 46:121-2 Mr 28'70. B 4033
Shakespeare's sonnets: the problems solved. by A. L. Rowse. (Steiner) 50:142-50 Mr18'74. B 4034
Shampoo. (Kael) 50:86-93 F17'75. CC 4035
The shark: splendid savage of the sea. by Jacques-Yves Cousteau [and] Philippe Cousteau. Francis Price, trans. (Anon.) 46: 182-4 N7'70. B 4036
The shattered dream: Herbert Hoover and the great depression. by Gene Smith. (Anon.) 46:120 Je20'70. B 4037
Shaw: an autobiography 1898-1950: the playwright years. by George Bernard Shaw. Stanley Weintraub, ed. (Anon.) 46:139 O3'70. B 4038
Shay Duffin as Brendan Behan. by Brendan Behan. Shay Duffin, adapt. (Oliver) 48:60 Ja13'73. T 4039
Sheila Levine is dead and living in New York. (Kael) 50:83-6 F3'75. CC 4040
Shenandoah. by James Lee Barrett [and] Peter Udell [and] Philip Rose [and] Gary Geld. (Gill) 50:61-2 Ja20'75. T 4041
Shelley: the golden years. by Kenneth Neill Cameron. (Anon.) 50:87 Jy15'74. B 4042
Shelter. by Gretchen Cryer [and] Nancy Ford. (Gill) 48: 79-80 F17'73. T 4043
Sheridan: the track of a comet. by Madeleine Bingham. (Anon.) 49:135 Mr10'73. B 4044
Sherlock Holmes. by Arthur Conan Doyle [and] William Gillette. Frank Dunlop, adapt. (Gill) 50:131 N25'74. T 4045
The shield and the sword. by Ernle Bradford. (Anon.) 49: 79 Jy16'73. B 4046
Shinbone Alley. (Gilliatt) 47:98 Ap17'71. CC 4047
The shoemaker's prodigious wife. by Federico García Lorca. (Oliver) 50:109 Mr18'74. T 4048
Shoes. by Ted Shine. (Oliver) 46:116 Mr21'70. T 4049
Short eyes. by Miguel Piñero. (Oliver) 50:107 Mr25'74; (Gill) 50:68 Je3'74. T 4050
The short victorious war: the Russo-Japanese conflict, 1904-1905. by David Walder. (Anon.) 50:191-2 O21'74. B 4051
Show me where the good times are. by Leonora Thuna [and] Kenneth Jacobson [and] Rhoda Roberts. (Oliver) 46:122 Mr

14'70. T 4052
Siamese connections. by Dennis J. Reardon. (Oliver) 48:59-60 F3'73. T 4053
A Siberian encounter. by Gaia Servadio. (Anon.) 48:106 Ap 1'72. B 4054
The Sicilian clan. (Gilliatt) 46: 165 Ap11'70. CC 4055
Siddhartha. (Gilliatt) 49:57-8 Jy 23'73. CC 4056
Siege and survival: the odyssey of a Leningrader. by Elena Skrjabina. Norman Luxenburg, trans. (Anon.) 47:181-3 O16'71. B 4057
The siege of Krishnapur. by J. G. Farrell. (Sissman) 50:193-4 N 25'74. B 4058
The sign in Sidney Brustein's window. by Lorraine Hansberry. (Gill) 47:69 F5'72. T 4059
Silence. by Harold Pinter. (Oliver) 46:84 Ap11'70. T 4060
The silencers. (Kael) 48:160 D 2'72. CC 4061
Silent running. (Gilliatt) 48:125 Ap15'72. CC 4062
The Silver Age of Venice. by Maurice Rowdon. (Anon.) 46:76 Ag1'70. B 4063
Single file. by Norman Fruchter. (Updike) 47:147-53 Ap10'71. B 4064
Sir Arthur Sullivan. by Percy M. Young. (Anon.) 48:108 Ap1'72. B 4065
Sir Walter Ralegh. by Robert Lacey. (Anon.) 50:144 Ap8'74. B 4066
Sir Walter Scott: the great unknown. by Edgar Johnson. (Auden) 47:117-23 F20'71. B 4067
The sirens. by Richard Wesley. (Oliver) 50:64-6 My27'74. T 4068
Sister Son/ji. by Sonia Sanchez. (Oliver) 48:97-8 Ap8'72. T 4069
Sisters. (TT) 47:33 My1'71; (Kael) 49:156-9 O29'73. CC 4070
Sisters of mercy: a musical journey into the words of Leonard Cohen. by Leonard Cohen [and] Zizi Mueller. (Oliver) 49:112 O8'73. T 4071
Six. by Charles Strouse. (Oliver) 47:95 Ap24'71. T 4072
6 rms riv vu. by Bob Randall. (Gill) 48:119 O28'72. T 4073
Sixties going on Seventies. by Nora Sayre. (Anon.) 48:95 Ja27'73. B 4074
Sizwe Banzi is dead. by Athol Fugard [and] John Kani [and] Winston Ntshona. (Gill) 50: 131 N25'74. T 4075
The sketchbooks of Reginald Marsh. by Edward Laning. (Rosenberg) 50:155-7 My13'74. B 4076
Skin game. (Kael) 47:154-7 O 9'71. CC 4077
Slag. by David Hare. (Oliver) 47: 68-9 Mr6'71. T 4078
Slaughterhouse-Five. (Gilliatt) 48:93 Ap1'72. CC 4079
Slayride. by Dick Francis. (Anon.) 50:124 Ap1'74. B 4080
Sleep. by Jack Gelber. (Oliver) 48:82-3 Mr4'72. T 4081
Sleep and his brother. by Peter Dickinson. (Anon.) 47:116 Je12'71. B 4082
Sleeper. (Kael) 49:47-9 D31'73. CC 4083
Sleuth. by Anthony Shaffer. (Gill) 46:103-104 N21'70. T 4084
Sleuth. (Kael) 48:53-4 D23'72. CC 4085
The slipway. by Graham Billing. (Anon.) 49:72 Ja7'74. B 4086
Slither. (Kael) 49:113 Mr10'73. CC 4087
Small craft warnings. by Tennessee Williams. (Oliver) 48: 110 Ap15'72. T 4088
Smith. by Dean Fuller [and] Tony

Hendra [and] Matt Dubey. (Gill) 49:54 My26'73. T 4089
Smith's gazelle. by Lionel Davidson. (Anon.) 47:126 My22'71. B 4090
Smokescreen. by Dick Francis. (Anon.) 49:136 Mr10'73. B 4091
Snakes. by Al Young. (Sissman) 46:77-9 Jy11'70. B 4092
So short a time. by Barbara Gelb. (Anon.) 49:95-6 Ja21'74. B 4093
Socialism. by Michael Harrington. (Anon.) 48:80 Ag12'72. B 4094
The socialist myth. by Peregrine Worsthorne. (Anon.) 47:143-4 S18'71. B 4095
Soldier. by Anthony B. Herbert [and] James T. Wooten. (Anon.) 49:130 Mr17'73. B 4096
Solitaire/double solitaire. by Robert Anderson. (Gill) 47:95-6 O9'71. T 4097
Soma the divine mushroom. by R. Gordon Wasson. (Sargeant) 46:90-8 My30'70. B 4098
Some call it loving. (Kael) 49:187 N26'73. CC 4099
Someone great. by Robert Grossbach. (Anon.) 47:184-5 N27'71. B 4100
Something for everyone. (Gilliatt) 46:55 Jy25'70. CC 4101
Something happened. by Joseph Heller. (Sissman) 50:193 N 25'74. B 4102
Something up a sleeve. by Richard Lockridge. (Anon.) 48:80 Jy 22'72. B 4103
Sometimes a hard head makes a soft behind. by J. E. Gaines. (Oliver) 48:58 Ag26'72. T 4104
Somewhere else. by Robert Kotlowitz. (Anon.) 48:78 D 23'72. B 4105
A song at twilight. by Noël Coward. (Gill) 50:102 Mr11'74. T 4106
Song of Norway. (Kael) 46:168-9 N14'70. CC 4107
Song of the earth. by Alexander Cordell. (Anon.) 46:136-7 Ap25'70. B 4108
Songs from the night before. by Anthony Tuttle. (Anon.) 48:115 Mr4'72. B 4109
Soon. by Martin Duberman. (Oliver) 46:66 Ja23'71. T 4110
The sorrow and the pity. (Kael) 48:116-21 Mr25'72. CC 4111
The sorrows of young Werther. by Johann Wolfgang von Goethe. Elizabeth Mayer, trans. [and] Louise Bogan, trans. (Anon.) 47:106-108 F27'71. B 4112
A sort of life. by Graham Greene. (Sissman) 47:126-30 O2'71. B 4113
Souls on fire: portraits and legends of Hasidic masters. by Elie Wiesel. Marion Wiesel, trans. (Anon.) 48: 148 Ap15'72. B 4114
Sounder. (Kael) 48:109-15 S30'72. CC 4115
South Africa: civilizations in conflict. by Jim Hoagland. (Anon.) 48:190-1 N11'72. B 4116
The South and the nation. by Pat Watters. (Coles) 46:147-55 O31'70. B 4117
South to a very old place. by Albert Murray. (Anon.) 47: 84-5 Ja8'72. B 4118
The southern strategy. by Reg Murphy [and] Hal Gulliver. (Anon.) 47:128 My22'71. B 4119
Southerners and other Americans. by Grady McWhiney. (Anon.) 49:91 Ag20'73. B 4120
A Soviet heretic. by Yevgeny Zamyatin. Mirra Ginsburg, ed. & trans. (Anon.) 46:163 My9'70. B 4121
Soylent Green. (Gilliatt) 49:126-31 Ap28'73. CC 4122

The space between. by Sharon Spencer. (Anon.) 49:154 S17'73. B 4123
The spawning run. by William Humphrey. (Anon.) 46:191 N 28'70. B 4124
Speaking to each other: Volume I, about society; Volume II, about literature. by Richard Hoggart. (Anon.) 46:84 Je27'70. B 4125
Specimen days. by Walt Whitman. (Anon.) 48:132-3 S23'72. B 4126
Spector. by Marc Davis. (Anon.) 46:75-6 Jy4'70. B 4127
Spies behind the pillars, bandits at the pass. by Kathleen Trautman. (Anon.) 48:132 Ap8'72. B 4128
The splendor of iridescence. by Hilda Simon. (Anon.) 47:148 My15'71. B 4129
The spoilers. by Desmond Bagley. (Anon.) 46:164 My9'70. B 4130
The sporting club. (Kael) 47:89-90 Mr13'71. CC 4131
Spreading fires. by John Knowles. (Anon.) 50:87 Ag5'74. B 4132
Spring snow. by Yukio Mishima. Michael Gallagher, trans. (Anon.) 48:78-9 Jy29'72. B 4133
The springtime of life. by Jean Dutourd. Denver Lindley, trans. [and] Helen Lindley, trans. (Sissman) 50:129-30 S9'74. B 4134
Spy story. by Len Deighton. (Anon.) 50:147 S23'74. B 4135
Squaw Point. by R. H. Shimer. (Anon.) 48:144 Ap22'72. B 4136
Stalin: the history of a dictator. by H. Montgomery Hyde. (Anon.) 47:91-2 Ja15'72. B 4137
Standard safety. by Julie Bovasso. (Gill) 50:65-6 Ja13'75. T 4138
Start the revolution without me. (Kael) 46:94-5 Mr7'70. CC 4139
A state of peace. by Janice Elliott. (Anon.) 47:170 O9'71. B 4140
State of siege. (Gilliatt) 49:141-4 Ap14'73; 49:118-21 My12'73; (Kael) 49:241-4 N19'73. CC 4141
The stately home murder. by Catherine Aird. (Anon.) 46: 140 Ap4'70. B 4142
Status quo vadis. by Donald Driver. (Gill) 49:80 Mr3'73. T 4143
Stavisky. (Kael) 50:76-8 Ja20'75. CC 4144
Stay of execution. by Stewart Alsop. (Sissman) 49:125-6 F11'74. B 4145
Steambath. by Bruce Jay Friedman. (Oliver) 46:48 Jy11'70. T 4146
The steel bonnets. by George MacDonald Fraser. (Anon.) 48:75 Jy1'72. B 4147
Steelyard blues. (Kael) 48:96-8 F17'73. CC 4148
Stendhal. by Joanna Richardson. (Pritchett) 50:99-102 Ja27'75. B 4149
Stephen A. Douglas. by Robert W. Johannsen. (Anon.) 49: 146-7 Ap28'73. B 4150
Sticks and bones. by David Rabe. (Oliver) 47:114-19 N 20'71; (Gill) 48:82 Mr11'72. T 4151
Stilwell and the American experience in China, 1911-45. by Barbara Tuchman. (N. Bliven) 47:141-6 My15'71. B 4152
The sting. (Kael) 49:49-50 D 31'73. CC 4153
The stone and the violets. by Milovan Djilas. Lovett F. Edwards, trans. (Anon.) 48: 131 Mr25'72. B 4154
The stone baby. by Ben Healey. (Anon.) 49:80 Jy23'73. B 4155
The stones of the abbey. by Fernand Pouillon. Edward

Gillott, trans. (Anon.) 46: 195-6 D12'70. B 4156

Storm of fortune. by Austin Clarke. (Anon.) 49:89 Ag20'73. B 4157

Storming heaven: the lives and turmoils of Minnie Kennedy and Aimee Semple McPherson. by Lately Thomas. (Anon.) 46: 226-8 N21'70. B 4158

Story theatre. by Paul Sills. (Gill) 46:133 N7'70. T 4159

The strange last voyage of Donald Crowhurst. by Nicholas Tomalin [and] Ron Hall. (Anon.) 46:211 N14'70. B 4160

Strange meeting. by Susan Hill. (Anon.) 48:146-7 Ap15'72. B 4161

The stranger in Shakespeare. by Leslie A. Fiedler. (Anon.) 48:83-4 Ag5'72. B 4162

Straw dogs. (Kael) 47:80-5 Ja 29'72. CC 4163

The strawberry statement. (Lardner) 46:63-4 Je27'70. CC 4164

A streetcar named Desire. by Tennessee Williams. (Gill) 49: 81 My5'73; 49:102 O15'73. T 4165

Streets, actions, alternatives, raps. by John Stickney. (Anon.) 47:230-1 N20'71. B 4166

Streets of gold. by Evan Hunter. (Anon.) 50:90-3 Ja13'75. B 4167

The strenuous decade. Daniel Aaron, ed. [and] Robert Bendiner, ed. (Anon.) 46:120 Mr7'70. B 4168

Strictly speaking: will America be the death of English? by Edwin Newman. (Anon.) 50: 214-15 N11'74. B 4169

Stringer. by Ward Just. (Anon.) 50:105-106 My27'74. B 4170

The strong man. (Gilliatt) 47:130-4 Ap24'71. CC 4171

Strong opinions. by Vladimir Nabokov. (Anon.) 49:80 D24'73. B 4172

The stunt man. by Paul Brodeur. (Sissman) 46:117-18 Je13'70. B 4173

The sty of the blind pig. by Phillip Hayes Dean. (Oliver) 47:131 D4'71. T 4174

Style in history. by Peter Gay. (Anon.) 50:88 Jy15'74. B 4175

Subject to fits. by Robert Montgomery. (Oliver) 47:84 F 27'71. T 4176

Such a gorgeous kid like me. (Gilliatt) 49:104-107 Mr31'73. CC 4177

Such good friends. (Kael) 47: 77-8 Ja8'72. CC 4178

Sugar. by Peter Stone [and] Jule Styne [and] Bob Merrill. (Gill) 48:109-10 Ap15'72. T 4179

The sugarland express. (Kael) 50:130-5 Mr18'74. CC 4180

Suggs. by David Wiltse. (Oliver) 48:100-101 My13'72. T 4181

The sultan. by Joan Haslip. (Updike) 50:141-2 My6'74. B 4182

The sultans. by Noel Barber. (Updike) 50:138-41 My6'74. B 4183

The Summer before the dark. by Doris Lessing. (Anon.) 49:113-14 Je9'73. B 4184

Summer in Prague. by Zdena Salivarova. Marie Winn, trans. (Steiner) 49:142-6 My 12'73. B 4185

Summer wishes, Winter dreams. (Kael) 49:169-75 D10'73. CC 4186

The sun of York: a biography of Edward IV. by Mary Clive. (Anon.) 49:127-8 F11'74. B 4187

Sunday, bloody Sunday. (Kael) 47:93-7 O2'71. CC 4188

The sunlight dialogues. by John Gardner. (Anon.) 48:92 Ja 13'73. B 4189

The sunshine boys. by Neil Simon. (Gill) 48:47 D30'72. T 4190

Superfly. (Kael) 48:160-3 D2'72.

CC 4191
Superior person: a portrait of Curzon in late Victorian England. by Kenneth Rose. (Anon.) 46:168 Mr21'70. B 4192
Surfacing. by Margaret Atwood. (Anon.) 49:154-5 Ap14'73. B 4193
Surviving the long night: an autobiographical account of a political kidnapping. by Geoffrey Jackson. (Anon.) 50:212-13 N 11'74. B 4194
Svoy Ostrov. See One's own island. T 4195
The sway of the grand saloon: a social history of the North Atlantic. by John Malcolm Brinnin. (Sissman) 47:181-4 N27'71. B 4196
Sweet and low. by Emma Lathen. (Anon.) 50:135-6 S9'74. B 4197
Sweet dreams. by Michael Frayn. (Anon.) 49:97-8 Ja14'74. B 4198
Sweet Sweetback's baadasssss song. (Gilliatt) 47:68-9 Je19'71. CC 4199
Swinburne: portrait of a poet. by Philip Henderson. (Anon.) 50: 148-9 S16'74. B 4200
Sylvia Plath. by Sylvia Plath. (Oliver) 49:69 Ja28'74. T 4201
The symmetrical family. by Michael Young [and] Peter Willmott. (Anon.) 50:107 My27'74. B 4202
Sympathy for the devil. (Gilliatt) 46:104-109 My2'70. CC 4203

T

T. R. Baskin. (Kael) 47:144-6 O23'71. CC 4204
Table manners. by Alan Ayckbourn. (Panter-Downes) 50:142-4 D2'74. T 4205
Tajos: the story of a village on the Costa del Sol. by Ronald Fraser. (Anon.) 49:198 D 10'73. B 4206
Takeover bid. by Sarah Gainham. (Anon.) 47:99-100 Ja22'72. B 4207
The taking of Pelham one two three. by John Godey. (Anon.) 49:131-2 Mr17'73. B 4208
The taking of Pelham one two three. (Kael) 50:72-3 O28'74. CC 4209
Taking off. (Gilliatt) 47:107-109 Ap3'71. CC 4210
The tale of Lady Ochikubo: a tenth-century Japanese novel. by Anon. Wilfred Whitehouse, trans. [and] Eizo Yanagisawa, trans. (Anon.) 47:154 O30'71. B 4211
A tale of two families. by Dodie Smith. (Anon.) 46:82-3 Je 27'70. B 4212
Tales of Beatrix Potter. (Gilliatt) 47:86-8 Je26'71. CC 4213
The talking trees and other stories. by Sean O'Faolain. (Anon.) 46:189 N28'70. B 4214
The tall blond man with one black shoe. (Gilliatt) 49:46-7 S3'73. CC 4215
Talleyrand: the art of survival. by Jean Orieux. Patricia Wolf, trans. (N. Bliven) 50: 146-50 My20'74. B 4216
The tamarind seed. (Gilliatt) 50:58-61 Jy15'74. CC 4217
The taming of the shrew. by William Shakespeare. (Oliver) 47:69 F12'72; 50:108-109 Mr18'74. T 4218
Tangier buzzless flies. by John Hopkins. (Anon.) 48:147 Ap 15'72. B 4219
Taris. (Gilliatt) 48:71-3 S23'72. CC 4220
Teddy bear. by Georges Simenon. Henry Clay, trans. (Anon.) 47:114-15 F19'72. B 4221
Tell me that you love me, Junie Moon. (Gilliatt) 46:54-6 Jy11'70. CC 4222
The tempest. by William Shake-

speare. (Oliver) 50:83-4 F25'74. T 4223
Ten days' wonder. (Gilliatt) 48:94-6 My6'72. CC 4224
Ten from your show of shows. (Kael) 49:92-6 Mr3'73. CC 4225
10 Rillington Place. (Gilliatt) 47:72-3 My22'71. CC 4226
Ten years of exile. by Anne Louise Germaine Staël-Holstein. Doris Beik, trans. (Anon.) 48:111-12 F17'73. B 4227
The tenants. by Bernard Malamud. (Anon.) 47:130 O2'71. B 4228
Terminal. by Susan Yankowitz. (Oliver) 46:50-1 Je6'70. T 4229
The terminal man. by Michael Crichton. (Anon.) 48:145 My 13'72. B 4230
Terraces. by Steve Carter. (Oliver) 50:103-104 Ap22'74. T 4231
That championship season. by Jason Miller. (Oliver) 48:99-100 My13'72; (Gill) 48:119 O 28'72. T 4232
That simple light may rise out of complicated darkness. by Bread and Puppet Theatre. (Oliver) 48:50 D23'72. T 4233
That's entertainment. by Howard Dietz [and] Arthur Schwartz. (Gill) 48:108-10 Ap22'72. T 4234
That's entertainment! (Gilliatt) 50:104-107 Je10'74. CC 4235
Theophilus North. by Thornton Wilder. (Anon.) 49:179-80 O29'73. B 4236
There was a crooked man... (Kael) 46:65 Ja9'71. CC 4237
There will be a short interval. by Storm Jameson. (Anon.) 49:135 My26'73. B 4238
There's one in every marriage. by Georges Feydeau. (Gill) 47:70 Ja15'72. T 4239
These splendored isles: the scenic beauty of Japan. by Magoichi Kushida. (Anon.) 46:190-1 O17'70. B 4240
They call me Mister Tibbs! (Gilliatt) 46:47 Jy18'70. CC 4241
They can't hang me! by Jacqueline Mallet. (Anon.) 50:203 O14'74. B 4242
They could not trust the king. by William V. Shannon. (Anon.) 49:111 F4'74. B 4243
The thief who came to dinner. (Kael) 49:113-15 Mr10'73. CC 4244
Thieves. by Herb Gardner. (Gill) 50:104-106 Ap15'74. T 4245
Thieves like us. (Kael) 49:92-6 F4'74. CC 4246
Thing to love. by Geoffrey Household. (Sissman) 47:128 My1'71. B 4247
The things of life. (Gilliatt) 46:64-6 S5'70. CC 4248
Things to come: thinking about the Seventies and Eighties. by Herman Kahn [and] B. Bruce-Briggs. (Anon.) 48:80 Ag19'72. B 4249
Thinking is child's play. by Evelyn Sharp. (Coles) 46:166-70 Ap11'70. B 4250
The third book of criticism. by Randall Jarrell. (Anon.) 46:156 Mr14'70. B 4251
The third life of Grange Copeland. by Alice Walker. (Coles) 47:104-106 F27'71. B 4252
36. (Flanner) 46:90-1 Mr7'70. CC 4253
This bright day: an autobiography. by Lehman Engel. (Anon.) 50:136 Ap29'74. B 4254
This earth, my brother... by Kofi Awoonor. (Updike) 47:190-2 N13'71. B 4255
This man must die. (Kael) 46:131-2 O31'70. CC 4256
Thoughts. by Lamar Alford. (Oliver) 49:77 Mr31'73. T 4257

Three. by Sylvia Ashton-Warner. (Anon.) 46:100 My30'70. B 4258
365 days. by Ronald J. Glasser. (Anon.) 47:140-1 S25'71. B 4259
Three mobs: Labor, Church, and Mafia. by Wilfrid Sheed. (Anon.) 50:84 D23'74. B 4260
The three musketeers. (Gilliatt) 50:111-12 Ap8'74. CC 4261
Three sisters. by Anton Chekhov. (Gill) 49:42 D31'73. T 4262
Three trapped tigers. by G. Cabrera Infante. Donald Gardner, trans. [and] Suzanne Jill Levine, trans. (Updike) 47:91-3 Ja29'72. B 4263
Thunder on Sunday. by Karen Campbell. (Anon.) 49:132 Mr 17'73. B 4264
Tied up in tinsel. by Ngaio Marsh. (Anon.) 48:116 My27'72. B 4265
Tigers are better-looking. by Jean Rhys. (Moss) 50:166 D 16'74. B 4266
Time on the cross: the economics of American Negro slavery. by Robert William Fogel [and] Stanley L. Engerman. (N. Bliven) 50:128-30 S30'74. B 4267
The time that was then. by Harry Roskolenko. (Anon.) 47:88 Jy17'71. B 4268
Time was. by Richard Berczeller. (Anon.) 47:131-2 My1'71. B 4269
The "Times" of London anthology of detective stories. by Times (London). (Anon.) 49:220 N 12'73. B 4270
Tinker, tailor, soldier, spy. by John le Carré. (Anon.) 50:83 Jy22'74. B 4271
To die of love. (Kael) 48:92-3 Mr4'72. CC 4272
To kill a cat. by W. J. Burley. (Anon.) 46:96 Ja30'71. B 4273
To live another Summer, to pass another Winter. by Hayim Hefer [and] Dov Seltzer. (Gill) 47:102 O30'71. T 4274
To serve them all my days. by R. F. Delderfield. (Anon.) 48:195 N4'72. B 4275
To the Finland Station. by Edmund Wilson. (Pritchett) 48:75-8 D23'72. B 4276
Together: a reporter's journey into the new black politics. by L. H. Whittemore. (Anon.) 47:141-2 S25'71. B 4277
Tokyo story. (Gilliatt) 48:102-106 Ap8'72. CC 4278
The toll. by Michael Mewshaw. (Anon.) 50:140-1 Ap8'74. B 4279
Tolstoy, my father. by Ilya Tolstoy. Ann Dunnigan, trans. (Anon.) 48:146-7 My6'72. B 4280
Tolstoy: the making of a novelist. by Edward Crankshaw. (Anon.) 50:135-6 Ap29'74. B 4281
Tomorrow. (Gilliatt) 48:124-5 Ap15'72. CC 4282
The tooth merchant. by C. L. Sulzberger. (Anon.) 49:114 Mr3'73. B 4283
The tooth of crime. by Sam Shepard. (Oliver) 49:92-4 Mr17'73. T 4284
Toro! Toro! Toro! by William Hjortsberg. (Anon.) 50:175-7 O7'74. B 4285
Total eclipse. by Christopher Hampton. (Oliver) 50:102-104 Mr11'74. T 4286
Touch. by Kenn Long [and] Jim Crozier. (Oliver) 46:132 D12'70. T 4287
The touch. (Gilliatt) 47:57-8 Jy24'71. CC 4288
A touch of class. (Gilliatt) 49:57-9 Jy9'73. CC 4289
A touch of danger. by James Jones. (Anon.) 49:136 My 26'73. B 4290
Touch the water touch the wind. by Amos Oz. Nicholas de Lange, trans. (Anon.) 50:

233-4 N18'74. B 4291
Touching. by Gwen Davis. (Anon.) 47:135 Mr13'71. B 4292
Tough to get help. by Steve Gordon. (Gill) 48:99 My13'72. T 4293
The towering inferno. (Kael) 50: 59 D30'74. CC 4294
The traces of Thomas Hariot. by Muriel Rukeyser. (Anon.) 47: 147-8 Ap17'71. B 4295
Traffic. (Kael) 48:132 D16'72. CC 4296
The tragi-comedy of Pen Browning. by Maisie Ward. (Anon.) 48:92 Ja13'73. B 4297
Train whistle guitar. by Albert Murray. (Anon.) 50:83 Jy22'74. B 4298
Tramp, tramp, tramp. (Gilliatt) 47:133-4 Ap24'71. CC 4299
Transparent things. by Vladimir Nabokov. (Updike) 48:242-5 N18'72. B 4300
Trash. (Kael) 46:132-7 O10'70. CC 4301
Travelers. by Ruth Prawer Jhabvala. (Pritchett) 49:106-109 Je16'73. B 4302
Travels in the south of France. by Marie Henri Beyle. Elisabeth Abbott, trans. (Anon.) 46:209 N14'70. B 4303
Travels with my aunt. by Graham Greene. (Sissman) 46:110-14 F28'70. B 4304
Travels with my aunt. (Kael) 48:85-6 Ja13'73. CC 4305
Treasure. by A. E. Hotchner. (Anon.) 46:119 Je20'70. B 4306
The treasure of Sutton Hoo. by Bernice Grohskopf. (Anon.) 46:155 My16'70. B 4307
Trelawney of the Wells. by Arthur Wing Pinero. (Oliver) 46:129-30 O24'70. T 4308
Trial and terror. Joan Kahn, ed. (Anon.) 49:184 O29'73. B 4309
The trial of Billy Jack. (Kael) 50:180-3 N25'74. CC 4310
The trial of the Catonsville Nine. by Saul Levitt [and] Daniel Berrigan. (Oliver) 47:90 F 20'71. T 4311
The trial of the Catonsville Nine. (Gilliatt) 48:107-108 My20'72. CC 4312
The trials of OZ. by Geoff Robertson. (Oliver) 48:47 D30'72. B 4313
Trick baby. (Kael) 48:92-4 F 10'73. CC 4314
Tricks. by Jean Baptiste Pouquelin Molière [and] Jon Jory [and] Jerry Blatt [and] Lonnie Burstein. (Gill) 48: 59 Ja20'73. T 4315
The trilogy of Alexander Sukhovo-Kobylin. by Alexander Sukhovo-Kobylin. Harold B. Segal, trans. (Wilson) 48:153 Mr18'72. B 4316
Trio. by Nathan Teitel. (Oliver) 50:60 O21'74. T 4317
Triple echo. (Kael) 49:183-5 N26'73. CC 4318
Tristana. (Gilliatt) 46:123-4 S 26'70. CC 4319
Tristes tropiques. by Claude Lévi-Strauss. John Weightman, trans. [and] Doreen Weightman, trans. (Steiner) 50:100-108 Je3'74. B 4320
Troilus and Cressida. by William Shakespeare. (Oliver) 49:100 D17'73. T 4321
The Trojan women. (Kael) 47: 155-61 O16'71. CC 4322
Trojan women. by Euripides. Andrei Serban, adapt. [and] Elizabeth Swados, adapt. (Oliver) 50:124-6 N4'74. T 4323
Tropic of Cancer. (Kael) 46:95-8 Mr7'70. CC 4324
Trouble in paradise. (Gilliatt) 48:50 Jy22'72. CC 4325
Troubles. by J. G. Farrell. (Anon.) 47:139-40 S25'71. B 4326
Truck. by Katherine Dunn. (Anon.) 47:140 S25'71. B 4327

True patriotism. by Dietrich Bonhoeffer. Edwin H. Robertson, ed. and trans. [and] John Bowden, trans. (Anon.) 49: 110 F4'74. B 4328

Truth to life: the art of biography in the Nineteenth Century. by A. O. J. Cockshut. (N. Bliven) 50:62-3 D30'74. B 4329

Tuesday the rabbi saw red. by Harry Kemelman. (Anon.) 50: 152 Mr18'74. B 4330

Twelfth night. by William Shakespeare. (Gill) 48:83 Mr11'72. T 4331

The twelve chairs. (Kael) 46:162-3 N7'70. CC 4332

Twelve trains to Babylon. by Alfred Connable. (Anon.) 47: 180 O23'71. B 4333

Twentieth-century Germany: from Bismark to Brandt. by A. J. Ryder. (Anon.) 49:154-5 S17'73. B 4334

The twenty-fifth hour. by Mary Kelly. (Anon.) 48:125 Mr11'72. B 4335

Twice over lightly: New York then and now. by Helen Hayes [and] Anita Loos. (Anon.) 48: 134-5 S23'72. B 4336

Twice retired. by Richard Lockridge. (Anon.) 46:120 Je13'70. B 4337

Twigs. by George Furth. (Gill) 47:112-14 N20'71. T 4338

Twilight of the day. by Mervyn Jones. (Anon.) 50:97-8 Ja 20'75. B 4339

The twilight of the presidency. by George Reedy. (Anon.) 46: 166-8 Ap18'70. B 4340

Two: a phallic novel. by Alberto Moravia. Angus Davidson, trans. (Anon.) 48:141 Ap29'72. B 4341

Two by two. by Martin Charnin [and] Richard Rodgers [and] Peter Stone. (Gill) 46:103 N 21'70. T 4342

Two English girls. (Kael) 48: 148-51 O14'72. CC 4343

Two gentlemen of Verona. by William Shakespeare. John Guare, adapt. [and] Mel Shapiro, adapt. (Gill) 47:101 D 11'71. T 4344

Two if by sea. by Priscilla B. Dewey [and] Charles Werner Moore [and] Tony Hutchins. (Oliver) 47:82 F19'72. T 4345

Two mules for Sister Sara. (Gilliatt) 46:56 Jy11'70. CC 4346

Two or three things I know about her. (Gilliatt) 46:102-104 My2'70. CC 4347

Two people. (Kael) 49:127-8 Mr24'73. CC 4348

Two virgins. by Kamala Markandaya. (Anon.) 49:174 O22'73. B 4349

A two-car funeral. by John Hough, Jr. (Anon.) 49:180 O29'73. B 4350

Two-lane blacktop. (Gilliatt) 47:55 Jy10'71. CC 4351

U

The ultra secret. by F. W. Winterbotham. (Anon.) 50: 64 D30'74. B 4352

Ulysses in nighttown. by James Joyce. Marjorie Barkentin, adapt. (Gill) 50:107 Mr18'74. T 4353

Unbidden guests. by Lael Wertenbaker. (Anon.) 46:195 D12'70. B 4354

Uncle Vanya. (Gilliatt) 48:103-106 My27'72. CC 4355

Uncle Vanya. by Anton Chekhov. (Gill) 49:88 Je9'73. T 4356

Under Milk Wood. (Kael) 48:94-5 F10'73. CC 4357

Under the guns: New York: 1775-76. by Bruce Bliven, Jr. (Anon.) 48:79 Ag26'72. B 4358

Undercurrent. by Bill Pronzini. (Anon.) 49:156 S17'73. B 4359

The underground woman. by Kay

Boyle. (Anon.) 50:97 Ja20'75. B 4360
The understudy. by Elia Kazan. (Anon.) 50:102 Ja27'75. B 4361
Une femme douce. (Gilliatt) 47: 79-81 My29'71. CC 4362
The uneasy chair: a biography of Bernard De Voto. by Wallace Stegner. (Anon.) 50:143 Mr25'74. B 4363
The unexpected universe. by Loren Eiseley. (Auden) 46:118-25 F 21'70. B 4364
United Nations journal: a delegate's odyssey. by William F. Buckley, Jr. (Anon.) 50:201 O14'74. B 4365
Unlikely heroes. by Larry Arrick. (Gill) 47:115 N6'71. T 4366
The unnatural history of the nanny. by Jonathan Gathorne-Hardy. (Anon.) 49:88 Ag13'73. B 4367
Unsecular man: the persistence of religion. by Andrew M. Greeley. (Anon.) 49:114-15 Mr3'73. B 4368
The unseen hand. by Sam Shepard. (Oliver) 46:82-3 Ap11'70. T 4369
An unsuitable job for a woman. by P. D. James. (Anon.) 49:80 Jy23'73. B 4370
The unwritten war: American writers and the Civil War. by Daniel Aaron. (Anon.) 49:199-200 N26'73. B 4371
Up in the cellar. (Gilliatt) 46: 51-2 Ag29'70. CC 4372
Up the organization. by Robert Townsend. (Sissman) 46:161-6 Ap18'70. B 4373
Up the sandbox! by Anne Richardson Roiphe. (Sissman) 47:145-7 Ap17'71. B 4374
Up the sandbox! (Kael) 48:48-9 D30'72. CC 4375
The upstart. by Piers Paul Read. (Anon.) 49:87 Ag13'73. B 4376
Uptown Saturday night. (Gilliatt) 50:88-90 Je17'74. CC 4377

V

V. Sackville-West's garden book. by Victoria Sackville-West. Philippa Nicolson, ed. (White) 46:125-6 Mr28'70. B 4378
Valdez is coming. (Gilliatt) 47: 98 Ap17'71. CC 4379
The vantage point: perspectives of the presidency 1963-1969. by Lyndon Baines Johnson. (Anon.) 47:199-200 N13'71. B 4380
Variety Obit. by Ron Whyte. (Oliver) 49:82-3 F24'73. T 4381
Vegas: a memoir of a dark season. by John Gregory Dunne. (Anon.) 50:135-6 Mr 11'74. B 4382
The velvet jungle. by Gene Horowitz. (Anon.) 47:82 Ag 7'71. B 4383
The Venice train. by Georges Simenon. Alastair Hamilton, trans. (Anon.) 50:92 Ag19'74. B 4384
Veronica's room. by Ira Levin. (Gill) 49:89 N5'73. T 4385
Via Galactia. by Christopher Gore [and] Judith Ross [and] Galt MacDermot. (Gill) 48: 109 D9'72. T 4386
The victim is always the same. by I. S. Cooper. (Coles) 50: 131-4 Ap29'74. B 4387
Victoria and her daughters. by Nina Epton. (Anon.) 47:95 Ja29'72. B 4388
Victorian and Edwardian London from old photographs. by John Betjeman. (Anon.) 46: 140 My23'70. B 4389
Victorian children. by Graham Ovenden [and] Robert Melville. (Anon.) 49:119 Mr31'73. B 4390
Victorian outsider: a biography of J. A. M. Whistler. by Roy McMullen. (Anon.) 49:199-200 D10'73. B 4391
The Victorian woman. by Duncan Crow. (Anon.) 48:143 Ap22'72.

B 4392
Viet journal. by James Jones.
 (Anon.) 50:142-3 Ap8'74. B
 4393
The virgin and the gypsy. (Gilliatt)
 46:71 Jy4'70. CC 4394
Virginia Fly is drowning. by
 Angela Huth. (Anon.) 49:114-15
 Je9'73. B 4395
Virginia Woolf. by Quentin Bell.
 (Maxwell) 48:88-96 F3'73. B
 4396
Visions of Cody. by Jack Kerouac.
 (Anon.) 48:110 F17'73. B
 4397
Visions of eight. (Gilliatt) 49:69-
 71 Ag20'73. CC 4398
The visit. by Friedrich Dürren-
 matt. (Gill) 49:111 D10'73.
 T 4399
A visit to Portugal, 1866. by
 Hans Christian Andersen. Grace
 Thornton, trans. (Anon.) 49:
 176 O22'73. B 4400
Vivat! Vivat Regina! by Robert
 Bolt. (Panter-Downes) 46:160-1
 N14'70; (Gill) 47:72 Ja29'72.
 T 4401
Vladimir and Rosa. (Gilliatt) 47:
 116-19 My8'71. CC 4402
The voice of the crab. by
 Charlotte Jay. (Anon.) 50:130
 S30'74. B 4403
Voices. by Richard Lortz. (Gill)
 48:108 Ap15'72. T 4404
The voices of the silent. by
 Cornelia Gerstenmaier. Susan
 Hecker, trans. (Anon.) 49:
 115 Mr3'73. B 4405
The von Richthofen sisters: the
 triumphant and the tragic modes
 of love. by Martin Green.
 (Anon.) 50:142-3 Mr25'74. B
 4406
Voyage in the dark. by Jean Rhys.
 (Moss) 50:161-6 D16'74. B
 4407
The voyage of the Franz Joseph.
 by James Yaffe. (Anon.) 46:
 83 Jy18'70. B 4408
Voyage to the first of December.
 by Henry Carlisle. (Anon.) 47:
 115 F19'72. B 4409

W

WUSA. (Kael) 46:164-5 N7'70.
 CC 4410
The wager. by Mark Medoff.
 (Oliver) 50:124 N4'74. T
 4411
Wait, just you wait. by Evelyn
 Berckman. (Anon.) 50:92
 Ag19'74. B 4412
Waiting for Godot. by Samuel
 Beckett. (Oliver) 46:78-80
 F13'71. T 4413
Waiting for the party: the life
 of Frances Hodgson Burnett.
 by Ann Thwaite. (Anon.) 50:
 190 O21'74. B 4414
Waiting out a war: the exile of
 Private John Picciano. by
 Lucinda Franks. (Anon.) 50:
 98-9 Ag12'74. B 4415
Wake up dead men. by Bruce
 Jackson. (N. Bliven) 48:74
 Jy8'72. B 4416
A walk in the Dolomites. by
 Caroline Neilson. (Anon.)
 46:162-3 My9'70. B 4417
Walkabout. (Gilliatt) 47:55
 Jy10'71. CC 4418
Walking Davis. by David Ely.
 (Anon.) 48:245 N18'72. B
 4419
Walking tall. (Kael) 50:100-106
 F25'74. CC 4420
Walls: resisting the third Reich
 --one woman's story. by
 Hiltgunt Zassenhaus. (Anon.)
 50:113-14 Mr4'74. B 4421
The waltz emperors. by Joseph
 Wechsberg. (Anon.) 49:59
 D31'73. B 4422
The waltz of the toreadors. by
 Jean Anouilh. (Gill) 49:59
 O1'73. T 4423
Wanda. (Kael) 47:138-40 Mr20'
 71. CC 4424
The wanderers. by Ezekiel
 Mphahlele. (Updike) 47:192-4
 N13'71. B 4425
The wanderers. by Richard
 Price. (Anon.) 50:150 My
 20'74. B 4426
Wanted. by David Epstein [and]

Al Carmines. (Oliver) 47:74 Ja29'72. T 4427
The war against Russia, 1854-1856. by A. J. Barker. (Anon.) 47:88 Ag14'71. B 4428
The war between men and women. (Gilliatt) 48:68 Je17'72. CC 4429
The war between the Tates. by Alison Lurie. (Anon.) 50:89 Ag19'74. B 4430
War of time. by Alejo Carpentier. Frances Partridge, trans. (West) 46:188-9 N28'70. B 4431
War without heroes. by David Douglas Duncan. (Sissman) 46:188-95 D12'70. B 4432
Warp. by Bury St. Edmund [and] Stuart Gordon. (Gill) 49:81 F 24'73. T 4433
The wartime journals of Charles A. Lindbergh, 1938-45. by Charles A. Lindbergh. (Anon.) 46:155-6 O31'70. B 4434
The waste land. by T. S. Eliot. Valerie Eliot, ed. (Steiner) 48:138-42 Ap22'72. B 4435
Watcher in the shadows. by Geoffrey Household. (Sissman) 47:127-8 My1'71. B 4436
Waterloo. (Gilliatt) 47:130-5 Ap10'71. CC 4437
Watermelon man. (Gilliatt) 46:85 Je6'70. CC 4438
The water-method man. by John Irving. (Anon.) 48:78 Jy22'72. B 4439
Watership Down. by Richard Adams. (Anon.) 50:122-3 Ap 1'74. B 4440
The way of the world. by William Congreve. (Oliver) 50:85 F 25'74. T 4441
The way we were. (Kael) 49:158-60 O15'73. CC 4442
We all went to Paris. by Stephen Longstreet. (Anon.) 48:143 Ap 29'72. B 4443
We can't breathe. by Ronald Fair. (Anon.) 47:103 F5'72. B 4444
We have all gone away. by Curtis Harnack. (Anon.) 49:131 Mr 17'73. B 4445
We talk, you listen: new tribes, new turf. by Vine Deloria, Jr. (Anon.) 46:176 O24'70. B 4446
The web and the rock. Dolores Sutton, adapt. (Oliver) 48:67-8 Ap1'72. T 4447
Wedding band. by Alice Childress. (Oliver) 48:105 N4'72. T 4448
Wedding in blood. (Gilliatt) 50: 97 Je3'74. CC 4449
Wedding in white. (Gilliatt) 49: 81-3 My19'73. CC 4450
The wedding of Iphigenia plus Iphigenia in concert. by Euripides. Doug Dyer, adapt. [and] Peter Link, adapt. [and] Gretchen Cryer, adapt. (Oliver) 47:57 D25'71. T 4451
Weeds. by Edith Summers Kelley. (Anon.) 48:177 D9'72. B 4452
Weeds and wildflowers of Eastern North America. by T. Merrill Prentice [and] Elizabeth Owen Sargent. (Anon.) 49:200 D10'73. B 4453
The weekend man. by Richard B. Wright. (Anon.) 47:114 Je12'71. B 4454
Weekend murders. (Gilliatt) 48: 69-70 Je17'72. CC 4455
Welcome to Andromeda. by Ron Whyte. (Oliver) 49:82 F24'73. T 4456
Wellington: pillar of state. by Elizabeth Longford. (N. Bliven) 49:131-3 Ap21'73. B 4457
Wellington: the years of the sword. by Elizabeth Longford. (N. Bliven) 46:76-82 Je27'70. B 4458
A well-told lie. by Christina Hobhouse. (Anon.) 49:134 Ap21'73. B 4459
West of the Rockies. by Daniel Fuchs. (Updike) 47:176-9 O23'71. B 4460

The Western coast. by Paula Fox. (Anon.) 48:158 O28'72. B 4461
Westworld. (Kael) 49:183 N26'73. CC 4462
What became of Jane Austen? and other questions. by Kingsley Amis. (Anon.) 47:230 N20'71. B 4463
What if it had turned up heads. by J. E. Gaines. (Oliver) 48: 120-1 O28'72. T 4464
What the butler saw. by Joe Orton. (Oliver) 46:106-107 My 16'70. T 4465
What the wine sellers buy. by Ron Milner. (Oliver) 49:56 My 26'73; (Gill) 50:83 F25'74. T 4466
What the woman lived: selected letters of Louise Bogan, 1920-70. by Louise Bogan. Ruth Limmer, ed. (Anon.) 49:219-20 N12'73. B 4467
Whatever became of sin? by Karl Menninger. (Anon.) 49:175 O 22'73. B 4468
What's a nice country like you doing in a state like this? by Ira Gasman [and] Cary Hoffman. (Oliver) 49:81-2 My5'73. T 4469
What's up, doc? (Kael) 48:121-5 Mr25'72. CC 4470
When even angels wept: the Senator Joseph McCarthy affair--a story without a hero. by Lately Thomas. (Anon.) 48:112 F17'73. B 4471
When in Rome. by Ngaio Marsh. (Anon.) 47:116 Je12'71. B 4472
When the snow comes, they will take you away. by Eric Newby. (Sissman) 48:108-109 Je3'72. B 4473
When you comin' back, Red Ryder? by Mark Medoff. (Oliver) 49: 99 D17'73. T 4474
Where am I now--when I need me? by George Axelrod. (Anon.) 47:91 My29'71. B 4475
Where do we go from here? by John Ford Noonan. (Oliver) 50:107 N11'74. T 4476
Where has last July gone? by Drew Middleton. (Anon.) 50: 151-2 Mr18'74. B 4477
Where has Tommy Flowers gone? by Terrence McNally. (Oliver) 47:101 O16'71. T 4478
Where the wasteland ends: politics and transcendence in postindustrial society. by Theodore Roszak. (Anon.) 48:126 S30'72. B 4479
Where's Charley? by George Abbott [and] Frank Loesser. (Gill) 50:52-3 D30'74. T 4480
Where's Poppa? (Kael) 46:166-8 N14'70. CC 4481
Whiskey. by Terrence McNally. (Oliver) 49:69 My12'73. T 4482
Whispers on the wind. by Lor Crane [and] John B. Kuntz. (Oliver) 46:90-2 Je13'70. T 4483
Whistler: a biography. by Stanley Weintraub. (Anon.) 49:119 F18'74. B 4484
The white dawn. by James A. Houston. (Anon.) 47:126-7 My22'71. B 4485
The white generals. by Richard Luckett. (Anon.) 47:231-2 N20'71. B 4486
A White House diary. by Lady Bird Johnson. (Anon.) 46:64 D26'70. B 4487
The White House murder case. by Jules Feiffer. (Oliver) 46:78-9 F28'70. T 4488
White knight: the rise of Spiro Agnew. by Jules Witcover. (Anon.) 48:142-3 Ap22'72. B 4489
The white land. by William Dieter. (Anon.) 46:154 My 16'70. B 4490
White niggers of America: the precocious autobiography of a Quebec "terrorist." by

Pierre Vallières. Joan Pinkham, trans. (Anon.) 47:147-8 My15'71. B 4491
The white use of blacks in America. by Dan Lacy. (Anon.) 48:131 Ap8'72. B 4492
Who is Harry Kellerman and why is he saying those terrible things about me? (Gilliatt) 47:56-7 Jy10'71. CC 4493
Who killed the British Empire? by George Woodcock. (Anon.) 50:82-3 Ja6'75. B 4494
Who needs the Democrats; and what it takes to be needed. by John Kenneth Galbraith. (Anon.) 46:80 Jy25'70. B 4495
Who pushed Humpty Dumpty?: dilemmas in American education today. by Donald Barr. (Anon.) 47:171-2 O9'71. B 4496
Who's who in hell. by Peter Ustinov. (Gill) 50:53 D23'74. T 4497
Why can't they be like us? America's white ethnic groups. by Andrew M. Greeley. (N. Bliven) 47:225-9 N20'71. B 4498
Why justice fails. by Whitney North Seymour, Jr. (Anon.) 49:154 D17'73. B 4499
Wide Sargasso Sea. by Jean Rhys. (Moss) 50:161-6 D16'74. B 4500
The Wilby conspiracy. by Peter Driscoll. (Anon.) 48:184 O14'72. B 4501
Wild excursions: the life and fiction of Laurence Sterne. by David Thomson. (Anon.) 49:132 F24'73. B 4502
Wild flowers of Connecticut. by John E. Klimas, Jr. (White) 46:116-20 Mr28'70. B 4503
Wild flowers of the United States, volume III: Texas. by Harold William Rickett. (White) 46:116 Mr28'70. B 4504
Wild flowers of the United States, volume IV: the south-western states. by Harold William Rickett. (Anon.) 46:192 N28'70. B 4505
A wild justice. by Francis Clifford. (Anon.) 48:77-8 Ag12'72. B 4506
Wild pitch. by A. B. Guthrie, Jr. (Anon.) 49:130 F24'73. B 4507
Will Rogers' U.S.A. by Will Rogers. Paul Shyre, adapt. (Gill) 50:100 My20'74. T 4508
Willard. (Gilliatt) 47:65 Ag7'71. CC 4509
Willem de Kooning drawings. by Thomas B. Hess. (Anon.) 49:119-20 Mr31'73. B 4510
William and Mary. by Henri van der Zee [and] Barbara van der Zee. (Anon.) 49:71 Jy 9'73. B 4511
William Cullen Bryant. by Charles H. Brown. (Anon.) 47:95 Ja29'72. B 4512
William Dean Howells: an American life. by Kenneth S. Lynn. (Anon.) 47:88 Je19'71. B 4513
Willy remembers. by Irvin Faust. (Anon.) 47:229 N20'71. B 4514
Wilson in the promise land. by Roland Van Zandt. (Gill) 46:49-50 Je6'70. T 4515
Winckelmann. by Wolfgang Leppmann. (Anon.) 46:190 N28'70. B 4516
The winds of war. by Herman Wouk. (Anon.) 47:135 D18'71. B 4517
The wine of astonishment. by Rachel MacKenzie. (Anon.) 50:108 Je3'74. B 4518
Wings. (Gilliatt) 47:104-106 S25'71. CC 4519
Winslow Homer. by John Wilmerding. (Anon.) 48:248 N 18'72. B 4520
Winter in Castille. by Honor Tracy. (Anon.) 49:110 F4'74. B 4521
Winter in the blood. by James Welch. (Anon.) 50:84 D23'74. B 4522
A Winter in the hills. by John

Wain. (Sissman) 46:206-207 N 14'70. B 4523
The Winter of the fisher. by Cameron Langford. (Anon.) 47:92 Je26'71. B 4524
The Winter soldiers. by Richard M. Ketchum. (Anon.) 49:115 Je9'73. B 4525
Wise child. by Simon Gray. (Gill) 47:69 F5'72. T 4526
The wise minority. by Leon Friedman. (Anon.) 47:132 Mr 27'71. B 4527
Without apparent motive. (Kael) 48:88-9 Mr4'72. CC 4528
Without cloak or dagger: the truth about the new espionage. by Miles Copeland. (Anon.) 50: 144-5 S23'74. B 4529
Without Marx or Jesus. by Jean-François Revel. J. F. Bernard, trans. (Flanner) 47:92-3 F 27'71; (Anon.) 47:179-80 O 23'71. B 4530
Without stopping: an autobiography. by Paul Bowles. (Anon.) 48:131-2 Mr25'72. B 4531
Witness to history: 1929-69. by Charles E. Bohlen. (Anon.) 49:110-11 Je16'73. B 4532
Wittgenstein's Vienna. by Allan Janik [and] Stephen Toulmin. (Steiner) 49:73-7 Jy23'73. B 4533
The wiz. by William F. Brown [and] Charlie Smalls. (Gill) 50:64-5 Ja13'75. T 4534
Wolves in the city: the death of French Algeria. by Paul Henissart. (Anon.) 46:139 O 3'70. B 4535
The woman alone. by Patricia O'Brien. (Anon.) 49:135 S10'73. B 4536
A woman named Solitude. by André Schwarz-Bart. Ralph Manheim, trans. (Anon.) 48: 114 F10'73. B 4537
Woman of the year. (Gilliatt) 48:71 S23'72. CC 4538
A woman under the influence. (Kael) 50:172-8 D9'74. CC 4539
The women. by Clare Boothe. (Gill) 49:81 My5'73. T 4540
Women in love. (Kael) 46:97-101 Mr28'70. CC 4541
The wonder-worker. by Dan Jacobson. (Sissman) 50:101-102 Je24'74. B 4542
The wood demon. by Anton Chekhov. Ronald Hingley, trans. (Oliver) 49:71 F11'74. T 4543
Woodstock. (Gilliatt) 46:161-5 Ap11'70. CC 4544
Words & faces. by Hiram Haydn. (Anon.) 50:202 O 14'74. B 4545
Words and music. by Sammy Cahn. (Gill) 50:63 Ap29'74. T 4546
Words and occasions: an anthology of speeches and articles selected from his papers by the right honourable Lester B. Pearson. by Lester B. Pearson. (Anon.) 46:88 Ja 9'71. B 4547
Words for a deaf daughter. by Paul West. (Anon.) 46:176 O24'70. B 4548
Words with music. by Lehman Engel. (Anon.) 48:112 Je 3'72. B 4549
The workhouse. by Norman Longmate. (Anon.) 50:194-6 N25'74. B 4550
The world of Charles Dickens. by Angus Wilson. (Anon.) 46:137 S19'70. B 4551
The world of George Orwell. Miriam Gross, ed. (Anon.) 48:156 Mr18'72. B 4552
The world of the Japanese garden, from Chinese origins to modern landscape art. by Loren Kuck. (White) 46:120 Mr28'70. B 4553
World without borders. by Lester R. Brown. (Anon.) 48: 247-8 N18'72. B 4554
World without end, amen. by Jimmy Breslin. (Sissman) 49:168-9 O8'73. B 4555

The wreck of the Penn Central. by Joseph R. Daughen [and] Peter Binzen. (Anon.) 47:68 D 25'71. B 4556

The writings of Anna Freud. by Anna Freud. (Coles) 48:129-31 S23'72. B 4557

X

X Y & Zee. (Kael) 47:84-7 F 12'72. CC 4558

Xerxes at Salamis. by Peter Green. (Anon.) 47:151 Mr20'71. B 4559

Xingu: the Indians, their myths. by Orlando Villas Boas [and] Claudio Villas Boas. Susana Hertelendy Rudge, trans. (Updike) 50:140-7 S16'74. B 4560

Y

The year of the dragon. by Frank Chin. (Oliver) 50:64 Je10'74. T 4561

The yellow Summer. by Suzanne Prou. (Anon.) 48:146 My13'72. B 4562

Yerma. by Federico García Lorca. (Oliver) 48:119-20 O28'72. T 4563

Yet she must die. by Sara Woods. (Anon.) 50:114-15 Mr 4'74. B 4564

Yin yang. by Joseph A. Walker [and] Dorothy A. Dinroe. (Oliver) 49:89 Je9'73. T 4565

Yonnondio: from the Thirties. by Tillie Olsen. (Anon.) 50:140-1 Mr25'74. B 4566

Young Frankenstein. (Kael) 50: 58-9 D30'74. CC 4567

The young Lenin. by Leon Trotsky. Max Eastman, trans. Maurice Friedberg, ed. (Anon.) 48:127 S16'72. B 4568

Young Mr. Pepys. by John E. N. Hearsey. (Anon.) 50:84 Jy22'74. B 4569

Young Winston. (Kael) 48:147-8 O14'72. CC 4570

Your mirror to my times. by Ford Madox Ford. Michael Killigrew, ed. (Steiner) 47: 98-102 F12'72. B 4571

Youth and dissent: the rise of a new opposition. by Kenneth Keniston. (Anon.) 47:201 N 13'71. B 4572

Z

Z. (Kael) 49:238-44 N19'73. CC 4573

Zabriskie Point. (Kael) 46:95-9 F21'70. CC 4574

Zardoz. (Kael) 49:98-100 F18'74. CC 4575

Zelda: a biography. by Nancy Milford. (Anon.) 46:80 Jy 25'70. B 4576

Zen and the art of motorcycle maintenance: an inquiry into values. by Robert M. Pirsig. (Steiner) 50:147-50 Ap15'74. B 4577

The Zuñis: self portrayals. by Anon. Alvina Quam, trans. (Coles) 48:109-14 F10'73. B 4578

Part III

NAME INDEX

Aaron, Daniel
4168, 4371
Aaron, Jonathan
334, 340, 548
Abbey, Edward
2095
Abbott, Elisabeth
2037, 4303
Abbott, George
3706, 4480
Abel, Elie
3936
Abell, Tyler
2514
Ableman, Paul
2891
Abraham, Henry J.
3125
Abrams, Charles
3175
Achebe, Chinua
2811
Ackerman, Robert Allan
3068
Acton, Harold
3464
Adams, Alice
1392, 1410, 1595, 2647
Adams, John
3102
Adams, Lee
1973
Adams, Leonard P., II
3795
Adams, Richard
4440
Adelman, Clifford
3610
Adelson, Leonard
3496
Adler, Alfred
1025
Adler, Renata
35, 230, 260, 318, 444, 653,
1339
Adler, Richard
3706
Aeschylus
2219, 3748
Aird, Catherine
4142
Ajayi, Afolabi
1886
Al Fann Theatrical Ensemble
3437
Albee, Edward
39, 1905, 4000
Albert, Allan
3832
Albertson, Chris
2065
Alexander, Herbert E.
3497
Alexandre, Philippe
2524
Alford, Lamar
4257
Alfred, William
2365, 2959
Alinsky, Saul D.
3948
Allegro, John M.
3960
Allen, Woody
462, 511, 656, 675, 753,
968, 978, 1444, 1458, 1782
Alonso, Nina
359
Alpers, Antony
3223
Alsop, Stewart
4145
Althaus, Keith
1818
Alvarez, A.
1133
Amabile, George
598, 660, 1106, 1777

Amadi, Elechi
2883
Ambler, Eric
2488, 3259
Amis, Kingsley
2582, 2810, 2892, 3924, 4463
Amis, Martin
3854
Amphoux, Nancy
2476
Anagnostopoulos, Athan
3793
Andersen, Hans Christian
4400
Anderson, Jervis
234, 446, 464
Anderson, Maxwell
3339
Anderson, Robert
4097
Angell, Roger
8, 141, 240, 466, 565, 697, 768, 770, 792, 853, 966, 1126, 1223, 1241, 1258, 1286, 1288, 1429, 1453, 1526, 1588, 1635, 1680, 2016r
Angelou, Maya
2781
Ann-Elizabeth
523
Anouilh, Jean
4423
Antonacci, Greg
2384
Aranha, Ray
3550
Arbib, Robert
3334
Arbus, Diane
2454
Arendt, Hannah
125, 305, 1367, 2354, 3658
Ariosto, Lodovico
3682
Aristophanes
3371, 3890
Arking, Linda
271, 1281
Arlen, Michael J.
36, 104, 513, 1243
Armbrister, Trevor
3632
Armstrong, Hamilton Fish
3734
Aronson, Theo
3128, 3845
Arrabal, Fernando
1946
Arrick, Larry
4366
Arrighi, Mel
2213
Arthur, Eric
2027
Artom, Guido
3564
Ashbery, John
301, 537, 1733, 1821
Asher, Linda
2670
Ashton, Dore
3590
Ashton-Warner, Sylvia
4258
Aston, Paul
2212
Astrachan, Anthony
3990r
Atwood, Margaret
425, 4193
Auchincloss, Louis
3003, 3722
Auden, W. H.
4, 14, 42, 227, 281, 378, 990, 1147, 1476, 1482, 1604, 1690, 1702, 1872r, 1964r, 2063r, 2220, 2699r, 2909r, 3249r, 3252r, 3254r, 4067r
Austin, Anthony
3813
Austin, Paul Britten
1957
Avery, Gillian
2541
Awoonor, Kofi
4255
Axelrod, George
4475
Ayckbourn, Alan
1843, 2991, 3299, 3621, 3945, 4205
Ayrton, Michael
2632

B

Bagley, Desmond
4130
Bailey, Anthony
886, 957, 1191, 1531, 1723
Bailey, John
38, 955, 1617
Bainbridge, Beryl
2921
Bainbridge, John
336
Baird, Thomas
3740
Baker, Leonard
2145
Bald, R. C.
3103
Baldwin, James
3015, 3862
Balliett, Whitney
43, 269, 385, 396, 639, 668, 725, 739, 810, 838, 937, 1057, 1076, 1078, 1131, 1216, 1316, 1333, 1337, 1405, 1623, 2065r
Baraka, Imamu Amiri
See Jones, Le Roi
Barber, Noel
4183
Barber, Richard J.
1923
Barber, Richard W.
3153
Barbour, Philip L.
3791
Barham, Richard Harris
3048
Barkentin, Marjorie
4353
Barker, A. J.
4428
Barker, Dudley
2770
Barlow, Anna Marie
1917
Barlow, Elizabeth
2723
Barnes, Djuna
1743
Barnes, Peter
3732
Barnet, Richard
617
Barr, Donald
4496
Barrault, Jean-Louis
3853
Barrett, James Lee
4041
Barry, Julian
3230
Barry, Philip
2961
Barry, Richard
4030
Barth, Alan
3831
Barth, John
2250
Barthelme, Donald
33, 214, 262, 303, 357, 391, 406, 423, 432, 470, 491, 544, 567, 610, 750, 871, 936, 1010, 1084, 1101, 1114, 1127, 1158, 1197, 1220, 1227, 1242, 1268, 1273, 1300, 1393, 1445, 1462, 1525, 1569, 1578, 1614, 1773, 1824, 1825, 1831, 1832
Barthes, Roland
3560
Barton, John
2963
Barzini, Luigi
2756
Bassani, Giorgio
2049
Bates, H. E.
2111
Batki, John
1107, 1571, 1629
Bawden, Nina
2084
Bayer, Carol
2792
Beaglehole, J. C.
3268
Beare, George
2040
Beattie, Ann
456, 528, 1285, 1811
Bebey, Francis
1874

Becerra de Jenkins, Lyll
1232, 1693
Beck, Evelyn Torton
1042
Beckett, Samuel
1850, 2048, 2581, 2913, 3081, 3155, 3624, 4413
Bedford, Sybille
1891
Beekman, E. M.
3729
Beerbohm, Max
3737
Behan, Brendan
2979, 4039
Behlmer, Rudy
3460
Behrman, S. N.
1259
Beik, Doris
4227
Belitt, Ben
490, 526, 1536, 1542, 1826
Bell, Daniel
2295
Bell, J. Bowyer
3559
Bell, Marvin
1535
Bell, Quentin
4396
Belloc, Hilaire
2055
Bellwood, Peter
2776
Beloff, Max
3021
Benchley, Nathaniel
3176
Benchley, Peter
1323, 3089
Bendiner, Robert
4168
Bennett, James V.
3002
Bennett, Michael
4009
Berckman, Evelyn
4412
Berczeller, Richard
1029, 1246, 1518, 4269
Berg, Stephen
743
Bergamini, David
3087
Berger, John
2769
Berger, Marilyn
926
Berger, Raoul
2621
Berger, Thomas
3882
Berger-Rioff, Suzanne
1675
Bergman, Ingmar
355
Bergstein, Eleanor
1856
Berle, Adolph A.
3576
Berle, Beatrice Bishop
3576
Bermant, Chaim
2345, 3191
Bernard, J. F.
4530
Bernstein, Burton
1153
Bernstein, Carl
1909
Bernstein, Jeremy
51, 414, 868, 1196, 1371, 1456, 1863r, 2079r, 3304r, 3730r, 3757r, 3956r
Bernstein, Leonard
2188
Berrigan, Daniel
2389, 4311
Berryman, John
403, 467, 842, 3875
Berteaut, Simone
3759
Berthier, Louis-Alexandre
1922
Beteta, Ramón
3088
Bethel, Nicholas
3189
Betjeman, John
962, 3762, 4389
Bettelheim, Bruno
2970

Beyle, Marie Henri
4303
Biddle, Sheila
2121
Billing, Graham
4086
Bingham, Madeleine
4044
Binzen, Peter
4556
Birstein, Ann
2460
Bishop, Elizabeth
267, 369, 562, 780, 1077, 1130, 1163, 1293, 1537, 1682, 1686
Bissell, Richard
3545, 3706
Bittker, Boris I.
2208
Black, Charles L., Jr.
2191
Blair, Alan
355
Blais, Marie-Claire
3421
Blanch, Leslie
3731
Blatt, Jerry
4315
Blau, Alan
355
Bliven, Bruce, Jr.
208, 1340, 1443, 2696, 2791r, 4358
Bliven, Naomi
1881r, 1968r, 1994r, 1999r, 2128r, 2225r, 2262r, 2280r, 2295r, 2300r, 2329r, 2339r, 2349r, 2359r, 2370r, 2459r, 2482r, 2542r, 2711r, 2820r, 2875r, 2943r, 2953r, 3038r, 3042r, 3087r, 3250r, 3383r, 3407r, 3421r, 3439r, 3455r, 3603r, 3653r, 3807r, 3846r, 3887r, 3910r, 3932r, 3935r, 4152r, 4216r, 4267r, 4329r, 4416r, 4457r, 4458r, 4498r
Blood Company
2108
Bloodworth, Dennis
2628
Blotner, Joseph
2664
Blount, Roy, Jr.
571
Blunt, Wilfrid
2842, 3659
Bluth, Fred
2510
Blyth, Henry
2203
Boas, Claudio Villas
Boas, Orlando Villas
See Villas Boas, Claudio
Villas Boas, Orlando
Bobrick, Sam
3608, 3622
Bock, Jerry
3943
Boelcke, Willi
4005
Bogan, Louise
3630, 4112, 4467
Bohlen, Charles E.
4532
Böll, Heinrich
2242
Bolt, Robert
4401
Bolton, Guy
3646
Bond, Edward
3567, 3980
Bonhoeffer, Dietrich
4328
Booker, Christopher
3581
Booth, George
798
Booth, Philip
1805
Boothe, Clare
4540
Boretz, Allen
3931
Borges, Jorge Luis
7, 22, 90, 131, 186, 273, 329, 472, 489, 508, 540, 631, 752, 817, 823, 1013, 1037, 1075, 1385, 1406, 1543, 1683, 1752, 2126
Borich, Michael
1596
Bosse, Malcolm
3417

Boswell, James
2137
Bothmer, Gerry
3556
Boucicault, Dion
3306
Boulle, Pierre
2037, 2443
Bouton, Jim
2016
Bovasso, Julie
3627, 4138
Bowden, John
4328
Bowen, Catherine Drinker
2650, 3511
Bowen, Elizabeth
3763
Bowers, John
2290, 3611
Bowles, Chester
3830
Bowles, Paul
3225, 4531
Boxer, Charles R.
3803
Boyd, Malcolm
1987
Boyer, Richard O.
3222
Boylan, Brian Richard
2058
Boyle, Kay
4360
Bradford, Ernle
4046
Bragg, Melvyn
3772
Braine, John
3843
Brandel, Marc
3416
Brandon, Johnny
2076
Braswell, John
2437, 2795
Braudel, Fernand
3455
Brauer, Jerold C.
3551
Bray, Barbara
2155, 3644
Brazell, Karen
2313
Bread and Puppet Theatre
4233
Brecht, Bertolt
2852, 3394, 3448
Brée, Germaine
2183
Brennan, Maeve
294, 527, 1555
Breslin, Jimmy
4555
Brewster, Townsend
3786
Brickman, Marshall
63, 837, 1356, 1707, 1770
Bridge, Ann
3120
Bridges, Lawrence
769
Bridgman, Richard
2796
Brillat-Savarin, Jean Anthelme
3758
Brinnin, John Malcolm
1438, 4196
Brisbane, Robert H.
2098
Brittan, Robert
3861
Broad, Jay
3142
Broch, Hermann
2898
Brock, Edwin
317
Brock, Van K.
1414
Brockett, Eleanor
3471
Brodeur, Paul
76, 261, 415, 492, 4173
Brodkey, Harold
1566
Bromell, Henry
139, 463, 684, 814, 1056,
1174, 1274, 1502
Brooke, Dinah
3353
Brooke, Sylvia
3844
Brookhouse, Christopher

3953
Brooks, Jeremy
2583
Brooks, John
75, 87, 243, 620, 809, 1019, 1559
Brophy, Brigid
3044
Brother Jonathan
2618
Broudy, Harry S.
3870
Brough, James
3933
Brower, Brock
3196
Brown, Anne S. K.
1922
Brown, Charles H.
4512
Brown, Dee
2171
Brown, Edward J.
3444
Brown, Joe David
1853
Brown, Lennox
2017
Brown, Lester R.
4554
Brown, Lew
2849
Brown, Michael
589, 2463
Brown, Steve
2657
Brown, William F.
4534
Browne, Michael Dennis
589
Browning, Elizabeth Barrett
3254
Browning, Robert
3254
Bruce, Robert V.
2053
Bruce-Briggs, B.
4249
Brund, Jerry
1855
Brundage, James A.
3899
Buchan, Perdita
976
Buckley, William F., Jr.
1764, 2731, 4365
Budberg, Moura
2736, 3687
Budgen, Frank
3555
Buechner, Frederick
3348, 3674
Buffet-Challié, Laurence
2705
Bulgakov, Valentin
3194
Bullins, Ed
2331, 2529, 2634, 2833, 2989, 3027, 3767, 3884
Bullitt, Orville H.
2718
Bullitt, William C.
2718
Burby, John
2873
Burckhardt, Carl J.
3902, 3903
Burford, William
1346
Burgess, Anthony
2373, 2606, 3565, 3664
Burke, Thomas
3278
Burley, W. J.
2420, 4273
Burney, Fanny
2413
Burnford, Sheila
3668
Burns, James MacGregor
3932
Burns, Robert Grant
705, 1797
Burr, Anne
3475
Burroughs, William S.
2627, 3099
Burroughs, William, Jr.
3135
Burrows, Abe
2730
Burstein, Lonnie
4315
Butler, Jack
1143, 1238, 1577
Byron, Lord

See Gordon, George

C

Cable, Mary
2091
Cadogan, Alexander
2455
Caesar, Irving
3613
Cahn, Sammy
3325, 4546
Calisher, Hortense
2532
Cameron, Kenneth Neill
4042
Cameron, Nigel
2024
Campbell, Alan
1772
Campbell, Gurney
2774
Campbell, Joseph
3561
Campbell, Karen
4264
Camus, Albert
2914
Canetti, Elias
3127
Cardozo, Joaquim
267, 1686
Carlisle, Henry
4409
Carlson, Joel
3612
Carmichael, Harry
3512
Carmines, Al
2640, 2768, 3097, 3117, 3267, 3283, 3321, 3401, 4427
Caro, Robert A.
81, 1309
Carpenter, Edmund
3647
Carpentier, Alejo
4431
Carrière, Jean-Claude
3286
Carrington, Dorothy
2334
Carroll, Vinnette
2357, 2498
Carter, Anne
3495
Carter, Steve
4231
Casares, Adolfo Bioy
508
Casey, John
1618
Casey, Warren
2871
Cassill, R. V.
2486
Castelot, André
3563
Cate, Curtis
1968
Catledge, Turner
3543
Catton, Bruce
2801
Caudill, Harry M.
3540
Cauley, Harry
3243
Cavafy, C. P.
514, 602, 664, 1648
Cavanaugh, Arthur
3218
Céline, Louis-Ferdinand
3623, 3910
Chandler, Raymond
3478
Chapman, John
3625
Chaquet, Virginia
2839
Charles, Gerda
2444
Charney, Shulamith
222
Charnin, Martin
3568, 4342
Charters, Ann
3137
Chase, Mary
2925
Chasin, Helen
1150
Chekhov, Anton
2237, 3251, 3999, 4262, 4356 4543
Cherry, Paul

3719
Chessman, Rex
3156
Chikamatsu
2166
Childress, Alice
4448
Chin, Frank
2239, 4561
Chisholm, Anne
3756
Chomsky, Noam
2716
Chopin, Kate
2303
Churchill, Caryl
3702
Ciardi, John
481
Clark, Kenneth
2267, 3930
Clark, Ron
3608, 3622
Clark, Ronald W.
2557
Clarke, Austin
3457, 4157
Clay, Henry .
4221
Clements, Otis
3071
Clephane, Irene
2670
Clermont-Crèvecoeur, Jean-François-Louis
1922
Clifford, Francis
1937, 4506
Clinton-Baddeley, V. C.
2428
Clive, John
3373
Clive, Mary
4187
Cluchey, Rick
2178
Clurman, Harold
3654
Cobb, Jonathan
2947
Cockburn, Alexander
3014
Cockburn, Claud
2450
Cockshut, A. O. J.
4329
Cocteau, Jean
2281
Cohen, Arthur A.
3035
Cohen, Jerry S.
1919
Cohen, Larry
3575
Cohen, Leonard
4071
Cohen, Richard M.
2930
Cohen, Rosemary Gerber
1118
Cohen, Stephen F.
2165
Colebrook, Joan
1757
Coleman, Cy
4009
Coleman, Lonnie
3771
Coles, Robert
1034, 1575, 1700, 1924r, 1936r, 2140r, 2217r, 2241r, 2294r, 2457r, 2555r, 2654, 2789r, 2799r, 3040r, 3065r, 3485r, 3600r, 3619r, 3648, 3651r, 3668r, 3881r, 3883r, 4117r, 4250r, 4252r, 4387r, 4557r, 4578r
Colette, Sidonie Gabrielle
2289, 2610, 3114, 3774, 3893
Coley, W. B.
2960
Collier, John
3481
Collier, Richard
2521
Collingwood, Charles
2434
Collins, Larry
3633
Collins, Michael
2206
Colodny, Lester
2766
Coltman, Derek
3383, 3421, 3709

Colton, John
3858
Colum, Padriac
85
Colwin, Laurie
71, 366, 394, 998, 1066, 1626
Combs, Frederick
2246
Comden, Betty
1973, 3657
Commoner, Barry
308
Condon, Richard
1945, 1979
Congreve, William
3349, 4441
Connable, Alfred
4333
Connell, Evan S., Jr.
2316
Connell, Maureen
821
Connelly, Marc
2046
Connolly, Cyril
2608
Conrad, Borys
3537
Conrad, L. K.
2648
Conroy, Frank
266, 1098
Cook, Adrian
1981
Cook, Olive
2588, 2591
Cook, Peter
2846
Cookson, Catherine
3692
Cookson, William
4011
Cooley, Peter
1059
Cooney, Ray
3625
Coons, William R.
1997
Cooper, Henry S. F., Jr.
6, 74, 927, 1498
Cooper, I. S.
4387
Cope, Jack
1724
Copeland, Miles
4529
Coppel, Alfred
3171
Cordell, Alexander
4108
Corn, Alfred
1324
Cortázar, Julio
1900
Cost, March
3139
Costello, David F.
2440
Cotler, Gordon
532, 1628, 1713
Courtney, C. C.
2533
Courtney, Ragan
2533
Cousteau, Jacques-Yves
4036
Cousteau, Philippe
4036
Covert, Paul
2179
Coward, Noël
2293, 2928, 3618, 3645, 3822, 4106
Cowles, Virginia
3944
Cowley, Malcolm
4003
Cox, Stephen
3343
Coxe, Louis
224
Crane, Hart
3253
Crane, Lor
4483
Crankshaw, Edward
4281
Crapanzano, Vincent
2678
Crawford, T. S.
2956
Crémieux, Francis
3538
Crews, Harry
2197, 2903

Crichton, Michael
2697, 4230
Crichton, Robert
2182
Croce, Arlene
2740
Crosland, Margaret
2281, 2288, 3893
Cross, Amanda
3792
Crouse, Timothy
2144
Crow, Duncan
4392
Crowley, Mart
2150
Croxford, Judi
1023
Crozier, Brian
2407
Crozier, Jim
4287
Cryer, Gretchen
4043, 4451
Cullinan, Elizabeth
5, 777, 1151, 1207, 1262, 1828
Curtin, Sharon R.
3616
Curtiss, Ursula
3246
Cushing, Tom
2895

D

Daglish, Robert
2868
Dahlberg, Edward
2312
Daiches, David
3190, 3926
Dale, Celia
2388
Dale, Jim
3982
Dana, Robert
1727, 1753, 1802, 1813
Daniels, Guy
3563
Daniels, Jonathan
3681
Daniels, Steven
2994
Dann, Martin E.
2093
Darling, Amanda
3305
Darlington, C. D.
2620
Dathorne, O. R.
1864
Daughen, Joseph R.
4556
David, Mack
3496
David, Michael Robert
3124
Davidson, Angus
4341
Davidson, Basil
1865
Davidson, Lionel
4090
Davidson, Marshall B.
1927
Davidson, N. R., Jr.
2559
Davies, John Paton, Jr.
2508
Davies, Robertson
2677, 3420
Davin, Dan
2153
Davis, Al
2096
Davis, Angela
1956
Davis, David Brion
2666
Davis, Gwen
4292
Davis, Johanna
3273
Davis, John Gordon
3676
Davis, Marc
4127
Davis, Ossie
3837
Davis, Sammy, Jr.
3966
Davison, Peter
384
Day, Douglas

3404
De Anda, Peter
3163
de Beauvoir, Simone
1907, 2294
de Beer, Gavin
2910
de Filippo, Eduardo
3975
de Gaulle, Charles
3220, 3466
de la Barca, Fanny Calderón
3266
de la Grange, Henri-Louis
3395
de la Mazière, Christian
2196
de Lange, Nicholas
4291
de Lanux, Eyre
1332
De Lillo, Don
608, 2580
de Madariaga, Salvador
3508
de Mattos, Alexander Teixeira
3272
de Mauny, Erik
3954
De Moraes, Vinícius
1537, 1686
de Rachewiltz, Mary
2473
De Sylva, B. G.
2849
de Tocqueville, Alexis
3873
De Vries, Peter
320, 698, 2725, 2818, 3493
Dean, Phillip Hayes
2746, 4174
Decter, Midge
3584
Dedijer, Vladimir
2033
Degler, Carl N.
3691
Deighton, Len
2123, 2276, 4135
del Castillo, Michel
4014
del Vayo, Julio Alvarez
2812
Delbanco, Nicholas
2662
Delderfield, R. F.
3491, 4275
Delmar, Viña
2747
Deloria, Vine, Jr.
4446
Dennis, Carl
1365, 1420, 1514
Dennison, George
3297
Deutsch, Helene
2315
Deutscher, Isaac
3229
Deutschman, Deborah
1344
Devine, Jerry
2244
Dewey, Priscilla B.
4345
di Giovanni, Norman Thomas
7, 22, 90, 131, 186, 273, 329, 472, 489, 508, 540, 631, 752, 817, 823, 1013, 1037, 1075, 1385, 1406, 1543, 1683, 1752, 2126
Dias, Robert Vas
See Vas Dias, Robert
Dickey, James
1345, 1368, 2435
Dickey, William
840, 1079
Dickinson, Peter
4082
Dieter, William
4490
Dietz, Howard
4234
Diggins, John P.
3534
Dilks, David
2455
Dinroe, Dorothy
3638, 4565
Dintenfass, Mark
2679
Djilas, Milovan
4154
Dobyns, Stephen
637
Donaldson, Gordon

2694
Donis, Miles
2644
Donleavy, J. P.
2643
Donnay, H.
3366
Donoso, José
3635
Dos Passos, John
2537
Dostoevski, Fydor
2771
Dougherty, Richard
2854
Douglas, David C.
3620
Douglas, Ellen
1972
Douglas, William O.
2820
Douglas, Frederick
2741
Dowdey, Clifford
2840
Doyle, Arthur Conan
4045
Drabble, Margaret
1983, 3578
Draper, Theodore
3879
Drew, Elizabeth
132, 338, 339, 1373
Drinnon, Richard
3463
Driscoll, Peter
4501
Driver, Donald
4143
Drucker, Peter F.
3472
Drummond, Ivor
3418
Drummond, June
3739
du Camp, Maxime
2699
du Maurier, Daphne
3947
Duberman, Martin
4110
Dubey, Matt
4089
Dubin, Arthur D.
3505
Dubos, René
2826, 3871
Dubus, Andre
27
Duckworth, Elisabeth
3258
Ducrot, Nicolas
1949
Dufault, Peter Kane
123, 872
Duffin, Shay
4039
Dumas, Henry
1980
Dunbar, Janet
3079
Duncan, David Douglas
4432
Dunlop, Frank
4045
Dunn, Douglas
749, 773, 1167
Dunn, Katherine
4327
Dunne, John Gregory
4382
Dunnigan, Ann
3194, 4280
Durant, Mary
2341
Duras, Marguerite
3170, 3773
Durel, René
1714
Dürrenmatt, Friedrich
3780, 4399
Dutourd, Jean
4134
Dutton, Fredrick G.
2228
Duvignaud, Jean
2226
Dyer, Doug
4451
Dyson, Freeman J.
885, 1361, 1459

E

Eastman, Max

4568
Eastwood, James
2940
Eban, Suzy
250, 253, 707, 806
Ebb, Fred
4025
Eberhart, Richard
111, 479, 558, 710, 1506, 1582
Eça de Queiroz, José
3247
Edel, Leon
3439
Edelman, Lily
2045
Edelman, Maurice
1904
Edwards, Lovett F.
4154
Edwards, Samuel
2477
Eglesfield, Robert
3399
Eiseley, Loren
3065, 4364
Elegant, Robert S.
3423
Eliot, T. S.
4435
Eliot, Valerie
4435
Elizabeth Charlotte, Princess Palatine
3248
Ellenbogen, Eileen
2520, 3397
Ellin, Stanley
2077
Elliott, Bob
2117
Elliott, Janice
4140
Ellis, H. F.
438, 1749
Ellsberg, Daniel
3713
Elman, Richard M.
2742
Elman, Robert
2874
Elmslie, Kenward
2867
Elon, Amos
2068, 3077
Ely, David
4419
Emmet, Lily
2726
Engel, Lehman
4254, 4549
Engerman, Stanley L.
4267
England, Barry
2307
Ephron, Nora
49, 342, 1124
Epstein, Daniel Mark
1061
Epstein, David
4427
Epstein, Edward Jay
416, 1237, 1457, 2484r
Epstein, Joseph
607, 1402
Epton, Nina
4388
Erdman, Jean
3502
Erlanger, Philippe
3343
Esfandiary, F. M.
3680
Estes, Winston M.
1962
Ettlinger, Don
1917
Euripides
2735, 3451, 3452, 4323, 4451
Evans, Christopher
2371
Evans, Roland, Jr.
3604
Evans-Charles, Martie
3084
Eveling, Stanley
2411, 3083
Evers, Charles
2616
Everwine, Peter
310, 449
Everyman Company
2107
Eyen, Tom
2468

F

Fabre, Jean Henri
3272
Fager, Charles E.
4013
Fainlight, Ruth
1486
Fair, Ronald
4444
Fairbank, John K.
2252
Fairlie, Henry
3134
Faludy, George
2599
Fandel, John
1305
Farago, Ladislas
2773
Farrell, J. G.
4058, 4326
Faulkner, William
2698
Faure, Edgar
2929
Faust, Irvin
4514
Feeley, Constance
55
Feibleman, Peter
2292
Feifer, George
2809
Feiffer, Jules
4488
Feinstein, Elaine
1533, 2369
Feldkamp, Fred
298, 409, 2847
Feldkamp, Phyllis
2847
Feldman, Irving
21, 666, 774, 1739
Feldman, Susan
735
Ferris, Paul
2988
Feuser, Willfried
1864
Feydeau, Georges
2236, 4239
Fick, Carl
2386
Fiedler, Leslie A.
4162
Fieger, Addy O.
2414
Field, Edward
997
Fields, Dorothy
4009
Fields, Jeff
2366
Fields, Joseph
3335
Finkel, Donald
169, 1156
Finkel, Ruth Schachner
192, 497
Finley, Joseph E.
2333
Fischer, David Hackett
2952
Fischoff, George
2792
Fisher, Howard T.
3266
Fisher, M. F. K.
177, 483, 839, 843, 946, 980, 1071, 1236, 1338, 1573, 1761, 1794, 1938, 2332r, 2712r, 3521r, 3758
Fisher, Marion Hall
3266
Fisher, Robert
3483
FitzGerald, Frances
84, 551, 1503, 1720
Fitzgerald, Geraldine
2618
FitzGibbon, Constantine
2304, 3034
Flaherty, Doug
715
Flanner, Hildegarde
1788
Flanner, Janet
67, 148, 154, 689, 797, 822, 916, 942, 956, 1009, 1330, 1474, 1621, 1671, 1699, 1952r, 2048r, 2060r, 2240r, 2277r, 2294r, 2308r, 2314r, 2605r, 2908r, 2958r, 3170r, 3205r, 3209r, 3214r, 3220r, 3227r, 3261r, 3450r, 3644r, 3682r,

3705r, 4253r, 4530r
Flaubert, Gustave
2699
Fleming, Amalia
3766
Fleming, Thomas
2059
Fletcher, Lucille
3599
Flexner, James Thomas
2790, 2791
Flint, R. W.
3428
Flory, Sheldon
864, 1117, 1806
Floyd, David
2717
Fogel, Robert William
4267
Foot, Michael
1954
Foote, Audrey C.
3856
Foote, Shelby
2266
Ford, Ford Madox
4571
Ford, Nancy
4043
Foreman, Richard
2490, 2983
Forster, E. M.
1889, 3441
Forster, John
3814
Forster, Margaret
3487
Forsyth, Frederick
2403
Foss, Michael
1879
Foster, Alan S.
2853
Foster, Paul
2567
Foulke, Adrienne
3711
Fowles, John
2540
Fox, Henry
2322
Fox, Paula
4461
Frame, Janet
2394
Francis, Dick
2125, 2593, 3863, 4080, 4091
Frank, Gerold
1925
Frank, Larry
2738
Frank, Waldo
3469
Frankel, Sandor
2069
Franklin, Benjamin
2059
Franklin, J. E.
2089, 3825
Franks, Lucinda
4415
Fraser, Antonia
2359
Fraser, George Mac Donald
4147
Fraser, James
2409
Fraser, Kennedy
2094r, 3578r, 3953r
Fraser, Ronald
3026, 4206
Frater, Alexander
1002, 1448
Frayn, Michael
4198
Frederic, Harold
2378, 2816, 3431
Freed, Donald
3054
Freeling, Nicolas
2001
Freeman, Arthur
377
Freeman, David E.
2348
Freeman, Stan
3359
Freemantle, Brian
2855
Freidel, Frank
2739
Freidin, Seymour K.
4018
Frenaye, Frances
2226

Freud, Anna
3619, 4557
Freud, Ernst L.
3256
Freud, Sigmund
2752, 3256
Friedberg, Maurice
4568
Friedenthal, Richard
3367
Friedman, Bruce Jay
880, 4146
Friedman, Gary William
3445
Friedman, Leon
4527
Friedrich, Otto
2043
Friel, Brian
2368, 2745
Frisch, Max
1576
Fromm, Erich
1940
Frost, Elinor
2649
Frost, Robert
2649
Fruchter, Norman
4064
Fruman, Norman
2286
Fry, Roger
3255
Fuchs, Daniel
4460
Fugard, Athol
2120, 3075, 3738, 4075
Fulbright, J. William
782
Fuller, Charles
3036
Fuller, Dean
4089
Fuller, Henry Blake
2064, 3626
Furth, George
2299, 2710, 4338
Fusero, Clemente
2130
Fussell, Paul
3968

G

Gaines, Frederick
2987
Gaines, J. E.
2500, 2934, 4104, 4464
Gainham, Sarah
3823, 4207
Galante, Pierre
3385
Galbraith, John Kenneth
2251, 2542, 2543, 4495
Galef, Jack
1152
Gall, Peter
2160
Gallagher, Michael
3952, 4133
Gallagher, Tess
218, 324
Gallant, Mavis
41, 77, 703, 761, 778, 799,
865, 1161, 2641
Gallo, Max
2719
Gallois, Claire
3986
Galvin, Brendan
151, 404, 1173
Garber, Charles
709
García Lorca, Federico
<u>See</u> Lorca, Federico García
García Marquez, Gabriel
<u>See</u> Marquez, Gabriel García
Gardner, Donald
4263
Gardner, Herb
4245
Gardner, Howard
3848
Gardner, John
2893, 3593, 4189
Garland, Patrick
2157
Garnett, Constance
3549
Garrigue, Jean
635, 1181, 1184, 1641
Garve, Andrew
2209, 3241
Gary, Romain
2240, 2780

Gasman, Ira
4469
Gathorne-Hardy, Jonathan
4367
Gay, John
2047
Gay, Peter
4175
Gaylin, Willard
3040
Gaynor, Charles
3071
Geist, Eileen
3385
Gelb, Barbara
4093
Gelbart, Larry
2767
Gelber, Jack
2025, 4081
Geld, Gary
3837, 4041
Gelman, Woody
3156
Genet, Jean
2706, 3847
Genovese, Eugene D.
3030, 3929
Gentry, Curt
3675
Geoffrey, Christopher
254
Gerald, John Bart
2326
Gerber, Dan
1827
Gerber, Rosanna
974, 1681
Gérin, Winifred
2976
Gerstenmaier, Cornelia
4405
Gibbs, Angela
3642
Gies, Joseph
2356
Gilbert, Anthony
3488, 3529
Gilbert, Michael
2119
Gilder, George F.
4028
Giles, Kenneth
2418
Gill, Brendan
533, 615, 671, 754, 1007, 1186, 1303, 1785, 1823, 1840r, 1843r, 1882r, 1905r, 1906r, 1908r, 1917r, 1930r, 1941r, 1943r, 1965r, 1973r, 1991r, 1998r, 2012r, 2046r, 2092r, 2103r, 2109r, 2117r, 2135r, 2141r, 2157r, 2166r, 2173r, 2185r, 2188r, 2194r, 2214r, 2223r, 2227r, 2236r, 2244r, 2248r, 2254r, 2270r, 2293r, 2299r, 2307r, 2340r, 2347r, 2362r, 2364r, 2365r, 2373r, 2380r, 2384r, 2414r, 2452r, 2463r, 2487r, 2496r, 2497r, 2502r, 2515r, 2523r, 2533r, 2561r, 2567r, 2574r, 2583r, 2585r, 2587r, 2594r, 2598r, 2611r, 2641r, 2646r, 2663r, 2683r, 2685r, 2706r, 2710r, 2730r, 2738r, 2745r, 2765r, 2766r, 2767r, 2776r, 2792r, 2806r, 2808r, 2829r, 2845r, 2846r, 2849r, 2852r, 2867r, 2880r, 2895r, 2902r, 2915r, 2925r, 2926r, 2928r, 2933r, 2942r, 2961r, 2968r, 2977r, 2983r, 2991r, 2997r, 3010r, 3013r, 3028r, 3033r, 3045r, 3050r, 3054r, 3071r, 3075r, 3095r, 3100r, 3108r, 3121r, 3158r, 3159r, 3170r, 3183r, 3215r, 3230r, 3234r, 3236r, 3243r, 3279r, 3291r, 3306r, 3323r, 3325r, 3335r, 3339r, 3349r, 3358r, 3359r, 3371r, 3376r, 3384r, 3391r, 3411r, 3415r, 3424r, 3436r, 3443r, 3452r, 3459r, 3473r, 3475r, 3476r, 3479r, 3483r, 3496r, 3501r, 3503r, 3514r, 3517r, 3518r, 3520r, 3528r, 3533r, 3536r, 3567r, 3568r, 3573r, 3599r, 3608r, 3613r, 3618r, 3622r, 3625r, 3627r, 3641r, 3649r, 3657r, 3669r, 3677r, 3682r, 3686r, 3693r, 3695r, 3700r, 3706r, 3719r, 3754r, 3755r, 3769r, 3771r, 3781r, 3790r, 3802r, 3805r,

3814r, 3819r, 3822r, 3825r, 3827r, 3837r, 3852r, 3853r, 3860r, 3861r, 3912r, 3918r, 3920r, 3922r, 3931r, 3943r, 3949r, 3966r, 3975r, 3982r, 3988r, 3995r, 3999r, 4000r, 4004r, 4009r, 4025r, 4041r, 4043r, 4045r, 4050r, 4059r, 4073r, 4075r, 4084r, 4089r, 4097r, 4106r, 4138r, 4143r, 4151r, 4159r, 4165r, 4179r, 4190r, 4232r, 4234r, 4239r, 4245r, 4262r, 4274r, 4293r, 4315r, 4331r, 4338r, 4342r, 4344r, 4353r, 4356r, 4366r, 4385r, 4386r, 4399r, 4401r, 4404r, 4423r, 4433r, 4466r, 4480r, 4497r, 4508r, 4515r, 4526r, 4534r, 4540r, 4546r

Gillette, William
4045

Gilliatt, Penelope
47, 88, 114, 263, 519, 575, 657, 704, 802, 835, 1070, 1146, 1231, 1287, 1304, 1326, 1369, 1481, 1549, 1551, 1561, 1608, 1731, 1837r, 1852r, 1860r, 1861r, 1880r, 1894r, 1916r, 1926r, 1944r, 1960r, 1969r, 1971r, 1974r, 1983r, 1996r, 2004r, 2014r, 2019r, 2020r, 2022r, 2057r, 2083r, 2100r, 2106r, 2114r, 2116r, 2134r, 2146r, 2161r, 2180r, 2186r, 2200r, 2205r, 2229r, 2235r, 2253r, 2264r, 2271r, 2277r, 2327r, 2330r, 2360r, 2377r, 2385r, 2392r, 2395r, 2398r, 2404r, 2419r, 2427r, 2432r, 2436r, 2438r, 2441r, 2442r, 2445r, 2449r, 2456r, 2466r, 2485r, 2495r, 2516r, 2538r, 2563r, 2576r, 2579r, 2595r, 2600r, 2601r, 2614r, 2615r, 2619r, 2658r, 2680r, 2695r, 2713r, 2715r, 2720r, 2725r, 2729r, 2744r, 2751r, 2753r, 2755r, 2763r, 2800r, 2822r, 2830r, 2832r, 2836r, 2865r, 2872r, 2877r, 2879r, 2882r, 2890r, 2900r, 2905r, 2907r, 2922r, 2935r, 2938r, 2939r, 2941r, 2945r, 2949r, 2950r, 2957r, 2958r, 2999r, 3004r, 3007r, 3039r, 3080r, 3091r, 3094r, 3096r, 3101r, 3107r, 3110r, 3122r, 3138r, 3149r, 3157r, 3160r, 3161r, 3172r, 3174r, 3178r, 3184r, 3204r, 3210r, 3213r, 3227r, 3233r, 3242r, 3294r, 3295r, 3314r, 3330r, 3345r, 3347r, 3352r, 3354r, 3360r, 3361r, 3363r, 3377r, 3378r, 3380r, 3381r, 3406r, 3409r, 3412r, 3429r, 3458r, 3470r, 3486r, 3493r, 3498r, 3499r, 3519r, 3547r, 3548r, 3552r, 3553r, 3577r, 3580r, 3583r, 3634r, 3662r, 3678r, 3710r, 3715r, 3717r, 3723r, 3724r, 3725r, 3728r, 3745r, 3752r, 3768r, 3778r, 3784r, 3785r, 3800r, 3806r, 3811r, 3817r, 3829r, 3836r, 3839r, 3864r, 3878r, 3880r, 3896r, 3907r, 3911r, 3915r, 3919r, 3923r, 3950r, 3972r, 3974r, 3978r, 3984r, 3993r, 4006r, 4007r, 4008r, 4031r, 4047r, 4055r, 4056r, 4062r, 4079r, 4101r, 4122r, 4140r, 4171r, 4177r, 4199r, 4203r, 4210r, 4213r, 4215r, 4217r, 4220r, 4222r, 4224r, 4226r, 4235r, 4241r, 4248r, 4261r, 4278r, 4282r, 4288r, 4289r, 4299r, 4312r, 4319r, 4325r, 4346r, 4347r, 4351r, 4355r, 4362r, 4372r, 4377r, 4379r, 4394r, 4398r, 4402r, 4418r, 4429r, 4437r, 4438r, 4449r, 4450r, 4455r, 4493r, 4509r, 4519r, 4538r, 4544r

Gillott, Edward
4156

Ginsberg, Allen
3126

Ginsburg, Mirra
4121

Ginzburg, Natalia
3615

Giovene, Andrea
2127, 2459

Giraudoux, Jean
3368, 3388

Giroud, Françoise
3006
Gishford, Anthony
2862
Gladwyn, Hubert Miles Gladwyn Jebb
3467
Glanville, Brian
2367
Glassco, Bill
2977
Glasser, Ronald J.
4259
Glatzer, Nahum
2302
Glazer, Nathan
3885
Glenny, Michael
1999, 3435
Glimcher, Arnold B.
3344
Glover, Michael
3221
Glück, Louise
44, 451
Godden, Jon
3492
Godey, John
4208
Godwin, Gail
2815, 3637
Goehring, George
3164
Goethe, Johann Wolfgang von
3630, 4112
Goggin, Dan
2919
Gohman, Don
1917
Gold, Herbert
3541
Goldberg, Gerald Jay
3369
Golding, William
3992
Goldman, Marshall I.
1297
Goldman, Peter
2415
Goldman, William
3816
Goldsmith, Lee
4026
Goodman, Paul
3292, 3588
Goodman, Walter
3742
Goodrich, Lloyd
2546
Goodwin, Richard N.
54, 133, 435, 516
Gorchov, Robert D.
1067
Gordimer, Nadine
1783
Gordon, George
1888, 2174
Gordon, R. L.
1091, 3921
Gordon, Steve
4293
Gordon, Stuart
4433
Gore, Christopher
4386
Gorky, Maxim
2583, 2736
Goss, Clay
1950
Gottlieb, Elaine
437
Gould, Heywood
2738
Gould, Lois
2682
Goulden, Joseph C.
3447
Goulding, Ray
2117
Goytisolo, Juan
2338
Grade, Arnold
2649
Graff, Gerald
607, 1402
Graham, Fred P.
4012
Graham, Loren R.
3990
Grant, Michael
1942
Grant, Micki
2357, 3825
Grass, Günter
2761, 3302
Graves, John

2916
Graves, Robert
221, 430, 560, 646, 824, 1691, 1808
Gray, Francine du Plessix
10, 172, 174, 760, 1418, 1580
Gray, Martin
2719
Gray, Simon
2173, 4526
Greeley, Andrew M.
4368, 4498
Green, Adolph
1973, 3657
Green, David
3842
Green, Hannah
860
Green, Julian
3690
Green, Martin
2262, 4406
Green, Paul
3108
Green, Peter
2130, 3951, 4559
Green, Roger Lancelyn
2176
Green, William M.
3965
Greenberg, Joanne
3917
Greenburg, Dan
395, 402
Greene, A. C.
3749, 3971
Greene, Bob
2074
Greene, Felix
2586
Greene, Graham
3333, 4113, 4304
Greene, Joseph
3156
Greene, Naomi
1970
Greenfield, Jeff
1855, 3614, 3798
Greenhalgh, Robert
3916
Greger, Debora
1012
Gregor, Arthur
969, 1787
Gregory, Andre
3999
Grierson, Edward
2424
Griest, Guinevere L.
3522
Grindrod, Muriel
3564
Grissmer, John
2189
Grogan, Emmett
3913
Grohskopf, Bernice
4307
Gross, Joel
1598
Gross, Miriam
4552
Grossbach, Robert
4100
Grosser, Maurice
3705
Grossman, Leonid
2352
Grossman, Vasily
2724
Grossman, Viktor
2210
Grossmann, Suzanne
2236
Grotowski Troupe
2605
Gruber, Howard E.
2393
Grumberg, Jean-Claude
2515
Grunfeld, Frederic V.
1985
Guare, John
2986, 4344
Guareschi, Giovanni
2648
Guerrier, Victor
2387
Guest, Christopher
3224
Guibert, Rita
4023
Guillemin, Henri
3098
Guinness, Desmond

3072
Gulliver, Hal
4119
Gunn, Bill
2092
Gunther, John
3046
Gurganus, Allan
1058
Gurney, A. R., Jr.
3985
Gussow, Alan
4017
Guthrie, A. B., Jr.
4507
Guthrie, Ramon
1008
Guttridge, Leonard F.
2876

H

Hackady, Hal
1917
Hacks, Peter
1939
Hahn, Emily
386, 1195, 1279, 1750, 3660
Hailey, Oliver
2663
Hale, J. R.
3886
Hall, Ron
4160
Halle, Kay
2863
Halliday, Mark
721, 1776
Halper, Albert
2856
Halperin, Elaine P.
2524
Halpern, Daniel
504, 849
Halsband, Robert
3331, 4010
Halsell, Grace
2616
Hamburger, Philip
24, 441, 442, 1125, 1280
Hamilton, Alastair
4384
Hamilton, Nancy
3663
Hamilton, William
1435
Hammer, Richard
2344
Hampton, Christopher
3754, 4286
Hamsun, Knut
3556
Han Suyin
3507
Handelsman, J. B.
521, 751
Handke, Peter
2821, 3130, 3906
Handler, Philip
2079
Hands, Terry
3787
Hanley, William
2112
Hannah, Barry
2794
Hansberry, Lorraine
3234, 4059
Hansen, Joseph
2417, 2639
Harbach, Otto
3613
Harbaugh, William H.
3202
Harding, James
2138
Hare, Bill
2824
Hare, David
4078
Harnack, Curtis
4445
Harnick, Sheldon
3943
Harper, Wally
4015
Harriman, W. Averell
1918
Harrington, Michael
4094
Harris, Bertha
2311
Harris, Fred R.
3587
Harris, Joseph D.

2387
Harris, Louis
1959
Harris, Neil
2099, 2328, 3782
Harris, Richard
78, 82, 307, 412, 605, 736, 766, 1113, 1142, 1314, 1447, 1669, 1754, 2136r, 3712r
Harrison, Gordon
2535
Harrison, Jim
2844
Harrison, Paul Carter
2881
Hart, Philip
3685
Harwood, Michael
2341
Harwood, Richard
3370
Haslip, Joan
2363, 4182
Hassan, Sana
2068
Hatherill, George
2446
Hawke, David Freeman
3704
Hay, Roy
2291
Hayden, Julie
397, 781, 1659, 1742
Haydn, Hiram
4545
Hayes, Helen
4336
Haylock, John
2703
Haynes, Mary
232
Hayter, Alethea
3679
Hayward, Max
2717, 2974, 2975
Hazzard, Shirley
1491, 2034
Healey, Ben
4155
Heaney, Seamus
124, 552, 712
Hearsey, John E. N.
4569
Hecht, Anthony
23, 641, 1266
Hecker, Susan
4405
Hefer, Hayim
4274
Heilbroner, Robert L.
3055
Heim, Michael Henry
3251
Heinz, G.
3366
Heisenberg, Werner
3757
Heller, Joseph
4102
Hellman, Geoffrey T.
31, 272, 469, 812, 939, 1222, 1265, 1320
Helpmann, Robert
2933
Helprin, Mark Henry
477, 716, 873, 1789
Hemenway, Robert
465, 1676
Hemingway, Ernest
3076
Hemming, John
2317
Henderson, Alexander
2602
Henderson, Elizabeth
2602
Henderson, Philip
4200
Henderson, Ray
2849
Henderson, Robert
1018, 1744
Hendra, Tony
3224, 4089
Hendry, J. F.
1684
Hendry, Tom
2490
Henissart, Paul
4535
Hennessy, James Pope
1964
Hentoff, Nat
275, 1955r, 2992r, 2994r, 3297r,
Herbert, Anthony B.

4096
Heren, Louis
3607
Herlihy, James Leo
4001
Herman, Jerry
3376
Herman, Judith
2332
Herman, Marguerite Shalett
2332
Herndon, James
2992
Herriman, George
3156
Herrod, Bro
2517
Hersey, John
1579
Hersh, Seymour M.
349, 1374
Hertzberg, Hendrik
1296, 3666
Herzen, Alexander
3549
Hess, Hans
2785
Hess, Thomas B.
4510
Heyen, William
306, 319, 587
Heyworth, Peter
1600
Hibbert, Christopher
2509, 2784, 3307
Higgins, George V.
2282, 2465, 2754
Highsmith, Patricia
2493, 3914
Hiken, Gerald
2760
Hill, Carol
3244
Hill, Christopher
3991
Hill, Susan
2081, 3041, 4161
Hillerman, Tony
2379, 2708
Hillier, Caroline
3245
Hilsman, Roger
2361
Himes, Chester
3840
Hine, Daryl
9, 1633
Hingley, Ronald
4543
Hirson, Roger O.
3769
Hiss, Anthony
1306, 3835r
Hjortsberg, William
4285
Hoagland, Edward
663
Hoagland, Jim
4116
Hobhouse, Christina
4459
Hochman, Sandra
1736
Hodes, Aubrey
3434
Hodge, Jane Aiken
3672
Hodgson, Godfrey
2484
Hoffman, Cary
4469
Hoffman, Daniel
439
Hoffman, Jill
1085, 1398
Hofstadter, Daniel
3570
Hofstadter, Richard
1934
Hoggart, Richard
3653, 4125
Höhne, Heinz
2782
Hollander, John
37, 486, 702, 958, 1470, 1779
Hollis, Christopher
3482
Hollo, Anselm
3847
Hollywood, Daniel
1908
Holm, Hans Axel
3688
Holman-Hunt, Diana
3539

Holt, Will
3700
Holton, Leonard
3824
Home, William Douglas
3100
Hooper, Walter
2176
Hoopes, Townsend
2447
Hopkins, John
1606, 2683, 4219
Horgan, Paul
1975, 2578, 3442
Horovitz, Israel
1845, 3281
Horowitz, Gene
4383
Horwitz, Julius
3433
Hotchner, A. E.
3148, 4306
Hough, John T.
3736
Hough, John, Jr.
4350
Hough, Richard
2105, 2193
House, Ron
2558
Household, Geoffrey
2503, 2673, 3928, 4247, 4436
Housman, A. E.
3249
Houssaye, Arsène
3410
Houston, James A.
4485
Houston, James D.
2653
Houston, Jeanne Wakatsuki
2653
Howar, Barbara
3198
Howard, Edmund
1986
Howard, Elizabeth Jane
3636
Howard, Jane
2465
Howard, Maureen
2042
Howard, Richard
600, 1313, 2914, 3368
Howe, Quincy
1992
Howes, Barbara
903
Hoy, Bernard
3903
Hoyer, Linda Grace
1317
Hsu, Francis L. K.
1935
Hughes, Ted
361, 362, 363, 364, 365, 367, 368, 410, 563, 987, 1000
Hugo, Richard F.
857, 1203
Hull, R. F. C.
2752
Humphrey, William
4124
Hunt, Andrew
1347
Hunt, Morton
905, 3523
Hunt, William
17, 731
Hunter, Evan
4167
Hunter, John Dunn
3463
Hunter, Richard
2789
Hunter-Blair, Kitty
2583
Hurwit, Lawrence
4026
Hussey, Anne
296, 407, 457
Hutchens, John K.
2066
Hutchins, Tony
4345
Hutchinson, Joyce A.
1874
Hutchison, Harold H.
2547
Huth, Angela
4395
Huxley, Aldous
3250
Huxley, Ann
2728

Huxley, Elspeth
3300
Hyams, Edward
2954
Hyde, H. Montgomery
4137
Hyde, Mary
3022
Hynes, Samuel
2551

I

Ibsen, Henrik
2494, 2585, 2937, 3167, 3438
Iduarte, Andrés
3603
Iglauer, Edith
183, 755
Illich, Ivan D.
2217
Infante, G. Cabrera
4263
Ingrassia, Anthony J.
2646
Ionesco, Eugène
2223, 2943, 3068, 3158, 3159
Irving, John
4439
Irwin, James
3998
Isherwood, Christopher
3133
Itō, Aiko
3000

J

Jackson, Bruce
4416
Jackson, Geoffrey
4194
Jacob, Dorothy
2707
Jacob, François
3304
Jacobs, Jim
2871
Jacobs, Paul
3224
Jacobs, Travis Beal
3576
Jacobsen, Josephine
1048, 1135
Jacobson, Dan
4542
Jacobson, Kenneth
4052
James, P. D.
4370
Jameson, Storm
3115, 3721, 4238
Janik, Allan
4533
Jarrell, Randall
4251
Jarrett, Derek
2589
Jay, Charlotte
4403
Jensen, Laura
70, 772
Jessup, Richard
3851
Jhabvala, R. Prawer
207, 775, 1182, 1328, 1409, 1688, 2625, 4302
Johannsen, Robert
4150
Johnson, Diane
3240
Johnson, Edgar
4067
Johnson, Haynes
3370
Johnson, Herman
3631
Johnson, Josephine W.
4022
Johnson, Lady Bird
4487
Johnson, Lyndon Baines
4380
Johnson, Nicholas
2993
Johnson, Pamela Hansford
2962
Johnson, Richard T.
1908
Jolas, Maria
2482
Jonas, Gerald
57, 541, 794, 1428, 1446, 1534, 1726

Jones, Elinor
2287
Jones, Howard Mumford
1876
Jones, James
4290, 4393
Jones, Le Roi
3872
Jones, Mervyn
4339
Jones, Tom
2287, 3755
Jones, Walter
2522, 3090
Jong, Erica
2667
Jory, Jon
4315
Joyce, James
4353
Judson, Horace Freeland
225
Jullian, Philippe
2703
Jung, C. G.
2752
Jurkowski, John
1440
Just, Ward
4170
Justice, Donald
474

K

Kael, Pauline
299, 399, 683, 685, 834, 1014, 1090, 1188, 1348, 1766, 1839r, 1849r, 1858r, 1884r, 1885r, 1892r, 1896r, 1897r, 1910r, 1926r, 1948r, 1953r, 2002r, 2008r, 2011r, 2015r, 2030r, 2032r, 2038r, 2039r, 2075r, 2090r, 2104r, 2122r, 2124r, 2133r, 2142r, 2143r, 2151r, 2168r, 2175r, 2177r, 2201r, 2222r, 2231r, 2249r, 2256r, 2259r, 2269r, 2273r, 2275r, 2308r, 2314r, 2318r, 2346r, 2350r, 2358r, 2397r, 2402r, 2405r, 2429r, 2453r, 2469r, 2472r, 2491r, 2501r, 2536r, 2554r, 2560r, 2566r, 2572r, 2590r, 2624r, 2626r, 2655r, 2671r, 2672r, 2676r, 2689r, 2693r, 2740r, 2748r, 2749r, 2762r, 2772r, 2778r, 2779r, 2797r, 2807r, 2814r, 2827r, 2828r, 2834r, 2835r, 2838r, 2858r, 2887r, 2896r, 2897r, 2918r, 2931r, 2973r, 2978r, 2981r, 2985r, 2998r, 3008r, 3009r, 3011r, 3012r, 3017r, 3018r, 3049r, 3063r, 3074r, 3093r, 3119r, 3146r, 3152r, 3162r, 3165r, 3168r, 3177r, 3180r, 3182r, 3187r, 3192r, 3193r, 3199r, 3200r, 3203r, 3207r, 3231r, 3238r, 3265r, 3277r, 3285r, 3286r, 3287r, 3290r, 3293r, 3308r, 3312r, 3319r, 3328r, 3338r, 3357r, 3362r, 3364r, 3374r, 3375r, 3379r, 3385r, 3389r, 3392r, 3408r, 3413r, 3414r, 3446r, 3500r, 3513r, 3526r, 3530r, 3532r, 3585r, 3586r, 3592r, 3598r, 3698r, 3700r, 3708r, 3714r, 3733r, 3743r, 3750r, 3753r, 3770r, 3779r, 3804r, 3821r, 3828r, 3838r, 3855r, 3889r, 3957r, 3976r, 3977r, 3979r, 3996r, 4016r, 4021r, 4024r, 4035r, 4040r, 4061r, 4070r, 4077r, 4083r, 4085r, 4087r, 4099r, 4107r, 4111r, 4115r, 4131r, 4138r, 4140r, 4144r, 4148r, 4153r, 4163r, 4178r, 4180r, 4186r, 4188r, 4191r, 4204r, 4209r, 4225r, 4237r, 4244r, 4246r, 4256r, 4272r, 4294r, 4296r, 4301r, 4305r, 4310r, 4314r, 4318r, 4322r, 4324r, 4332r, 4343r, 4348r, 4357r, 4375r, 4410r, 4420r, 4424r, 4442r, 4462r, 4470r, 4481r, 4528r, 4539r, 4541r, 4558r, 4567r, 4570r, 4573r, 4574r, 4575r
Kafka, Franz
2302, 3258
Kahler, Erich
2793, 3067
Kahn, E. J., Jr.
79, 153, 199, 206, 429, 495,

577, 870, 910, 914, 915, 1031, 1035, 1050, 1097, 1283, 1760, 1769, 1781, 2691
Kahn, Herman
2571, 4249
Kahn, Joan
4309
Kahnweiler, Daniel-Henry
3538
Kaiko, Takeshi
2391
Kalb, Bernard
3150
Kalb, Marvin
3150, 3936
Kalcheim, Lee
2997
Källberg, Sture
3642
Kander, John
4025
Kanfer, Stefan
3112
K'ang-hsi
2575
Kani, John
3075, 4075
Kanin, Garson
2515, 2964
Kaplan, Justin
3280, 3430
Karlinsky, Simon
3251
Karshan, Donald H.
1977
Katayev, Valentin
2868
Kaufman, George S.
2046, 3641
Kaufman, Sue
2645
Kavanagh, P. J.
1164
Kawabata, Yasunari
3440
Kayden, Mildred
3068
Kazan, Elia
1995, 4361
Keating, H. R. F.
3058
Keeley, Edmund
514, 602, 664, 1648
Keillor, Garrison
107, 119, 143, 330, 581, 590, 597, 729, 960, 988, 1108, 1194, 1229, 1260, 1284, 1351, 1468, 1504, 1512, 1615, 1695, 1786
Keller, Werner
2602
Kelley, Edith Summers
4452
Kelly, Katie
2777
Kelly, Mary
4335
Kelly, Sean
3224
Kelman, Steven
894, 922
Kemelman, Harry
4330
Kemp, Arnold
2539
Kemp, Lindsay
2706
Kendall, Paul Murray
3342
Keneally, Thomas
2110
Keniston, Kenneth
4572
Kennan, George F.
380, 1574, 3462
Kennebeck, Edwin
3123
Kennedy, Duncan
251
Kennedy, Raymond
2850
Kenner, Hugh
2164, 3807
Kenny, Sean
2942
Kent, Stephen
3084
Kern, Jerome
3646
Kerouac, Jack
4397
Kerr, A. P.
3873
Kerr, Jean
2685
Kerr, Jessica

4033
Kessle, Gun
1957
Kessler, Charles
3042
Kessler, Harry
3042
Ketcham, Ralph
2757
Ketchum, Richard M.
2636, 4525
Keveson, Peter
3579
Khrushchev, Nikita
3140
Kidel, Boris
2701
Kiely, Benedict
959, 1003, 1139, 1404, 1622
Killens, John Oliver
2335
Killigrew, Michael
4571
Kilmartin, Joanna
3983
Kilmartin, Terence
3466
Kilty, Jerome
3286 3323
Kim, Richard E.
3340
Kimball, Robert
2285
Kimber, Rita
2793
Kimber, Robert
2793
King, Larry L.
2310
Kinglake, A. W.
2596
Kinkead, Eugene
34, 180, 188, 315, 1219, 1419, 1556
Kinnell, Galway
1248
Kintner, Elvan
3254
Kirk, Lydia
2570
Kirkup, James
3780
Klappert, Peter
795
Klein, Martin
3730
Kleiner, Isador
2660
Klimas, John E., Jr.
4503
Klonsky, Milton
2633
Knef, Hildegard
2805
Knepler, Henry
3410
Knowles, John
4132
Koch, Kenneth
3939
Koenig, Laird
3289
Koestler, Arthur
2071, 2181, 2211, 3935
Kohlmeier, Louis M.
2823
Kolodny, Robert
3175
Koning, Hans
2421
Konrád George
2212
Koren, Edward
787
Kosinski, Jerzy
2052
Kosner, Edward
417
Kotker, Zane
2118
Kotlowitz, Robert
4105
Kotzwinkle, William
2565, 2651
Kozol, Jonathan
2743
Kraft, Joseph
59, 285, 286, 887, 890, 892, 896, 901, 909, 913, 919, 928, 989, 1230, 1372, 1391, 1830, 1911r, 1966r, 1999r, 2044r, 2702r, 3510r, 3667r, 3671r
Kramer, Jane
418, 582, 719, 877, 893, 895, 900, 902, 1696
Kramer, Richard

862
Krock, Arthur
2320
Krohn, Herbert
636
Kroll, Maria
3248
Kuck, Loren
4553
Kumin, Maxine
13, 696, 1421
Kunitz, Stanley
999
Kuntz, John B.
3164, 4483
Kupferberg, Tuli
1988
Kushida, Magoichi
4240
Kuzma, Greg
557, 1140, 1396, 1501, 1685

L

LM
3132
La Guma, Alex
3037
Lacey, Robert
3927, 4066
Lacouture, Jean
3570
Lacy, Dan
4492
Lahr, John
2003, 2046, 2982
Laing, R. D.
2475, 3154
Lamb, Myrna
3494
Lambert, Derek
3877
Lamming, George
3574
Landau, David
3151
Lane, Helen R.
1915, 2338
Lane, Robert M.
2722
Lang, Daniel
1, 144, 714, 985, 1221, 1591
Lange, Monique
3288
Langford, Cameron
4524
Laning, Edward
4076
Lapierre, Dominique
3633
Lardner, Susan
252, 2215, 2336r, 3390r, 3652r, 3699r, 4164r
Larkin, Philip
3703
Larner, John
2372
Larsen, Lance
2926, 3084
Lash, Joseph P.
2561, 2562
Lasson, Frans
3262
Lathen, Emma
1993, 3318, 3527, 3761, 4197
Latta, Gordon
3687
Laurence, Charles
3536
Laurence, Dan H.
2063
Laurence, Margaret
2479
Laurents, Arthur
2577, 2902
Lavallee, David
2613
Laver, James
1877
Lavers, Annette
3560
Lavin, Mary
1654, 1663
Lawrence, Barbara
1249
Lawrence, D. H.
3106
Lawrence, George
3873
Lawrence, Jerome
3045
Lazard, Naomi
100, 972, 1807
le Carré, John
4271

Le Vay, David
2289, 2610, 3114, 3774
Leach, Joseph
2158, 2437
Leach, Wilford
2795
Lean, E. Tangye
3566
Leasor, James
2711
Lebowsky, Stanley
2776
Leduc, Violette
3383
Lee, Robert E.
3045
Lee, Ta-ling
3895
Lees-Milne, James
1963
Lefebvre, Georges
2878
Leggett, John
3942
Legros, G. V.
2631
Lehmann, John
2545
Leigh, Mitch
2365
Leighton, Ann
2534
Leitch, David
2825
Lelchuk, Alan
1931
Lemay, Harding
3056
Leonard, Hugh
1998
Leonard, John
2087
Leontiev, Konstantin
1872
Leontovich, Eugenie
1961
Leppmann, Wolfgang
4576
Lerner, Alan Jay
2806, 3533
Lerner, Gerda
2894
Leroux, Etienne
2556
Lessing, Doris
4184
Levi, Peter
3275
Levin, Ira
4385
Levine, Al
50, 210
Levine, David
3609
Levine, Philip
159, 219, 387, 473, 622,
866, 1294, 1426, 1650, 1763
Levine, Suzanne Jill
2278, 4263
Levison, Andrew
1819
Lévi-Strauss, Claude
2759, 4320
Levitin, Isabella
3640
Levitt, Saul
4311
Levy, Diana Shalet
2078
Lewin, John
2109, 2219
Lewis, Arthur H.
2202
Lewis, Michael J.
2373
Lewis, Morgan
3663
Lewis, Thomas S. W.
3253
Libbey, Elizabeth
670
Lichtenberg, Georg Christoph
2960
Liddell Hart, B. H.
2955
Lidderdale, Jane
2412
Lieberman, Laurence
1215
Lifton, Robert Jay
2140, 2971
Limmer, Ruth
4467
Lindbergh, Anne Morrow
2159, 2984, 3303
Lindbergh, Charles A.

4434
Lindley, Denver
3461, 4134
Lindley, Helen
4134
Lindsay, John V.
2263
Ling, Ken
3895
Linington, Elizabeth
3809
Link, Peter
2533, 4451
Linklater, Eric
3946
Linney, Romulus
3358
Lister, R. P.
393
Little, Stuart W.
3643
Litvinoff, Emanuel
2426
Litvinov, Ivy
91, 212, 223, 708, 1178
Livingston, Jerry
3496
Lockridge, Richard
3059, 4103, 4337
Loeser, Katinka
717, 728
Loesser, Frank
4480
Loewe, Frederick
2806
Loewen, James W.
3485
Lofts, Norah
3582
Logan, Andy
97, 103, 105, 130, 136, 289, 348, 434, 505, 550, 662, 720, 722, 765, 776, 1111, 1128, 1157, 1160, 1192, 1321, 1325, 1395, 1584, 1592, 1593, 1619, 1632, 1647, 1665, 1709, 1711, 1722, 1747, 1767, 1873
Logan, William
1477
London, Miriam
3895
Long, Kenn
4287
Longford, Elizabeth
4457, 4458
Longhi, V. J.
3279
Longmate, Norman
4550
Longstreet, Stephen
4443
Loomis, Stanley
2659
Loory, Stuart H.
2433
Loos, Anita
3335, 4336
López, Francisco Pérez
See Pérez López, Francisco
Lorca, Federico García
4048, 4563
Lord, John
2530
Lord, Walter
2396
Lorenz, Konrad
2268
Lorick, Robert
2919
Lortz, Richard
4404
Lottman, Herbert
248, 1105
Lowe, Alfonso
2029
Lubell, Samuel
2946
Luce, Clare Boothe
See Boothe, Clare
Luckett, Richard
4486
Ludlum, Robert
3897
Lukas, J. Anthony
2028
Lurie, Alison
1422, 4430
Lurie, Morris
255
Luxenburg, Norman
4057
Lynes, Russell
2851
Lynn, Kenneth S.
4513

M

Maas, Henry
3249
Maas, Peter
4020
Mabee, Carlton
2088
Macalpine, Ida
2789
McCabe, John
2786
McCall, Dan
3082
McCarry, Charles
3480
McCarten, John
95, 328, 742, 801, 961
McCarthy, Abigail
3820
McCarthy, Cormac
2241
McCarthy, Joe
2996
McCarthy, Mary
1662
McCarty, Ernest
3005
McCluskey, John
3326
McCoy, Alfred
3795
McCullers, Carson
2630, 3459
McCullough, David
2875
MacDermot, Galt
2423, 3129, 4386
Macdonald, Dwight
2474, 3175r, 3549
McGivern, William P.
2192
McGovern, George S.
2876
MacGowran, Jack
2048
McGrath, Charles
175, 1244, 1412, 1822
McGuane, Thomas
2172, 3602
McGuire, Ken
2895
McGuire, William
2752
Machado de Assis, Joachim Maria
2337
McHale, Tom
1898, 2656
McHugh, Heather
341, 807
McIntyre, Alice T.
375, 408
Mack, John E.
3600
McKee, Alexander
3145
McKenna, Siobhan
2942
MacKenzie, Rachel
4518
MacKenzie, Ruth
1394
McKeown, Tom
1570
Mackey, William Wellington
2051, 2076
MacKinnon, John
3031
Maclean, Alistair
2195, 2199
Maclean, Fitzroy
2305
Maclean, Virginia
3521
MacLeish, Archibald
3995
McLeod, Enid
2230
McMahon, Frank
2135
McMahon, Thomas
3818
Macmillan, Harold
3909
McMullen, Roy
4391
McMurtry, Larry
1902
McNally, Terrence
2012, 2528, 3865, 3918, 4478,
4482
McNamee, Thomas
633
McNeal, Claude
2669
McNeil, Lily
343, 447, 1620
McNulty, Faith

524, 973, 1310
McPhee, John
379, 413, 484, 553, 601, 993, 1322, 1349, 1353, 1417, 1452, 1550, 1666
McPherson, Harry
3794
McPherson, Sandra
1771
McWhiney, Grady
4120
Madden, David
2073
Maddow, Ben
2549
Maddox, Everette H.
1471
The Madhouse company of London
3386
Magee, David
3047
Magoon, Eaton, Jr.
2933
Magruder, Jeb Stuart
1929
Maher, Ernie
3181
Mailer, Norman
2623, 3427, 3639, 3962
Mainwaring, Marion
3801
Maisel, Carolyn
566
Malamud, Bernard
1366, 4228
Malcolm, Janet
1055, 1895r, 2549r
Maling, Arthur
2467, 3329
Mallet, Jacqueline
4242
Mallet-Joris, Françoise
3709
Maloff, Saul
2932
Malone, Dumas
3092
Malraux, André
2670
Mandel, Frank
2849, 3613
Mandel, George
3981
Mandelstam, Nadezhda
2974, 2975
Mandelstam, Osip
586
Manfull, Helen
1854
Mangione, Jerre
2511
Manheim, Ralph
1939, 2139, 2752, 2761, 2898, 3302, 3623, 4537
Manilow, Barry
2517
Mankiewicz, Frank
3744
Mankiewicz, Tom
2792
Mann, Theodore
2630
Mann, Thomas
3257
Mannes, Marya
3696
Manning, Gill
2929
Mano, D. Keith
3833
Manvell, Roger
3973
Marasco, Robert
2248
Marceau, Félicien
2349
Marcham, George
3365
Marchand, Leslie A.
1888, 2174
Markandaya, Kamala
4349
Marks, S. J.
121, 1132
Marlowe, Christopher
2548
Marlowe, Derek
2483
Márquez, Gabriel García
1449, 3217, 3665
Marre, Albert
2365
Marric, J. J.
2803, 2804
Marsh, Ngaio
2086, 4265, 4472
Marshack, Alexander
3934

Marshall, Garry
2849
Marshall, John
3857
Marshall-Cornwall, James
2866
Martel, Tom
2915
Martí-Ibáñez, Félix
3484
Martin, Jay
3572
Martin, Norman L.
4025
Marx, Arthur
3483
Massin
3245
Massingham, Harold
32
Masterman, J. C.
2506
Masteroff, Joseph
4025
Masterson, Whit
2422
Matchett, William
1269
Mathers, Michael
3908
Matthews, Herbert L.
2906
Matthews, T. S.
2885
Matthiessen, Peter
690, 1667
Maugham, W. Somerset
2260, 3858
Mauriac, Claude
3687
Mauriac, François
3407
Maurois, André
3461
Maxtone-Graham, John
3673
Maxwell, William
1226, 1815, 1941, 2787r, 3477r, 3874r, 4396r
May, Rollo
3808
Mayer, Elizabeth
3630, 4112
Mayer, J. P.
3873
Mayer, Martin
2023
Mayfield, Sara
2622
Mayor, A. Hyatt
3797
Mays, Benjamin E.
2132
Mead, Margaret
2101, 3862, 3956
Mead, Matthew
187, 290, 291, 292, 293, 732
Mead, Ruth
187, 290, 291, 292, 293, 732
Meadows, Jersey
1908
Mednick, Murray
2995
Medoff, Mark
4411, 4474
Medvedev, Zhores A.
3456
Meehan, Thomas
2, 1022, 1276
Mehta, Ved
287, 304, 382, 419, 784, 816, 912, 933, 1371
Mellow, James R.
2234
Melville, Robert
4390
Menaker, Charles
175
Menaker, Daniel
648, 967, 1244, 1412, 1485, 1822
Menashe, Samuel
1800
Mendelssohn, Kurt
3904
Menen, Aubrey
2261
Menkes, Vivienne
3245
Menninger, Karl
4468
Meredith, William
116, 458
Meriwether, Louise
2375
Merriam, Eve

3050
Merrill, Bob
4179
Merrill, James
767, 975, 1701, 1706
Merwin, W. S.
140, 194, 216, 244, 270, 279, 295, 300, 345, 360, 370, 426, 436, 440, 500, 502, 520, 536, 556, 559, 564, 578, 584, 586, 603, 616, 655, 667, 677, 723, 790, 825, 830, 856, 863, 881, 1064, 1087, 1116, 1159, 1172, 1177, 1189, 1190, 1201, 1264, 1302, 1401, 1450, 1466, 1483, 1517, 1546, 1607, 1637, 1653, 1692, 1705, 1729, 1756, 1759, 1762
Metcalf, Steven
2510
Metzker, Isaac
2078
Mewshaw, Karl E.
4279
Meyer, Karl E.
1291
Meyer, Michael
3010
Miall, Bernard
2631
Michaels, Sidney
2531
Michel, Henri
4030
Michelson, Peter
1862
Middleton, Christopher
3127
Middleton, Drew
4477
Mihaly, Csikszentmihalyi
1505
Milford, Nancy
4576
Millar, Ronald
1840
Miller, Arthur
1903, 2347, 2364, 2585
Miller, Betty
3925
Miller, Helen
3050
Miller, Jason
3617, 4232
Miller, Merle
3776
Miller, Wright
3228
Millett, Kate
2709, 4027
Milligan, Spike
2857
Millstein, Gilbert
3197
Milner, Ron
4466
Milns, R. D.
1893
Milton, David Scott
2147
Mintz, Morton
1919
Mishima, Yukio
3952, 4133
Mitchell, Adrian
2353
Mitchell, David
3601
Mizener, Arthur
3961
Moir, Lyn
3398
Mojtabai, A. G.
3525
Molette, Barbara
3937
Molette, Carlton
3937
Molière, Jean Baptiste Pouquelin
2489, 2496, 3236, 3982, 3988, 4315
Molnár, Ferenc
3783
Monod, Jacques
2225
Montagu, Mary Wortley
4010
Montgomery, Robert
3341, 4176
Mooney, Michael M.
2948
Moore, Barrington
3881
Moore, Brian
2216
Moore, Charles Werner

4345
Moore, Dudley
2846
Moore, Honor
3518
Moore, Marianne
1001
Moorehead, Alan
3195
Moravia, Alberto
4341
Morea, Douglas
93, 176, 314, 572, 676, 952, 1183, 1748
Morgan, Berry
274, 699, 1245, 1277, 1529, 1672
Morgan, Elaine
2439
Morgan, Frederick
515, 1295 1377
Morin, Edgar
3876, 3951
Morison, Samuel Eliot
2603, 2604, 3967
Morreale, Ben
2675
Morris, Ivan
3387
Morris, James
3812
Morris, Jeremiah
2997
Morris, John
61, 771, 1875
Morris, John N.
284
Morris, Willie
3186
Morris, Wright
543, 695, 1355, 2686, 3346
Morrison, Toni
2115
Mortimer, Penelope
963, 986, 2967
Moseley, Maboth
3069
Mosley, Nicholas
3571
Mosley, Oswald
3542
Moss, Howard
69, 118, 152, 237, 280, 665, 1041, 1082, 1104, 1154, 1176, 1187, 1329, 1342, 1362, 1384, 1436, 1439, 1557, 1609, 1638, 1664, 1674, 1698, 1803, 1867r, 2054r, 2631r, 2848r, 3060, 3272r, 3336r, 3426r, 3841r, 4266r, 4407r, 4500r
Mossman, James
3274
Mostert, Noël
1590
Mountzoures, H. L.
53, 977, 1052, 1301, 1387, 2154
Mousnier, Roland
1994
Moyers, Bill
3284
Moyes, Patricia
3422
Moyles, Lois
679
Moynihan, Daniel
83, 783, 2329
Mphahlele, Ezekiel
4425
Mrabet, Mohammed
3225
Muchnic, Helen
3955
Mueller, Elaine
984
Mueller, Zizi
4071
Muir, Edwin
3902
Muir, Willa
3902
Mulcahy, Lance
3719
Muller, Herbert J.
2243, 3029
Müller, Ronald
617
Mumford, Lewis
1038
Munro, Alice
2382, 3298
Munro, James
3051
Murdoch, Iris
1844, 2094, 3959
Murphy, Michael

2843
Murphy, Reg
4119
Murray, Albert
2944, 3651, 4118, 4298
Murray, John
3931
Murray, William
908, 911, 917, 921, 1541
Murray-Brown, Jeremy
3136
Myrdal, Gunnar
2224
Myrdal, Jan
1957

N

Nabokov, Dmitri
297, 1263, 1697, 2817
Nabokov, Vladimir
297, 730, 1263, 1697, 2817, 3322, 3435, 4172, 4300
Nader, Ralph
422
Naipaul, Shiva
2255
Naipaul, V. S.
3337
Namier, Julia
3260
Narayan, R. K.
1099, 3535
Nardi, Marcia
156
Nash, Ogden
1100, 1198, 1833, 3568
Nathan, Leonard
678, 882
Natsume, Sōseki
3000
Neal, Avon
2597
Nee, Brett de Bary
3320
Nee, Victor G.
3320
Neilson, Caroline
4417
Nemerov, Howard
155, 231, 333, 1370, 1463, 1812
Nemiroff, Robert
3234, 3861
Neruda, Pablo
490, 526, 1193, 1536
Neugeboren, Jay
3718
Neustadt, Richard E.
1911
Nevel, Blanche
669, 1235
Nevel, Joseph
669, 1235
New York 21
3324
Newby, Eric
4473
Newfield, Jack
3798
Newhouse, John
73, 1427
Newlove, Donald
2518, 3232
Newman, Edwin
4169
Newman, Montgomery
1170
Nichols, Peter
3078, 3573
Nicholson, Mary
2412
Nicolson, Nigel
3802
Nicolson, Philippa
4378
Nijō, (Lady)
2313
Nin, Anaïs
2458
Nissenson, Hugh
851
Nizan, Paul
1967
Noble, Joan Russell
3874
Nolen, William A.
3400
Noonan, John Ford
3650, 4476
Norman, Barbara
3891
Norman, Dorothy
1895
Norman, Gurney

2478
Norris, Leslie
238, 313, 1088, 1261, 1497
Norton, Lucy
2953
Novak, Robert D.
3604
Novosti Press Agency
3468
Nowell, John
3367
Ntshona, Winston
3075, 4075
Nutting, Anthony
3569, 3994

O

Oates, Joyce Carol
2481
O'Brian, Patrick
1907, 2294
O'Brien, Conor Cruise
3528
O'Brien, Edna
354, 535, 727, 820, 981,
992, 1225, 3596
O'Brien, Lawrence
3606
O'Brien, Patricia
4536
O'Brien, Tim
3016
Obst, David
3038
O'Casey, Sean
3790, 4029
O'Connor, Richard
3073
Odets, Clifford
2006, 2340
Odier, Daniel
3099
O'Donnell, Richard W.
1644
Oerke, Andrew
779
O'Faolain, Sean
4214
O'Hara, J. D.
102
O'Leary, Brian
3402
Oliver Edith
1845r, 1850r, 1868r, 1886r,
1903r, 1913r, 1939r, 1946r,
1947r, 1950r, 1961r, 1978r,
1991r, 2006r, 2012r, 2017r,
2025r, 2035r, 2047r, 2051r,
2062r, 2076r, 2085r, 2089r,
2096r, 2097r, 2099r, 2107r,
2108r, 2120r, 2147r, 2150r,
2162r, 2178r, 2187r, 2188r,
2189r, 2204r, 2213r, 2219r,
2232r, 2233r, 2237r, 2238r,
2239r, 2246r, 2260r, 2283r,
2287r, 2323r, 2324r, 2325r,
2328r, 2331r, 2348r, 2353r,
2357r, 2368r, 2384r, 2399r,
2401r, 2410r, 2411r, 2413r,
2437r, 2448r, 2468r, 2480r,
2489r, 2490r, 2494r, 2498r,
2500r, 2510r, 2512r, 2517r,
2522r, 2526r, 2528r, 2529r,
2531r, 2548r, 2553r, 2558r,
2559r, 2577r, 2581r, 2612r,
2618r, 2630r, 2634r, 2640r,
2657r, 2661r, 2669r, 2681r,
2721r, 2722r, 2733r, 2735r,
2741r, 2746r, 2750r, 2760r,
2768r, 2774r, 2795r, 2798r,
2824r, 2831r, 2833r, 2837r,
2841r, 2871r, 2881r, 2891r,
2901r, 2908r, 2911r, 2912r,
2913r, 2919r, 2934r, 2937r,
2942r, 2951r, 2959r, 2963r,
2972r, 2979r, 2980r, 2986r,
2987r, 2989r, 2995r, 3005r,
3025r, 3027r, 3036r, 3068r,
3081r, 3083r, 3084r, 3085r,
3090r, 3097r, 3117r, 3124r,
3126r, 3129r, 3130r, 3142r,
3147r, 3154r, 3155r, 3163r,
3164r, 3166r, 3167r, 3173r,
3224r, 3226r, 3235r, 3263r,
3264r, 3267r, 3281r, 3283r,
3309r, 3321r, 3341r, 3355r,
3373r, 3388r, 3394r, 3401r,
3437r, 3438r, 3445r, 3448r,
3451r, 3490r, 3494r, 3502r,
3506r, 3515r, 3520r, 3550r,
3557r, 3575r, 3579r, 3594r,
3617r, 3624r, 3628r, 3631r,
3638r, 3645r, 3646r, 3650r,
3663r, 3670r, 3683r, 3697r,

3702r, 3727r, 3738r, 3746r, 3747r, 3751r, 3764r, 3767r, 3773r, 3777r, 3780r, 3782r, 3783r, 3786r, 3787r, 3832r, 3858r, 3859r, 3865r, 3867r, 3872r, 3890r, 3900r, 3901r, 3905r, 3906r, 3922r, 3937r, 3940r, 3941r, 3980r, 3982r, 3985r, 3987r, 3998r, 4015r, 4019r, 4026r, 4029r, 4039r, 4048r, 4049r, 4050r, 4052r, 4053r, 4060r, 4068r, 4069r, 4071r, 4072r, 4078r, 4081r, 4088r, 4104r, 4110r, 4146r, 4151r, 4174r, 4176r, 4181r, 4201r, 4218r, 4223r, 4229r, 4231r, 4232r, 4233r, 4257r, 4284r, 4286r, 4287r, 4308r, 4311r, 4313r, 4317r, 4321r, 4323r, 4345r, 4369r, 4381r, 4411r, 4413r, 4427r, 4441r, 4447r, 4448r, 4451r, 4456r, 4464r, 4465r, 4466r, 4469r, 4474r, 4476r, 4478r, 4482r, 4483r, 4488r, 4543r, 4561r, 4563r, 4565r

Olsen, Tillie
4566

O'Neill, Eugene
2880, 3013, 3309, 3501, 3517

Opie, Iona
2245

Opie, Peter
2245

Oppenheimer, George
2066, 3697

Orieux, Jean
4216

Origo, Iris
3019

Orkin, Harvey
3997

Ornstein, Robert E.
3835

Ortega y Gasset, José
3454

Orton, Joe
4465

Ortzen, Len
4002

Osers, Edward
4005

Oudoguem, Yambo
2139

Ovenden, Graham
4390

Ovid
3476

Owen, Harold
1870

Owen, John
538

Owens, Iris
1866

Owens, Rochelle
3129

Oyamo
2951

Oz, Amos
4291

P

Pace, Tom
1871

Pack, Robert
1548

Packard, Frederick
869

Page, Bruce
2484

Painter, Charlotte
2309

Palastanga, David Cameron
2805

Palsgrave, John
3239

Panetta, Leon E.
2160

Panter-Downes, Mollie
120, 126, 246, 904, 1597, 1755, 2161r, 2419r, 2455r, 2544r, 2598r, 3299r, 3621r, 3649r, 3707r, 3754r, 3945r, 4205r, 4401r

Papp, Charles S.
2297

Parent, Gail
3335

Parker, Ann
2597

Parker, Derek
2545

Parker, Rod
1947

Parker, Tony
2764
Parkinson, Roger
2272, 2406
Parmelin, Hélène
3760
Partridge, Eric
2461
Partridge, Frances
4023, 4431
Pascal, Valerie
2470
Patai, Raphael
1976
Paterson, John
3629
Patrick, John
3359
Paz, Octavio
1163, 1881, 1915
Peabody, James Bishop
3102
Pearsall, Ronald
2550
Pearson, Drew
2514
Pearson, Lester B.
4547
Peck, John
29, 405, 744, 874, 1540, 1552
Peck, Robert Newton
2400
Peech, John
935
Pelikan, Maria
3551
Pentecost, Hugh
2499
Percy, Walker
3351
Perelman, S. J.
65, 106, 650, 661, 1033, 1063, 1199, 1257, 1282, 1350, 1354, 1500, 1507, 1775, 1780, 2035
Perera, Padma
26
Pérez López, Francisco
2387
Perkinson, Coleridge-Taylor
2881
Perkis, Susan
2997
Perr, Harvey
3940, 4026
Perrey, Cassandra
2556
Perrin, Noel
162, 388, 786, 1216, 1631, 3239r
Peterson, William S.
3061
Petrie, Paul
756
Pfaff, William
197, 1560, 1721, 2306
Phillips, John
3415
Piaget, Jean
2247, 3449
Piercy, Marge
2383
Pinero, Arthur Wing
4308
Piñero, Miguel
4050
Pinkham, Joan
4491
Pinkus, Oscar
2257
Pinter, Harold
2085, 2972, 3173, 3649, 4060
Pippin, Don
2657
Pirandello, Luigi
2574, 3949
Pirsig, Robert M.
4577
Plath, Sylvia
92, 135, 241, 347, 568, 613, 1270, 1493, 2054, 4201
Pletzke, Marvin
2283
Plimpton, George
1928, 3382
Plomer, William
2451
Plumb, J. H.
2425, 2692
Plumly, Stanley
614, 803, 1740
Pogue, Forrest C.
2783
Pohl, Frederick J.
3276
Poliakov, Léon
1986

Pomerans, Arnold J.
3757
Porambo, Ron
3605
Porter, Cole
3697
Posner, David
1432, 1581
Poston, Richard W.
2775
Potok, Chaim
3546
Pottle, Frederick A.
2137
Pouillon, Fernand
4156
Pound, Ezra
4011
Pound, Reginald
1890
Powell, Adam Clayton, Jr.
1851
Powell, Anthony
2128
Powell, Lily
2082
Powell, Margaret
2056
Powers, Francis Gary
3675
Powers, J. F.
529
Powledge, Fred
302, 1115
Predmore, Richard L.
2221
Prentice, T. Merrill
4453
Prescott, Peter S.
2390
Prévert, Jacques
796
Price, Anthony
1887
Price, Francis
4036
Price, Richard
4426
Prideaux, James
3183, 3805
Priestley, J. B.
2544, 2552
Pritchett, V. S.
178, 525, 621, 1021, 1378, 1563, 1790, 2018, 2338r, 2476r, 2575r, 2787, 3477, 4149r, 4276r, 4302r
Proetz, Victor
115
Prokosch, Frederic
1920
Pronzini, Bill
4359
Prou, Suzanne
3711, 4562
Pryce-Jones, David
2607, 2635
Purdy, James
3001
Putnam, Emily James
3169
Pynchon, Thomas
2870

Q

Quam, Alvina
4578
Quasar, Basheer
3124
Queneau, Raymond
2026, 2704
Quennell, Peter
2207, 3426, 3969
Quest, Rodney
2218
Quigg, Philip W.
1921

R

Raab, Lawrence
1728
Rabassa, Gregory
1449, 3217
Rabe, David
2031, 3033, 3683, 4151
Racine, Jean Baptiste
1952, 2060
Rado, James
3859
Rado, Ted
3859
Ragni, Gerome

2523
Rahman, Aishah
3166
Raine, Kathleen
1211
Ramer, Jack
3005
Randall, Bob
3391, 4073
Rattigan, Terence
2750, 3028
Raven, Simon
3707
Ravitch, Diane
2884
Raw, Charles
2484
Rawlins, Dennis
3735
Read, Cathleen B.
3795
Read, Piers Paul
1899, 3826, 4376
Réalités, Editors
3023
Reardon, Dennis J.
2911, 4053
Reavey, George
1872
Rébuffat, Gaston
3471
Reck-Malleczewen, Friedrich Percyval
2457
Redman, Eric
2381
Redwine, Skip
2738
Reed, Ishmael
3179, 3524
Reed, J. D.
1166, 1204, 1212, 1834
Reedy, George
4340
Reich, Charles A.
643, 949
Reid, Alastair
549, 566a, 920, 1334, 1472, 1642
Reischauer, Edwin O.
3086
Reisner, Robert
2861
Reiss, James
371
Remarque, Erich Maria
2765
Rendell, Ruth
3661
Renek, Morris
2936
Renfrew, Colin
2041
Revel, Jean-François
4530
Reynolds, Siân
3455
Rhys, Jean
1867, 2848, 3841, 4266, 4407, 4500
Rice, Edward
3104
Rice, Howard C., Jr.
1922
Rice, Tom
3095
Richards, Paul
2760
Richardson, Claibe
2867
Richardson, Joanna
2592, 4149
Rickett, Harold William
4504, 4505
Ridley, Jasper
3332
Riegle, Donald
3632
Rintels, David W.
2270
Rivers, Joan
2766
Robbins, Jane Marla
2413
Roberts, Rhoda
4052
Robertson, D. W., Jr.
1841
Robertson, Don
2889
Robertson, Edwin H.
4328
Robertson, Geoff
4313
Robertson, Strowan
619
Robinson, Derek

2859
Robinson, George
4014
Robinson, Phyllis
2365
Robison, David V.
3827
Robson-Scott, Elaine
3256
Robson-Scott, William
3256
Roche, Paul
1298
Rodgers, Richard
4342
Rodinson, Maxime
3495
Rofheart, Martha
2727
Rogers, Will
4508
Rogin, Gilbert
15, 522, 848, 1138, 1363, 1433, 1544, 1602
Roiphe, Anne Richardson
3310, 4374
Roloff, Michael
2821
Roosevelt, Elliott
3933
Roosevelt, Franklin D.
2718
Rose, Kenneth
4192
Rose, Philip
4041
Rosen, Kenneth
1074
Rosenberg, Edgar
2766
Rosenberg, Harold
1848, 2408, 2511r, 4076r
Rosenberg, John
2504
Rosenberg, Samuel
3562
Rosengarten, Theodore
1901
Rosenkranz, Richard
1847
Roskolenko, Harry
4268
Ross, E.
2732
Ross, Jerry
3706
Ross, Judith
4386
Rostand, Edmond
2373
Roszak, Theodore
4479
Roth, Philip
2149, 3544
Rothman, David J.
2471
Rothman, Esther P.
1955
Rothschild, Emma
3716
Rothstein, Raphael
2668
Roueché, Berton
80, 110, 580, 596, 628, 652, 741, 791, 1252, 1397, 1434, 1490, 1508, 1522, 1795, 2674
Rovere, Richard H.
907, 932, 1909r, 3020r
Rowdon, Maurice
4063
Rowe, Jack
3084
Rowse, A. L.
2568, 2569, 4032, 4034
Royko, Mike
2136
Ruark, Gibbons
1603
Rubens, Paul
2457
Rubinstein, Arthur
3554
Rudge, Susana Hertelendy
4560
Rudorff, Raymond
3558
Ruesch, Hans
2009
Rukeyser, Muriel
800, 4295
Rutsala, Vern
245
Ryan, Cornelius
2156
Ryan, Michael
884

Ryan, William
2102, 3072
Ryder, A. J.
4334
Ryton, Royce
2362

S

Sachs, Nelly
187, 290, 291, 292, 293, 732
Sackville-West, Victoria
4378
Sagan, Françoise
3983
St. Edmund, Bury
4433
Saint-Simon, Louis De Rouvroy
2953
Sajer, Guy
2726
Salemson, Harold J.
3098
Salinger, Pierre
3655
Salivarova, Zdena
4185
Salter, Elizabeth
2376
Sanchez, Sonia
2099, 4069
Sandbach, Mary
2799
Sanders, Lawrence
2690
Sandy, Stephen
570
Sansom, William
3834
Sarduy, Severo
2278
Sargeant, Winthrop
3, 625, 691, 785, 1308, 1589, 1718, 1774, 3032, 3393r, 4098r
Sargent, Elizabeth Owen
4453
Saroyan, William
3775
Sarraute, Nathalie
2482
Sarton, May
1990, 3144
Sartre, Jean-Paul
3261
Saxon, Charles
757
Sayre, Nora
4074
Scammon, Richard M.
3869
Scerbanenco, Giogio
2520
Schecter, Leonard
2016
Schiff, Zeev
2668
Schiller, Johann Christoph
3436
Schisgal, Murray
1906, 1930, 2254, 2487
Schlesinger, Arthur, Jr.
3020
Schmidt, Harvey
2287, 3755
Schoenstein, Ralph
808, 970, 1289, 1624
Scholem, Gershom
3958
Schrag, Peter
2431
Schramm, Richard
424, 833, 1487, 1516
Schultz, Philip
1735
Schuyler, James
198, 507, 945
Schwab, Laurence
2849
Schwartz, Arthur
4234
Schwartz, Stephen
2831, 3391, 3769
Schwarz, Boris
3531
Schwarz-Bart, André
4537
Schwarz-Bart, Simone
2155
Scott, Eleanor M.
1914
Scott, John
3905
Scott, Winfield Townley
1914
Scott-Heron, Gil

3595
Seale, Douglas
3164
Seaver, Richard
2943, 3006
Seelye, John
3141
Seferis, George
3793
Segal, Erich
2642, 3356
Segal, Harold B.
4316
Segal, Lore
1576
Segalen, Victor
3887
Seigle, Cecilia Segawa
2391
Seitz, Jane Clark
3366
Seltzer, Dov
4274
Selznick, David O.
3460
Semprun, Jorge
4002
Seneca
3451
Sennett, Richard
2947
Serban, Andrei
2735, 3451, 4323
Seroff, Victor
3868
Serrin, William
2300
Servadio, Gaia
4054
Sewall, Richard B.
3269
Seward, Desmond
2687
Sewell, Richard
875
Sexton, Anne
201, 606, 638, 829, 1202, 1390
Seyersted, Per
2303, 3131
Seymour, Whitney North, Jr.
4499
Shackelford, Rudy
1804
Shaffer, Anthony
4084
Shaffer, Peter
2598
Shakespeare, William
1991, 2908, 3147, 3374, 3473, 3479, 3520, 3686, 3746, 3900, 3901, 4218, 4223, 4321, 4331, 4344
Shannon, William V.
4243
Shapiro, David
944, 1234
Shapiro, Fred C.
420, 460, 1036
Shapiro, Karl
740
Shapiro, Mel
4344
Shapiro, Stanley
2587
Shaplen, Robert
190, 889, 897, 898, 899, 906, 918, 923, 929, 931, 1110, 1247, 1251, 1758
Sharp, Evelyn
4250
Sharp, Margery
3052
Shattuck, Roger
3425
Shaw, George Bernard
2063, 2185, 2194, 2497, 3411, 4038
Shaw, Irwin
2609, 2898
Shawcross, William
2351, 2519
Shawn, Wallace
3693
Shearer, James F.
3603
Shearer, Toni
3514
Sheed, Wilfrid
3443, 3741, 4260
Sheehan, Edward R. F.
2860
Sheehan, Neil
1982
Sheehan, Susan
1254
Shelton, Richard

288, 323, 640, 680, 1319, 1375, 1381, 1431, 1467, 1539, 1610, 1658, 1715, 1801
Shepard, Sam
2721, 3677, 4284, 4369
Shepp, Archie
3166
Sheridan, Richard Brinsley
3920, 3987
Sheridan-Smith, A. M.
3876
Sherman, Richard M.
3700
Sherman, Robert B.
3700
Sherrard, Philip
514, 602, 664, 1648
Shevelove, Burt
2767, 3613
Shimer, R. H.
4136
Shine, Ted
2325, 3777, 4049
Shogan, Robert
3849
Shulman, Alixkates
3465
Shyre, Paul
2103, 3764, 4508
Silberman, Charles E.
2355
Sillitoe, Alan
40, 3866
Sills, Paul
4159
Silman, Roberta
137, 282
Silverman, Stanley
2046, 2490, 2983
Simenon, Georges
2067, 2813, 3396, 3397, 3398, 3399, 4221, 4384
Simic, Charles
713, 1586
Simon, Greg
268
Simon, Hilda
4129
Simon, Neil
2808, 2829, 2845, 3819, 4190
Simon, Peter
3025
Simpson, Bland
2452
Simpson, Louis
11, 346, 943, 1479, 1717
Singer, Alma
248
Singer, Isaac Bashevis
16, 192, 222, 248, 366, 394, 437, 471, 497, 669, 693, 818, 974, 998, 1042, 1105, 1118, 1180, 1235, 1327, 1430, 1532, 1626, 1634, 1681, 2584
Singer, Joseph
16, 693, 1634
Sissman, L. E.
52, 60, 64, 128, 181, 312, 327, 337, 411, 454, 482, 506, 512, 626, 762, 763, 891, 982, 1026, 1089, 1119, 1149, 1318, 1469, 1553, 1613, 1643, 1719, 1817, 1898, 1928r, 1931r, 2034r, 2115r, 2172r, 2375r, 2435r, 2503r, 2565r, 2582r, 2584r, 2607r, 2643r, 2656r, 2673r, 2809r, 2857r, 2870r, 2892r, 2917r, 3106r, 3143r, 3197r, 3351r, 3478r, 3489r, 3572r, 3602r, 3615r, 3644r, 3703r, 3844r, 3854r, 3928r, 4001r, 4017r, 4058r, 4092r, 4102r, 4113r, 4134r, 4145r, 4173r, 4196r, 4247r, 4304r, 4373r, 4374r, 4432r, 4436r, 4473r, 4523r, 4542r, 4555r
Sithole, Ndabaningi
3796
Sitwell, Edith
2545
Skinner, B. F.
2070
Skrjabina, Elena
4057
Slater, Jerome
3062
Smalls, Charlie
4534
Smith, Dave
373
Smith, Dennis
3888
Smith, Dodie
4212

Smith, Edwin
2588
Smith, Gene
4037
Smith, Grover
3250
Smith, John Holland
2321
Smith, Mark
2423
Smith, Mason
2617
Smith, Shelley
2869
Smith, Vern E.
3111
Smith, W. H. S.
2517
Smith, Walt
1978
Smith, William Edgett
1315
Smith, William Gardner
3894
Smythies, J. R.
2071
Snapp, Thomas
583, 827, 1137
Snodgrass, W. D.
1171
Snow, C. P.
3043, 3405
Snow, Edgar
3315
Sochen, June
3589
Sokoloff, Alice Hunt
2904
Solley, Marvin
2919
Solms, Kenny
3335
Solomon, Barbara Probst
1984
Solzhenitsyn, Alexander
1999, 2184, 2688, 2717, 2899
Sondheim, Stephen
2710, 2767, 2902, 3291
Sontag, Susan
94, 109
Sophocles
1965, 2735
Sorell, Walter
2637
Soustelle, Jacques
2732
Southgate, Patsy
3288
Spaak, Paul-Henri
2322
Spacks, Barry
461, 498, 947
Spark, Muriel
450, 1838
Speer, Albert
3057
Spence, Jonathan D.
2575
Spencer, Elizabeth
547, 1475
Spencer, Joan
1994
Spencer, Sharon
4123
Spender, Stephen
2374, 3436
Spigelgass, Leonard
3325
Spike, Paul
2013
Spivak, Talbot
2152
Spock, Benjamin
2430
Sprigge, Elizabeth
3270
Squire, Geoffrey
2513
Staël-Holstein, Anne Louise Germaine
4227
Stafford, Jean
2258r
Stafford, William
509, 1679, 1835
Stanford, Ann
706, 1065, 1704
Starbird, Kay
3282
Starbuck, George
149, 1538
Starkie, Enid
2700
Starr, Kevin
1936
Stead, Christina

1051
Steane, J. B.
2864
Steegmuller, Francis
236, 372, 1208, 2280, 2699
Stegner, Page
2927
Stegner, Wallace
1958, 4363
Stein, Aaron Marc
1912, 2684
Stein, Gertrude
3283
Stein, Jean
1928
Stein, Joseph
3071
Steinbeck, John
3641
Steiner, George
209, 316, 475, 542, 573, 579, 747, 832, 1416, 1738, 1751, 1857r, 1862r, 1891r, 2071r, 2112r, 2126r, 2245r, 2286r, 2302r, 2620r, 2629r, 2769r, 2802r, 2899r, 2974r, 2975r, 3024, 3057r, 3260r, 3333r, 3387r, 3440r, 3441r, 3464r, 3818r, 3958r, 4032r, 4034r, 4185r, 4320r, 4435r, 4533r, 4571r, 4577r
Steinman, Jim
3506
Stendhal
See Beyle, Marie Henri
Stent, Gunther S.
2296
Stern, James
3258
Stern, Richard
3689
Stevens, Ann
3247
Stevens, Edmund
1967
Stevens, William
2190
Stevenson, Frances
3301
Stevenson, James
28, 184, 326, 433, 494, 759, 954, 995, 1016, 1046, 1047, 1162, 1275, 1360, 1484, 1734, 1784
Stewart, George R.
1932
Stewart, J. I. M.
2005
Stewart, Jean
3396, 3407
Stewart, Michael
3376
Stewart, Natacha
649, 796, 1765
Stickney, John
4166
Stimac, Anthony
2324, 2657
Stokes, Terry
1640
Stoloff, Carolyn
599, 1656
Stone, Peter
2765, 4179, 4342
Stone, Robert
2492
Stone, Ronald
3883
Stoppard, Tom
1868, 2594, 3121, 3867, 3941
Storey, David
2227, 2323, 2968, 3726
Strand, Mark
134, 220, 448, 627, 654, 700, 1155, 1357, 1403, 1499, 1567, 1655, 1778
Straus, Dorothea
471, 818, 1180, 1327, 1430, 1532, 1973
Strindberg, August
2380, 2661, 2799
Strong, Jonathan
3694
Strouse, Charles
1973, 4072
Strunk, William, Jr.
2564
Stuart, Dabney
1148, 1668
Stuart, Francis
2196
Stuhlmann, Gunther
2458
Styne, Jule
2902, 3325, 4179

Sukhovo-Kobylin, Alexander
3765, 4316
Sullivan, Frank
647
Sulzberger, C. L.
1878, 3185, 4283
Sundgaard, Arnold
1072, 1376
Sutton, Denys
3255
Sutton, Dolores
4447
Suyin, Han
See Han Suyin
Svendsen, Clara
3262
Swados, Elizabeth
2735, 4323
Swan, Jon
758, 1044, 1179, 1206, 1379
Swan, Lester A.
2297
Swenson, May
1331, 1423, 1464, 1547
Swerdlow, Robert
3355
Swinnerton, Frank
3656, 3938
Symons, Julian
3509, 3788
Synge, John Millington
3781
Synge, Patrick M.
2291
Szarkowski, John
3327
Szulc, Tad
924, 3053

T

Taborski, Boleslaw
3271
Tagliacozzo, Giorgio
2802
Talbott, Strobe
3140
Tannahill, Reay
2712
Taper, Bernard
501
Tate, James
1473
Tauke, M. S.
233
Taylor, A. J. P.
2036
Teal, Thomas
1883, 3688
Tebelak, John-Michael
2831
Teichmann, Howard
2788
Teitel, Nathan
2526, 2681, 4317
Terkel, Studs
2917
Terras, Victor
2771
Terry, Megan
2342
Tesich, Steven
2204, 3628
Theroux, Paul
3963
Thomas, Brandon
2232
Thomas, Gordon
3970
Thomas, Hugh
2370, 3105
Thomas, Lately
3815, 4158, 4471
Thomas, Lewis
1185, 3296
Thomas, Ross
2010, 2714, 3799
Thompson, Hunter S.
2665
Thompson, Kent
1846
Thompson, Robert
1496
Thomson, David
4502
Thomson, George H.
1889
Thorburn, David
2319
Thornton, Grace
4400
Thronson, Ron
3514
Thuna, Leonora
3243, 4052

Thwaite, Ann
4414
Tidyman, Ernest
2527
Tillich, Paul
3551
Times (London)
4270
Tindall, Gillian
2131
Tobias, Fred
2776
Tokyo Kid Brothers
2841
Tolstoy, Ilya
4280
Tolstoy, Leo
1961
Tomalin, Nicholas
4160
Tomkins, Calvin
46, 193, 259, 353, 358, 459, 624, 733, 941, 971, 1030, 1039, 1092, 1093, 1095, 1208, 1383, 1408, 1611, 1625, 1646, 1793, 3264r, 3474, 3540r
Topp, Sylvia
1988
Topping, Seymour
3113
Toronto Workshop Company
2238
Total Loss Farm
2969
Toulmin, Stephen
4533
Tournier, Michel
3644
Towle, Tony
1820
Townsend, Peter
2525
Townsend, Robert
4373
Trachtenberg, Alan
3469
Tracy, Honor
3850, 4521
Tracy, Stephen
1307
Trahey, Jane
3912
Trautman, Kathleen
4128
Tremblay, Michel
2977
Triana, José
2353
Trillin, Calvin
164, 443, 787, 1670, 1694, 2050r
Trollope, Anthony
3707
Trollope, Christine
3760
Trotsky, Leon
4568
Trow, George W. S.
182, 202, 203, 1073
Troyat, Henri
2476
Truax, Hawley
321, 398, 1796
Truman, Harry S.
3776
Truman, Margaret
2923
Trumbo, Dalton
1854
Tryon, Thomas
2924
Tsvetayeva, Marina
1533
Tucci, Niccolò
1358
Tuchman, Barbara
4152
Tullius, F. P.
356, 1015, 1568, 1605, 1657, 1703
Turnbull, Colin M.
3516
Turner, Dennis
2233
Tuten, Frederic
1859
Tuttle, Anthony
4109
Twombly, Robert C.
2737
Tyler, Anne
845, 2274
Tyler, Royall
2324
Tynan, Kenneth
99, 826

Tyne, John
3489
Tyrmand, Leopold
1267, 1361

U

Udell, Peter
3837, 4041
Udoff, Yale M.
2901
Uhnak, Dorothy
3201
Underwood, Franklin
3359
Underwood, J. A.
2349, 3887
Ungar, Sanford J.
3712
Unsworth, Barry
3504
Unterecker, John
844
Updike, John
142, 157, 179, 257, 258, 325, 390, 400, 476, 503, 555, 658, 681, 726, 737, 789, 813, 983, 1213, 1271, 1290, 1389, 1521, 1530, 1708, 1838r, 1859r, 1874r, 1900r, 2013r, 2026r, 2052r, 2139r, 2155r, 2163, 2383r, 2478r, 2632r, 2667r, 2704r, 2761r, 2771r, 2794r, 2817r, 2843r, 2883r, 2885r, 2914r, 3037r, 3067r, 3270r, 3296r, 3302r, 3322r, 3337r, 3481r, 3535r, 3665r, 3729r, 3852, 3959r, 3983r, 4064r, 4182r, 4183r, 4255r, 4263r, 4300r, 4425r, 4460r, 4560r
Upton, John
3088
Uris, Leon
1978
Urquhart, Brian
2909
Ustinov, Peter
4497

V

Vallierês, Pierre
4491
van Buitenen, J. A. B.
3393
Van Burek, John
2977
van der Zee, Barbara
4511
van der Zee, Henri
4511
van der Zee, John
2888
Van Doren, Mark
629
Van Duyn, Mona
487, 1741
van Itallie, Jean-Claude
3557, 4019
van Ostaijen, Paul
3729
Van Peebles, Melvin
1882, 2502
van Thal, Herbert
2055
Van Zandt, Roland
4515
Vance, Samuel
2343
Vas Dias, Robert
1639
Vennewitz, Leila
2242
Vercors
3856
Verger, Jean-Baptiste-Antoine de
1922
Vidal, Gore
2170, 2611, 2965
Vietor, Dean
217, 1062, 1494
Vilar, Esther
3419
Villas Boas, Claudio
4560
Villas Boas, Orlando
4560
Vivante, Arturo
117, 160, 168, 189, 427, 480, 718, 805, 828, 858, 883, 1169, 1240, 1519, 1673
Volanakis, Minos
3452
Voltaire
2187
Vonnegut, Kurt, Jr.

2148, 2912
Voznesensky, Andrei
1966
Vroom, Barbara
1228

W

Wagoner, David
569, 609, 612, 734, 847, 878, 1006, 1513, 1661, 1678
Wain, John
4523
Wainhouse, Austryn
2225
Walcott, Derek
1094, 1585, 1651, 2512
Walder, David
4051
Waldman, Marguerite
2127
Waldron, Eli
204, 1636, 1687
Waldrop, Keith
239, 1652
Walker, Alice
4252
Walker, David
145
Walker, Joseph A.
3638, 3922, 4565
Walker, Robert
3084
Walker, Ted
19, 30, 101, 112, 127, 161, 211, 256, 265, 431, 499, 701, 934, 1011, 1134, 1136, 1200, 1495, 1515, 1564, 1594, 1627, 1725
Wall, Bernard
2459, 3690
Wall, Joseph Frazier
1951
Wallace, Anthony F. C.
2416
Wallace, Michael
1934
Walsh, Donald D.
2812
Walter, Elizabeth
3986
Walton, Richard J.
2284
Wambaugh, Joseph
2113
Wann, Jim
2452
Ward, Douglas Turner
2162, 2401
Ward, Maisie
4297
Warner, Philip
3453
Warner, Sylvia Townsend
25, 122, 166, 167, 196, 478, 561, 574, 585, 630, 642, 788, 953, 979, 1083, 1096, 1272, 1336, 1382, 1441, 1442, 1528, 1730, 1798
Warren, Joyce
496
Warren, Robert Penn
12, 191, 1103, 1352, 1520, 2966
Wasiolek, Edward
2771
Wasson, R. Gordon
4098
Wästberg, Per
1883
Wattenberg, Ben J.
3869
Watters, Pat
4117
Weaver, Helen
3538
Weaver, William
2049
Webb, Charles
3432, 3684
Webber, Andrew Lloyd
3095
Webster, Noah
2167
Wechsberg, Joseph
888, 930, 1081, 1210, 1224, 2819, 3810, 4422
Weesner, Theodore
682, 2198
Weidman, Jerome
3188
Weightman, Doreen
4320
Weightman, John
4320

Weil, Gordon L.
3316
Weill, Kurt
2062, 3108, 3339, 3394
Weinberg, Herman G.
2301
Weinberger, Eliot
1881
Weiner, Leslie
2612
Weinstein, Arnold
3476
Weintraub, Stanley
3118, 4038, 4484
Weis, Charles McC.
2137
Weiss, Theodore
18, 276, 859
Welch, James
1205, 4522
Weller, Michael
3503, 3506
Welsh, Alexander
2265
Welty, Eudora
3336, 3669
Wensinger, Arthur S.
2960
Wertenbaker, Lael
4354
Wertenbaker, William
517, 1509
Wescott, Howard B.
3454
Wesley, Richard
2097, 2099, 2798, 2837, 3727, 4068
West, Anthony C.
1989, 2337r, 4431r
West, Cristy
745
West, Jessamyn
1086
West, Morris
2920, 3964
West, Paul
4548
Westlake, Donald E.
2021
Wetzel, Donald
2080
Wheeler, Hugh
2188, 3071, 3291
Wheelock, John Hall
242, 793, 861, 1630
Whitcomb, Ian
1869
White, Alan
3311, 3317
White, Anthony
2719
White, Antonia
2813
White, Diz
2558
White, E. B.
229, 644, 764, 925, 1364, 2564
White, Edgar
3235, 3263
White, Joan
2878
White, Katharine S.
2291r, 2298r, 2534r, 2705r, 2707r, 4033r, 4378r, 4503r, 4504r, 4553r
White, Patrick
2629
White, Theodore H.
3403
Whitehead, E. A.
1913, 2733
Whitehead, James
3109
Whitehead, Paxton
2236
Whitehouse, Wilfred
4211
Whiteside, Thomas
72, 344, 381, 389, 421, 1322, 1511, 3064
Whitman, Walt
4126
Whitney, Arthur
2480
Whitney, Thomas P.
2724
Whittemore, L. H.
4277
Whittemore, Reed
879
Whittle, Tyler
2298
Whitworth, William
98, 226, 1278, 1527
Whyte, Ron

4381, 4456
Wicker, Tom
2638
Wiesel, Elie
2045, 4114
Wiesel, Marion
4114
Wigginton, Eliot
2734
Wilbur, Richard
588, 815, 1565, 1649, 2188, 3988
Wilder, Alec
1933
Wilder, Thornton
4236
Willeford, Charles
2169, 2279
Williams, Alan
2061
Williams, C. K.
836
Williams, Emlyn
2573
Williams, Eric
2758, 3066
Williams, Jill
3860
Williams, John
2000
Williams, Raymond
2339
Williams, Tennessee
2214, 3695, 4088, 4165
Williamson, Alan
108, 247, 1554
Williamson, Nicol
3594
Willmott, Peter
4202
Wilmerding, John
4520
Wilson, Angus
2588, 4551
Wilson, Arthur M.
2462
Wilson, Colin
3989
Wilson, Dick
3313
Wilson, Earl, Jr.
2399
Wilson, Edmund
146, 147, 592, 604, 1524, 1583, 1710, 2064r, 2184r, 2210r, 2352r, 2378r, 2660r, 2688r, 2816r, 3048r, 3076r, 3431r, 3442r, 3626r, 3765r, 4276, 4316r
Wilson, Graeme
3000
Wilson, Lanford
2980, 3226, 3515
Wilson, Robert M.
2410, 3264
Wilson, Robley, Jr.
1745
Wilson, Sandy
2141
Wiltse, David
4181
Winchester, Barry
2072
Wind, Herbert Warren
129, 277, 309, 374, 493, 518, 554, 623, 645, 1005, 1024, 1054, 1068, 1112, 1214, 1255, 1256, 1380, 1415, 1550, 1612, 1616, 1660, 1689, 1716, 1799, 1810
Winn, Marie
4185
Winston, Clara
3057, 3067, 3257, 3720
Winston, Richard
3057, 3067, 3257, 3720
Winterbotham, F. W.
4352
Winters, Shelley
3670
Witcover, Jules
2930, 3892, 4489
Witney, Dudley
2027
Witt, Harold
1209, 1829
Witts, Max Morgan
3970
Wode, Ed
3890
Wodehouse, P. G.
3646, 3783, 3789
Woiwode, L.
163, 235, 1017, 1175, 1292, 1572
Woldin, Judd

3861
Wolf, Patricia
2443, 4216
Wolff, Jessica
1576
Wood, G.
2630
Wood, Jessie
3385
Woodcock, George
4494
Woodham-Smith, Cecil
3846
Woods, Sara
4564
Woods, William Crawford
3143
Woodward, Bob
1909
Woodward, C. Vann
1924
Woolf, Leonard
3116
Wooten, James T.
4096
Woroszylski, Wiktor
3271
Worsthorne, Peregrine
4095
Wouk, Herman
4517
Wright, Barbara
2026, 2704
Wright, Charles
1424, 1842
Wright, Constance
2652
Wright, James
468, 595, 1165, 1311, 1359, 1455
Wright, Richard B.
4454

Y

Yaffe, James
4408
Yanagisawa, Eizo
4211
Yankowitz, Susan
4229
Yanovsky, V. S.
2886, 3640
Yarmolinsky, Avrahm
2505, 3252
Yeats, W. B.
3502
Yellen, Sherman
3943
Yglesias, Helen
831, 1461, 2990
Yglesias, Jose
335, 659, 1400, 2507
Youmans, Vincent
3613
Young, Al
4092
Young, Caryl Gabrielle
2414
Young, Clarence, III
3747
Young, Michael
4202
Young, Percy M.
4065
Younger, Calton
3070

Z

Zakrzewski, Paul
4015
Zaltzberg, Charlotte
3861
Zamyatin, Yevgeny
4121
Zaslavsky, Claudia
1863
Zassenhaus, Hiltgunt
4421
Zhukov, Georgii K.
3468
Zimmerman, Ed
3350
Zindel, Paul
1943, 2553, 4004
Zolling, Herman
2782
Zuckmayer, Carl
3720
Zweig, Arnold
3256
Zweig, Paul
20, 724, 1712, 1857